GROWING
UP
WITH
PHILOSOPHY

This is the first sourcebook designed for the growing field of philosophy and children, a discipline which promises to enrich both childhood and philosophical thinking. It seeks to motivate children to think in ways that will increase the meaningfulness of their lives and, as a consequence, help them see the importance of their own education. In addition, it entails a reappraisal of the entirety of philosophical literature in search of those parts most useful in doing philosophy with children.

The approximately thirty essays are organized in topical sections and provide a foundation for building new learning experiences through philosophy. The first group is an historical selection of works by major philosophers. The relationship between developmental theories and philosophy for children is the theme of the next section, and is

GROWING
UP
WITH
PHILOS

followed by sections on children
and moral philosophy, children
and aesthetics, and children and
ethics. A final section on the role of
the teacher in the philosophical
education of the child rounds out
the anthology.

Philadelphia

OPHY

by

MATTHEW LIPMAN

and

ANN MARGARET SHARP

Temple University Press

Temple University Press, Philadelphia 19122
© 1978 by Temple University. All rights reserved
Published 1978
Printed in the United States of America

Library of Congress Cataloging in Publication Data

Main entry under title:

Growing up with philosophy.

    Bibliography: p.
    1. Education—Philosophy—Addresses, essays, lec-
tures. 2. Philosophy—Study and teaching (Elementary)
—Addresses, essays, lectures. 3. Child development
—Addresses, essays, lectures. 4. Motivation in
education—Addresses, essays, lectures. I. Lipman,
Matthew. II. Sharp, Ann Margaret, 1942-
LB17.G73   107   77-93451
ISBN 0-87722-118-9

CONTENTS

PREFACE

Within barely half a dozen years, a new branch of philosophy has emerged: philosophy and children. As a discipline, it is still in its formative years, and it is much too early to foretell its eventual direction, or how much momentum it may acquire. But already it can be seen to be surprisingly complex, for while in some ways it resembles what happens when philosophy is applied to a particular profession (for example, philosophy and medicine) or what happens when the philosophy of a particular social group is identified (for example, philosophy and women), in other ways it is sharply different and unique.

What especially distinguishes the new field of philosophy and children is its *educational* dimension. It represents what may be both the last and the most important subject to be removed from its academic shelter in the university and readied for introduction into the elementary school. Thus, in addition to the recognition of the fact that children's thinking often has a philosophical cast—that there is such a thing as philosophy *by* children—it is also recognized today that there is such a thing as philosophy *for* children. This latter involves an appraisal of the entire literature of philosophy so as to discover what there is in that literature which would lend itself to the enhancement of children's philosophical experience. These promising aspects of the philosophical tradition must then be processed so as to construct a sequential curriculum which would be the basis for exposing children to philosophy.

Once it is admitted that philosophy is no longer reserved for adults—that children want it, can understand it, and can profit from it—then it becomes important to discover afresh what had long been taken for granted: the methodology of philosophical education. After all, if elementary school teachers are to be instructed and rehearsed in the procedures of teaching philosophy, which had never before been permitted to cross the elementary school threshold, then it would seem necessary to distinguish the pedagogy and the content of this discipline. But this turns out to be very difficult to accomplish. The pedagogy of philosophy can be distinguished from its content for purposes of analysis, but in practice the two are inseparable. The content of philosophy is not just the history of philosophy nor is it critical thinking. It is both of these things and more. It involves wondering about things with a view to thinking for oneself. To learn philosophy, one must become actively involved in the life of philosophy and this can only be accomplished by children's appropriating the philosophical tradition for themselves, reenacting it in terms of their own experience, critically reflecting upon it and incorporating the meanings thus acquired into the ongoing conduct of their lives.

In order for children to experience philosophy in this sense, it must be taught by teachers who themselves appreciate the craft of philosophical reflection and dialogue, as well as the tradition of philosophical ideas. But how should the future teachers of elementary school philosophy be educated in such a way as to make this feasible? It cannot be a matter of adding a few philosophy courses to the present teacher education sequence. What is needed is that philosophy should permeate the entire process of teacher preparation.

To put philosophy into the classroom is an important step towards reuniting method and content in education, for the philosophic combination of wonder and reasonableness in the candid consideration of alternatives is precisely the atmosphere which should prevail when students are being introduced to the arts, sciences and humanities which make up their cultural heritage. If we want to inspire children to emulate greatness, it would seem that we must try to arrange for them to study the great cultural products of the critical, imaginative and scientific spirit—the scientific and humanistic achievements of mankind—under conditions resembling as much as possible those in which such achievements were created. The discovery technique is not the only technique in the arsenal of education, but surely the atmosphere of creativity and invention and reenactment is a suitable one for learning of any kind. To insist upon the opposite—to compel students to study the inventions, the discoveries, the works of art, all of them products of wondering and exploring, experimentation and imagination, in a fashion that is wholly different from the manner in which such artifacts came into being, would seem to be counter-productive—if not downright perverse.

The primary purpose of the present volume is to make available to both teachers and students in the areas of philosophy and philosophy of education a body of writings which will serve to acquaint them with some of the peculiar problems of this new branch of philosophy, and with some of the approaches to those problems which are now being explored. The book is therefore well-suited for use as a college text. But there is much in it, we feel, which the interested lay person would be able to profit from, particularly if such a person is concerned to know what happens when the thought of a child intersects with the ideas of a civilization.

I

LANDMARKS IN PHILOSOPHY FOR CHILDREN

INTRODUCTION

Seldom in the history of philosophy has children's capacity for philosophical reflection even been considered, much less encouraged in any systematic way. The fact is somewhat puzzling. One would have thought that recent, more enlightened attitudes toward children would have led to greater appreciation of children's capacity to be aware, to think for themselves, and to reason about metaphysical and epistemological issues. It is well known that before Romanticism, the thoughts of children were considered unimportant; children themselves had little social status. Romanticism took a big step from considering children as nonpersons to considering them as persons in their own right. In the late eighteenth and early nineteenth century, the child came to be portrayed as a natural, feeling creature of tender innocence and naïve charm, living in a world of playful fantasy, removed from the serious workaday world of adults.

Romanticism saw childhood as a valid experience in itself and not as a mere preparation for adulthood. But the quality of childhood experience was held to be sharply different—different in kind—from adult experience. Childhood's combination of naïveté and natural spontaneity was a priceless state to be preserved for as long as possible. This insistence on the idiosyncratic character of childhood experience liberated the child from treatment as an underdeveloped adult at school and at home. The discovery by Romanticism of the richness of the life of children was invaluable, as was its appreciation of the emotional and developmental factors in education and its sense of the importance of synchronizing the educational curriculum with the child's changing needs and capacities. Yet the Romantic view of childhood (as epitomized by Wordsworth) created new difficulties when it conceived of the thought processes of the child as being somehow discontinuous with those of the adult. Paradoxically, what began as a liberating movement became in many ways a barrier to understanding the capacities of children to think for themselves and to think philosophically.

As Romanticism asserted the uniqueness and integrity of the child's experience, it also came to stress the developmental view of human behavior. It was no accident that Romanticism shared its domination of nineteenth century thought with historicism and evolutionary concepts. A contradiction threatened. How could the developmental approach, which assumes a gradual transition from childhood to adulthood, be reconciled with the notion that the end of childhood is a rupture of what was once pure and innocent and happy, a falling off rather than a cumulative development? The clash was avoided by a double strategy. On the one hand,

the cognitive capacities of children were seen as subject to laws of development. The very young child's thinking was deemed to be rudimentary,
hardly comparable with the adult achievement but capable of steady and
sustained growth. On the other hand, the capacity of children to think
philosophically was scarcely considered because the very conception of
philosophy, widely shared for many centuries, was that of a discipline so
complex and formidable as to be unintelligible to most adults, much less
children. This helps to explain why, during a period in which virtually
every other academic discipline was reformulated to be made available to
children, philosophy remained cloistered in the university. Philosophy was
believed to require seasoned, informed thinkers, and children were by
definition too immature to cope with so formidable a discipline.

Models for Philosophy

Philosophers of the Enlightenment had been content to allow philosophy
to remain the avocation of an intellectual and professional minority. They
sought a universal understanding through dissemination of the mathematical and physical sciences, and philosophy itself soon was reshaped in the
image of those models. Nevertheless, the Enlightenment writers implied
that mankind universally was educable, a notion radically different from
the traditional view that only a small portion of mankind was capable of or
deserved education. By the middle of the nineteenth century, the possibility of philosophy as a vital component of a newly formulated mass education was undermined still further by Marxist disparagement and ridicule of
philosophy as an ineffectual means of dealing with the important problems
of modern life. Such critics did not destroy the philosophical tradition but
redirected it into more practical channels. The pragmatic tradition in its
turn applied itself very specifically to educational problems, holding to the
Enlightenment notion that universal education had to be identified with
the dissemination of scientific knowledge. The pragmatists attempted to
bring to education not so much the results of science as the method of
science. Even in Dewey, education apparently is to be revitalized through
a sweeping commitment to the method of inquiry. That commitment was
an enormous advance over the traditional conception of education, but
Dewey's constant encouragement of the child's engagement in independent reflection about all dimensions of experience was not maintained by
his followers. Dewey's superb grasp of the possibilities of education became
limited solely to the inquiry method, which was seen as a rational tech-

nique for problem-solving to be applied to the manageable areas of human life. This almost by definition excluded philosophical concerns, and metaphysical and epistemological issues were ignored. The formulation and resolution of problematic situations was proposed as the only valid paradigm for exploring and understanding the world.

The logical positivists in the first third of the twentieth century sought to assimilate philosophy completely to science. This attempt collapsed and opened the way for the ordinary language movement. Where the logical positivists sought to construct an ideal language on the model of science, ordinary language philosophers encouraged attention to everyday colloquial language, discovering in it the users' underlying philosophical presuppositions and meanings. But if the assumptions of philosophy are to be discovered in ordinary language, then they can be discovered in the everyday language of children as well as of adults. Indeed, it may be even more profitable to investigate the acquisition of philosophical concepts in childhood than to penetrate the more elaborate and esoteric formulations in the language of grown-ups. There are those today who dispute the view that children's concepts of the world are crude distortions of what they have learned from adults; they contend that adults' concepts of the world are frequently only elaborate, sophisticated versions of the intuitions they had had in childhood. The proponents of ordinary language never contemplated a venture into philosophy for children, but their approach lent substance and credibility to the idea when it occurred.

What we are discussing is the revision and redefinition of philosophy so as to bring about its increasing involvement with the lives and problems of all people, rather than an academic and technical exercise for a detached and philosophical few. The process of redefining philosophy to be more democratically available perhaps has not gone very far. Some contemporary philosophers continue to speculate systematically about the nature of things, and many pursue their specialized studies as part of their discipline's traditional quest for clarified understanding. But certainly the ordinary language movement on the one hand and the pragmatic, existentialist and phenomenological movements on the other have compelled philosophers to concentrate more on the varieties of ordinary experience rather than on the ideals of perfection characteristic of some periods of the philosophical enterprise. The application of philosophy to law, to medicine, to education, and to other realms of contemporary life represents only the outermost fringe of what is going on in philosophy today. But what is fringe today may be closer to the center in the future.

Philosophy and Educational Change

The perception of the relevance of philosophy to childhood could not have been the product just of the redefinition of philosophy by philosophers. What was needed was the redefinition of education. The ancient and medieval world did not doubt the capacity of children to study, absorb and master intellectual skills, and engage effectively in numerous mental acts. What children were not trusted to do was to reflect upon, appraise, and evaluate the content of the materials learned. For the most part, the learning process was to be a passive absorption by the child of adult erudition. Adults of the time could perceive perfectly well that children possessed the thinking skills necessary to memorize and apply the principles of mathematics, music, rhetoric, and foreign languages. But (like women and members of certain races) children were thought to be lacking in judgment, discretion, and the ability to think for themselves about matters of importance. Encouraging them to do so could lead only to chaos. Paternalistic authorities simply excluded such a possibility from consideration. Most other adults had no access to philosophy and were unable to hear the philosophical dimensions of their children's discourse. Thus, for many centuries, we know a great deal about what children were required to learn but have hardly any record of childhood speculations about metaphysical, epistemological, moral, and aesthetic perplexities. They were not thought to merit preservation.

The past hundred and fifty years have witnessed struggles to abolish slavery and to emancipate women. Both struggles have attempted to enfranchise fully developed adults on the apparent assumption that personhood is synonymous with achievement of a certain chronological age. As long as immaturity was the fundamental criterion of dependency, children were excluded from the rights of personhood.

What eroded this assumption? A number of trends have contributed to a drastically revised conception of childhood in the twentieth century. Freud discovered a sexual dimension to childhood and, significantly, did not imply that childhood sexual impulses are different in kind from adult sexual impulses. He revealed the full seriousness of childhood, not only for its effect on later life but as an authentic experience in itself. Freud himself was capitalizing on a century of insights into the powerful impulses of the child and the active role of the child in the learning process. Vico, Rousseau, Pestalozzi, Froebel, and many others had denounced the tradition of the child as a passive recipient of external sensations and had urged instead that children be seen as active agents who learn by doing and creating, full partners with the teacher in learning. Dewey enlarged on this development by recognizing the child's intellectual readiness; he portrayed more judiciously and more realistically the balance between the child's intellectual and creative propensities and the traditional disciplines of the culture.

The changing conception of philosophy, coupled with the changing conception of childhood, prepares the ground for necessary revisions in the prevailing conception of education. Just as Freud argued, contrary to prevalent beliefs, that the child's sexual dispositions had to be taken seriously, so the changing conception of the child leads to a new awareness of children's philosophical propensities. If philosophy is seen to represent the natural fulfillment and culmination of childhood curiosity and wonder, of childhood speculation about the nature of things, and of childhood concern for truth about reality, then nothing could be more in keeping with children's own intellectual dispositions than philosophical activities. Thus, the first justification for introducing philosophy into elementary education is that, properly redefined, philosophy and childhood are eminently congenial.

A second justification is that children need critical tools that will enable them to assess effectively the philosophical dimension of the present curriculum. Critical thinking in itself cannot accomplish this end because by itself it is merely an inventory of scrupulous precautions, the prudence born of past experience. Critical thinking fails to give children an avenue for their own unique efforts to comprehend the richness and complexity of the world, so that they can then compare their own perspectives with one another and with the perspective of the curriculum being presented to them.

Take a subject like history. If the child's mind is conceived to be completely passive and docile, then a mass of information can be poured into it to be accepted uncritically. On the other hand, if children are merely encouraged to be wary of fallacies, skeptical about claims, and critical of assumptions—if, in other words, they are taught to be critical but not philosophical—then the full impact of the pageantry and richness and complexity and mysteriousness of history is lost on them. The sweep and grandeur of history cannot be appreciated without a sense of proportion by which certain facts can be recognized as trivial and others as important and fundamental. If children's sympathies and imagination are not brought into play so that they can identify with those human beings who were engaged in making history, and if children do not bring to the study of history a sharpened intelligence whose aesthetic, ethical, and metaphysical dispositions have been alerted to these dimensions of human experience, then history will be no more important to them than it is to a child only force-fed on the data of history.

A third justification for doing philosophy with children is their need to find meaning in their own lives. Their having a philosophical impulse does not necessarily mean that they can discover by themselves the meanings they seek. This is where the enormous repertoire of philosophical ideas can be valuable. Children are curious, and we can show them an enormous amount, in ways they can understand, that will fascinate them and train their curiosity to work constructively. To children's impressive capacity for wonder, philosophy can add awareness of the fundamental enigmas of existence that most children unaided can only suspect. Children need the help with logic we can give them, in order to evaluate their own reasoning and the evidence on which their judgments must be based. Children need sets of interconnected ideas to show them that their own thinking need not remain fragmentary. Logic alone cannot help children find meaning in their lives; critical thinking alone cannot help children find meaning in their lives; but philosophy in combination with formal and informal logic can open the possibility of their finding meaning. Even if philosophy does not provide ultimate meanings, it conveys to the child that the quest is feasible and worthwhile. Explanations of the physical world are not enough; children need a context in which the explanation is meaningful and which includes the sorts of concerns that they are curious about. The child's persistant "Why?" expresses a profound need to get at whatever meanings the world has to offer. This is why the child cannot make do with less than philosophy.

The fourth justification follows from the third. If children find the education they are being given meaningless, they will come to distrust it. A society that wishes its children to take education seriously must provide better incentives than ours has so far. It is true that a few children have been intensely motivated toward educational achievement and have managed to succeed in the worst of circumstances. It is also true that some children have been fortunate enough to enjoy delightful educational environments in which they prosper despite their own lack of motivation. But the masses of children fall between these extremes. They need to be motivated—not to think, for they are already doing so continuously and intensely—but to think in ways that increase the measure of meaning in their lives. Here, philosophy offers benefit to all children. It would be utterly wrong to see it merely as an enrichment, suitable for only a small aristocracy of students and too esoteric for the mediocre many. It can help to provide what all students need: their own sense of the importance of learning.

Reason and Imagination

In including Locke's work among the landmarks that point the way to philosophy for children, we do not claim that Locke advocates either teaching philosophy to children or engaging children in long philosophical discourses. He makes clear that he would regard such proposals as pedagogical absurdities. Nevertheless, Locke provides a setting appropriate to a pedagogy in which philosophy would play an important role. Locke does here what he sought to do in epistemology—to clear the ground effectively for those who would follow.

Treat the child, Locke counsels us, as a rational creature. Instead of asserting rules and principles to teach children how to reason, engage them in practices that call for reasoning behavior. At the same time, expose them to models of what you advocate. Appeal to motives that are "level to their thoughts"—appropriate to their age and inclinations. Indeed, he tells us to be guided by the inclinations of children, for they should not be compelled to do what they do not have a mind and disposition to do. We have to learn how to arrange what we want to teach children so that they will of their own accord want to learn it. Children's curiosity is impressive evidence of their desire to learn. Therefore, their questions should not be laughed at but should be taken seriously as the beginning of inquiry, and they should be responded to in their own terms. Adults themselves have much to learn from the questions of children: "the native and untaught suggestions of inquisitive children . . . often offer things that may set a considering man's thoughts on work."

The atmosphere of trust and mutual respect that Locke urges in dealing with children is indispensable to a meaningful dialogue. Recognition of the child's capacity to reason, sensitivity to the child's interests, appreciation of the child's questionings and awareness that the child may have a much more open and interesting outlook than do many conventional adults—in all of these emphases Locke contributes much to our understanding of the educational process.

Vico's approach to education is one that seeks an improved balance between the instruction of the child in traditional disciplines and liberation of the child's imagination. He urges that we recognize imagination to be important in education because it enables children to grasp more effectively the materials to be learned. Children imaginatively reenact the subject matter in their minds, they live it and see it vividly. In reenacting it, children appropriate it for themselves and are able to think it through in their own fashion. This is in contrast to the dry, alien way in which the material has been presented to them. Even logic and mathematics, and especially geometry, when properly taught, can liberate the poetic imagination while at the same time teaching, Vico argues.

Vico opposes the notion that the fallibility of childhood judgments is due to children's inability to reason. On the contrary, he remarks, "The age of childhood is reasonable but it has no material on which to reason."[1] In other words, what children lack is experience of the world; their logical powers are sufficient to process adequately the information they acquire. Thus, education should concentrate on giving children this experience. Vico is very critical of the practice of teaching children formal logic at too early an age. He feels that the critical use of logic—its utilization for the purpose of appraising the validity of arguments—should be postponed until the later years of adolescence. In the earlier period, children should be encouraged to devise arguments (i.e. discover the connections between reasons and beliefs), and they should be encouraged to develop a practical sagacity with respect to the *probable* results of their actions, instead of being compelled to consider ideal courses of thought and conduct that have little relevance to the actual world.

Education as Dialogue

Like Locke and Vico, Pestalozzi demands that children be respected as active agents in their own education. Teaching is not merely a matter of carefully arranging the environment to present proper sequences of stimuli that will provoke children into reading, writing and other forms of learning. It is considerably more important to provoke the child to think and to develop the habit of thinking, as a self-initiated and regular process of reflection. Like Locke, Pestalozzi sees the value of dialogue with children for eliciting their own opinions on the subject under discussion. There is even a hint of Leibniz in Pestalozzi's suggestion that the aim of educational dialogue is to develop the native dispositions of the child's mind: once such development is activated, the intellectual processes of the child will continue to advance on their own. While perhaps Pestalozzi's approach is not very elaborate, he does recognize the readiness of children to think for themselves, as well as their need to be respected as intellectual agents in their own right. The educational process must evoke the child's own cognitive creativity while, as Pestalozzi insists, the cognitive and emotional dimensions of the child's life must be treated as an indissoluble unity.

From Augustine to Sartre, a number of writers have glowingly described their first encounter with philosophical ideas. One of the most vivid of these accounts is that of Tolstoy. For him in his boyhood, the exploration of philosophy was a continuous and wonderful adventure. Every metaphysical notion that he encountered—whether it was symmetry or eternity, solipsism or nothingness—struck him as a fresh and marvelous discovery. Tolstoy demonstrates that the impact of philosophical ideas in childhood can be excruciatingly intense. Far from being overwhelming, wrestling with philosophical ideas in childhood can be a formative and inspiring experience that will illuminate the remainder of one's life.

Is Childhood a Stage of Life or a Part of Life?

The Groethuysen essay attempts to indicate certain similarities between what children experience and what metaphysicians seek to understand. The metaphysician, says Groethuysen, is wary of the interpretations that the adult world places on any particular experience. When adults try to recall what it was like to be children, the result always turns out to be an assemblage of information derived from later experience, which was not part of the child's original awareness. Our interpretations represent the child's world as shot through with ambiguities or incongruities. But children themselves do not necessarily understand their experience as ambiguous or feel it to be incongruous with other experiences. As we search for an initial, original form of experience existing before the overlay of later interpretations, we should listen to children patiently and scrupulously and refrain from bursting in with information intended to put their insights into "more realistic" perspective— the perspective of our own adult world.

Another point made by Groethuysen is that it is a serious error to divide a human life into stages and then to consider the mature stage as somehow "normal," so that childhood and old age are merely a leading up to and a falling away from the norm. Once we conceive of a human life as a totality, then every period has its intrinsic importance, because the whole life is expressed in a distinctive way through each of its periods. A life is no less validly expressed in old age or childhood than in its mature years. This realization—of the unity of a life—leads Groethuysen to the further thought that what the child expresses is not limited in value to an understanding of childhood alone but helps in an understanding of life in its entirety: "That is why we must also ask the child what life is and what the world is." If we fail to take account of how the child perceives and understands things, then we deprive ourselves of the light that the child can throw on our own understanding.

Philosophy, Jaspers remarks, should be accessible to everyone, but it is not something that one person can somehow provide to another: all individuals must do philosophy for themselves. We must realize that any human being is capable of insights "which penetrate to the very depths of philosophy." This is no less true of children, and Jaspers does not hesitate to speak categorically of "children's philosophy." The child, like anyone else, can directly confront such ultimate philosophical problems as the mystery of the self. Moreover, the child questions incessantly in a way that most adults have long since ceased to do. Jaspers suggests that the philosophical disposition to appraise and freely express one's own experience is to be found as authentically in childhood as in any other phase of human life.

Setting the Stage for Thinking

In 1901, early in his career as a philosopher of education, Dewey was able to write that the ideas of the disciples of Pestalozzi had everywhere become commonplace: "the supremacy of self-activity, the symmetrical development of all the powers, the priority of character to information, the necessity of putting the real before the symbol, the concrete before the abstract, the necessity of following the order of nature and not the order of human convention"[2] had come to be accepted by teachers everywhere. Dewey observed, however, that while reformers were victorious in the field of theory, those who in fact determined the nature of educational practice were those who retained actual control of school conditions. He cited school conditions such as the grouping of children in classes, grading, curriculum, teacher training, selection of teachers, and teacher pay and promotion as the factors that underlay the actual fact-to-face contact of teacher and child.

What is the connection between such factors and the possibility of children doing philosophy in the classroom? Dewey draws our attention to the social setting of the educational process. Implicit in his every line is confidence in the child's ability to think, given a provocative environment congenial to thought. It is we and not the child who control these conditions. If we ask that children seek solutions to our problems rather than to their own, we foil any effort they might make to think for themselves. If we lecture them instead of involving them in dialogue and listening to what they have to say, if we conceive of education as restricted solely to mental and cognitive matters, if we isolate curricular subjects from one another so that children lose track of any possible connections, and if we fail to relate in-class topics to out-of-class experience, then we frustrate children's natural bent to think for themselves for the sheer enjoyment of the process.

We cannot give the child ideas:

> What he *directly* gets cannot be an idea. Only by wrestling with the conditions of the problem at first hand, seeking and finding his own way out, does he think. When the parent or teacher has provided the conditions which stimulate thinking and has taken a sympathetic attitude toward the activities of learning by entering into a common or conjoint experience, all has been done which a second party can do . . . the rest lies with the one directly concerned. If he cannot devise his own solution and find his own way out, he will not learn.

Implicit in Dewey's educational philosophy is the premise that children will think freely and creatively about whatever problems concern them if only the conditions of their educational lives are properly arranged. The environment to be created is not to be permissive; rather, educators must make it challenging and provocative. The teacher and the curriculum must instigate and promote the child's native tendency to inquire. Dewey stresses that all thinking begins in reflection upon one's personal experience. To think for oneself about one's own experience is to engage in genuine philosophical activity. More extensively and empathetically than any other philosopher, Dewey recognizes the immense complexity and significance of the child's intellectual possibilities as well as the child's urgent need to find meaning in life. But Dewey is not content simply to point to children's capacities. He shows what must be done in the way of remaking the social environment, and the school environment in particular, so that children are challenged to engage all of their powers in ways that will liberate them for still further growth and creativity.

NOTES

1. Giambattista Vico *The Autobiography of Giambattista Vico* translated from the Italian's Max H. Fisch and Thos. G. Bergin, (Ithaca: Great Seal Books, Cornell U. Press, 1944) p. 145.

2. *John Dewey, The Middle Works, 1899–1924*, vol. 1, edited by Jo Ann Boydston (Carbondale and Edwardsville: Southern Illinois University Press, 1976), p. 260.

⤐ 1 ⥱

ANTICIPATIONS OF PHILOSOPHICAL THINKING AMONG CHILDREN

⤐   JOHN LOCKE

Some Thoughts Concerning Education

§ 188. *Rhetorick* and *Logick* being the Arts, that in the ordinary method usually follow immediately after Grammar, it may perhaps be wondered that I have said so little of them. The reason is because of the little advantage young People receive by them. For I have seldom or never observed any one to get the Skill of reasoning well, or speaking handsomely by studying those Rules, which pretend to teach it. And therefore I would have a young Gentleman take a view of them in the shortest Systems could be found, without dwelling long on the contemplation and study of those Formalities. Right Reasoning is founded on something else than the *Predicaments* and *Predicables*, and does not consist in talking in *Mode* and *Figure* it self. But 'tis besides my present Business to enlarge upon this Speculation. To come therefore to what we have in hand; if you would have your Son *Reason well*, let him read *Chillingworth*; and if you

From *Some Thoughts Concerning Education,* and from *Locke's Letters to Edward Clarke.*

would have him speak well, let him be conversant in *Tully*, to give him the true *Idea* of *Eloquence*, and let him read those things that are well writ in *English*, to perfect his Style in the purity of our Language.

§ 189. If the use and end of right Reasoning, be to have right Notions, and a right Judgement of things; to distinguish betwixt Truth and Falsehood, Right and Wrong; and to act accordingly: be sure not to let your Son be bred up in the Art and Formality of Disputing, either practising it himself, or admiring it in others: unless instead of an able Man, you desire to have him an insignificant Wrangler, Opiniater in Discourse, and priding himself in contradicting others; or, which is worse, questioning every thing, and thinking there is no such thing as truth to be sought, but only Victory in Disputing. There cannot be any thing so disingenuous, so mis-becoming a Gentleman, or any one who pretends to be a rational Creature, as not to yield to plain Reason, and the Conviction of clear Arguments. Is there any thing more inconsistent with civil Conversation, and the end of all Debate, than not to take an Answer, though never so full and satisfactory; but still to go on with the Dispute as long as equivocal Sounds can furnish [a *Medius terminus*] a Term to wrangle with on the one side, or a Distinction on the other? whether pertinent or impertinent, Sense or Nonsense, agreeing with or contrary to what he had said before, it matters not. For this in short, is the Way and Perfection of Logical Disputes, That the opponent never take any Answer, nor the respondent ever yield to any Argument. This neither of them must do, whatever becomes of Truth or Knowledge; unless he will pass for a poor baffl'd Wretch, and lie under the Disgrace of not being able to maintain whatever he has once affirm'd, which is the great Aim and Glory in Disputing. Truth is to be found and supported by a mature and due Consideration of Things themselves, and not by artificial Terms and Ways of Arguing: These lead not Men so much into the discovery of Truth, as into a captious and fallacious use of doubtful Words, which is the most useless and most offensive way of talking, and such at least suits a Gentleman or a lover of Truth of any thing in the World.

Locke to Clarke, 1 September 1685

Sir,

Your son's temper by the account you give of it is I find not only such as I guessed it would be, but such as one would wish, and the qualities you already observe in him require nothing but right management whereby to be made very useful.

Curiosity in children is but an appetite after knowledge, and therefore ought to be encouraged in them, not only as a good sign, but as the great instrument nature has provided, to remove that ignorance they brought into the world with them, and which without this busy inquisitiveness would make them dull and useless creatures. The ways to encourage and keep it active and vigorous are, I suppose, these following:

1st. Not to check or discountenance any enquiries he may make, or suffer them to be laughed at; but to answer all his questions and explain matters he desires to know, so as to make them as much intelligible to him, as suits the capacity of his age and knowledge. But confound not this understanding with explications or notions that are above it, or with the variety or number of things that are not to his present purpose. Mark what it is he aims at in the question, and when you have informed and satisfied him in that, you shall see how his thoughts will proceed on to other things, and how by fit answers to his enquiries he may be led on farther than perhaps you could imagine. For knowledge to the understanding is as acceptable as light to the eyes; and children are pleased and delighted with it exceedingly, especially if they see that their enquiries are regarded, and that their desire of knowing is encouraged and commended. And I doubt not but one great reason why many children abandon themselves wholly to silly play, and spend all their time in trifling, is, because they have found their curiosity baulked and their enquiries neglected. But had they been treated with more kindness and respect, and their questions answered as they should to their satisfaction, I doubt not but they would have taken more pleasure in learning several things, and improving their knowledge, wherein there would be still newness and variety, which they delight in than in returning over and over to the same playthings.

2nd. To this serious answering their questions, and informing their understandings in what they desire, as if it were a matter that needed it, should be added some ways of commendation. Let others whom they esteem be told before their faces of the knowledge they have in such and such things; and since we are all even from our cradles vain, and proud creatures, let their vanity be flattered with things that will do them good; and let their pride set them to work on something which may turn to their advantage. Upon this ground you shall find that there can not be a greater spur to anything you would have your son learn or know himself, than to set him upon teaching it his sisters.

3rd. As children's enquiries are not to be slighted, so also great care is to be taken, that they never receive deceitful and deluding answers. They easily perceive when they are slighted or deceived, and quickly learn the trick of neglect, dissimulation, and falsehood which they observe others to make use of. We are not to entrench upon truth in our conversation, but least of all with children. Since if we play false with them, we not only deceive their expectation, and hinder their knowledge, but corrupt their innocence, and teach them the worst of vices. They are travellers newly arrived in a strange country of which they know very little: we should therefore make conscience not to mislead them. And though their question seem sometimes not very material, yet they should be seriously answered; for however they may appear to us to whom they are long since known, enquiries not worth the making, they are of moment to them who are wholly ignorant. Children are strangers to all we are acquainted with, and all the things they meet with are at first unknown to them, as they were to us; and happy are they who meet with kind people, that will comply with their ignorance, and help them to get out of it.

If you or I should be set down in Japan, with all our prejudice and knowledge about us, a conceit whereof makes us perhaps apt to slight the thoughts and enquiries of children; should we, I say, be set down in Japan, we should no doubt (if we would inform ourselves of what is there to be known) ask a thousand questions, which, to a supercilious and inconsiderate Japanese, would seem very idle and impertinent; and yet to us would be very material, and we would be glad to find a man so kind and humane, as would answer them, and instruct our ignorance.

When any new thing comes in their way, children usually ask the common question of a stranger, What is it? Whereby they commonly mean nothing but the name; and therefore to tell them how it is called is usually the proper answer to that demand. The next question usually is, What is it for? And this it should be answered truly and directly: the use of the thing told, and the way explained, how it serves to such a purpose, as far as their capacities can comprehend it; and so of any other circumstances they shall ask about it; not turning them going, till you have given all the satisfaction they are capable of, leading them by the answers into farther questions. And perhaps to a grown man such conversation will not altogether be so idle and insignificant as he may imagine. The native and untaught suggestions of inquisitive children do often offer things that may set a considering man's thoughts on work. And I think there is often more to be learnt from the unexpected questions of a child, than the discourses of men, who talk in a road, according to the fashions and customs of their country.

4th. Perhaps it may not, however, be amiss to exercise their curiosity concerning strange and new things in their way, on purpose that they may enquire and be busy to inform themselves about them; and if by chance their curiosity leads them to ask what they should not know, it is a great deal better to tell them plainly, that it is a thing that belongs not to them to know, than to pop them off with a falsehood, or a frivolous answer.

Locke to Clarke, 28 January 1688[-9]

Sir,

You may remember that I have formerly told you that children whilst very young should be treated as rational [creatures], and that therefore you should always carry this in your mind in all the management and discipline of your son. This I perceive [needs some] little explication, it being liable to some mistake. It is true your son and all children should be treated as rational creatures, therefore argued with as grown men. Long discourses and philosophical reasonings at best do but amaze and confound but do not instruct them. When I say, therefore, that they must be treated as rational creatures, I mean that you should make them sensible by the mildness of your carriage and your composure, even in your correction of them, that what you do is reasonable in you, and useful and necessary for them; and that it is not out of caprichio, passion, or fancy that you command or forbid them anything. This they are capable of understanding; and there is no virtue they should be excited to, nor fault they should be kept from, which I do not think they may be convinced of; but it must be by such reasons as their age and understandings are capable of, and those proposed always in a very few and plain words. The foundations on which several duties are built, and the fountains of right and wrong from which they spring, are not, perhaps, easily to be let into the minds of grown men not used to abstract their thoughts from common received opinions. Much less are children capable of reasonings from remote principles. They cannot conceive the force of long deductions: the reasons that move them must be obvious, and level to their thoughts, and such as may (if I may say so) be felt and touched. But yet if their age, temper and inclinations be considered, there will never want such motives as may be sufficient to convince them. If there be no other more particular, yet these will always be intelligible, and of force, to deter them from any fault fit to be taken notice of in them, viz. that it will be a discredit and disgrace to them, and displease you. But of all the ways whereby the children are to be instructed and their manners formed, the plainest, easiest, and most efficacious, is to set before their eyes the examples of those things you would have them do or avoid; which, when they are pointed out to them in the practice of persons within their knowledge, with some reflection on their beauty or unbecomingness, are of more force to draw or deter their imitation than any philosophical discourses can be made to them. Virtue and vices can by no words be so plainly set before their understandings as the actions of other men will show them, when you direct their observation and bid them view this or that good or bad quality in the practice. And the gracefulness or ungracefulness of many things in good or ill breeding will be better learnt, and make deeper impressions on them, in the examples of others, than from any rules or instructions can be given about them. This is a method to be used, not only whilst they are young, but to be continued even as long as they shall be under another's tuition or conduct. Nay, I know not whether it be not the best way to be used by a father as long as he shall think fit, on any occasion to reform anything he wishes mended in his son; nothing sinking so gently and so deep into men's minds as example, And what ill they either overlook or indulge in themselves, they cannot but dislike and be ashamed of when [they see] it in another.

⤳ GIAMBATTISTA VICO

On the Study Methods of Our Time

In the past, all arts and disciplines were interconnected and rested in the lap of philosophy; subsequently, they were sundered apart. Those responsible for this separation can be compared to a tyrannical ruler who, having seized mastery of a great, populous, and opulent city, should, in order to secure his own safety, destroy the city and scatter its inhabitants into a number of widely strewn villages. As a consequence, it is impossible for the townsmen to feel inspired, through the bold pride awakened by the sight of the splendor and wealth of their city and by the awareness of their number, to band together and conspire against him, lending one another help in their fight against the common oppressor. . . .

Translated by Elio Gianturco, (Indianapolis, Ind: The Bobbs-Merrill Co., Inc., 1965), pp. 47, 13–15, 19, 24, 33, 35, 42.

Philosophical criticism is the subject which we compel our youths to take up first. Now, such speculative criticism, the main purpose of which is to cleanse its fundamental truths not only of all falsity, but also of the mere suspicion of error, places upon the same plane of falsity not only false thinking, but also those secondary verities and ideas which are based on probability alone, and commands us to clear our minds of them. Such an approach is distinctly harmful, since training in common sense is essential to the education of adolescents, so that that faculty should be developed as early as possible; else they break into odd or arrogant behavior when adulthood is reached. It is a positive fact that, just as knowledge originates in truth and error in falsity, so common sense arises from perceptions based on verisimilitude. Probabilities stand, so to speak, midway between truth and falsity, since things which most of the time are true, are only very seldom false.

Consequently, since young people are to be educated in common sense, we should be careful to avoid that the growth of common sense be stifled in them by a habit of advanced speculative criticism. I may add that common sense, besides being the criterion of practical judgment, is also the guiding standard of eloquence. It frequently occurs, in fact, that orators in a law court have greater difficulty with a case which is based on truth, but does not seem so, than with a case that is false but plausible. There is a danger that instruction in advanced philosophical criticism may lead to an abnormal growth of abstract intellectualism, and render young people unfit for the practice of eloquence. . . .

Just as old age is powerful in reason, so is adolescence in imagination. Since imagination has always been esteemed a most favorable omen of future development, it should in no way be dulled. Furthermore, the teacher should give the greatest care to the cultivation of the pupil's memory, which, though not exactly the same as imagination, is almost identical with it. In adolescence, memory outstrips in vigor all other faculties, and should be intensely trained. Youth's natural inclination to the arts in which imagination or memory (or a combination of both) is prevalent (such as painting, poetry, oratory, jurisprudence) should by no means be blunted. Nor should advanced philosophical criticism, the common instrument today of all arts and sciences, be an impediment to any of them. The Ancients knew how to avoid this drawback. In almost all their schools for youths, the role of logic was fulfilled by geometry. Following the example of medical practitioners, who concentrate their efforts on seconding the bent of Nature, the Ancients required their youths to learn the science of geometry which cannot be grasped without a vivid capacity to form images. Thus, without doing violence to nature, but gradually and gently and in step with the mental capacities of their age, the Ancients nurtured the reasoning powers of their young men.

In our days, instead, philosophical criticism alone is honored. The art of "topics," far from being given first place in the curriculum, is utterly disregarded. Again I say, this is harmful, since the invention of arguments is by nature prior to the judgment of their validity, so that, in teaching, that invention should be given priority over philosophical criticism. In our days, we keep away from the art of inventing arguments, and think that this skill is of no use. We hear people affirming that, if individuals are critically endowed, it is sufficient to teach them a certain subject, and they will have the capacity to discover whether there is any truth in that subject. It is claimed that, without any previous training in the *ars topica*, any person will be able to discern the probabilities which surround any ordinary topic, and to evaluate them by *the same standard employed in the sifting of truth*. But who can be sure that he has taken into consideration every feature of the subject on hand? . . .

I think, young men should be taught the totality of sciences and arts, and their intellectual powers should be developed to the full; thus they will become familiar with the art of argument, drawn from the *ars topica*. At the very outset, their common sense should be strengthened so that they can grow in prudence and eloquence. Let their imagination and memory be fortified so that they may be effective in those arts in which fantasy and the mnemonic faculty are predominant. At a later stage let them learn criticism, so that they can apply the fullness of their personal judgment to what they have been taught. And let them develop skill in debating on either side of any proposed argument. . . .

The geometrical method enables us to set forth matters in a purely geometrical, apodeictic form, and gives us the possibility of teaching them in a plain, unadorned way, devoid of any aesthetic charm. All of the modern physicists affect a style of exposition which is as severe as it is limited. Our theory of physics (in the process of learning as well as when mastered) moves forward by a constant and gradual series of small, closely concatenated steps. Consequently, it is apt to smother the student's specifically philosophic faculty, i.e., his capacity to perceive the analogies existing between matters lying far apart and, apparently, most dissimilar. It is this capacity which constitutes the source and principle of all ingenious, acute, and brilliant forms of expression. It should be emphasized that tenuity, subtlety, delicacy of thought, is not identical with acuity of ideas. That which is tenuous, delicately refined, may be represented by a single line; "acute" by two. Metaphor, the greatest and brightest ornament of forceful, distinguished speech, undoubtedly plays the first role in acute, figurative expression.

But the greatest drawback of our educational methods is that we pay an excessive amount of attention to the natural sciences and not enough to ethics. Our chief fault is that we disregard that part of ethics which treats of human character, of its dispositions, its passions, and of the manner of adjusting these factors to public life and eloquence. We neglect that discipline which deals with the differential features of the virtues and vices, with good and bad behavior-patterns, with the typical characteristics of the various ages of man, of the two sexes, of social and economic class, race and nation, and with the art of seemly conduct in life, the most difficult of all arts. . . .

Our young men, because of their training, are unable to engage in the life of the community, to conduct themselves with sufficient wisdom and prudence. . . .

Therefore, it is an error to apply to the prudent conduct of life the abstract criterion of reasoning that obtains in the domain of science. A correct judgment deems that men—who are, for the most part, but fools— are ruled, not by forethought, but by whim or chance. The doctrinaires judge human actions as they *ought* to be, not as they actually are (i.e., performed more or less at random). Satisfied with abstract truth alone, and not being gifted with common sense, unused to following probability, those doctrinaires do not bother to find out whether their opinion is held by the generality and whether the things that are truths to them are also such to other people. . . .

If adolescents whose imagination and memory have been previously strengthened are taught philosophical criticism, their poetical powers, I think, would derive benefit from the process. Poets keep their eyes focused on an ideal truth, which is a universal idea, as I shall presently explain. Even the geometrical method is conducive to the contriving of poetical figments, if the writer makes an effort to preserve throughout the continuity of the plot, the identical psychological traits which he has given to his characters at the beginning of the play. This is an art of which Homer was the earliest instructor, said Aristotle. The Philosopher points out that there are certain paralogisms *a consequente*, such as: *Daedalus flies, if he has wings.* Poetic figments cannot be handled in the correct fashion except by artists who can link properly point to point, so that the second point seems to proceed naturally from the first, and the third from the second. It was acutely but truthfully said that figments of this kind can be invented only by persons intimately familiar with philosophic truths. This is done outstandingly by geometricians who, working from hypothetical or incorrect premises and data, are able to deduce conclusions which are true.

∾§ JOHANN HEINRICH PESTALOZZI

The Child as Thinker

Letter XXIX

APRIL 4, 1819.

MY DEAR GREAVES,

The second rule that I would give to a mother, respecting the early development of the infant mind is this: Let the child not only be *acted upon* but let him be an *agent* in intellectual education.

I shall explain my meaning. Let the mother bear in mind that her child has not only the faculties of attention to and retention of certain ideas or facts, but also a faculty of reflection, independent of the thoughts of others. It is well done to make a child read, and write, and learn, and repeat,—but it is still better to make a child *think*. We may be able to turn to account the opinions of others, and we may find it valuable or advantageous to be acquainted with them: we may profit by their light; but we can render ourselves most useful to others and we shall be most entitled to the character of valuable members of society by the efforts of our own minds; by the result of our own investigations; by those views and their application which we may call our own intellectual property.

I am not now speaking of those leading ideas which are from time to time thrown out, and by which science is advanced or society benefited at large. I am speaking of that stock of intellectual property which every one may acquire, even the most unpretending individual and in the humblest walks of life. I am speaking of that habit of reflection which guards against unthinking conduct under any circumstances, and which is always active to examine that which is brought before the mind; that habit of reflection

From J. H. Pestalozzi, *Letters on Early Education* (Syracuse, N.Y.: C.W. Bardeen, 1898)

which excludes the self-sufficiency of ignorance or the levity of "a little learning";—which may lead an individual to the modest acknowledgement that he knows but little, and to the honest consciousness that he knows that little well. To engender this habit, nothing is so effective as an early development in the infant mind of thought,—regular, self-active thought.

Let not the mother suffer herself to be detained from this task by the objections of those who deem the infant mind altogether incapable of any exertion of that kind. I will venture to say that those who propose that objection, though they may be the profoundest thinkers or the greatest theorists, will be found to have no *practical* knowledge whatsoever of the subject nor any moral interest in the investigation of it. And I, for one, would trust more in the experimental knowledge of a mother, proceeding from exertions to which she was prompted by maternal feeling—in that experimental knowledge, even of an illiterate mother, I would trust more than in the theoretical speculations of the most ingenious philosophers. There are cases in which sound sense and a warm heart see farther than a highly refined, cold, and calculating head.

I would therefore call upon the mother to begin her task, in spite of any objections that may be raised. It will be enough if she is persuaded to *begin;* she will then continue of herself; she will derive such gratification from her task that she will never think of relaxing.

While she unfolds the treasures of the infant mind and uncloses the world of hitherto slumbering thought, she will not envy the assurance of philosophers who would have the human mind to be a "universal blank". Engaged in a task which calls into activity all the energies of her mind and all the affections of her heart, she will smile at their dictatorial speculations and their supercilious theories. Without troubling herself about the knotty question whether there are any *innate ideas,* she will be content if she succeeds in developing the *innate faculties of the mind.*

If a mother asks for the designation of the subjects which might be profitably used as vehicles for the development of thought, I would answer her that any subject will do if it be treated in a manner suitable to the faculties of the child. It is the great art in teaching, never to be at a loss for the choice of an object for the illustration of a truth. There is not an object so trivial that in the hands of a skilful teacher it might not become interesting, if not from its own nature, at least from the mode of treating it. To a child everything is new. The charm of novelty, it is true, soon wears off; and if there is not the fastidiousness of matured years there is at least the impatience of infancy to contend with. But then there is for the teacher the great advantage of a combination of simple elements, which may diversify the subject without dividing the attention.

If I say that any subject will do for the purpose, I mean this to be understood literally. Not only there is not one of the little incidents in the life of a child, in his amusements and recreations, in his relations to his parents and friends and playfellows,—but there is not actually anything within the reach of the child's attention, whether it belong to nature or to the employments and arts of life, that might not be made the object of a lesson by which some useful knowledge might be imparted, and, which is still more important, by which the child might not be familiarized with the habit of thinking on what he sees and speaking after he has thought.

The mode of doing this is not by any means to talk much *to* a child, but to enter into conversation *with* a child; not to address to him many words, however familiar or well chosen, but to bring him to express himself on the subject; not to exhaust the subject, but to question the child about it, and to let him find out and correct the answers. It would be ridiculous to expect that the volatile spirits of an infant could be brought to follow any lengthy explanations. The attention of a child is deadened by long expositions but roused by animated questions.

Let these questions be short, clear, and intelligible. Let them not merely lead the child to repeat in the same or in varied terms what he has heard just before. Let them excite him to observe what is before him, to recollect what he has learned, and to muster his little stock of knowledge for materials for an answer. Show him a certain quality in one thing, and let him find out the same in others. Tell him that the shape of a ball is called round; and if, accordingly, you bring him to point out other objects to which the same character belongs you have employed him more usefully than by the most perfect discourse on rotundity. In the one instance he would have had to listen and to recollect; in the other he has to observe and to think.

◄§ LEV TOLSTOY

My Encounter with Philosophical Ideas

I can scarcely believe what were the favorite and most constant subjects of my meditations during my boyhood—they were so incompatible with my age and position. But, in my opinion, incompatibility between a man's position and his moral activity is the truest proof of sincerity.

During the course of the year, when I led an isolated moral life, concentrated within myself, all the abstract questions concerning the destination of man, the future life, the immortality of the soul, already presented themselves to me; and, with all the fervor of inexperience, my weak childish mind endeavored to solve these questions, the presentation of which represents the highest stage to which the mind of man can attain, but the solution of which is not granted to him.

It seems to me that the human mind, in every separate individual, traverses the same path during development by which it is developed in whole races; that the thoughts which serve as a foundation for the various philosophical theories form the inalienable attributes of the mind; but that every man has recognized them, with more or less clearness, even before he has known of the philosophical theories.

These thoughts presented themselves to my mind with such clearness, and in such a striking light, that I even tried to apply them to life, fancying that I was the *first* to discover such great and useful truths.

Once the thought occurred to me that happiness does not depend upon external conditions, but on our relations to them; that man, after he is accustomed to endure suffering, cannot be unhappy; and, in order to accustom myself to pain, I held Tatischeff's lexicon for five minutes in my outstretched hands, in spite of dreadful pain, or I went into the garret and castigated myself on the bare back with a rope so severely that tears sprang involuntarily to my eyes.

On another occasion, remembering, all of a sudden, that death awaited me at any hour, at any moment, I made up my mind, not understanding how people had hitherto failed to understand it, that man can be happy only by making use of the present, and not thinking of the future; and for three days, under the influence of this though, I neglected my lessons, and did nothing but lie on the bed, and enjoy myself by reading a romance and eating gingerbread with Kronoff mead, for which I spent the last money I had.

On another occasion, while standing before the blackboard engaged in drawing various figures upon it with chalk, I was suddenly struck by the thought: Why is symmetry pleasing to the eye? What is symmetry?

It is an inborn feeling, I answered myself. But on what is it founded? Is there symmetry in everything in life? On the contrary here is life—and I drew an oval figure on one side of the blackboard. After life the soul passes into eternity; here is eternity—and from one side of the oval I drew a line which extended to the very edge of the board. Why not another similar line from the other side? Yes, and, as a matter of fact, what kind of eternity is that which is on one side only? for we certainly have existed before this life, although we have lost the memory of it.

This reasoning, which appeared to me extremely novel and lucid, and whose thread I can now only catch with difficulty, pleased me excessively, and I took a sheet of paper with the idea of setting it forth in writing; but, in the process, such a mass of thoughts suddenly entered my mind, that I was obliged to rise and walk about the room. When I approached the window, my attention turned on the water-carrier horse which the coach-man was harnessing at the moment; and all my thoughts were concentrated upon the solution of the question, Into what animal or man will the soul of that horse migrate, when it is set free? At that moment, Volodya was passing through the room, and smiled, perceiving that I was meditating something; and that smile was sufficient to make me comprehend that all I had been thinking about was the most frightful nonsense.

I have related this, to me, memorable occasion, merely for the purpose of giving the reader to understand the nature of my reflections.

But in none of all the philosophical directions was I drawn so far as by skepticism, which at one time brought me into a state bordering on madness. I fancied that, besides myself, nothing and nobody existed in the whole world; that objects were not objects, but images which only appeared when I directed my attention to them; and that, as soon as I ceased to think of them, the objects disappeared.

In a word, I agreed with Schelling in the conviction that objects do not exist, but only my relation to them exists. There were moments when, under the influence of this *fixed idea*, I reached such a stage of derangement that I sometimes glanced quickly in the opposite direction, hoping suddenly to find nothingness (*néant*) where I was not.

A pitiful, worthless spring of moral action is the mind of man!

My weak mind could not penetrate the impenetrable; but in this labor, which was beyond its strength, I lost, one after the other, the convictions which, for the happiness of my own life, I never should have dared to touch upon.

From all this heavy moral toil I brought away nothing except a shiftiness of mind which weakened the force of my will, and a habit of constant moral analysis which destroyed freshness of feeling and clearness of judgment.

Abstract thoughts take shape, in consequence of man's capacity to seize with his perceptions the state of his soul at any given moment, and transfer it to his memory. My tendency to abstract meditation developed the perceptive faculties in me to such an unnatural degree that frequently, when I began to think of the simplest sort of thing, I fell into an inextricable circle of analysis of my thoughts, and no longer considered the question which had occupied me, but thought of what I was thinking about. When I asked myself, Of what am I thinking? I replied, I think of what I am thinking. And now what am I thinking of? I think that I am thinking of what I am thinking, and so on. Intellect gave way before ratiocination.

Nevertheless, the philosophical discoveries which I made were extremely flattering to my self-conceit. I often fancied myself a great man, who was discovering new truths for the benefit of mankind, and I gazed upon other mortals with a proud consciousness of my worth; but, strange to say, when I came in contact with these mortals, I was shy in the presence of every one of them, and the higher I rated myself in my own opinion, the less capable I was of displaying my consciousness of my own merit to others, and I could not even accustom myself not to feel ashamed of my every word and movement, however simple.

ᴈᔈ BERNARD GROETHUYSEN

The Child and the Metaphysician

He has a particular fondness for childhood which he considers the inspired age of man.

M. Saint-Clair

We are scarcely conscious of what we were in our childhood. Most of the time, it seems to us that the world which we then contemplated was the same as that which we know at the present time, the only difference being that we did not know it. Here is approximately how it seems to us: first, there was the world, the world such as we conceive of it today and, in the beginning, when we had just arrived in the world, we knew of it but very little. It was only little by little that we learned to know it. That is why almost all stories of childhood begin by giving the town in which we were

The original German text, dating from before 1910, was translated into French by Alix Guillain and was published in *Deucalion*, vol. 2, 1947, pp. 11–20. The present version has been translated from the French version by Robert M. Glick.

born, who our parents were, and a general description of our surroundings. Yet it is evident that we did not know all of these facts in the same way at that time. The "town" was then not a town, the "parents" were not the individuals in question, and all that surrounded us was not this objectivity of which we are currently speaking. The world is thus, we think, but we did not know it; this was a time of apprenticeship.

It is true that we are also able to recognize something like the soul of the child, and particular ways of conceiving and feeling which are peculiar to the child. However in doing this we start from the idea that our world is there, and that only the manner in which the soul understands it is different. It is for this reason that we feel that stories of youth are of interest to us only insofar as they instruct us on the character of the man, or on the human soul in general. There is no question whatever of our believing that these stories could shed some new light on our understanding of the world. When we glance backward at our childhood, it is not in order to understand the world but rather to understand ourselves. We were at that time beginners in the art of interpreting the world, and who would even consider questioning a beginner? Childhood is an age at which we do not yet know anything. And this is indeed true, for if the world were something that we were able to know or to grasp, we could no longer continue to ask questions and childhood, strictly speaking, would be no more than a time of preparation, an age useless in itself, at least as far as the comprehension of things is concerned. We agree that the child has a particular joy of his own and that we must take care to assure that childhood maintains its proper character. We must, we are told, let the child be a child, but as far as his experience with the world is concerned, the child is merely a schoolboy; and in what way can a schoolboy instruct us, at least in regard to what we need to learn?

That is why we have such a special relationship to our childhood. We do not ask the child we were how the world appeared to him at that time, but from the depths of the knowledge we have acquired we reconstruct for him the world which he then saw, at the time he was beginning to speak— that world which made him suffer or made him happy. For example, we remember stained-glass windows and soft light. We say at present: "The stained-glass windows were in such and such a room, in such and such a house, in such and such a town." But these are so many facts of which we knew nothing at the time. Moreover are we truly certain that we knew the stained-glass windows were there and that the light was soft? Not only do we not speak of what we really remember—at best we sometimes utter parenthetically: "I still remember" or "If I remember correctly," but this is in order to project immediately beyond memory the object that we remember—but also we do not cling to the way in which we remember. And that seems impossible, moreover. The words we use are the words of grown-ups. We can no longer shake the notions of "man" or "thing" that are solidly anchored within us. There is a sort of contradiction in wishing to be a child again, now that we already know everything, in using words, and at the same time letting things act within us, without naming them, in knowing things and in visualizing images differently from the way in which they are visualized by a being who still knows nothing. A psychologist will perhaps tell you: "You are undertaking the impossible, for even the memories you are still able to retain have been transformed into knowledge in the adult." And yet it is not so. There remains the "visionary," the obscure, the thing of another essence: all that in each of us preceded knowledge. But it is precisely this that we cannot know, or at least that we have no way of knowing, without losing the nature of our being.

It is evident that this cannot be known. It is also certain that it is not a matter of simply erasing what we have learned since then. What is it, then, in truth, that makes the state of childhood so foreign to us? It is knowledge; not, strictly speaking, the fact of knowing more, but rather the particular manner of knowing.

Let me explain: we did not know formerly that this was a room and that it was possible to enumerate all of the different objects in it according to the role they play in life, that this was an armoire, that a chair, this a picture, but to our eyes all these objects had an existence of their own, as independent objects. We were unaware that they had a reason to exist. Now, we know their reason for being. We have acquired the experience and assurance that life gives, and for this reason we live as strangers in an undefined world, or rather in a world otherwise defined. But we have this assurance only so long as we do not seek to get our bearings in the world.

And if, therefore, we begin to be astonished, are we not then drawing closer to that first world, the world of the child, and farther from the world of the grown-up? We feel ourselves strangers in the defined world, yet it is odd that there was a time when this world was not defined. We speak of the man stranded on a desert island and no longer knowing from whence he had come. But was this not once true of each of us? What is known to us at present must have once been unknown to us. And at that time we were children. It is one of the oddities of the human condition that we recognize ourselves as complete individuals when we have behind us a being, a state preceding knowledge. This was not, in reality, a slumbering, nor was it a gradual exploration in order to know the region better and better, as if we had seen at first only a small part of the island and had little by little discovered it in its entirety. Someone will say: "It was first a kind of slumbering, but a slumbering in which we were dreaming." The man would have been carried, asleep, from the place of the shipwreck to the island, following which he would have roamed the island for a long time, sluggish, and as soon as he had awakened completely, his surroundings would no longer in any way seem strange to him. Far better. He would have already become familiar with things before really knowing what they were. Exactly! But now that these things as a whole seem strange to him does it not seem to him that this is once again the beginning? Certainly this awareness of the strangeness is not the act of the child. But there is somehow a special relationship between metaphysics and the state of childhood, or in any event there can be one between the world which would somehow be beyond interpretation and the world not yet interpreted. It is thus that the metaphysician is perhaps able to take a step back toward childhood, since he does not believe that it is possible to know life and since he will not attribute to the child interpretations given by knowledge. He will not start out from the awareness that he knows better at present what the world is about and will not begin sermonizing to the child he was. It will sometimes seem to him—wrongly, perhaps—that there was already something like a question asked by the child about the world and to which life was unable to give an answer. And then it will perhaps seem to him as well that all that he had forgotten in between was close, was coming back to him. There will then be something in him that will induce him to interpret this former world as a metaphysician. This will be an act of faithfulness. He will not say to the child: "What you saw then was a flower of such and such a far-off country, I know now, and that being who appeared before you at that time was of this profession or that or belonging to one or another social class: Mr. So-and-So, I know him now." But he will say: "Far from wishing to define your world for you, I shall try to explain to you as a metaphysician what was given to you and how it was given to you. I shall not seek to exchange for another the image you have of life, but I shall confine myself to this reflection and inquire of the world which is reflected. If philosophy is a reflecting consciousness, there must be a 'reflection' of this world as well. In your world there were things, and there were beings endowed with souls, there was distance and proximity, there were things which were fixed and others which were not."

But why am I inquiring into all of this? In order to better understand life. If, by reflecting on ourselves, we start with the 'man' and the 'soul,' our attitude toward the child must be other than that which we would have if we start with life. The 'man,' the 'soul,' the 'I' are in truth words without age, without life. Rather, we picture a kind of normal age which was preceded by youth and followed by old age. There is in that picture something which isolates man from what happens in the world as well as from other men. He becomes a personality having specific qualities; he wonders unceasingly: "How am I" and the other man is no longer the same as he. Yes, they are related and resemble one another. They speak of a human nature that they have in common. But this resemblance is not something that unites them. The same is true of anyone's life. All people divide their life, for how would they conceive of the whole of it when they begin from the point of view of the personality? The child is not what the man will be, and even if you think you can recover your qualities in childhood, there is nothing there out of which to constitute a unity of life. For what has given unity to my life is not that I was this or that, but this life itself, such as it unfolds. The fact that I am a man among other men does not mean that we are similar but rather that we share the same destiny. And it is thus that I would like to grasp the whole of my life and the world that I am experiencing. And that is why we must also ask the child what life is and what the world is.

I choose the story of the youth of Sören Kierkegaard because it offers many remarkable things. What it was, when Sören Kierkegaard was still very, very young, he scarcely realizes. He knows that there was something "like that" and which went along on its own, and next to that there were a thousand strange things. But he is aware only of what is strange. There were rooms that one entered only infrequently; they were strange. One of them had bottle-green windows. He attached little importance to the fact that there were other people in those rooms, for he still knew nothing of the special significance which people have. No. There were large rooms, and some were bright while others were somber. He did not know very well what was happening outside as he was not curious about it. That was not familiar to him; it was not part of his world. If someone told him this or that about it, he retained something of it, but something distant and nothing at all like what he felt in those rooms which constantly soak up our glances and of which we are a part. In order for that to enter inside you, it had to be something strange, yet something near. Later, he noticed that the same was true of grown-ups who do not see the starry heavens because they are too far off and because they have nothing to do with them, people who also do not reflect on everyday happenings around them. And streets and cars and people were to him what starry skies were to grown-ups, while his room was his world.

Only once did he become aware of the vast world around him. On that day he was lost. It is then that we suddenly perceive that there are many, many people and that we are "elsewhere" and that we are unable to find ourselves in all of that. It seems a strange awakening. We know then that we are small and we become aware of the fact that there are other people.

In the same way, one day, in an exceptional moment, he became aware of everyday life. It was a day when it had begun to rain, endlessly. He was told that it was "drizzle," but it appeared to him to be a length of time, slow hours, obscurity. Something that was there, outside, was closing in on him. Otherwise he knew nothing of days and hours. The world was outside of time and, for him, this did not happen first and that later. Afterwards he realized that grown-ups, too, have difficulty understanding what belongs to time and that they speak of themselves as if time had no hold on them. And yet, with all of its strange contents, that was truly his world.

One time, however, he realized that alongside of his world there was something else. Sören Kierkegaard still knew nothing of night at that time. He knew it only at a later date. But one morning he awoke very early and there was a greyish light in the room, also a large bed, and not the slightest noise. He was no longer able to distinguish different directions. He no longer knew what was in front and what was behind, or where the door was, or the window. He abandoned himself completely to the haziness in which all was bathed. It was as if he had discovered something entirely new. It might have been called the soul, or else the sense of being carried along by something, and also the feeling of an absolute solitude. It seems to him now that it was only then for the first time that he had been fully himself and that, today also, he would have only to forget many things in order to be once again what he was then. There are thus moments in life from which everything happening afterward seems a series of dreams from which one awakens with the same feeling as one about to fall asleep. In his life, this was such a moment; or it can be said that it is in such instants that a kind of astonishment, or a question, comes over a person, and all that follows is only a series of interpretations or explanations and not an answer.

We must however continue our story and see how Sören Kierkegaard found out that things and people existed. For at that time it was still not people and things nor even himself that was part of life, but only generalities of a certain dimension and always containing many, many diverse things. First it was one's surroundings, if that be the proper term for it, the place where one does not live. One does not go to this one's place or to that one's; one does not go to his grandmother's, for example, but one goes somewhere where there are a lot of people without being able to distinguish the unity from the number, and it does not seem that this or that person is anything special within the group. But there it is, I am 'elsewhere' and this 'elsewhere' is something about which Sören Kierkegaard was unable to be precise, even later while speaking to grown-ups. Still later this vision of the whole remained with him, although he had learned to separate the unity from the whole and to distinguish this individual from that. For that was not sufficient to cause the impression of the whole to disappear or to exhaust it; it receded somewhat into the background, yet it always remained an undefined whole that was different here or there. Occasionally it seems to him now that his first manner of contemplating the world was more profound, more definitive, and that as far as the rest was concerned, he had only arranged it haphazardly as it came, as life brought it to him; and it was certainly true of what had happened later, with 'knowledge' filling him in on this or that.

There are things and there are people, but things were closer to him than people, and that is why I must begin to speak to you of things, or rather before that, of what we call a quality particular to things; I mean color. There are colors that we know; we see them again and again, but we do not pay attention to them; moreover, we cannot grasp them since they are everywhere and we do not question them. Sometimes, though, there is a color that comes from somewhere else; Sören Kierkegaard knew several of them. There was a shade of green on a map which hung on the wall, and this shade was not this or that specifically, it was not unusual, but if one looked at it for a long time it became something other than what it was; one was astonished that it was different, and one went back to see it constantly. For this reason we are wrong to speak of colored things, but, as Sören Kierkegaard experienced it, there is color that exists outside of things, by itself, and it is precisely when it is a part of things that we do not really see it, as we do when it exists by itself, as on the map. What led Sören Kierkegaard to look at colors was, I repeat, his love for "the something else," the idea that there were worlds colored differently, and yet it was also possible to say that when he looked at a color he was closer to himself. We might say that this is a sensation similar to that which Sören Kierkegaard experienced on that beautiful morning when, rising at dawn, he entered into himself, a sensation that also would accompany him throughout his life. 2065004

In fact such colors remain what is undefined. And so, later, we no longer know anything of what we knew of them before. They differ in this from things about which we are always learning something new, things that we never stop trying to define better. What is undefined is always something seeming to have preceded all the rest. And it is because people are not able to comprehend what is not defined that they are so far from children. They continue to believe that the child does not know what the world is about and that they know much more at present than he. But it is precisely to what we did not know, to what is undefined, that we must return in order to understand life in its entirety, to know what it is truly about, and what our knowledge has added to it since, in order to find behind all of our interpretations that which preceded every interpretation.

Nevertheless, there was something else as well that morning when Sören Kierkegaard awakened at dawn. His eyes fell on something in particular, next to which there were many other objects, such as things and people. It was in the contact with things that he sensed what it is to have a feeling for an object outside of himself. It happened thus: he had to choose a toy, which he did, but scarcely had he done so than he was seized with remorse over the thought of the other toys that he had not chosen. It seemed to him that he had committed some injustice toward them, that he had rejected them. There was no reason why he should not have chosen them. We say, it is true, "I prefer *this* toy," but that must not mean that we are *against* the others; on the contrary, they become dearer to us. Our relationship to the toy we have chosen is not the same as our relationship to the others. We have still decided *against* them. It is not normal to say no to something simply because we have said yes to something else. This was for him a kind of first love, a love for things that he had repudiated. I know of no other love he had at that time, whether for things or people.

As far as people were concerned, his relationships with them were strange. People are difficult to understand and it is impossible to become familiar with them as we can with things. We stop in front of a thing, look at it, touch it, come back to it, and it is always there, ever the same. Not so, people; we cannot look at them and touch them. They are not simple. We feel that each time they are different. Their comings and goings always mean something, and for our part we cannot relate to them as we relate to things; we do not know what meaning is in their faces—they are not familiar to us, not something which is simply there, so that we can say: "This is the object that is here or there, an object that is in the room, or even, this man whom you see on this picture." No, their faces remain foreign to us, their eyes, their noses different from all we are familiar with; they have no fixed contours or forms as do all the other objects here in the room or hanging on the walls; and if it happens that they are extremely still, so that we can look at them leisurely—when they are sitting, or sleeping, for example—they have something disquieting about them.

Sören Kierkegaard was unable to succeed in having true relationships with people. The world of colors and things was closer to him; he felt somehow freer with them, more directly drawn to them. To this must be added as well the idea that people do something to you, they speak to you, or else they speak about you among themselves, while you continue to look at them or be surprised at the strange sound of their voices; and while they are still there—as we would say later, objects of pure perception—they advance toward you and begin to speak, and this is exactly what at first seems to you an astonishing vision, because it is your first, and yet it is something that caresses you and seems as if it has been with you for quite some time. And then it always seems a bit strange to hear ourselves spoken about; we never imagine that we were like that, moreover we never thought that we were such-and-such. What difference could it possibly make to Sören Kierkegaard that he was a child, that he was small, that he had this or that quality? To him, he was not 'small,' he was not a 'child.' These were new notions to him, something he was learning, acquiring because someone was telling it to him or because he heard one person speaking about it to another. This belongs to those things that we hear and therefore come to know, things that determine our conduct when we are among others and when they are all like that. But they are quickly forgotten when we are alone, or when we are among things. When people are present, we represent something, we are different—we are a child among grown-ups, but in reality it is only for grown-ups and because of grown-ups that we are thus; when we are with objects or colors, we forget all about it and cease being big or small.

It was only later that Sören Kierkegaard began to reflect on himself. It was after he had been told of heaven and hell that he had not slept all night. Afterward he began to think that there were good and bad days in life. When he tried to understand all of this, reviewing the days one by one, one after the other, he tried to picture to himself what it would be like to be on a boat or in a far-off country.

The child thus leads a strange double life and for this reason it is difficult to know a child. Furthermore he is what we make of him; we give him form, the existence in which he appears and the expressions he must use. But besides that there is something else which we cannot express, which is not part of what can be communicated, such as it has been formed in grown-ups, something that has nothing to do with what we are with or for others. When the child learns to speak, he learns to be "such," in a completely defined and artificial way. In speaking, we express only what is defined and in a defined way, but we do not express *ourselves*. It is a matter of something that has become artificial, something that we only learn to be. This remains the secret that things alone would know if they were able to understand and that they themselves would perhaps not know fully. Later on, we will forget it more and more and each of us will have difficulty believing in the unity of our life.

But there is yet another thing that moved Sören Kierkegaard far from people: he was not able to conceive of human beings one by one. People told him: "Oh, him, he's So-and-So," Uncle Edward, for example. But in all truth such a statement did not mean very much. We know what a lion is, or a tiger; we recognize them in pictures. Sören Kierkegaard would then ask grown-ups whether the lion or the tiger was the stronger; everyone told him numerous things about this subject or about other similar ones. But when someone told him that Uncle Edward was a doctor, he remained in a fog. He could certainly imagine what a doctor or a schoolmaster was like—he had a clear idea even before going to school—but he could not comprehend the meaning of the statement "This is a doctor" or "This is a schoolmaster." It is easy to imagine that there are lions, tigers, soldiers, and sailors in this world, but the same does not hold for a particular individual to whom one gives a name and who is not a certain well-defined object. The gardener, or the coachman—we know them, we know who they are. But it is almost incomprehensible that a person exists in and of himself, and in any case, of what interest could that possibly be? That is why we understand people we see in pictures, because in reality they are never that particular individual who exists by himself but rather they are thus and so because they represent this or that. Once we have understood this, we know that this is such and such a person; we know him, we grasp him, he almost belongs to us.

This is the world as Sören Kierkegaard conceived of it according to what he had heard about it. There were animals in this world, and you could tell what they were like and which among them was the strongest; and then there were people of different countries, all dressed in particular ways and partially in different colors; and lastly there were mailmen, soldiers, sailors, coachmen, all of whom had recognizable attributes. You saw them in pictures or sometimes when you went for a walk. There were also books that you could open only occasionally and in which very strange people were to be found, but the people he saw around him were not like that and were not really a true part of the world such as it appeared to him.

There was also a time when Sören Kierkegaard heard the animals speaking, something which seemed to him an awesome thing. . . .

◄§ KARL JASPERS

The Philosophical Disposition in Children

In philosophical matters almost everyone believes himself capable of judgment. Whereas it is recognized that in the sciences study, training, method are indispensable to understanding, in philosophy men generally assume that they are competent to form an opinion without preliminary study. Our own humanity, our own destiny, our own experience strike us as a sufficient basis for philosophical opinions.

This notion that philosophy must be accessible to all is justified. The circuitous paths travelled by specialists in philosophy have meaning only if they lead man to an awareness of being and of his place in it.

Second: Philosophical thought must always spring from free creation. Every man must accomplish it for himself.

A marvellous indication of man's innate disposition to philosophy is to be found in the questions asked by children. It is not uncommon to hear from the mouths of children words which penetrate to the very depths of philosophy. A few examples:

A child cries out in wonderment, "I keep trying to think that I am somebody else, but I'm always myself." This boy has touched on one of the universal sources of certainty, awareness of being through awareness of

From *Way to Wisdom* (New Haven and London: Yale University Press, 1954), translated by Ralph Manheim.

self. He is perplexed at the mystery of his I, this mystery that can be apprehended through nothing else. Questioningly, he stands before this ultimate reality.

Another boy hears the story of the Creation: In the beginning God made heaven and earth . . . and immediately asks, "What was before the beginning?" This child has sensed that there is no end to questioning, that there is no stopping place for the mind, that no conclusive answer is possible.

A little girl out walking in the woods with her father listens to his stories about the elves that dance in the clearings at night . . . "But there are no elves . . . " Her father shifts over to realities, describes the motion of the sun, discusses the question of whether it is the sun or the earth that revolves, and explains the reasons for supposing that the earth is round and rotates on its axis . . . "Oh, that isn't so," says the little girl and stamps her foot. "The earth stands still. I only believe what I see." "Then," says her father, "you don't believe in God, you can't see Him either." The little girl is puzzled for a moment, but then says with great assurance, "If there weren't any God, we wouldn't be here at all." This child was seized with the wonder of existence: things do not exist through themselves. And she understood that there is a difference between questions bearing on particular objects in the world and those bearing on our existence as a whole.

Another little girl is climbing the stairs on her way to visit her aunt. She begins to reflect on how everything changes, flows, passes, as though it had never been. "But there must be something that always stays the same. . . . I'm climbing these stairs on my way to see my aunt—that's something I'll never forget." Wonderment and terror at the universal transience of things here seek a forlorn evasion.

Anyone who chose to collect these stories might compile a rich store of children's philosophy. It is sometimes said that the children must have heard all this from their parents or someone else, but such an objection obviously does not apply to the child's really serious questions. To argue that these children do not continue to philosophize and that consequently such utterances must be accidental is to overlook the fact that children often possess gifts which they lose as they grow up. With the years we seem to enter into a prison of conventions and opinions, concealments and unquestioned acceptance, and there we lose the candour of childhood. The child still reacts spontaneously to the spontaneity of life; the child feels and sees and inquires into things which soon disappear from his vision. He forgets what for a moment was revealed to him and is surprised when grownups later tell him what he said and what questions he asked.

❧ JOHN DEWEY

Thinking in Education

The Essentials of Method. No one doubts, theoretically, the importance of fostering in school good habits of thinking. But apart from the fact that the acknowledgment is not so great in practice as in theory, there is not adequate theoretical recognition that all which the school can or need do for pupils, so far as their *minds* are concerned (that is, leaving out certain specialized muscular abilities), is to develop their ability to think. The parceling out of instruction among various ends such as acquisition of skill (in reading, spelling, writing, drawing, reciting); acquiring information (in history and geography), *and* training of thinking is a measure of the ineffective way in which we accomplish all three. Thinking which is not connected with increase of efficiency in action, and with learning more about ourselves and the world in which we live, has something the matter with it just as thought. And skill obtained apart from thinking is not connected with any sense of the purposes for which it is to be used. It consequently leaves a man at the mercy of his routine habits and of the authoritative control of others, who know what they are about and who are not especially scrupulous as to their means of achievement. And information severed from thoughtful action is dead, a mind-crushing load. Since it simulates knowledge and thereby develops the poison of conceit, it is a most powerful obstacle to further growth in the grace of intelligence. The sole direct path to enduring improvement in the methods of instruction and learning consists in centering upon the conditions which exact, promote, and test thinking. Thinking *is* the method of intelligent learning, of learning that employs and rewards mind. We speak, legitimately enough, about the method of thinking, but the important thing to bear in mind about method is that thinking is method, the method of intelligent experience in the course which it takes.

1

The initial stage of that developing experience which is called thinking is *experience.* This remark may sound like a silly truism. It ought to be one;

From John Dewey, *Democracy and Education* (New York: Macmillan Co., 1916), chapter 12.

but unfortunately it is not. On the contrary, thinking is often regarded both in philosophic theory and in educational practice as something cut off from experience, and capable of being cultivated in isolation. In fact, the inherent limitations of experience are often urged as the sufficient ground for attention to thinking. Experience is then thought to be confined to the senses and appetites; to a mere material world, while thinking proceeds from a higher faculty (of reason), and is occupied with spiritual or at least literary things. So, oftentimes, a sharp distinction is made between pure mathematics as a peculiarly fit subject matter of thought (since it has nothing to do with physical existences) and applied mathematics, which has utilitarian but not mental value.

Speaking generally, the fundamental fallacy in methods of instruction lies in supposing that experience on the part of pupils may be assumed. What is here insisted upon is the necessity of an actual empirical situation as the initiating phase of thought. Experience is here taken as previously defined: trying to do something and having the thing perceptibly do something to one in return. The fallacy consists in supposing that we can begin with ready-made subject matter of arithmetic, or geography, or whatever, irrespective of some direct personal experience of a situation. Even the kindergarten and Montessori techniques are so anxious to get at intellectual distinctions, without "waste of time," that they tend to ignore—or reduce—the immediate crude handling of the familiar material of experience, and to introduce pupils at once to material which expresses the intellectual distinctions which adults have made. But the first stage of contact with any new material, at whatever age of maturity, must inevitably be of the trial and error sort. An individual must actually try, in play or work, to do something with material in carrying out his own impulsive activity, and then note the interaction of his energy and that of the material employed. This is what happens when a child at first begins to build with blocks, and it is equally what happens when a scientific man in his laboratory begins to experiment with unfamiliar objects.

Hence the first approach to any subject in school, if thought is to be aroused and not words acquired, should be as unscholastic as possible. To realize what an experience, or empirical situation, means, we have to call to mind the sort of situation that presents itself outside of school; the sort of occupations that interest and engage activity in ordinary life. And careful inspection of methods which are permanently successful in formal education, whether in arithmetic or learning to read, or studying geography, or learning physics or a foreign language, will reveal that they depend for their efficiency upon the fact that they go back to the type of the situation which causes reflection out of school in ordinary life. They give the pupils something to do, not something to learn; and the doing is of such a nature as to demand thinking, or the intentional noting of connections; learning naturally results.

That the situation should be of such a nature as to arouse thinking means of course that it should suggest something to do which is not either routine or capricious—something, in other words, presenting what is new (and hence uncertain or problematic) and yet sufficiently connected with existing habits to call out an effective response. An effective response means one which accomplishes a perceptible result, in distinction from a purely haphazard activity, where the consequences cannot be mentally connected with what is done. The most significant question which can be asked, accordingly, about any situation or experience proposed to induce learning is what quality of problem it involves.

At first thought, it might seem as if usual school methods measured well up to the standard here set. The giving of problems, the putting of questions, the assigning of tasks, the magnifying of difficulties, is a large part of school work. But it is indispensable to discriminate between genuine and simulated or mock problems. The following questions may aid in making such discrimination. (a) Is there anything but a problem? Does the question naturally suggest itself within some situation or personal experience? Or is it an aloof thing, a problem only for the purposes of conveying instruction in some school topic? Is it the sort of trying that would arouse observation and engage experimentation outside of school? (b) Is it the pupil's own problem, or is it the teacher's or textbook's problem, made a problem for the pupil only because he cannot get the required mark or be promoted or win the teacher's approval, unless he deals with it? Obviously, these two questions overlap. They are two ways of getting at the same point: Is the experience a personal thing of such a nature as inherently to stimulate and direct observation of the connections involved, and to lead to inference and its testing? Or is it imposed from without, and is the pupil's problem simply to meet the external requirement?

Such questions may give us pause in deciding upon the extent to which current practices are adapted to develop reflective habits. The physical equipment and arrangements of the average schoolroom are hostile to the existence of real situations of experience. What is there similar to the conditions of everyday life which will generate difficulties? Almost everything testifies to the great premium put upon listening, reading, and the reproduction of what is told and read. It is hardly possible to overstate the contrast between such conditions and the situations of active contact with things and persons in the home, on the playground, in fulfilling of ordinary responsibilities of life. Much of it is not even comparable with the questions which may arise in the mind of a boy or girl in conversing with others or in reading books outside of the school. No one has ever explained why children are so full of questions outside of the school (so that they pester grown-up persons if they get any encouragement), and the conspicuous absence of display of curiosity about the subject matter of school lessons. Reflection on this striking contrast will throw light upon the question of how far customary school conditions supply a context of experience in which problems naturally suggest themselves. No amount of improvement in the personal technique of the instructor will wholly remedy this state of things. There must be more actual material, more *stuff*, more appliances, and more opportunities for doing things, before the gap can be overcome. And where children are engaged in doing things and in discussing what arises in the course of their doing, it is found, even with comparatively indifferent modes of instruction, that children's inquiries are spontaneous and numerous, and the proposals of solution advanced, varied, and ingenious.

As a consequence of the absence of the materials and occupations which generate real problems, the pupil's problems are not his; or, rather, they are his *only as* a pupil, not as a human being. Hence the lamentable waste in carrying over such expertness as is achieved in dealing with them to the affairs of life beyond the schoolroom. A pupil has a problem, but it is the problem of meeting the peculiar requirements set by the teacher. His problem becomes that of finding out what the teacher wants, what will satisfy the teacher in recitation and examination and outward deportment. Relationship to subject matter is no longer direct. The occasions and material of thought are not found in the arithmetic or the history or geography itself, but in skillfully adapting that material to the teacher's requirements. The pupil studies, but unconsciously to himself the objects of his study are the conventions and standards of the school system and school authority, not the nominal "studies." The thinking thus evoked is artificially one-sided at the best. At its worst, the problem of the pupil is not how to meet the requirements of school life, but how to *seem* to meet them—or, how to come near enough to meeting them to slide along without an undue amount of friction. The type of judgment formed by these devices is not a desirable addition to character. If these statements give too highly colored a picture of usual school methods, the exaggeration may at least serve to illustrate the point: the need of active pursuits, involving the use of material to accomplish purposes, if there are to be situations which normally generate problems occasioning thoughtful inquiry.

2

There must be *data* at command to supply the considerations required in dealing with the specific difficulty which has presented itself. Teachers following a "developing" method sometimes tell children to think things out for themselves as if they could spin them out of their own heads. The material of thinking is not thoughts, but actions, facts, events, and the relations of things. In other words, to think effectively one must have had, or now have, experiences which will furnish him resources for coping with the difficulty at hand. A difficulty is an indispensable stimulus to thinking, but not all difficulties call out thinking. Sometimes they overwhelm and submerge and discourage. The perplexing situation must be sufficiently like situations which have already been dealt with so that pupils will have some control of the meanings of handling it. A large part of the art of instruction lies in making the difficulty of new problems large enough to challenge thought, and small enough so that, in addition to the confusion naturally attending the novel elements, there shall be luminous familiar spots from which helpful suggestions may spring.

In one sense, it is a matter of indifference by what psychological means the subject matter for reflection is provided. Memory, observation, reading, communication, are all avenues for supplying data. The relative proportion to be obtained from each is a matter of the specific features of the particular problem in hand. It is foolish to insist upon observation of objects presented to the senses if the student is so familiar with the objects that he could just as well recall the facts independently. It is possible to induce undue and crippling dependence upon sense-presentations. No one can carry around with him a museum of all the things whose properties will assist the conduct of thought. A well-trained mind is one that has a maximum of resources behind it, so to speak, and that is accustomed to go over its past experiences to see what they yield. On the other hand, a quality or relation of even a familiar object may previously have been passed over, and be just the fact that is helpful in dealing with the question. In this case direct observation is called for. The same principle applies to the use to be made of observation on one hand and of reading and "telling" on the other. Direct observation is naturally more vivid and vital. But it has its limitations; and in any case it is a necessary part of education that one should acquire the ability to supplement the narrowness of his immediately personal experiences by utilizing the experiences of others. Excessive reliance upon others for data (whether got from reading or listening) is to be depreciated. Most objectionable of all is the probability that others, the book or the teacher, will supply solutions ready-made, instead of giving material that the student has to adapt and apply to the question in hand for himself.

There is no inconsistency in saying that in schools there is usually both too much and too little information supplied by others. The accumulation and acquisition of information for purposes of reproduction in recitation and examination is made too much of. "Knowledge," in the sense of information, means the working capital, the indispensable resources, of further inquiry; of finding out, or learning, more things. Frequently it is treated as an end itself, and then the goal becomes to heap it up and display it when called for. This static, cold-storage ideal of knowledge is inimical to educative development. It not only lets occasions for thinking go unused, but it swamps thinking. No one could construct a house on ground cluttered with miscellaneous junk. Pupils who have stored their "minds" with all kinds of material which they have never put to intellectual uses are sure to be hampered when they try to think. They have no practice in selecting what is appropriate, and no criterion to go by; everything is on the same dead static level. On the other hand, it is quite open to question whether, if information actually functioned in experience through use in application to the student's own purposes, there would not be need of more varied resources in books, pictures, and talks than are usually at command.

3

The correlate in thinking of facts, data, knowledge already acquired, is suggestions, inferences, conjectured meanings, suppositions, tentative explanations:—*ideas*, in short. Careful observation and recollection determine what is given, what is already there, and hence assured. They cannot furnish what is lacking. They define, clarify, and locate the question; they cannot supply its answer. Projection, invention, ingenuity, devising come in for that purpose. The data *arouse* suggestions, and only by reference to the specific data can we pass upon the appropriateness of the suggestions.

But the suggestions run beyond what is, as yet, actually *given* in experience. They forecast possible results, things *to* do, not facts (things already done). Inference is always an invasion of the unknown, a leap from the known.

In this sense, a thought (what a thing suggests but is not as it is presented) is creative,—an incursion into the novel. It involves some inventiveness. What is suggested must, indeed, be familiar in some context; the novelty, the inventive devising, clings to the new light in which it is seen, the different use to which it is put. When Newton thought of his theory of gravitation, the creative aspect of his thought was not found in its materials. They were familiar; many of them commonplaces—sun, moon, planets, weight, distance, mass, square of numbers. These were not original ideas; they were established facts. His originality lay in the *use* to which these familiar acquaintances were put by introduction into an unfamiliar context. The same is true of every striking scientific discovery, every great invention, every admirable artistic production. Only silly folk identify creative originality with the extraordinary and fanciful; others recognize that its measure lies in putting everyday things to uses which had not occurred to others. The operation is novel, not the materials out of which it is constructed.

The educational conclusion which follows is that *all* thinking is original in a projection of considerations which have not been previously apprehended. The child of three who discovers what can be done with blocks, or of six who finds out what he can make by putting five cents and five cents together, is really a discoverer, even though everybody else in the world knows it. There is a genuine increment of experience; not another item mechanically added on, but enrichment by a new quality. The charm which the spontaneity of little children has for sympathetic observers is due to perception of this intellectual originality. The joy which children themselves experience is the joy of intellectual constructiveness—of creativeness, it the word may be used without misunderstanding.

The educational moral I am chiefly concerned to draw is not, however, that teachers would find their own work less of a grind and strain if school conditions favored learning in the sense of discovery and not in that of storing away what others pour into them; nor that it would be possible to give even children and youth the delights of personal intellectual productiveness—true and important as are these things. It is that no thought, no idea, can possibly be conveyed as an idea from one person to another. When it is told, it is, to the one to whom it is told, another given fact, not an idea. The communication may stimulate the other person to realize the question for himself and to think out a like idea, or it may smother his intellectual interest and suppress his dawning effort at thought. But what he *directly* gets cannot be an idea. Only by wrestling with the conditions of the problem at first hand, seeking and finding his own way out, does he think. When the parent or teacher has provided the conditions which stimulate thinking and has taken a sympathetic attitude toward the activities of the learner by entering into a common or conjoint experience, all has been done which a second party can do to instigate learning. The rest lies with the one directly concerned. If he cannot devise his own solution (not of course in isolation, but in correspondence with the teacher and other pupils) and find his own way out he will not learn, not even if he can recite some correct answer with one hundred per cent accuracy. We can and do supply ready-made "ideas" by the thousand; we do not usually take much pains to see that the one learning engages in significant situations where his own activities generate, support, and clinch ideas—that is, perceived meanings or connections. This does not mean that the teacher is to stand off and look on; the alternative to furnishing ready-made subject matter and listening to the accuracy with which it is reproduced is not quiescence, but participation, sharing, in an activity. In such shared activity, the teacher is a learner, and the learner is, without knowing it, a teacher—and upon the whole, the less consciousness there is, on either side, of either giving or receiving instruction, the better.

4

Ideas, as we have seen, whether they be humble guesses or dignified theories, are anticipations of possible solutions. They are anticipations of some continuity or connection of an activity and a consequence which has not as yet shown itself. They are therefore tested by the operation of acting upon them. They are to guide and organize further observations, recollections, and experiments. They are intermediate in learning, not final. All educational reformers, as we have had occasion to remark, are given to attacking the passivity of traditional education. They have opposed pouring in from without, and absorbing like a sponge; they have attacked drilling in material as into hard and resisting rock. But it is not easy to secure conditions which will make the getting of an idea identical with having an experience which widens and makes more precise our contact with the environment. Activity, even self-activity, is too easily thought of as something merely mental, cooped up within the head, or finding expression only through the vocal organs.

While the need of application of ideas gained in study is acknowledged by all the more successful methods of instruction, the exercises in application are sometimes treated as devices for *fixing* what has already been learned and for getting greater practical skill in its manipulation. These results are genuine and not to be despised. But practice in applying what has been gained in study ought primarily to have an intellectual quality. As we have already seen, thoughts just as thoughts are incomplete. At best they are tentative; they are suggestions, indications. They are standpoints and methods for dealing with situations of experience. Till they are applied in these situations they lack full point and reality. Only application tests them, and only testing confers full meaning and a sense of their reality. Short of use made of them, they tend to segregate into a peculiar world of their own. It may be seriously questioned whether the philosophies which isolate mind and set it over against the world did not have their origin in the fact that the reflective or theoretical class of men elaborated a large stock of ideas which social conditions did not allow them to act upon and test. Consequently men were thrown back into their own thoughts as ends in themselves.

However this may be, there can be no doubt that a peculiar artificiality attaches to much of what is learned in schools. It can hardly be said that many students consciously think of the subject matter as unreal; but it assuredly does not possess for them the kind of reality which the subject matter of their vital experiences possesses. They learn not to expect that sort of reality of it; they become habituated to treating it as having reality for the purposes of recitations, lessons, and examinations. That it should remain inert for the experiences of daily life is more or less a matter of course. The bad effects are twofold. Ordinary experience does not receive the enrichment which it should; it is not fertilized by school learning. And the attitudes which spring from getting used to and accepting half-understood and ill-digested material weaken vigor and efficiency of thought.

If we have dwelt especially on the negative side, it is for the sake of suggesting positive measures adapted to the effectual development of thought. Where schools are equipped with laboratories, shops, and gardens, where dramatizations, plays, and games are freely used, opportunities exist for reproducing situations of life, and for acquiring and applying information and ideas in the carrying forward of progressive experiences. Ideas are not segregated, they do not form an isolated island. They animate and enrich the ordinary course of life. Information is vitalized by its function; by the place it occupies in direction of action.

The phrase "opportunities exist" is used purposely. They may not be taken advantage of; it is possible to employ manual and constructive activities in a physical way, as means of getting just bodily skill; or they may be used almost exclusively for "utilitarian," *i.e.*, pecuniary, ends. But the disposition on the part of upholders of "cultural" education to assume that such activities are merely physical or professional in quality is itself a product of the philosophies which isolate mind from direction of the course of experience and hence from action upon and with things. When the "mental" is regarded as a self-contained separate realm, a counterpart fate befalls bodily activity and movements. They are regarded as at the best mere external annexes to mind. They may be necessary for the satisfaction of bodily needs and the attainment of external decency and comfort, but they do not occupy a necessary place in mind nor enact an indispensable role in the completion of thought. Hence they have no place in a liberal education—*i.e.*, one which is concerned with the interests of intelligence. If they come in at all, it is as a concession to the material needs of the masses. That they should be allowed to invade the education of the elite is unspeakable. This conclusion follows irresistibly from the isolated conception of mind, but by the same logic it disappears when we perceive what mind really is—namely, the purposive and directive factor in the development of experience.

While it is desirable that all educational institutions should be equipped so as to give students an opportunity for acquiring and testing ideas and information in active pursuits typifying important social situations, it will, doubtless, be a long time before all of them are thus furnished. But this state of affairs does not afford instructors an excuse for folding their hands and persisting in methods which segregate school knowledge. Every recitation in every subject gives an opportunity for establishing cross connections between the subject matter of the lesson and the wider and more direct experiences of everyday life. Classroom instruction falls into three kinds. The least desirable treats each lesson as an independent whole. It does not put upon the student the responsibility of finding points of contact between it and other lessons in the same subject or other subjects of study. Wiser teachers see to it that the student is systematically led to utilize his earlier lessons to help understand the present one, and also to use the present to throw additional light upon what has already been acquired. Results are better, but school subject matter is still isolated. Save by accident, out-of-school experience is left in its crude and comparatively irreflective state. It is not subject to the refining and expanding influences of the more accurate and comprehensive material of direct instruction. The latter is not motivated and impregnated with a sense of reality by being intermingled with the realities of everyday life. The best type of teaching bears in mind the desirability of affecting this interconnection. It puts the student in the habitual attitude of finding points of contact and mutual bearings.

Summary

Processes of instruction are unified in the degree in which they center in the production of good habits of thinking. While we may speak, without error, of the method of thought, the important thing is that thinking is the method of an educative experience. The essentials of method are therefore identical with the essentials of reflection. They are first that the pupil have a genuine situation of experience—that there be a continuous activity in which he is interested for its own sake; secondly, that a genuine problem develop within this situation as a stimulus to thought; third, that he possess the information and make the observations needed to deal with it; fourth, that suggested solutions occur to him which he shall be responsible for developing in an orderly way; fifth, that he have opportunity and occasion to test his ideas by application, to make their meaning clear and to discover for himself their validity.

II

PHILOSOPHY
IN THE
EARLY
YEARS

INTRODUCTION

It is important to distinguish between recognizing the philosophical dimension already characteristic of children's thought and considering what must be done to encourage children to think philosophically. In this section, the essays deal with children's own philosophical tendencies; those in Part Four will more specifically analyze the problems encountered when philosophical questions are treated in the classroom.

Some of the issues that emerge when viewing the relationship of philosophy and children are these: Can children do philosophy? Can they deal with philosophy as we know it, or only a crude and rudimentary version of it? If children can do philosophy, should they? What is its value for children, and what is its value for us? Is the freedom to engage in philosophical inquiry a right of childhood? Is the commitment of educators to education furthered by encouraging children's tendencies to philosophize? If the essays in this section do not successfully answer these questions, they at least draw attention to them and initiate inquiry regarding them.

Inexperience and Openness

As if in response to Groethuysen's suggestion that the metaphysician is attempting to regain a childlike openness to experience, Matthews sets out to identify the similarities and differences between the philosophical thinking of children and adults. Matthews is unable to agree with Groethuysen's contention that childhood experience is somehow more true to reality than later experience—that what is "purely given" might be more accessible to the child than to the adult. Matthews does speculate, however, that the child may experience the problematic aspects of experience very intensely. Children often wrestle with problems (such as whether the distant object is really smaller) with a seriousness that adults can only pretend to. Such immediacy does not hinder children as philosophers, of course; on the contrary, it may well help them. Matthews has a wonderful sensitivity to the nuances of children's language that enables him to document his thesis persuasively.

Matthews acknowledges that the adult repertoire of philosophical concepts is considerably more extensive than that of children, but agrees that this fact in itself does not mean that philosophy for children and adults must differ substantially. He wonders what would happen if children were introduced to concepts now entertained only by adults. What kind of adults might they become if as children they were systematically stimulated by a representative selection from the full range of ideas in the philosophical repertoire?

Matthews concludes that children philosophize naturally while adults do so in a manner that must be described as cultivated or institutionalized. If this distinction—between the child as a natural philosopher and the adult as an institutionalized philosopher—is intended to rule out the thesis that philosophy for children and philosophy for adults are one and the same thing, then it raises as many issues as it resolves. Are we sure, for example, that eight-year-olds do not wonder how they viewed things when they were four? Is there not a difference between how one does philosophy and why? Two adults may do philosophy in much the same way but for different reasons. Might not children and adults both do philosophy in the same fashion but with very different motivation? If children's philosophy is to be distinguished from adult philosophy, might we not inquire into the different psychological motives involved?

Like Matthews, Toulmin recognizes that the anxieties of childhood are not always capable of being explained away psychologically. Matthews takes as philosophical the child's statement of dismay at the idea of infinity; Toulmin recognizes the serious epistemological concern of the child who has just realized that there is no largest number. Both Toulmin and Matthews point to something that Sartre observed some decades earlier: that many problems usually classified as psychological are meaningful only when seen and analysed as philosophical problems.

Toulmin contends that children can ask reflective questions to which straightforward factual answers are inappropriate. Such questions deal with philosophical issues to which there are no known answers. Philosophical perplexities, says Toulmin, are perplexities because the very tests and criteria needed to resolve them are unknown. Confronted in this way, the child experiences wonder—according to Toulmin, many kinds of wonder: exploratory wonder that produces science, creative wonder that produces art, mystified wonder that produces theology, and "reflective, self-critical, perplexed wonder" that produces philosophy. One may wonder about the existence of so many different kinds of wonder. But whether wonder is one or many, the central problem before us is to discover the meaning of the child's questioning behavior. In this record, it is better to seek out the implications of children's questions than merely to explain their concerns by listing their causal antecedents.

One point that emerges is that children's comparative shortage of experience may work to their disadvantage in some philosophical respects but to their advantage in others. The disadvantages may show up in a lack of tact or astuteness in dealing with delicate interpersonal matters. (Freud cites the example of the child who opens a conversation with the remark, "Grandma, when you die. . . . " and then is hushed up by grown-ups.) But the advantages are qualities such as the child's openness to those enigmatic and perplexing aspects of existence that most adults have rationalized away, a natural openness, as Groethuysen and Matthews might agree, due to lack of experience rather than a deliberate, hard-won openness gained by temporary suspension of learned assumptions.

The Competence of Children

Neither the essay by French on the philosophy of mind nor the paper by Olsen on epistemology are centrally concerned with philosophy for children. They deal rather with the broader epistemological implications of philosophy for children. They represent efforts by philosophers to take the thought of children into account when dealing with general approaches to mind and knowledge. French argues that children's conceptions of the relationship of 'mind' and 'body' are sometimes treated by adults—even by adult philosophers—as absurd even though there is nothing strange or implausible in the views as such. French believes that children (at least in the American culture) tend to take a Cartesian position on the mind-body relationship, which of course shocks proponents of mind-brain identity, and he invokes Kripke's argument to show that the dualistic position has not been refuted, thus suggesting that there may be more to be said for children's intuitions than is at first apparent.

Whether children's literature and children's intuitions are as pervasively Cartesian as French contends is a matter requiring further empirical study. The evidence is relatively scanty, and the testimony so far collected from children is subject to many different interpretations. For example, here is a remark of a twelve-year-old boy who was asked about the body-mind relationship: "It's the difference between the grapefruit and the taste of the grapefruit." Is such a statement Cartesian or materialistic? Further, are these the only two options open to children? Could there not be others? As more and more children begin to do philosophy in a disciplined fashion, we may discover that interpreting children's philosophical formulations is less simple than it appears at first glance.

By bringing in Wittgenstein's 'forms of life', Olsen seeks to show that the extent to which one can be said to have knowledge is dependent on the relevant cultural context as well as the active and sensory capacities of the individual. In the case of the child, the cultural context is the situation in which the child is reared and educated and includes the criteria of judgment that children have somehow acquired. Whether or not children have knowledge is not to be ascertained by measuring their understanding against an adult standard, but rather by judging how far their knowledge is sufficient to deal with their own world. Thus, the task of tying shoelaces involves action, understanding, and awareness of what the culture accounts to be an adequate knot. The child who knows what is to be done, does it, and does it in fulfillment of the relevant cultural requirements can be said to possess objective knowledge to no less an extent than does the adult who understands and performs a task more strictly associated with adults.

By introducing the notion of 'forms of life', Olsen also calls attention to the social dimension of knowledge, which is neglected by those who see cognitive development as strictly biological, a matter of a unilinear progression of stages. Olsen's essay points toward a more pluralistic understanding of knowledge. He is fundamentally dubious about the Piagetian assumption that the acquisition of knowledge moves from egocentricism to objectivity, arguing that it makes more sense to see objectivity (like the concept of knowledge itself) as always relative to a given context. To attribute total subjectivity to childhood knowledge is gratuitous and unfounded because forms of life must always be taken into account.

Olsen's essay may give epistemologists cause to wonder whether, once childhood intellectual performance is assessed by standards appropriate to that level of development, children's understanding may be found worthier than it has traditionally been held to be. His thesis calls into question the theory of childhood incompetence, which has been one of the basic justifications for denying children intellectual and other rights.

The Question of Autonomy

The notion of childhood incompetence is implicit in David Norton's characterization of childhood as a period of complete dependency, one in which children are incapable of self-management, distracted by external stimulii, unaware of the question of personal identity, and incapable of autonomous activity. Norton sees personal freedom as beginning only in adolescence when children, no longer problems for others, become problems to themselves. It is evident that Norton, seeing childhood as a state of complete dependency, believes paternalism, indoctrination, and denial to the child of rights to philosophical inquiry to be quite justified.

And yet, Norton states that children as early as their fourth year become aware of the central problems of metaphysics, such as the paradox of being and nonbeing, the contingency of existence, and the tension between appearance and reality. (For instance, children encounter the appearance-reality problem through experiencing their own ability to lie.) Norton sees the great metaphysical questions as unanswerable. When confronted with them, one can only take a stand and express one's autonomy. But, according to Norton, this is precisely what children in their utter dependency cannot do. Since they cannot, they must be protected. To encourage children to think philosophically about metaphysical issues would jeopardize their childhood. Norton does concede that children should be taught to think logically and clearly, asserting that logic "consists entirely in conforming to wholly authoritative rules," but he holds that moral knowledge and metaphysical attitudes should be inculcated.

The rich cluster of contentions in Norton's article raises many questions. First and foremost among them, does childhood, as Norton supposes, consist of a fixed series of developmental stages? Is the characterization of childhood as a period in which the dependent child is incapable of self-management a matter of definition or of empirical generalization? Even if there were evidence to justify such a generalization, the child's deficiencies could still be due to a lack of proper education rather than to some intrinsic quality of childhood. If, on the other hand, dependency is a matter of definition, then it would seem that Norton should show why so defining children is more appropriate than recognizing their early personhood and their potential for at least the beginnings of autonomy and critical reflection on their own experience.

A second question is whether Norton is consistent in seeing children as sensitive to metaphysical issues while proposing to protect them from philosophical exploration, even in the company of their peers and their teachers. One wonders whether Norton is right to think that children cannot entertain the problem of their personal identities. On this notion rests his argument that children lack the autonomy necessary for doing philosophy. Rather than make such a categorical assumption, it would seem more appropriate to watch very closely what actually happens as philosophy proceeds to enter the elementary school curriculum. Experience should soon show whether Norton's fears are warranted, or whether, on the contrary, children are able to employ philosophy to think for themselves about matters they find important, and in the process immeasurably enrich the period of childhood.

Michael Gillespie asserts that children most certainly engage in metaphysical questioning. Indeed, he argues that conflicts among belief-systems are bound to erupt in the classroom and that children must be encouraged to think philosophically in order to find their way among such conflicts. To Gillespie, metaphysical questions are those concerned with the ultimate status of things, or ultimate generalizations about all there is, or an individual's overall way of looking at the world. All of these concerns engage children as well as metaphysicians because the metaphysical is a universal dimension of experience; that is, it represents one set of meanings that are revealed by experience. (Other areas of philosophy, such as ethics, aesthetics and epistemology, deal with other dimensions of human experience.) It is natural that children, in attempting to understand their experience, should reach out for the meanings that philosophers also explore. Gillespie acknowledges that children's metaphysical questioning is often playful, but this in no way means that the child is not serious. Children may seek to deal with the metaphysical dimension of their experience in various ways. Philosophy can make them more conscious both of the metaphysical dimension of life and of ways in which they can more effectively deal with it.

Gillespie in fact recommends for children exactly what Norton would deny, namely, educational support for dealing with intellectual conflicts—conflicts which Gillespie sees as inherent in the curriculum, in a pluralistic society, and simply in living, experiencing and thinking at any age. To defend his position against the kind of questions Gillespie raises at the end of his article, Norton would seem to need to present clear evidence to support the stage theory of development that for him precludes any institutional encouragement for metaphysical inquiry by children.

The Role of Ethics

What is the relationship between ethics and childhood? To Joseph Flay, moral education is itself immoral. To Clyde Evans, ethics for children is both feasible and desirable.

Like Norton, Flay argues for the Romantic view that childhood is a stage of life that must be protected in all its innocence and dependence. It is a world organized and stabilized by adult authority. Eventually this world will shatter and the child will be confronted by fragmentation and chaos. It is only then that a rational ethic can help them. To introduce it earlier would hasten the very fragmentation that reason will later have to heal. Ethics prematurely introduced can lead only to cynicism, skepticism, boredom, and alienation.

It may be wondered whether Flay is realistic in contending that American children in the final years of the twentieth century are free of moral doubt and conflict and unaware of the pluralistic character of the society in which they live. Is it really adult authority that holds the world of children together and is the need to make moral choices really foreign to their experience? Even if such concerns were to wait until childhood is ended, how would children then find themselves in possession of the capacity for moral perception, sensitivity, and practice—in short, with the ability to pursue ethical inquiry—when they have never been educated in these skills? Withholding moral education during childhood could well deny children the tools they must have to handle personal encounters requiring moral discrimination.

Evans is experienced as a teacher of third, fourth, and fifth grade school children as well as a practicing philosopher. His observations of children doing philosophy lead him to conclusions that differ sharply from those of Norton and Flay. He has found it not only feasible but also beneficial for children to study philosophy through philosophical dialogue with each other under the auspices of a trained teacher. Small children have shown themselves able to bring forth reasons for their views, analyze the arguments of others, distinguish good reasons from poor ones, and develop commitments to the same criteria of inquiry used by adult philosophers. Evans demonstrates that philosophy can bring children to a mastery of skills and a fruition of attitudes that are valuable to their development as moral individuals. Far from making children into cynics or skeptics, the meaningful and disciplined exploration of important philosophical issues that arise in the classroom can help them perceive the strengths of their own commitments in ways that were not apparent to them before.

Social Issues in the Classroom

The relevance to children of social and political philosophy is discussed by Jane Roland Martin and Louis Katzner. Both believe that acquainting children with the notion of justice is the central organizing concept of social and political philosophy, but they disagree about how this is to be done. Katzner sees the traditional approach of philosophy, which encourages students to analyze the language and concepts appropriate to the field, as a viable model for elementary school children in the classroom. Martin maintains that the traditional model of philosophy, which prepares its practitioners for intellectual autonomy, fails to acquaint children with the social, economic, and political realities of which they are a part. In Martin's view, traditional philosophy fails to make children aware of the alternatives to those present realities that they are capable, even at their age, of considering.

Martin concentrates on a particular curriculum model of philosophy for children, one that takes novels written for children and embodying philosophical approaches as the point of departure. Merely to hint at underlying social injustices while modeling philosophical techniques is, she contends, quite insufficient. It is necessary to include the enormous inadequacies of the existing social system in any consideration; otherwise, children's discussions remain on the level of abstraction, sealed off from social and economic realities, constituting mere intellectual games. To Martin, if the existing situation is unjust, then true education must produce youthful social critics. If philosophy is to become a legitimate part of childhood education, it must deal with economic and social problems or else be deemed superfluous.

The problems created by Martin's approach appear to be formidable. The discipline of philosophy has traditionally been committed to objectivity and open discussion in which all points of view are invited and respected. To propose that in the particular variety of philosophy to be presented to children "the integrity of the discipline of philosophy should not be of prime concern" creates a distinct rupture between the existing philosophical community and those seeking to introduce philosophy into the schools. Other disciplines are not deemed to lose integrity when transposed from higher to elementary education: elementary school mathematics has no less integrity than college mathematics. To Martin's criticism, we can reply that philosophy is capable of broaching all issues; what is done with them after that depends upon the classroom situation. We do not see that present efforts to introduce philosophy to children in any way involve shielding social institutions from the students' critical scrutiny. Certainly, helping children understand the value of consistency between beliefs and actions is a step toward demonstrating the dangers of a society in which ideals and actions are tragically split. But this is not the same thing as urging students to commit themselves to social action. To do that would fly in the face not only of the practice of philosophy but also of the commitment of educators to impartiality. The educators' question might be, "If the traditional striving for objectivity and impartiality is abandoned, who is to decide which point of view is to be presented in the classroom?" The broad community consensus presented in most classrooms may be incomplete, but it at least offers the opportunity for giving the children the tools needed for constructing their own critique of society. For consensus to fail in a community or for one viewpoint to become "official" is usually for education to cease.

Katzner in defending social philosophy for children cites the value it would have for their understanding of why they are expected to attend school. If children do not comprehend why they should become educated individuals, it is not surprising that they should become restless and alienated. If we believe that our educational system is indeed justifiable, then we have nothing to fear in permitting children to examine the rationale for it. If, on the other hand, there are some of our social traditions, such as sexism and racism, to which Katzner alludes, about which public conflict has arisen, then there is nothing to be gained by evading these issues in the classroom. Katzner's article can be seen as a reply to Martin, in which philosophical reflection upon social issues by children is seen as a highly constructive activity. It is not enough to alert children to the inadequacies of our social, economic, and political systems without giving them an opportunity to explore the nature of justice or to discuss privilege, obligation, and many other fundamental categories of social life. A mere sense of injustice can lead to ill-advised and counterproductive activities. Katzner recognizes the dangers of introducing philosophical issues earlier than children can handle them, as well as the danger of not equipping them to understand the social forces that operate on them throughout their childhood. He does not minimize the new problems that are bound to emerge when social philosophy is brought into the elementary school classroom. But the lack of social philosophy has already resulted in a tendency for children to become skeptical or dogmatic, because they have not developed the critical skills to handle the authority conflicts that they certainly experience. In the long run, children who have learned to evaluate the criteria employed by those who wield rights and authority will be better able to deal with them intelligently than will be children who have had no such preparation.

Education and Science

As a philosopher of science, Tamny finds interesting similarities in the ways that both children and scientists come to terms with the world. He is even tempted to recommend childhood as a first step toward becoming a scientist! He sees children as scientists writ small, and he sees scientists as children writ large. Tamny considers to what extent children are or can become critically aware of notions that are current among scientists. He concludes that while children are not acquainted with concepts like hypothesis formation, testability, prediction, and explanation, they could easily come to recognize them through philosophical discussion. Children do consider patterns of conceptual development not unlike those of scientists: for example, they move from description to explanation and then to a revised, explanatory description. They may not be aware of such changes, but they can become aware of them, reflect on them, and discuss them, even if such changes were originally nonrational rather the result of than "good reasons." Tamny observes that it is not altogether clear that the situation with adult scientists is much different.

If Tamny is correct about the proclivity of children for scientific thinking, then engaging children in discussions of the philosophy of science would particularly benefit students likely to study science in high school. Despite their readiness, many young people today have little idea of what science is about. Budding scientists need a preliminary philosophical orientation toward the scientific enterprise if they are not to be narrow and inflexible. They need a sense of alternative values and goals that science might pursue. Perhaps if the philosophical dimension envisioned in Tamny's paper is realized, science may come to be conducted in a wholly critical spirit, so that the present scrupulous attention to procedure would be combined with a constant awareness of the potential for dogmatism inherent in the scientific approach.

❧ 2 ৡ❧

ARE CHILDREN

PHILOSOPHICAL?

❧ GARETH B. MATTHEWS

University of Massachusetts, Amherst

The Child As Natural Philosopher

Jordan (five years old), going to bed at 8. P.M., asked: "If I go to bed at 8 and get up at 7 in the morning, how do I really know that the little hand of the clock has gone around only once? Do I have to stay up all night to watch it?

"If I look away even for a short time maybe the small hand will go around twice."

How might one try to deal with Jordan's skepticism?

It's natural to construe Jordan's unease as a worry about not having enough evidence, or perhaps not enough evidence of the right sort, for a certain conclusion. Jordan's opening questions, in fact, suggest that just this is what bothers him.

In the normal case, one's observations of a clock will certainly be sporadic. Jordan may check on his clock from time to time during the day— but not, obviously, when he is out of the room, not when he has meals, watches television, goes out to play or off to school. Then there's that especially intriguing time during which, although he is in the room, perhaps even very near the clock, he is asleep. What happens then? And how can Jordan know? How could anyone know?

Insofar as Jordan's worry is an unease about what philosophers of science call the evidential base for a certain hypothesis, there are obvious remedies. Mummy and Daddy might be asked to check up on the clock when they go to bed at night. Jordan himself suggests staying up all night to keep the clock under surveillance.

The comment Jordan adds to his question ("If I look away even for a short time maybe the small hand will go around twice") suggests, however, that his worry is deeper than, or anyway different from, a worry about how extensive his evidential base is. Even the briefest period in which the clock goes unobserved is an opportunity for it to misbehave. How does he know that it won't take advantage of that opportunity?

Hovering around this last question may be a general concern about whether observed states are a reliable guide to unobserved states. Jordan may have a friend at kindergarten who manages to make faces at the teacher whenever her back is turned, but not otherwise. How do we know clocks are not like that? Perhaps induction rests on an assumption as naïve as the belief that what Jordan does under the watchful eye of the teacher is a reliable guide to what Jordan does when the teacher leaves the room, or even looks away.

Maybe Jordan's worries are even more fundamental than the problem of induction. Maybe he wants to know how he can be sure there is anything at all (!) when he looks away, or how he knows there is a world while he sleeps. Perhaps he is sufficiently worried about even having such a worry that he hasn't yet brought himself to express it; instead, he has expressed several less radical worries.

It may be hard, without actually talking to Jordan himself, to determine which of these traditional philosophical concerns lay behind his comments. That he was in the grip of at least one familiar philosophical problem, however, seems hardly debatable.

The Unitarian Thesis

At a recent workshop on philosophy for children[1] one symposiast remarked that philosophy for children is the same as philosophy for anyone else. Let's call that the Unitarian Thesis. It would be an application of the Unitarian Thesis to say that coping with Jordan's skepticism is basically the same kind of endeavor for Jordan as for anyone else—whether five years old or fifty. And that seems right. Consider the question of one's evidence base. What we are to say about a given evidence base, and whether it justifies a given induction, and, if so, why?—all this is a traditional concern in epistemology and the philosophy of science. An adult philosopher might, but needn't, use more sophisticated examples than Jordan's clock. Anyway, much of what one would have to say to, and to learn from, the adult philosopher could be said to, and learned from, Jordan.

Something similar, I think, is true about the question of how reasoning can ever justify the leap from observed instances to the unobserved. It's also true of the so-called "problem of the external world." Indeed the classical literature on the problem of the external world deals with familiar objects like Jordan's clock—what J. L. Austin in *Sense and Sensibilia* (Oxford, 1962, p. 8) calls "moderate-sized specimens of dry goods."

So Jordan's case seems to support the Unitarian Thesis. But let's now consider another example.

I am tucking my eight-year-old son, John, into bed. He looks up at me and asks, quite without warning, "Daddy, why don't I see you double, because I have two eyes and I can see you with each one by itself?"

What do I say?

First I try to make sure I understand what is puzzling him.

"You have two ears," I point out, "are you surprised you don't *hear* double?"

John grins. "What is hearing double?"

"Well, maybe my-my voi-voice wo-would s-sound li-like thi-this," I say.

He reflects. "But your ears both go to the same place."

"And couldn't it be that your eyes both go to the same place?" I suggest.

He gets serious, thinks, then grins again. "You're just giving me *another* problem," he protests; "I want to think about the one I already have."

Fair enough.

"Maybe," I suggest, "it's because the picture you get with your left eye comes together with the picture you get with your right eye; when they come together they make *one* picture."

We experiment with two fingers, one closer to our eyes, the other further away; we try focussing now on one, now on the other. The aim is to see how, by focussing on the near finger, one can see the further one double, and vice versa. The moral is supposed to be that sometimes the two pictures don't come together to make one, although in the normal case they do.

My son is not satisfied. It turns out that he has constructed for himself, elaborating in various ways on what he has learned at school about vision and the retinal image, a complex theory of vision according to which one image comes through each eye, is reversed, re-reversed and then projected out in front of the subject. No wonder he is worried about why we don't see double!

I suggest various ways of simplifying his theory, but he won't accept simplifications.

"I'll have to think about it some more," he says; "I'll talk to you again after I get it worked out."

John's question, 'Why don't I see you double?—I have two eyes', mixes optics, neurophysiology, and philosophy. John, I discovered, had seen on school television an episode in which a little man climbed into someone's eye to gaze at the retinal image. Ever since the retinal image was actually observed in the early seventeenth century people have worried about why they don't see things upside down, since their retinal images reverse the objects seen. The seldom-spoken assumption is that what one really sees is the retinal image.

John insisted that the television program he had seen in school had not given him his problem, that he had already had the problem before he saw the program. Certainly he seemed willing and able to think of the retinal image as being re-reversed by some later process in vision. His problem, he said, was to figure out how the images from the two separate eyes could merge.

Medieval theorists of vision, such as Alhazen and Roger Bacon, supposed that images travel from each eye back through the optic nerve to the optic chiasma, where the nerve from the two eyes cross and where, as Alhazen and Bacon supposed, the two images become one. They were led to their theory by a worry about why we don't see double, although we receive two images—one through each eye. Their theory is an answer to John's problem.[2]

In his brilliant *Paralipomena ad vitellionem* Johannes Kepler rejected, scathingly, this medieval account of vision; he said it was optically impossible. Light doesn't behave in the way the medieval theory requires, he explained. Kepler took enormous strides in accounting for the optics of vision, but he did so at a price. He renounced all ambition to give an account of what happens in vision after the image is formed on the retina that somehow results in someone actually seeing something.

My John wanted to account for the fact that one sees something by supposing that one somehow projects visual images out in front. If we are to think of images projected in this way as something like the image on a movie screen, nothing will have been explained. We will still want to know how the projected images can be seen. Doesn't that require vision— just what we first set out to explain? If, however, we are to think of the projecting out front as the seeing, then there may be more hope for a nonregressive explanation. But now the notion of projection will carry a great explanatory load.

I don't know whether John will ever sort out these basic perplexities to his own satisfaction. If he does, sophistication in neurophysiology, psychology, and optics will have to accompany sophistication in philosophy—as it would for anyone, whether young child or wizened adult. Again, the Unitarian Thesis seems right; philosophy for children is the same as philosophy for anyone else.

So far we have considered two examples. Both seem to support the Unitarian Thesis. But what now about this anecdote:

> Ian (six years old) found to his chagrin that the three children of his parents' friends monopolized the television; they kept him from watching his favorite program. "Mother," he asked in frustration, "why is it better for three people to be selfish than for one?"

Perhaps not very many of our contemporaries, except for professional philosophers, are, by any clear criteria, utilitarians. Still, utilitarian considerations commonly turn up in everyday ethical discussions. One suspects that Ian was quite familiar with the style of argument that would preempt his viewing rights by citing the three others that could be made happy by turning to their program while only one would be satisfied by turning to his. Ian sought to defuse this move by an ingenious reversal. "Why," he asked cleverly, "is it better for three people to be *selfish* than for one?"

Ian's question leads naturally to a consideration of utilitarianism. If Mother sought to justify the present state of affairs by pointing out that three people are made happy by this arrangement instead of only one, one might expect Ian to raise a problem of equity. "Suppose I always want to watch a program nobody else wants to watch," one can imagine him saying, "would it be right always to make other kids happy—even if there are tons and tons of them—and never make me happy?"

The question of equity is essential for a utilitarian, whether young or old, to deal with. Whatever difficulties stand in the way of answering it satisfactorily seem to have little to do with the age of the questioner. So in this respect the Unitarian Thesis still holds up.

There is, however, an interesting feature of Ian's original question ("Why is it better for three people to be selfish than for one?") that I have so far overlooked. In asking this question Ian seems to be assuming that being selfish is simply refusing to share some possession or some advantage one has over others.

This notion of selfishness is inadequate; however, it is neither perverse nor idiosyncratic. We teach children what being selfish is by pointing out cases in which, as we say, Joe or Janet is being selfish, perhaps being selfish about a toy. If Joe refuses to let Janet play with his toy and the parent or teacher snatches the toy away from Joe and gives it to Janet, Joe, in this primitive use of the term 'selfish' isn't allowed to be selfish about his toy; he is made to share the toy. Using the term 'selfish' in a more adult way, we might say that Joe remained quite selfish through the whole episode; his thoughts and actions were never tempered by altruism. But in the simple sense he wasn't selfish because he wasn't allowed to be selfish; he was made to share.

How many selfish people are there in Ian's household? Perhaps three, in Ian's primitive sense of 'selfish'. In a more interesting sense of the term the answer might be "all four" or perhaps "only one, namely, Ian."

I suspect that the simpler concept of being selfish offers itself as a way of avoiding difficult questions about intention; it is easier to teach to children than the adult concept, but it is also much less interesting for ethical reflection.

There emerges here not an absolute but a relative distinction between philosophy for adults and philosophy for children. In this case, and in perhaps others as well, the child may have only a simplified version of a philosophically interesting concept. A philosophical issue or difficulty that emerges for the child might disappear, or perhaps appear in quite a different form, if the child had available the more sophisticated concept.

This point is hardly fatal to the Unitarian Thesis. One can say that philosophy for children is the same as philosophy for anyone else while still acknowledging that one's individual conceptual repertory may be much more extensive than another's and that, in general, an adult's conceptual repertory will be more extensive than a child's.

Is there some more interesting way in which the Unitarian Thesis shows itself inadequate?

Perhaps so. Here is a suggestive anecdote concerning perception:

One day John Edgar (four years old), who had often seen airplanes take off, rise and gradually disappear into the distance, took his first place ride. When the place stopped its ascent and the seat-belt sign went out, John Edgar turned to his father and said in a rather relieved, but still puzzled, tone of voice, "Things don't really get smaller up here."

Philosophers and psychologists have often disagreed among themselves about whether an object gradually disappearing into the distance appears to be growing smaller and we interpret that appearance as mere appearance or whether it simply appears to be going further and further away. Obviously the first alternative is friendly to sense-datum theories and the second is not. Despite the efforts of gestalt psychologists and phenomenologists to regain for us the innocence of pure experience, some of us despair of determining how things really appear apart from interpretative accretions or even whether there is for us any such thing as the pure given.

John Edgar seems to be in a radically different position. Whereas for us adults the innocence of pure experience seems inevitably compromised by theory, John Edgar seems actually to have the epistemological problem we adults can only pretend we have when we try to work out a philosophical account of perception. For him it is not a matter of bracketing interpretation and getting down to the pure given element in perceptual experience. He seems to have immediately available, without need for any special discipline or act of reflection, a much purer "given" than is available to us. Moreover, he seems to have put a wrong interpretation on it and to be in the process of working out an alternative interpretation.

In this case it seems that philosophy for an adult cannot be quite the same thing as philosophy for John Edgar. We have lost our innocence. Our theories infect our ideas of what is given in experience. His do not, or at least they do not to quite the same extent.

Here, now, is an anecdote on the sky. It bears reflecting on.

Katherine (almost four years old) was given a helium-filled balloon at a fair. Carelessly she let it go. She was much upset. After going to bed that night she called her mother into her room and asked where the balloon was then: "what city is it over now? Is it in Vermont?" Mother: "I don't know where it is; it's probably not as far away as Vermont." Katherine: "Well, there aren't *three* skies, you know; there's only *one*."

How many skies are there? The question is an odd one. Superficially it's a bit like "How many oceans are there?" But unlike that question it can't be answered by looking in an atlas or an encyclopedia. It also seems a bit like 'How many moons are there?' But no book on meteorology or astronomy will tell us how many skies there are. The question is kooky.

United Air Lines tells us to "fly the friendly skies of United," but without telling us how many skies there are or even how many are covered by the United route map.

We distinguish skies in various ways. We speak of the morning sky and the evening sky; we may say that the morning sky is overcast and the evening sky is clear. A guide for stargazers may picture a summer sky and a winter sky, or perhaps a summer sky in northern latitudes, perhaps at midnight or just before dusk. Someone may say that Scottish skies are very different from mediterranean skies.

What is the concept that finds expression in these sentences? Perhaps it is primarily the notion of a visible hemisphere above the observer at a certain place and time and secondarily, maybe, the visible contents of that hemisphere. When 'sky' is understood to express the idea of a visible dome over some point on the earth's surface, one can say there are many, many different skies—an infinitely large number of them, in fact.

There is also an inclination to say that the sky is the envelope of atmosphere above building level that envelopes the globe. Anything that leaves the ground and goes up above buildings and trees goes up into the sky. When 'sky' is used to express this notion, there is only one sky.

A variation on this last idea has the sky as the clear air around the earth above the building level. When 'sky' is understood to express this idea, a hole in the clouds may be said to enable us to see the sky.

I said initially that the question, 'How many skies are there?' is a kooky question. Yet I've gone on to give it an answer of sorts. The sort of answer I've gone on to give it is a philosophical one, or at least the beginning of a philosophical one. I've started a sketch of two or three concepts that could be said to be expressed by the word 'sky'. Using one of these concepts, we could say with Katherine that there aren't three skies, there is only one. Using another we'd have to say there are an infinitely large number of skies.

Most people don't ask themselves or others how many skies there are. They learn early in life that this question, unlike the question 'How many oceans are there?' is a kooky question.

Children, such as Katherine, don't yet know that this is a kooky question. They stumble into philosophy from innocence, rather than from the cultivation of naïveté that adults are limited to.

So here is an important respect in which philosophy for children is not the same thing as philosophy for adults. Children have not yet learned to reject as queer and misbegotten those many questions that philosophers have taught themselves to rescue from the waste bin of inquiry. If a child pursues a philosophical question into reflection it will be from innocence. That possibility is no longer open to the adult. Again, the Unitarian Thesis breaks down.

Let me now try to bring the point about innocence and philosophy into line with a point about innocence and poetry.

In chapter 1 of his book, *The Child's Conception of the World* (London, 1929), Jean Piaget reports asking children between the ages of six and ten or eleven whether words are strong (pp. 55–60). Piaget expects them to say "Yes, some words are strong" at age six or so and "No, words are not strong" at age ten or eleven. He expects them to answer in these ways because he thinks they begin by confusing a word with its meaning, a sign with the thing signified, and later learn to master and appreciate this important distinction. Thus he thinks they will confuse the word 'wind' with the wind and, noting that the wind is, or may be, strong, will conclude that the word 'wind' is strong, or anyway may be strong. Piaget expects them to sort all this out eventually until they can say that, although words are not themselves strong, some of the things words name are strong.

Are words strong?

Well, some are. An irate customer might complain to a shopkeeper in strong words, even in very strong words. An English teacher might tell her pupils to favor Anglo-Saxon words over those of Latin origin on the ground that the latter are weak, the former strong. She would be right. Short words tend to be strong, long words weak.

'Strong' is itself a strong word and not because it means 'strong.' One of Piaget's young subjects pointed out that the word 'strong' is strong. But she seems not to have been given a chance to explain why she wanted to say that.

In addition to being a strong word, 'strong' is a word with an incredibly complex array of meanings and applications. Among the many things that may be correctly said to be strong are oxen, a good weight-lifter, sunlight, certain colors, coffee, an argument, a conviction, a custom, a market in a certain commodity, an irregular verb, and an ocean tide.

We adults naturally suppose that 'strong' has one basic literal sense and then a host of figurative senses and that the figurative ones can probably be accounted for somehow by reference to the literal one. I expect Piaget supposed this. Perhaps Charles Atlas and the wind are strong in the literal sense, whereas it is only in a figurative sense that the words of the irate customer or the stewed tea can be said to be strong.

In fact, the task of enumerating and sorting out all the senses of a rich and strong word like 'strong' is terribly difficult. Saying just which uses are literal and which figurative is also difficult and showing in any helpful way how the allegedly figurative uses are related to the allegedly literal ones may not even be possible.

The literal-figurative distinction, of which perhaps nobody can give an entirely clear and satisfactory account, is a distinction one learns to accept at an early age. Once one accepts it, one loses much of one's natural curiosity about the wonderfully intricate ways in which the meanings of words are related to each other.

A young child may be struck by the fact that both a horse and a cup of tea may be correctly said to be strong. Given opportunity or encouragement, the child may write a poem that teases out this curious fact. Or, given a different kind of stimulus or inclination, a child may wonder, philosophically, whether strong words are those that express strong feelings and strong feelings are those that move people to take strong actions. When a child assimilates from our culture the desensitizing thesis that many uses of words are merely figurative or metaphorical, she or he loses the fascination with the weft of words that inspires poetry and animates philosophy.

A late adolescent or adult who writes poetry or does philosophy has to cultivate innocence to puzzle and muse over the simplest ways we have of saying and seeing things. Cultivated innocence has many advantages over its natural counterpart. One advantage is that it is not so easily thrown off balance by pretentious learning. But calculated innocence is not the same thing as natural innocence. For at least this reason children's poetry is different from adult poetry. And for at least this reason philosophy for children can't be exactly like philosophy for adults.

In arguing for the importance of philosophy in modern life and society, Robert Spaemann has characterized philosophy as "institutionalized naïveté."[3] To institutionalize naïveté is presumably to find an institutional setting in which people will be encouraged to ask questions so basic that grappling with them seems to all of us some of the time, and some of us all of the time, hopelessly naïve.

Yet at most it is philosophy for adults that is institutionalized naïveté. Philosophy for children is natural naïveté. Children, if they are philosophers at all, are natural philosophers.

Philosophical Reflection in Children

I have concerned myself in this paper with the question whether philosophy for children is the same thing as philosophy for adults—the "Unitarian Thesis." I've said that in some ways it is the same, in some ways it isn't. In conducting my discussion I have ignored altogether the prior question,

'Are children capable of philosophical thinking at all?' Let me conclude by saying a word about that.

The only good way to find out whether all, or many, or some, or no children are capable of philosophical thinking is to talk to children and to listen to what they say, drawing them out a bit here and there, before they get old enough to assimilate the antiphilosophical bias of our society. If one does that one will discover, I think, that many children are indeed natural philosophers.

Here I must issue a warning. Most adults have no interest in and no patience for philosophical reasoning. I expect that many of them have had philosophy beaten out of them by a process of socialization. But, however they came to be that way, they now have no nose and no ear for philosophy. Some of them talk to children a great deal. They do not discover philosophical thinking in children for the very good reason that they are themselves largely immune to philosophical perplexity. They fail to recognize philosophy for what it is and they discourage its elaboration and development. An example from the writings of the most celebrated investigator of thinking in young children, Jean Piaget, will perhaps clarify my point.

In a conversation with a child nine and a half years old Piaget asked, "But before God gave it its name was there a sun?" (*The Child's Conception of the World*, London, 1929, p. 66)

"No," answered the child, "because he wouldn't know where to make it come from."

To me this child's answer is intriguing, even exciting. As a mere reader of Piaget's book, indeed a reader reading half a century after the actual interview took place, I am frustrated to realize that I can't get the child to share her reasoning with me. I can only imagine what that reasoning might have been. Several possibilities suggest themselves. This is one.

To create something, the child might have reasoned, one needs to think about what it is one is creating and about how to produce just that— including "where to make it come from." But one can't think about what one is going to create without giving it some sort of designation, however temporary: one must name it. Hence God would have had to name the sun—if only temporarily—before he could have created it.

Clearly Piaget had none of my enthusiasm for the child's answer. Instead he reacted with great condescension and no little impatience. "The idea of non-existence," he comments in his book with obvious irritation, "always causes difficulty." Of course it does! It caused difficulties for Parmenides and Plato. It causes difficulties for us. Those difficulties have bred some of the profoundest philosophical thoughts anybody has ever had—from Parmenides's and Plato's thoughts on being and nonbeing to Meinong's *Gegenstandsteorie*, Russell's Theory of Descriptions, Heidegger's reflections on *das Nichts*, Sartre's idea of the *pour soi*, contemporary "free" logics, and even possible-world semantics. The difficulty of the idea of nonexistence is one of the great glories of philosophy.

Seemingly innocent of the pitfalls as well as the grandeur of the topic, Piaget tries out the following question on his young interlocutor: "If a thing wasn't there [i.e., didn't exist] could it [sic] have a name?" And then he adds this explanation:

> Long ago men used to believe there was a certain fish in the sea which they called a 'chimera' but there wasn't really any such fish . . . . So can't a thing that doesn't exist have a name? (p. 66)

I'm sorry I can't report that Piaget's young interlocutor points out the paradox in saying, "A thing that doesn't exist can have a name." But we must remember that the conversation was both conducted and written up by an adult, a rather imposing adult at that, who saw nothing puzzling or intriguing about talk of nonexistents.[4]

We shall never learn whether a child has any interesting thoughts on this or any other philosophical topic unless we see to it that the child's conversational partner is sensitive to philosophical issues.

My own rather unsystematic investigations of the thinking of young children and my growing collection of anecdotes suggest that philosophical thinking in young children may indeed be serious, deep, and natural. I have given some of my evidence in this paper. One of the anecdotes I have recounted catches my son in the act of philosophical reflection—reflection that he undertook without specific encouragement (though I like to think my relationship to my son offers him support and encouragement for such reflection in at least a general sort of way). The other anecdotes I have recounted, except for those from Piaget, were told me by friends and acquaintances. These people reported, too, that their children's reflective explorations occurred without specific encouragement from them or from other adults. So here is significant evidence that some children are natural philosophers.

I conclude with a brief statement of one of the more moving accounts to have come to my attention of a child acting as a natural philosopher. I recently taught a course entitled "Philosophy and the Young Child" in which I assigned as lab work the project of reading a story to a young child and then discussing the story with the child afterward.[5] One of my students read a chapter of one of C. S. Lewis's Narnia tales to Michael, seven years old. There ensued a three-hour discussion that covered many of the most philosophical topics imaginable. I'm told the discussion would have gone on even longer if Michael's mother hadn't finally appeared to announce that enough was enough.

The discussion began with worries about evil and the origin of evil ("What makes people bad?" "Have people always been bad?" Etc.). Eventually talk turned to the universe and its character, and finally to whether or not the universe is infinite. My student, I judge, had never before worried seriously about whether the universe is infinite. Michael had.

"I don't like to [think] about the universe without an end," said Michael. "It gives me a funny feeling in my stomach. If the universe goes on forever there is no place for God to live, who made it."

Michael then mentioned an article his father had written on finite models for the universe. He said he hadn't read the article and, in effect, didn't want to comment until he had done so. Still, largely unknown to his parents (as I later learned) he had turned over in his mind the question as to whether the universe is finite.

"Why is that important?" asked my student, obviously surprised to find Michael concerned about it.

"It's nice to know you're *here*," replied Michael. "It is not nice to know about nothing. I hope [the universe] doesn't go on and on forever. I don't like the idea of it going on forever because it's obvious it can't be anywhere."

Breathtakingly concise, this bit of reasoning captures what seems to have mattered most to Michael about whether the universe is infinite. An infinite universe can't be located anywhere, nor, as Michael went on to muse, can there be any absolute location within an infinite universe.

Michael expressed his thoughts about this last point by an analogy of being lost in a foreign country without the linguistic means of getting one's bearings. Here are parts of his explanation of the analogy:

> It is like [being] in Japan and no one is English-speaking. No maps and without cash. Only . . . a car . . . . Like being in a big city and not having maps . . . . It is nice to know . . . [to] have security to know where you are.

I learned from Michael's mother that a short while before the interview took place the family had been traveling in France and that Michael had indeed been lost in a country in which he did not speak the language and for which he had no map. His mother had noticed that he was very relieved to get back to England again. But she hadn't appreciated fully the emotional impact the experience of being lost had made on Michael and she had, of course, no idea that the experience had provided for him an analogy for a universe in which there would be no absolute location and thus no way to find out, except in a disappointingly relative way, where one is.

Picking up Michael's remarks on insecurity in an infinite universe, my student asked, "What if there is no end? How can we have security? Say we [are] lost in a Chinese city . . . "

"That goes on forever?" Michael asked. "No maps? No English? [We] would have to try not to crash into cars and drive around like being lost."

"Does finding out if the universe has an end tell us who we are or what we are?" asked my student. "No," replied Michael, "but it makes us more secure."

"How do we react to space and death?" asked my student at a later point in the discussion.

"It is more important," said Michael firmly, "to know where you are than what happens after you die. Most people don't think about death. It is more important to think about maps in [a] Chinese city than dying. I think I would rather have the maps."

Some adults can, of course, bring much more sophisticated conceptual machinery, including, perhaps, non-Euclidian geometries, to the consideration of whether the universe is infinite than is available to Michael. But Michael exhibited in that interview a clear understanding of some of the basic implications of the question. And he clearly had a gut sense of the importance of some these matters that cannot be bettered, I suggest, by anyone—whether adult or child.

Of course Michael is not an entirely typical seven-year-old. Some of his intellectual preoccupations have to do, no doubt, with the fact that his mother is a computer scientist and his father a mathematician. His willingness to open up to an adult suggests that someone has shown both him and what he has to say real respect.

Though not entirely typical, Michael is not either, I suggest, entirely atypical. Such evidence as I have managed to assemble suggests that, for many young members of the human race, philosophical thinking is as natural as making music and playing games and quite as much a part of being human. To the great loss of us adults, and to the impoverishment of our children, we have not made any place in the family or in school for the child as natural philosopher.[6]

NOTES

1. At Harvard in August 1976, sponsored by the Institute for the Advancement of Philosophy for Children and directed by Matthew Lipman and Ann Margaret Sharp.
2. For more on the medieval account, see my "A Medieval Theory of Vision," *Studies in the History and Philosophy of Perception*, Robert Turnbull and Peter Machamer, eds., forthcoming.
3. "*Philosophie als institutionalisierte Navitaet,*" *Philosophisches Jahrbuch* 81 (1974): 139–42.
4. For more on Piaget and philosophical thinking in children see my "On Talking Philosophy with Children," *Proceedings of the Royal Institute of Philosophy for 1975–6*, forthcoming.
5. For more on how philosophy shows itself in children's stories, see my "Philosophy and Children's Literature," *Metaphilosophy* 7 (1976): 7–16.
6. I have tried to offer some tips on talking philosophy with children in my "Philosophy and the Young Child," *Metaphilosophy*, forthcoming.

✌§ STEPHEN TOULMIN

University of Chicago

Wonder, Puzzlement, and Perplexity

When I was a child the family used to go for holidays to a cottage in the country, some fifty miles northeast of London. In the normal way, I used to sleep in a tiny attic room, the only room on the top floor, with a bare dormer window looking out across the fields in front of the house. Yet on one occasion (as I recall) I found myself using the front bedroom, which was normally my elder sister's room and had a fine pair of heavy deep-red curtains across the window. Sitting up in the unaccustomed bed, I was intrigued by something about those richly colored curtains. What color were they? What was their color, *exactly?* I closed each eye in turn and found to my perplexity that they looked slightly different when I was using my left eye alone—a fraction richer, deeper, more saturated—than they did when I was using my right eye alone. As I moved my head around, the changes were even more marked. The play of the candlelight on the falling

From *Knowing and Acting* (New York: Macmillan Co., 1976), pp. 3–13.

folds of the drapery and the texture of the pile gave the curtains, seen from this way or that, a variety of appearances that were clearly beyond my own power to describe, and were, perhaps, wholly indescribable. Yet the oddest thing of all remained the difference between the ways the curtains looked to each of my two eyes separately. I simply did not know what to make of *that*. If those two natural allies—my two eyes—gave such different testimony, I just did not know *what* to believe. What color *did* the curtains have, really and truly?

Forty years later I am still not wholly clear about the answer to that question, or even whether the question has any straight-forward answer at all. Indeed it seems to me now quite as important to understand how the question arose for me initially—how I came to ask it in the first place—as to answer it. For there is something peculiar to be noticed about *reflective* questions such as this—questions like: "What is involved in recognizing the colors of things?" "How does the way things *look* tie up with the way they *really are?*" "If colors are primarily something we see, how can there be any difference between the way things look and the way they really are?" "How do we come to have a system of names for colors at all?" (After all, Adam had to give names not only to animals but also to colors, shapes, smells, and the rest!) The things that come to light when we reflect about such questions can lead us quite as much to a better understanding of ourselves as to a better understanding of the world around us. With the help of questions like these, we can look (so to say) into a mirror that shows us the workings of our own minds. And to do that is to do *philosophy*.

Why is this? Why were questions that I asked myself at the age of nine or ten reflective and philosophical questions, rather than being perfectly straightforward, factual questions entitled to equally straightforward, factual answers? As to that, notice one thing. There was simply no clear, established procedure by which those questions could have been answered, and even—as some would argue—no clear meaning to the questions themselves. Of course, the curtains did *have* a definite color. If my mother had wanted more fabric, of the identical color, to make another set of similar curtains, there were practical things she could have done to ensure that result; for example, she could have discovered the technical name used for this precise shade of fabric, she could have taken one of the existing curtains as a sample to match against the new fabric, she could have consulted expert lighting engineers—maybe even have had a spectrographic analysis done—and in these ways she could have carried as far as possible the straightforwardly factual and scientific component in my question, "What is the *real* color of the curtains?" But that would still have left unresolved the deeper part of the question—the part I found truly perplexing: namely, what the shade of color I saw with my left eyes alone had to do with the shade I saw with my right eye alone, and what either of these had to do with the curtains themselves. At that stage, the very tests for deciding what one should *say* was the "real" color of the curtains—the *criteria* for deciding this, as the jargon puts it—were quite unclear; in consequence, my initial perplexity was not merely unresolved, but unresolvable.

Let me connect this experience with the concerns of traditional philosophy. More than two thousand years ago one of the men who did most to establish our modern traditions of intellectual inquiry—not only philosophical inquiry but also scientific and political, aesthetic and ethical—traced the origins of philosophy back to a *sense of wonder* natural in human beings. The habits of questioning, arguing, reflecting, investigating, criticizing, deliberating, reconsidering, correcting, starting afresh—these habits of rational inquiry were, in his view, not just the property of exceptionally inquisitive or bookish academicians, "long-haired intellectuals" or their ancient Greek equivalents. On the contrary, the roots of philosophical debate, like those of scientific investigation, moral reflection, political theory, and artistic criticism, were to be discovered in the lives of all men alike. Yet Aristotle's epigram, to the effect that *Philosophy is the product of wonder*, leaves one thing unexplained. How is philosophical wonder to be told apart from scientific or aesthetic wonder, say? Just how many different things, indeed, does that term 'wonder' include? In 400 B.C. the word 'philosophy' was still a very general, comprehensive term covering most of what we ourselves would call physics, ethics, psychology, and theology, and even parts of politics—not merely logic, theory of knowledge, and those other areas that remain philosophical to this day. What, then, was Aristotle referring to? By 'wonder', did he mean those exploratory feelings of curiosity and puzzlement that may eventually lead a man into, say, physics or physiology? Would he include also the sense of awe and mystery at the very existence of a world, and of ourselves, that marks off the budding theologian? Or was he in fact speaking as a 'philosopher' in the narrower twentieth-century sense of the term? If so, something needs to be added to his epigram. Philosophy may be one product of wonder, but it is only one among others; in addition, we must be ready to ask further about the connections—and differences—between the exploratory, inquisitive, puzzled wonder that gives birth to natural science, the delighted, creative wonder that expresses itself through the arts, the mystified, grateful yet apprehensive wonder underlying theology, and the reflective, self-critical, perplexed wonder that remains the driving force of philosophy today.

Still, about philosophy, quite as much as about science and politics, something in what Aristotle said remains fundamentally true. If we come to philosophy from the right direction, we shall discover that it is not alien, recondite, elitist, scholastic, hostile. Like it or not, we are all of us "born" philosophers, just as we are "born" art critics, moralists, political thinkers, and even scientists. It may take much talk about the movies before we can handle aesthetic questions in an articulate manner, just as it may take an exceptional political situation (a Vietnam war, a Watergate, or whatever) to bring out the political theorists in us all. Yet, if we look back at our childhood with the right questions in mind, many of us will rediscover moments in our own early experience—like that moment of mine in the family weekend cottage—that represent the first clear stirrings of authenti-cally *philosophical* perplexity.

A few years later on—I must have been thirteen or fourteen—I embarked voraciously on a diet of books with titles like *The Restless Universe*. Some onlookers may have seen in this an indication that I was "a physicist in the making"; and yet, though it was at one stage touch and go, that is not how matters turned out. Rightly so, as I see in retrospect, since my motives for digesting all those books of popular physics and cosmology were less scientific than philosophical. If I had possessed the genuinely outward-looking curiosity that might eventually have made an astronomer or a particle physicist of me, that would already have shown itself in an appetite for factual details, mathematical ingenuities, and theoretical refinements, of a kind I lacked even in those days.[1] Instead, the questions that sprang up in my mind and took command of my inquisitiveness were, for instance:

> And what if *fish* did science? Living in water instead of air, experiencing buoyancy instead of gravity—finding themselves always having to thrust against a resisting fluid, instead of being free to move around—might not fish end up with a view of the natural world totally unlike our own? Or must some common route of inquiry—some shared procedure for dealing with the total body of accessible facts—carry both them and us eventually through to the same fundamental theories and ideas?

In the spirit in which I was asking it, of course, this was not really a question about *fish*—not an "ichthyological" question, at all. Suppose the focus of my interest had really been the intellectual capacities of fish, simply regarded as fish, my later life would once again have gone differently. In that case I might have ended up in, say, one of those contemporary research teams studying the mental powers of dolphins.[2] But my actual concerns were quite different. In wondering "What if fish did science?" my perplexity embraced dolphins, chimpanzees, and Martians alike, that is, any conceivable group of investigators capable in imagination of studying Nature from a scientific starting point other than our own. To introduce an ugly but useful word, the point of my question was an 'epistemological' one; my fundamental interest was to understand better what our scientific "knowledge" really is—how we come by it, what claims can be made on its behalf, how much freedom of choice we, or any other investigators, would have in developing a picture of the natural world.

> Does the fact that, as human scientists, we start from a specifically human situation and work ahead from there leave enduring traces on the science we build up as a result? Or must any "correct" or "valid" picture of Nature possess an absolute, anonymous neutrality that would be recognizable equally in the science of Martians, chimpanzees, and even dolphins?

So it was no accident that I pursued my original curiosity into the theory of knowledge ('epistemology') rather than ending up in animal behavior research and, in particular, that I became preoccupied with a whole string of questions about the nature and justification of scientific ideas and theories. If this fact seems odd—if it seems odd that a question about *fish* turned out to be the cover for questions about *knowledge*—that is simply one more thing we can bear in mind as we move more deeply into the terrain of philosophy. In philosophy as in psychoanalysis, the forms of questions, problems, and images can be misleading. Very often we have to ignore the manifest, apparent content of questions or problems, and dig more deeply. Why! The very first philosophical question I remember asking, about the *color* of the curtains, itself turns out to disguise some deeper questions about visual perception and its relation to language.

So much by way of autobiography. For others, the starting points of reflective philosophical thought lie elsewhere; yet the reasons for identifying their childhood reflections, too, as "philosophical" are the same as before. Thus a friend of mine recalls walking down a street at the age of four, wondering how it would have been if her parents had never met and married: "Would I still have been 'I'?" This recollection is still so vivid, she reports, that it colors all her memories of what it was like to *be* four years old. Now, a psychiatrist might pick on this vividness as a sign that the remembered experience was some kind of emotional "mask," veiling deeper, concealed anxieties; yet that would be to leave the manifest, philosophical content of the reflection untouched. For philosophical it surely is, in at least two respects. In the first place, it poses quite squarely the problem of *personal identity*, which remains a source of perplexities today as much as ever. (Perhaps more so today than ever before, since the more we find out about the psychiatric states of "split personality" and about the ways in which brain injury or disease can lead to the dissociation of our senses and our language, the harder it becomes to articulate any simple and straightforward account of the things that make a person a "unity," either at a moment in time or over a longer period.) In the second place, the crucial source of perplexity in the four-year-old child's experience was once again the lack of well-established *criteria:*

> Would I still have been "I"? How on earth are we to say? What conceivable tests could possibly serve to decide that this was—or was not—the "same" child as might in fact have been born to other parents in a different world?

In tough-minded moods and moments, we may even be tempted to doubt whether such questions as this one really have any meaning at all. *Yet even that doubt is itself philosophical.* For, at the outset, nearly all of us will surely understand perfectly well what the four-year-old child was asking. And how could that be so if the question itself were—strictly speaking—meaningless? Yet, supposing that we follow along this road; we shall find ourselves wondering before long whether we do, after all, have any clear and satisfactory tests or criteria for deciding what does, or does not, have a genuine "meaning." The problem about personal identity will not have been resolved; it will simply have been traded in for a prior problem about language.

Let us move along and explore some other pathways into philosophy. Here are three more children. One of them, a three-year-old boy, is weeping quietly to himself in the night. His mother asks him what he is weeping about. Answer: he has just realized that there is no largest number because, however large a number he imagined, he could always construct still larger numbers by adding to it. Why the weeping? "Surely," a psychologist might say, "some extraneous sense of loss must be finding expression through this perplexity." Yet, in itself, the philosophical perplexity is authentic enough. For even a three-year-old, at any rate one destined to become himself a talented mathematician, can see that the idea of *number* carries some built-in difficulties—a sequence that has a beginning, we naturally presume, should also be capable of having an end. If we can anchor down the start of the number sequence at 0 or 1, how come that it apparently unrolls endlessly at the other extremity? Yet, on the other hand, what would *count as* an end? What criteria could there possibly be for deciding, "Yes, *this* is where the sequence of numbers ends"?

The second child feels a similar perplexity about time. Yesterday I can understand, and last year, and even the time before my grandfather was born. But when did Time itself begin? And what happened before that?

In their own way, the difficulties built into the idea of *time* are as acute as those involved in *number*. Again, we find it natural to visualize the passage of time as the unrolling of a tape. Let us fasten it down with a thumbtack at *now*, then trace it backwards into the past. We get into equally severe difficulties, it seems, whether we imagine the tape going on forever, without limit, or coming to an abrupt, arbitrary stop—beyond which, what? (This is one of those points at which physical cosmology ceases to be purely scientific, and must come to grips with philosophical issues. Immanuel Kant, the eighteenth-century German philosopher, worked on cosmology in his younger days but later turned to confront the philosophical difficulties that he had earlier been ignoring. The whole attempt to argue in terms of, say, a 'beginning of time', he argued, precipitates us into *inescapable* perplexities. Whether we choose to say that Time does have a beginning, or that it does not, the result is a kind of *Catch-22*. We are caught out either way.)

The third child is at a different place. The television set is turned on, and on the screen four old men can be seen playing stringed instruments. From time to time the picture switches to show the faces of the audience. These display a sequence of emotions as striking as the sweep of the violinist's arm, or the thrust of the cellist's bow. So, we might say, the audience itself represents a symphony of feelings. Ah, yes; but that is the point. The sound is turned down, so all that the child is aware of are the sight of the quartet, the visual spectacle of the audience, and the evident harmony between them. "Why are those people alternately so happy and so sad?" Let us talk to him on the assumption that his puzzle is a psychological one, about the *changes* of mood. We may then explain how different kinds of music and different passages in music have the power to move people now one way, now another. Yet he may still be dissatisfied. The problem for him lies not in the differences or changes of mood but in the fact that there are *any* "moods" to be observed at all. Those four elderly men working away at their strings—and that great mass of people seated in semidarkness—how can there be any such relationship between them at all? If music *is* possible at all, then different pieces of music will no doubt elicit different reactions. But just *look*—turn the sound off, and simply use your *eyes*. What is going on, so that the noises from stringed instruments have the power to affect people in this way?

Notice, once again, the generality of this problem. If the question at issue were simply, "Why does *this* kind of music make people happy and *that* kind make them sad?" there need be nothing specially philosophical about the problem; and so we might turn to the music critic or the psychologist, or both, for theories about the character of music and the hearer's response. The child seated before the silent television set, however, has a different and deeper preoccupation. The question for him is, how *any* music whatever comes to have *any* such effect on people. And here again we may briefly refer to Kant, who had a masterly eye for issues of this general form. As he saw clearly, one specific task for the philosopher is to look behind all particular questions—questions about this natural effect or that, which may be dependent upon these conditions or those—and to bring to light other deeper aspects of human life and experience, which are entirely general yet often mysterious. "How is the whole business of *musical expression* possible at all?" That, in effect, is what the child is asking. And, once again, the philosophical nature of his initial bewilderment shows itself in the entirely general character of his question.

NOTES

1. This is not to say that the questions of physics can always be cut off from those of philosophy in any hard-and-fast way. On the contrary, several of the most significant steps in the development of physics and philosophy have been taken at the same time and in double harness; while some branches of physics—notably, cosmology—retain a serious philosophical component to this day.

2. Once again, there is no absolute, hard-and-fast line to be drawn in this case between scientific and philosophical curiosity. Anyone drawn into comparative studies of animal behavior is soon faced not only by questions of the form "What things can dolphins *in fact* do?" but also by questions of the form "How far do these things *count* as 'thinking', 'problem-solving', 'using language', and so on?" These latter questions—being once again questions about the *criteria* for calling something, say, *thinking*—are as much reflective and philosophical as they are exploratory and scientific.

❧ 3 ❧

THE ADEQUACY
OF CHILDHOOD
UNDERSTANDING

❧ PETER FRENCH

University of Minnesota, Morris

What The Scarecrow Thought He Didn't Have: Children and the Philosophy of Mind

Classical literature for children has been a motherlode for philosophers in this century. Clearly the favorite source of examples has been the rather quasi-philosophical *Alice* books of Lewis Carroll. I admit to sharing that fondness for Alice and to having gone to Carroll's bank of extraordinary personages and witty phrases for a handy withdrawal on more than one occasion. *Alice* has proved to be so popular among professional philosophers that there now exists, in fact, a philosophers' edition of the books.

Much to my surprise and chagrin, however, I have learned from discussions with my own children and others that *Alice* is not among their favorites and not by a long shot. My daughter positively detests the Carroll books, and her reaction is not uncommon. Alice is a lonely figure in a confused world with few friends, is beset on every side at every turn by quarrelsome grown-ups and rather sadistic if befuddled creatures. The humor, the puns, the logical twists of *Alice* seem to be lost, although a measure of unrelieved terror is not.

By far the more popular classic piece for children seems to be that other tale of a young girl caught in a dream world with nightmarish aspects, Frank

Baum's *The Wizard of Oz*. The famous Judy Garland movie based on the novel is no doubt to some extent responsible for its popularity, but it does have other aspects that appeal to children that are not to be found in Carroll's books. For one thing, there is much beauty in Oz: a fairy queen (or good witch), Glinda, who, as well as being beautiful, is an omniscient observer and merciful provider of escape routes when matters become too grave for a brave little girl to endure. Furthermore, and this seemed to be the telling difference, especially for my daughter, Dorothy is surrounded by kind and loyal friends. She is not alone against the terrors of her dream (even were those terrors merely bombastic logico-linguistic ones, as they are for Alice). She has the courage of a lion, albeit one who thinks himself a coward, the tenderness and love of Nick Chopper, the Tin Woodman, who thinks he has no heart, and the wit and cunning and downright good sense of the Scarecrow. I shall concentrate my attention in this paper on this curious character who thinks he has no brain. My reasons for doing so are many, and I hope they will become clear in what follows, but first I want to defend my choice of this or any other example from children's literature as a way of dealing with the topic "Children and the Philosophy of Mind."

I shall treat as an unquestioned assumption that children tend to adopt those of their views that are of interest to philosophical psychology as a result of a bombardment of a certain set of Cartesian assumptions from three primary sources: (1) conversations with family members and friends regarding life, death, spirits, and even sometimes thinking, believing, wanting, etc.; (2) either formal or informal religious training; and (3) children's literature (including movies and television programs for children). My experience is that most children tend to distinguish between minds and bodies in ways that may be properly described as—if unsophisticated—still Cartesian. They seem to find the Cartesian intuitions compelling.

It is certainly no revelation that much of the classic literature for children depends upon the Cartesian distinction between the mind and the body. The metamorphosis motif (frog/prince, etc.) is only one example. In his sequel to *The Wizard of Oz*, *Ozma of Oz*, Baum creates a most incredible and to adults, a grotesque character, Princess Langwidere, who keeps a cupboard of heads, one for every day of the month, each quite beautiful, which she, "by the aid of the mirror", changes on her neck each day. Different dispositions seem to accompany the various heads, much to Dorothy's displeasure, for the Princess dons one with a fiery temper when she meets Dorothy and behaves outrageously to the young Kansas girl. Oddly, perhaps, the Princess has a memory of what she does regardless of what head she chooses to wear and often regrets the things she did while wearing No. 17. How could a child make sense of this unless he had adopted some version of the Cartesian intuition that minds and mental events are not to be identified with physical entities and brain events? It makes no difference that Baum's intended joke might have been the conceptual one that mocks a Lockean or Cartesian concept of personal identity. Children tell me that what is really funny is the image of someone standing before a mirror with no head on her neck, about to don one, worrying all the time over whether it is the right one for the day, if it suits her, if it is on straight, etc.: the logical extension to nonsense of the preening of their mothers and older sisters or brothers. I suspect also then that the Cartesian intuitions are being reinforced by the tale.

What I want to explore specifically is whether or not those intuitions are reasonable ones, even though they are embedded in the undisguised nonsense that characterizes stories for children. To be more direct, I shall be concerned with whether those Cartesian intuitions can withstand the recent and seemingly telling challenge of twentieth-century materialism, specifically in the form of the Mind/Brain Identity Theory. In one sense, this could be to ask, "How unreasonable is it for the Scarecrow to think that he has no brain?" I hope to argue persuasively that it is not unreasonable for the Scarecrow to think that: that his thinking so does not diminish his stature, that he is indeed to be admired as the most intelligent of the trio of Dorothy's friends—indeed of the residents of Oz, as the Wizard well knew. In preparing my argument I rely rather heavily on some of the recent innovative work in the philosophy of language of Saul Kripke. I cannot show that all or even most of children's literature provides examples that contribute to the beginnings of a defensible philosophy of mind. This is intended only as a beginning. I shall limit my discussion to the Scarecrow's utterance. Perhaps at some future date some enterprising person will carry the task further.

2

Some years ago U. T. Place and J. J. C. Smart (among others) set forth to defend the thesis that consciousness is identical to a brain process as a reasonable scientific hypothesis. They argued that, in Place's words:

> The statement "Consciousness is a process in the brain," although not necessarily true, is not necessarily false . . . it is a reasonable scientific hypothesis, in the way that the statement "Lightning is a motion of electric charges" is a reasonable scientific hypothesis.[1]

Smart clarifies the sense of identity being expressed in the theory by saying, "When I say that a sensation is a brain process or that lightning is an electrical discharge, I am using 'is' in the sense of strict identity."[2] By that he means that the hypothesis is not that consciousness is to be identified *with* a spatially or temporally continuous brain event, but that consciousness is identical *to* a brain event. Using the standard name, I shall refer to this theory as the Identity Theory (or IT). I recognize that my account of its salient features will be brief in the extreme, but for my purposes that is not going to be important. I am not going to be interested in spelling out how the theory explains thinking or having sensations, etc. I am only interested in the very broad statement of IT. With avowed simplicity, IT may be stated thusly:

> Every sensation, experience or other mental event is strictly identical with some brain state or other and that identity relationship is a contingent one analogous to that of lightning and a motion of electric charges.

Proponents of IT tell us that the research leading to the discovery of the brain states that are identical with so-called mental events is already underway and is to some extent successful; in the near future, they say, IT will have been confirmed.

Obviously, IT is an outright denial of those Cartesian intuitions exemplified throughout classical children's literature and mentioned in Part 1 of this paper. I shall stipulate that IT is the most compelling as surely it is the most fashionable version of materialism. Clearly if IT is substantially the correct account of, for example, thinking, then the Scarecrow is expressing a proposition that is necessarily false when he utters the sentence, "I think that I do not have a brain," and the humor of the utterance is to be found in the conjunction of that fact with the obvious sincerity of the utterance. If it is true that the Scarecrow thinks (regardless of what he thinks), then he must have a brain, because IT tells us that for anyone to think is for there to be a process going on in his brain, and if he does not have a brain it cannot be true that he thinks, as the requisite brain process that is identical to thinking that thought cannot go on. (Even thinking that one does not have a brain is identical to some process in one's brain!) It all seems so elementary: the Scarecrow's utterance is a conceptual or, as Wittgenstein might have said, a grammatical joke.

Everyone will agree that self-discovery is one of the primary themes of *The Wizard of Oz*. The Tin Woodman has "heart" even if he has no heart. The Cowardly Lion is really courageous; he is just not foolheartedly so, as he shows by his actions. He cannot be given courage, which is, after all, a disposition and not a bodily organ or any other thing. And the Scarecrow is really quite thoughtful and intelligent. Right from Dorothy's first meeting him, the decisions which he makes are well-reasoned, despite his claim that he has no brain. Children, however, tell me that they do not think that the Scarecrow's desire to have a brain is funny because he must already have one or he would not have been able to think so well. They find the humor in the fact, as they see it, that the Scarecrow doesn't need a brain. This is not because he already has one; he demonstrably does not have one. Strictly analogous to his friends, however, he wants something he has no need of and with which he would be no better off if he did have it. For children the joke is not a grammatical one, as it would be for the proponents of IT. The humor is not so deep as that. It is a joke purely and simply of someone wanting something because other people have it, although he does not need it. The joke involves a commentary on the way people will put themselves through incredible difficulties and over great obstacles to get something that has no real utility for them if they were to attain it. In this respect the joke, as the children see it, does not nip their budding Cartesian intuitions, and it surely does not encourage them to adopt IT. It's not at all grammatical; it is axiological.

It is possible, however, that the children may be getting the joke wrong, laughing for the wrong reasons. Perhaps they should be brought round to see the joke of the Scarecrow's utterance as a grammatical joke. But if we were to believe that, then we believe that IT rests on a firm philosophical foundation. Does it? We must examine the underlying assumption of IT: the contingent identity of someone's thinking a certain thought with a certain process in his brain, that there exists and will be discovered a strict though contingent identity between mental events and brain processes akin to that which has been discovered to exist between lightning and the motion of electric charges. But is this analogy really a good one? I shall sketch the salient point of Kripke's way of showing that the analogy breaks down at the critical stage.

Essential to Kripke's objection to IT is the distinction that he draws between what he calls 'rigid' and 'non-rigid' designation. In "Naming and Necessity"[3] Kripke defines a rigid designator as "a term that designates the same object in all possible worlds."[4] A non-rigid designator does not or need not designate the same object in all possible worlds. Rigid designators turn out to be like names for things, whereas non-rigid designators are usually descriptions.[5] For example, suppose we imagine that Jimmy Carter is the husband of Queen Elizabeth II. In order to do that, it seems that we have to have some way of deciding which person in the possible world in which Carter is the husband of Queen Elizabeth is picked out by 'Jimmy Carter.' How would we do that? We can't do it simply by saying that 'Jimmy Carter' picks out the man from Georgia who raises peanuts, has a large toothy smile, and was elected president of the United States in 1976, because in the possible world we are thinking about, the one in which Carter is the husband of the queen, none or only some of those descriptions may be true of Carter. A confusion against which Kripke warns already may be stealing into this attempt to state the issue. Possible worlds are not 'counter-worlds.' When we suppose that Jimmy Carter is married to Queen Elizabeth II, it must be the same person, Jimmy Carter, who is picked out by the name 'Jimmy Carter' in the actual world, to whom we are referring. We are imagining that certain descriptions are no longer true of him and that other descriptions are true of him. On Kripke's account, a word or phrase is a rigid designator if it is necessary that it picks out the same entity in all possible worlds in which it has a use. 'Jimmy Carter' is, on this criterion, indeed a rigid designator because no matter what we say of Jimmy Carter, it is the object picked out in this world by 'Jimmy Carter' that we must be talking about. 'The husband of Queen Elizabeth II', on the other hand, is not a rigid designator. That phrase might pick out 'Philip' in this world and 'Jimmy Carter' in some other world. Schematically we shall say that R designates rigidly if $\Box$ (R = R) and N designates non-rigidly if $\Diamond$ (N $\neq$ N).

'The Scarecrow's thinking the thought that he has no brain' is a rigid designator (for easy reference let us substitute 'ST' for that longer phrase). ST picks out just and only just the thought of the Scarecrow that he has no brain, and it would do so in all possible worlds. Also 'the brain event that occurs at the same time as the Scarecrow has the thought ST' is a rigid designator (which, again for easy reference, will be written 'SB'). 'ST' and 'SB' are both rigid designators, and the identity theorists are maintaining that ST = SB but they are also claiming, first we must attempt to fix the referents of ST and SB. (By "fix the referent" is meant something like point out what is being referred to by the rigid designator.) We have many ways of fixing a referent, but most of them, other than simple ostensive teaching, invoke the use of non-rigid designation. To return to the earlier example, the referent of 'Jimmy Carter' might be fixed by 'the smiling peanut farmer from Georgia.' Clearly identities that are formulated by referent-fixing in this manner cannot be necessarily true. They seem to be paradigms of the contingent identity relationship that is basic to IT. Jimmy Carter in some possible world we might imagine might not ever smile or farm peanuts or be from Georgia. In effect, it is possible that the non-rigid designation that fixes the referent 'Jimmy Carter' in our example might not do so under a different set of circumstances, just as 'the last person to enter my office' fixes the referent of 'my son Sean' while it certainly is not part of the analysis of 'my son Sean' that it is necessarily true of him that he was the last person to enter my office. Seconds later, in fact, that phrase picks out my daughter Shannon and is then no longer true of Sean.

If rigid designators are joined in an identity claim that is true, however, the identity is necessary and not contingent. For example, if Marion Morrison is John Wayne, he is necessarily John Wayne. It may well be that someone meeting John Wayne is unaware that he is meeting Marion Morrison, although he could later be informed that he had met Marion Morrison or he could discover it for himself by, for example, consulting birth and court records or a copy of *Who's Who*. Nonetheless, if John Wayne is Marion Morrison, he has to be Marion Morrison. (John Wayne just could not be, for example, Bernie Schwartz unless "Bernie Schwartz" and "Marion Morrison" are co-referential.) If 'John Wayne' picked out one person and 'Marion Morrison' picked out another, then it would have to be false that John Wayne is Marion Morrison, but it is true that Wayne is Morrison, so it must be false that John Wayne picks out one thing and Marion Morrison another. If we apply this to the problem at hand, we see that insofar as 'ST' and 'SB' are rigid designators, the identity formulated between them must be necessary and not contingent. The identity theorist then is incorrect in his claim that the identity between mental phenomena and physical phenomena is a contingent one. If there is an identity, it must be a necessary one. That is to say, that if ST is identical to SB then it is not conceivable that in some other world, in another set of circumstances, it is true that the Scarecrow thought ST and SB did not occur. IT, if it demands contingent identity of these rigid designators, is indefensible. It may be, however, that proponents of IT are only confused about what they mean to call contingent.

Some necessary identities are discovered *a posteriori* and hence can and do become the proper subject of scientific investigation. The famous example of Hesperus and Phosphorus is a case in point. Also, to use the example cited by Place, lightning and a certain motion of electric charges is another case, and so is our example of John Wayne and Marion Morrison. What makes these necessary identities amenable to scientific research is that the referents of the two terms of the identity are or were originally fixed by radically different non-rigid designators. Suppose that the referent of John Wayne were fixed by 'the male actor whose first major movie role was in *Stagecoach*' and that the referent of Marion Morrison were fixed by 'the son of Michael Morrison who was born in Winterset, Iowa, in 1907.' Someone might well discover that the non-rigid designation 'the male actor . . . ' is the same person as—fixes the same referent as—'the son of Michael Morrison . . . .' This discovery is an a posteriori one, and it is contingent, for it is clearly not necessary that the son of Michael Morrison who was born in Winterset, Iowa, in 1907 would be the male actor whose first major movie role was in *Stagecoach*. It is easy enough to imagine that, given some other set of circumstances, Michael Morrison's son would have been injured in a childhood accident and have never been deemed suitable for the silver screen of the 1930s.

Based on an analysis not unlike the preceeding, Saul Kripke formulates the principle that:

A necessary condition for "$R^1 = R^2$ to be known *a posteriori* is that there be a non-rigid designator N^1 and another N^2 such that it is not the case that R^1 is necessarily N^1 and not the case that R^2 is necessarily N^2 and it is not the case that what has the properties of N^1 is necessarily identical to what has the properties of N^2 and N^1 fixes the referent of R^1 and N^2 fixes the referent of R^2.[6]

The lightning example and our Wayne/Morrison example satisfy these conditions and therefore can be known a posteriori. But the identity that is proposed by the identity theorist, the one we have represented as ST = SB, fails to satisfy all of these conditions. ST and SB, as already mentioned, are rigid designators; that is not the problem here. If they are identical, as we have seen, they are necessarily identical. The condition that is not satisfied is the one that calls for the referent of ST to be fixed by a non-rigid designator, one that might not have been true of it.

How can we fix the referent of ST? (Remember that ST is 'the Scarecrow's thinking the thought that he has no brain.') Suppose we try to fix its referent by 'what causes the Scarecrow to think he needs the aid of the Wizard.' It seems reasonable to say that ST might not have caused the Scarecrow to think he needs the aid of the Wizard. So we seem to have the requisite contingency and the conditions for the scientific discovery of the identity of ST and SB. But do we? Does 'what causes the Scarecrow to think he needs the aid of the Wizard' fix the referent of ST? I think it does not. Instead, it tells us of the causal relationship between the contents of two thoughts. It does not pick out ST, independent of references to some other "mental event," the thinking of another thought. Fixing the referent of ST would be to identify ST in some way analogous to picking out John Wayne from the cast of a cowboy movie. 'ST is the thinking of the thought that followed the thinking of ———' or 'it is the one that preceded XXX' cannot do the trick because they depend upon our ability to pick out the thinking of the thought identified as ——— or as XXX, and it is just that problem of picking out a certain thinking of a thought that is at issue in the case of ST.

The point, as Kripke makes it in a different context, is that if we pick out ST we necessarily do so by essential properties of ST.[7] There is no other way to isolate ST than by reference to its content and its being a thought in a sequence of thoughts of the Scarecrow. The physical states of the Scarecrow at the time he has ST might have been different, but it cannot be the case that ST might not have been the thinking of that thought: the thought with that content. It could not have been some other thought, for example, one with the propositional content that it is very cold. Only when the Scarecrow thinks that he has no brain is it true that ST is occurring. We cannot use their contingent properties to fix the reference of the rigid designators of mental events. We identify ST as the Scarecrow's thinking the thought that he has no brain, and ST is necessarily the thinking of the thought with that content. The thinking of a thought with any other propositional content simply cannot be ST. Kripke make an analogous case with 'pain.' He writes:

> The experience itself has to be *this experience*, and I cannot say that it is a contingent property of the pain I now have that it is a pain . . . . That is, whenever anything is such and such a pain, it is essentially that very object, namely, such and such a pain.[8]

It surely cannot be a contingent property of ST that it is the thinking of a thought and it cannot be a contingent property of any thought that it is a thought. We could not have fixed the referent of ST by any of the previously suggested methods and have it turn out that we were rigidly designating by ST something other than (1) the thinking of a thought and (2) the thinking of the thought that the Scarecrow has no brain. If this account is correct, then the only remaining condition necessary for the identity thesis to be a testable scientific hypothesis does not exist. There is no non-rigid designator that fixes the referent of ST to satisfy the contingency criterion.

This rather complicated argument, I think, provides, at least, strong reasons for questioning the program of the identity theorist. Kripke writes: "the analytical tools we are using go against the identity thesis and so go against the general thesis that mental states are just physical states."[9] If proponents of IT are guilty of committing a conceptual error, then, of course the description of the Scarecrow as thinking he has no brain is not conceptually outrageous in and of itself. It is of a class with Descartes' contention that he could exist without his body. Descartes wrote:

> I thought of myself first as having a face, hands, arms, and all this mechanism composed of bone and flesh and members, just as it appears in a corpse, and which I designated by the name of "body." . . . I am not this assemblage of members which is called a human body . . . Because I know certainly that I exist, and that . . . any other thing necessarily pertains to my nature or essence, excepting that I am a thinking thing, I rightly conclude that my essence consists solely in the fact that I am a thinking thing . . . Possibly . . . I possess a body with which I am very intimately conjoined, yet . . . it is certain that this I (that is to say, my soul by which I am what I am), is entirely and absolutely distinct from my body, and can exist without it.[10]

This quotation is sufficient to establish that Descartes understood 'body' to be a rigid designator for his body and 'mind' for his mind and that his argument is that because his essence is that of a thinking being, demonstrated by the famous *cogito* argument, it is possible that he (that essence) is not identical to his body,   ('Descartes' ≠ 'body'). (We need not explore the many fascinating ways in which Descartes did or could have secured this point using Kripke-like analyses of identity.) We may, I think, agree that the underlying assumption that partially motivates Descartes' argument is that unearthed by Kripke: identities between rigid designators are always necessary. What Descartes tried to show is that identifying oneself *with* a particular body is purely a contingent matter. What Kripke shows is that if there did exist an identity of a mind and body, of certain mental events and physical ones, it would have to be a necessary one, yet one that could not be discovered by experimental research. Descartes' argument then appears to be, surprisingly, productive of the weaker conclusion of the two. Descartes' argument purports to demonstrate only non-identity, albeit Descartes must still deal with the incredibly difficult task of explaining the contingent relationship of persons with particular bodies, the so-called mind-body problem, and at that he is not terribly convincing. Kripke, on the other hand, ought to be read as arguing that the conceptual onus falls, not on the Cartesian, but on the proponent of IT to show that what seems to us to be possible is not: that "I can exist without it (my body)." But even succeeding in that, and surely it could not be shown by experimentation, he is still trapped by the problem of fixing the referent of the rigid designator of mental phenomena other than by their essential properties. In the end then it would seem that one's decision in favor of adopting IT must rest on purely *a priori* grounds.

A criticism of the position I have taken has been mounted by Michael Levin.[11] Levin concentrates on Kripke's analysis of sensations (pain, in particular), but if his argument works as advertised for sensations, it should be transferable to other purported mental phenomena such as thinking certain thoughts. Briefly, Levin argues that Kripke's analysis does not show that the identity of some rigid designator of a mental phenomenon and a rigid designator of a physical phenomenon must violate Kripke's principle because it is consistent with Kripke's account that there could be a description that does fix the referent of that mental phenomenon rigid designator and it not be true that that description picks out that phenomenon by essential properties. If we can locate such a description for the rigid designators of mental phenomena, IT can be rescued as a scientific hypothesis. Levin offers, as candidates, topic-neutral descriptions, such as 'what goes on when my skin is damaged,' that many IT proponents have used in their statements of the theory.

It seems to me that a case for the topic-neutral description of 'pain' might be made; I shall not pursue that here. The program seems to falter, however, indeed to fail, when we try to locate such a description for the thinking of specific thoughts. If the general form of such topic-neutral descriptions is, as Levin suggests, 'what goes on when (public event),'[12] then I do not see what can be reasonably substituted for '(public event)' in the case, say, of ST. I have already suggested that causal attributions will do no good. What public, topic-neutrally described event can be relevantly associated with ST? Suppose it were true in *The Wizard of Oz* that every time the Scarecrow is described as thinking ST he is also described as losing the stuffing from the right side of his head. Might we then not fix the referents of ST by the topic-neutral description 'whatever happens when the Scarecrow loses the stuffing from the right side of his head'? It might seem to be a contingent property of ST that the stuffing on the right side of the Scarecrow's head falls out at those times when ST occurs. But this is not going to be a uniquely referring description, and whether it is a property, contingent or not, of ST is surely disputable. Indeed it is just the issue of mind/body identity itself. This description could fix, at the same time as it fixes the referent of ST, the referent of 'body state t' (the Scarecrow becomes tipsy or topples over to the right). We cannot assume that this non-rigid designator is uniquely referring, for if we did, then we would have prejudiced the case in favor of IT at just the point under dispute.

3

The case for materialism of the IT variety is in serious danger of collapse if arguments such as those discussed in Part 2 above are cogent, and I think they are. Of course, IT does not exhaust the ways of formulating an anti-Cartesian monistic theory. Nonetheless, my intention has not been to investigate the range of alternative philosophies of mind. It has been to explore the possibility that the Cartesian position, generally adopted by the writers of children's literature, cannot be explained away as a conceptual mistake or the uncritical acceptance of a myth. Although I have not shown that the Cartesian intuitions are correct, I have shown that they are not as assailable as many contemporary philosophers and scientists have supposed. Let us return to the question which launched this discussion: is the predominantly Cartesian philosophy of mind that is embedded in the classical literature for children archaic, indefensible, or indeed unintelligible? Of course a theory may well be archaic but still intelligible and defensible. The stylish theories may, in fact, be incorrect, based on weak or false assumptions, which does seem to be the case, as suggested above, with IT. To say that something is archaic is to say that it is out-of-date, out of step with the current trends. Traditional children's literature, when seen as embodying a philosophy of mind, is certainly archaic or at least it was until very recently out-of-date. The identity theorist and his materialist cousins, however, no longer stand unscathed. Populatiry is ever a fleeting d thing where scientific and quasi-scientific theories are concerned—although not where children's literature is concerned.

The Cartesian intuitions may not, in the end, be defensible, though they are, it would seem, intelligible, at least to a point. A subtly guided discovery of these intuitions and possibly some of their implications would indeed be a worthwhile exploration with children, using their literature as a common world of reference. It is indeed not surprising that some of the most attractive humor found in the philosophically interesting works of children's literature attempts to focus on the very point of intelligibility of those Cartesian intuitions, as I have outlined it in regard to the Scarecrow in *The Wizard of Oz*. Tik-Tok and Princess Langwidere of *Ozma of Oz*, the Frog Prince of the Brothers Grimm, and the Beast of de Beaumont's tale are only a few of the others who might lead children into the Cartesian environs. Of course children's literature abounds in the personifications of objects and animals—from Humpty Dumpty to the talking tugboat, Little Toot; to Winnie the Pooh ("The Bear of Little Brain") and Tigger; Horton and the Whos—all of which evidence Cartesian overtones.

The intelligibility of the notion of discrete mental and physical entities does not provide a complete solution to the mind-body problem. Indeed, it is just because that discreteness has been so intuitively appealing (and hence has become embedded in the literature for children) that there is in the philosophical literature so much space devoted to the mind/body problem. What I hope I have shown, using Kripke's tools of analysis, is that those Cartesian intuitions are not to be explained away as, for example, mere confusions of reference-fixing and synonymy. Only the first step toward the defense of a dualistic theory of mind has been successfully taken; in other words, what I hope has been shown is that the distinction between mind and body can be made without necessarily being nonsensical. What has not been shown is how minds and bodies could possibly interact and when doing so produce even the simplest of human acts. For example, I have not even suggested how reasons (or intuitions or motives) can be causes of physical events. I am content in this paper only to provide reasons for rejecting what I take to be the usual philosophical analysis of those motifs in children's literature that bear on the philosophy of mind. What I have tried to suggest is that philosophers, with their vision tunneled by devotion to a fashionable thesis, may well be laughing at children's literature for the wrong reasons.

In sum, I have tried to show that the intuitions about minds that are commonplace, indeed the very coin of the realm, in literature for children—the intuitions that may be expected to have a major effect in reinforcing or establishing a child's belief about minds—are not as foolish or unreasonable as they are made to seem by contemporary materialists. The pet theory of the latter thinkers is constructed over a conceptual San Andreas fault and is in imminent danger of total collapse.

NOTES

1. U. T. Place, "Is Consciousness a Brain Process?" *The British Journal of Psychology* 47 (February 1956), reprinted in John O'Connor, *Modern Materialism* (New York: Harcourt, Brace and World, 1969), p. 23.

2. J. J. C. Smart, "Sensations and Brain Process" *Philosophical Review* 67 (1959), revised and reprinted in O'Connor, p. 37.

3. Saul Kripke, "Naming and Necessity," *Semantics of Natural Language*, ed. by Harman and Davidson (Dordrecht: Reidel, 1972), pp. 253–355 (hereafter NN).

4. Saul Kripke, "Identity and Necessity," *Identity and Individuation*, ed. by M. Munitz (New York: New York University Press, 1971), reprinted in *Naming, Necessity, and Natural Kinds*, ed. by S. Schwartz (Ithaca: Cornell University Press, 1977), p. 78 (hereafter IN).

5. Of course, taking Kripke's position is to stand against Russell's theory that names are disguised descriptions. I shall not pursue that topic in this paper.

6. I have adapted for my purposes a statement of Kripke's principle as formulated by Michael Levin. "Kripke's Argument Against the Identity Thesis," *Journal of Philosophy* 72 (no. 6, March 27, 1975): 152.

7. Kripke is concerned with pain. See both NN and IN.

8. IN, pp. 98–99.

9. IN, p. 99.

10. René Descartes, *Discourse on Method and Meditations* (Indianapolis: Bobbs-Merrill, 1960), "Second Meditation," p. 83.

11. Levin, op. cit.

12. Ibid., p. 155.

ᵈ§ CHRISTOPHER OLSEN

Ontario Institute for Studies in Education

Epistemology and the Developing Child

With few exceptions, philosophical theories of knowledge have taken knowledge as it manifests itself in the thought, judgment, and action of the mature adult human being. Seldom are questions even raised about whether there are any philosophically significant differences between the knowledge of the developing child and that of the adult, whether the young child may properly be said to have knowledge at all, or whether, if yes to both questions, this would make any significant difference to an adequate philosophical account of the nature of knowledge. The failure even to raise these questions is no doubt partly due to the widely held view among philosophers that the *development* of knowledge is really a problem for psychologists and not one that philosophers can properly handle. Fortunately, this view is not universal. A prime example of philosophers' taking serious interest in problems about the development of knowledge is the collection of articles edited by Theodore Mischel arising from a conference held in 1969.[1] Most of the articles in this volume deal directly or indirectly with theoretical issues arising from the work of Jean Piaget. This is as it should be, for Piaget has made a significant, if controversial, contribution to both philosophical and psychological epistemology.

In the present article, I have chosen not to deal with Piaget except in some passing remarks. Those who are familiar with his ideas will nonetheless recognize his influence at certain points, and I freely admit my debt to him in that he has made me aware of the necessity of taking the development of knowledge into consideration in a philosophical account of the nature of knowledge. I have also chosen not to engage in a critique of traditional and contemporary nondevelopmental theories of knowledge. These are both serious but necessary omissions. Instead I shall simply present a framework for a theory of knowledge which not only makes provision for the development aspect of knowledge from very early childhood onwards but which would also be capable of incorporating acceptable features of contemporary nondevelopmental theories of knowledge. My account is admittedly no more than a sketch for a theory of knowledge. It is in need of far greater elaboration than is possible here. My purpose is more to offer a framework within which it becomes possible to raise significant questions about childhood knowledge than to answer those questions in any detail. One major question about childhood knowledge is whether it can be objective. Thus a main concern that will run throughout this article will be the problem of the objectivity of knowledge. While objectivity is also a problem for nondevelopmental theories of knowledge, they would be concerned primarily to account for the conditions under which knowledge *as an end state* could be objective. In a developmental theory of knowledge, on the other hand, the problem would also be to account for the conditions under which objective knowledge could arise.

The problem is briefly this. According to Piaget, one of the main characteristics of early childhood is the child's epistemological egocentrism, by which he means the child's inability to decenter from his own point of view; this prevents him from having an objective relation to, and an objective understanding of, the world. Thus Piaget sees the development of knowledge as involving a progression from egocentrism to objectivity. If we agree that objectivity is essential to knowledge, in that it would not make sense to speak of purely individualistic or logically private knowledge, and if Piaget is right about the young child's epistemological egocentrism, then how can the child be said to have *knowledge* of the world? It would seem that either we must deny that young children can be said to have knowledge or we must give up adherence to the criterion of objectivity in knowledge. These are not, however, the only alternatives. As I shall suggest later, we might better regard objectivity not as an all-or-nothing affair but as one which, like knowledge, can admit of degrees, as might be expected in a developmental theory of knowledge such as the one I shall now begin to sketch.

1. The Knower-Known Relationship

Most epistemologies postulate a duality between a knower and a known, between a knowing subject and objects of knowledge. Where various theories differ is in how they conceive of the knower and in what they take to be objects of knowledge. Thus traditional rationalism and empiricism view the subject as a noncorporeal mind, an inner stage on which conscious activities occur. Objects of knowledge, on the other hand, are considered to be the contents of consciousness—ideas, impressions, sense data and the like—which, in the case of empirical knowledge, are causally related to things in the external world. Things in the world can never, on this model, be directly known by the mind. Their existence and nature can only be inferred from what is directly given to consciousness. Such a view of the knowing subject and of objects of knowledge has been pretty thoroughly discredited in recent philosophy, even if remnants of it occasionally still appear dressed up in more sophisticated, usually linguistic, garb. What, then, can replace it?

Regarding the knower, while it is not my purpose in this article to delve into philosophy of mind or a theory of persons, I shall nonetheless have to provide some indication of the view I would advance. Eschewing on the one hand any form of incorporeal mentalism of a Cartesian or Lockean kind and on the other hand a reductionist physicalism or central state materialism, I should maintain that there must still be a place for the notion of consciousness in characterizing the knowing subject. Thus, in adumbrating my view, I shall simply claim that the *knowing* subject is an essentially active, conscious being whose consciousness, characterized by intentionality, manifests some level of conceptual activity as evidenced either through the nature of his overt physical action upon the world or his covert action of making judgments about the world, judgments which may be expressed overtly in language or in nonverbal behavior. Such a view, while not neutral as to the subject's necessary embodiment in human or something like human form, is neutral as to the specific physical basis or ultimate physical nature of conscious activity. Whatever this part of the story turns out to be, it is essential to note that the knowing subject must be conceived of as a totality in which his conscious activity is integrated with his sensory capacities and his physical action upon the world outside his body. In claiming the active conceptualizing nature of the knower, this view would deny a conception of the knowing subject as merely a recipient of "information" or an automatic processor of data from an external environment. It would equally deny that his activity is mere reactivity to external stimuli unmediated by a conceptual structure which is essential to his subjectivity. The idea of an active conceptualizing consciousness is that of a subject capable of being aware of things in the world *as* this or that and not something else, that is, as falling under certain concepts, thereby enabling the subject to make judgments about the world. In that the consciousness of a knowing subject is an intentional consciousness, it is always directed upon objects which it structures in a conceptual scheme. In order to explain this I shall now turn to discuss the opposite pole of the knower-known duality.

An object of knowledge may be regarded as a portion or fragment of the world—a thing, event, or relationship—carved (so to speak) out of the total world in an epistemic act of judgment in which a knowing subject brings particular features of the world under one or more of the objective concepts he has within his conceptual repertoire. In "bringing it under concepts," the knowing subject *structures* the world into objects of knowledge and so confers meaning on it in order to make it intelligible to himself. The idea of conceptually 'structuring' the world is difficult to illustrate because, in the ordinary course of events, we adults do it almost automatically or unreflectively unless we are faced with a problem that requires us to see things in different ways, that is, to 'structure' the world differently in order to cope with it. Such is the case in investigative activities like scientific research, solving a crime, or doing philosophy, different as these activities may be. But in order to see something as a problem in the first place we must structure a situation by means of an appropriate set of concepts. In order to resolve a problem, on the other hand, we may well have to restructure the world under a different set of concepts and thereby create new objects of knowledge. This will often involve modifying the concepts we do have or acquiring new concepts which will enable us to structure the world in different ways in order to achieve our purposes.

In order to illustrate the idea of structuring the world, I shall offer an example of ordinary nonproblematic knowledge in which we might well be aware of the process of structuring the world in accordance with our conceptual scheme. I will also suggest how this example might be seen as an analogy for the very young child's increasing ability to structure the world into objects of knowledge. The example is that of approaching a city from a very great height in an airplane. At first the city appears not even as a city but merely as a blob on the horizon: something different in our field of vision, something we know not what. We soon begin to see outlines of things which have more specific shapes and perhaps colors. On closer approach we distinguish larger buildings, roads, etc., which we bring under the concepts 'building', 'road', or whatever, and still later under more specific concepts: 'apartment building', 'office building', 'house', 'car', 'telephone pole', 'person'. In bringing these things under concepts, their nature, purpose, and relationships become intelligible to us in a way that was not possible when the city was no more than a blob on the horizon, when we were not able to see things *as* this or that. In structuring the world into objects of knowledge in order to make it intelligible to ourselves, we confer meaning on that which we make into objects of knowledge. To do this presupposes having the appropriate concepts within our conceptual repertoire. Otherwise we would not be able to see these things *as* apartment buildings, roads, or people. They would remain mere things which for us have no meaning.

This point is directly relevant to the conceptual situation of a very young child. Whereas in this example of an adult's structuring the world the normal adult would already have the appropriate concepts, the infant child (as I shall argue later) does not. Insofar as he does not he would be unable to structure the world into objects of knowledge. He would therefore not be able to make it intelligible to himself. However, as he comes to acquire a set of concepts and as his conceptual repertoire becomes more elaborate, he becomes progressively able to structure the world and thereby make it progressively intelligible to himself. The case of an adult's structuring the world as he progressively approaches the city could well be seen as an analogy for the case of a child. The analogue of the adult's progressive approach to the city is the child's progressive acquisition of an increasingly elaborate conceptual repertoire through which he becomes progressively more capable of structuring the world into objects of knowledge.

Before leaving the topic of objects of knowledge, I should introduce two points regarding the objectivity of knowledge. By 'objective knowledge' in this context I mean knowledge that is in principle sharable with other knowers and which could therefore be assessable as knowledge according to norms or standards shared within a community of knowers. A presupposition necessary to any theory of knowledge which can remain consistent in claiming the objectivity of knowledge is that there be a common world shared by, and hence theoretically open to, all knowers whatever the differences of extent or kind there may be among individual knowers. The fact that there are very significant differences in what a person's intelligence, conceptual capacities, training, and environment make him capable of knowing, or what his particular circumstances permit him to know, is in no way prejudicial to this presupposition of a common world theoretically open to all knowers. Given a common world, there is then the possibility of there being common points of reference among knowers to which all have access.

If objects of knowledge are fragments of a common (public) world so structured in acts of knowing, a condition of objectivity is that the knowers who do have access to this common world must be able to structure it into the same objects of knowledge, each in his own act of knowing. The possibility of their doing this depends upon their possessing a common conceptual scheme, that is, a repertoire of concepts which each possesses individually but which they all share, as evidenced by their applying these concepts in the same way in making judgments about the world. To the extent that they possess a common conceptual scheme by which they can structure the world into objects of knowledge, communication about one and the same thing as structured according to a common set of concepts becomes possible. Once communication becomes possible, objectivity also becomes possible, since only through communication on common ground among putative knowers can agreement or disagreement in the application of concepts and hence in judgments be detected and differences be amended or ameliorated in such a way that common judgments are reached.

There is much more to the problem of objectivity than I have been able to sketch here. I have tried to relate the story only as it concerns objects of knowledge. More of the story as it concerns common conceptual schemes and communication among knowers will have to await an account developed in the ensuing section on foundations of knowledge.

With this brief description of how the knowing subject and how objects of knowledge should be conceived, I now wish to suggest that knowledge itself be conceived as a dynamic relationship between knower and known. A relational conception of knowledge is to be contrasted with views that conceive of knowledge as a static inner state of a knower or as a fund of information stored away in a knower's mind or as merely a set of justified true beliefs or as a set of dispositions to behave in certain successful ways. Such views, though not totally misconceived, tend to focus attention away from the central feature of knowledge, its relational character. On a relational account of knowledge, when a knowledge claim is made by or about a putative knower, this would be construed as a claim that a certain kind of intentional relationship exists between the knower and what are said to be the objects of his knowledge. Since there are many different types of knowledge—empirical, scientific, logico-mathematical, aesthetic and moral knowledge, knowledge of the past, and self-knowledge, to name a few—the specific nature of the knowledge relationship will differ somewhat in the kind of relationship which is possible to establish between the knowing subject and the different types of knowledge. The details of these differences are matters to be elucidated in the epistemological accounts of the various types of knowledge just mentioned. Nonetheless, all knowledge relationships must satisfy three very general criteria which can be noted now and elaborated upon later.

First, a knowledge relationship between a knower and a known must be dynamic and intentional rather than static and merely extensional. By this I mean that it is a relationship which is established through the activity of the knower when, in an act of judgment, he structures the world into objects of knowledge through his conceptual scheme. In the process of establishing a knowledge relationship, both knower and known are altered or "transformed": the knower as the relationship alters and expands his conceptual capacities, and the known as it takes on significance through the intentionality of the knower's structuring the world. This criterion is particularly important in understanding the development in childhood where transformations of the child's conceptual structure are most apparent and most critical in their effect on later knowledge capacities.

Second, knowledge relationships must satisfy the criterion of objectivity. As suggested above, this means that such relationships must in principle be assessable by other persons according to the criteria accepted within the community of knowers for the type of knowledge in question.

The third criterion, which is closely connected to the objectivity criterion, is that a knowledge relationship must be intelligible to an appropriate community of knowers. By this I mean that the relationship must be such that it could be cited in explanation of how a knower came by his knowledge or in justification of a claim that a knowledge relationship obtains. Where the nature of the claimed relationship cannot be made intelligible to the relevant community of knowers, they are justified either in denying the knowledge claim or at least in withholding judgment on its epistemic validity until its intelligibility as a knowledge relationship has been established within the community. For example, claims to telepathic or clairvoyant knowledge, at this time, would fail on the intelligibility criterion because we have no way of understanding the nature of the claimed relationship between the subject and the supposed objects of knowledge. On the other hand, there is no such similar problem in understanding the basics, if not the details, of the claimed knowledge relationship in the case of perceptual knowledge or in the case of knowledge of the past where this is based on perceptual memory or on the compilation of adequate evidence. Since both the objectivity criterion and the intelligibility criterion involve norms established within an appropriate community of knowers, I shall defer further elaboration until I have had the opportunity to introduce the notion of forms of life.

At this point, however, I can begin to say a bit more about why epistemology ought to concern itself with the development of knowledge in childhood. Regarding the question of childhood knowledge, three positions might be advanced. At one extreme it might be claimed that, strictly speaking, it does not make sense to attribute knowledge to young children up to the age of ten or twelve. Such a view might have received some credence a century or two ago when children were not seriously regarded as fully persons until they had reached the "age of reason." Fortunately for children and thanks to a liberalized epistemology—I say this with tongue only partly in cheek—this idea no longer merits serious counterargument even though one suspects that some parents and educators still tend to think that way at times. At the opposite extreme, it might be claimed that insofar as children can be said to have knowledge at all, their knowledge is formally identical to adult knowledge. But since it is quite obvious that there are significant differences between an adult's actual knowledge and knowledge capacity and those of a child, it is simply that children do not have the length of experience in dealing with the world that adults do. Put as a relational account of knowledge, this would mean that regarding the knowledge children do have, a knowledge relationship between a child knower and an object of knowledge would be formally identical to a knowledge relationship between an adult knower and an object of knowledge. Given his shorter experience in the world, however, the child has simply not established as many knowledge relationships as a normal adult, nor, perhaps, has he established them as firmly. In either a standard or a relational version, it would be something like this kind of answer that I suspect philosophers who do not take a developmental approach to epistemology would have to give if they are willing to attribute knowledge to young children.

While an argument could be given for such a view—and certainly it could be made more plausible with greater elaboration than I have provided—I would argue that it does serious injustice to an understanding of childhood knowledge to account for the marked differences between an adult's epistemic abilities and a child's simply by citing lack of experience. A preferable approach would be to account for the differences by means of the nature and kinds of knowledge relationships that the developing child is capable of establishing between himself and objects of knowledge. While the child, as knowing subject, would still have to be regarded as a conscious, intentional conceptualizing being (as described above), where he differs from a normal adult is, first, in his actional capacities by which he establishes knowledge relationships, and second, in his conceptual capacities, that is, the complexity and extent of his conceptual repertoire, in relation to which he structures the world. This much is hardly new and might very well figure in a standard nondevelopmental account of childhood knowledge. But it takes on a different significance in the kind of developmental, relational account of knowledge that I am espousing. Thus, insofar as a child's conceptual and actional capacities are different from an adult's, this will mean that his ability to structure the world into objects of knowledge will be different from an adult's. This in turn makes a difference to the knowledge relationships that the child is capable of establishing. Simply to assert this does not take us very far. How, it might be asked, do a child's conceptual capacities differ and how, in consequence, do the claimed knowledge relationships differ from an adult's? If they are significantly different, will the knowledge relationships a child is supposedly capable of establishing be able to satisfy the three general criteria mentioned above? While I shall not attempt to answer these questions here, if I take the account a stage further and examine the conditions of the possibility of conceptual development through childhood, I will have provided the basis from which detailed investigation into these questions can begin. I shall therefore outline the main features of a second major segment of the theory of knowledge I am advancing.

2. The Foundations of Knowledge

In the previous section, I suggested that knowledge must be conceived as a dynamic relationship between a knower and a known. In this section, my argument will be that the possibility of knowledge relationships, that is, the possibility of objective human knowledge, rests jointly on three foundations,[2] namely, sensory capacities or 'sensibility', actional capacities or 'action', and, to use Wittgenstein's term, 'forms of life'. To some extent I shall have to discuss these three foundations of knowledge separately, but it should be made clear at the outset that it is only through their mutual involvement in the development of knowledge that they could constitute the conditions of the possibility of knowledge. As foundations they function jointly from infancy onwards to effect a progressive elaboration of the individual's conceptual repertoire and thereby become the basis of his capacity to establish objective knowledge relationships.

Though clearly far less ambitious in scope, my purposes in this section are somewhat similar to part of Kant's program in the *Critique of Pure Reason*.[3] It will therefore be useful in explaining my scheme to contrast it with Kant's at certain points. In the final paragraph of his introduction to the *Critique*, Kant asserts that "there are two stems of human knowledge, namely, sensibility and understanding . . . . Through the former, objects are given to us; through the latter they are thought" (B 29). In the "Transcendental Aesthetic" he defines 'sensibility' as "the capacity (receptivity) for receiving representations through the mode in which we are affected by objects" (B 33). The modes he refers to are the five sensory modalities which constitute a subject's receptive dimension. If we had no receptive capacities through which we are affected by things outside our bodies, empirical knowledge as we understand it would clearly be impossible. Even a rationalist epistemology recognizes this much in allowing that innate structures must be activated through sensation in order to provide knowledge its empirical content. If, to put it in my terms, knowledge relationships are to be established with things in the world, sensory capacities play a fundamental role because such relationships are intentional relationships involving the subject's consciousness of objects. My main disagreement with Kant on the matter of sensibility concerns his acceptance of a representative theory of perception in which he regards the objects of empirical intuition as appearances. As noted earlier, my claim is that objects of knowledge are quite literally things in the world and, however much the mind may be involved in structuring the world into objects of knowledge, they are not merely appearances of an underlying reality.

Nonetheless Kant was quite correct to view sensibility as one "stem of human knowledge," but he also recognized that it could not be the only stem, as an empiricist account would have it. He saw the necessity of positing something else, which he called the understanding, by which what is received via sensibility is structured conceptually in such a way that it becomes intelligible to us as knowledge. In speaking of sensibility and the understanding, he tells us that it is

> just as necessary to make our concepts sensible . . . as to make our intuitions intelligible, that is, to bring them under concepts. These two powers or capacities cannot exchange their functions . . . . Only through their union can knowledge arise. (B 75–76)

Much more ought to be said about the way in which our sensory capacities make knowledge possible and yet—given the sensory capacities that we as human beings happen to have—place certain limits on the kind of conceptual repertoire that is possible for us. But for present purposes it is more important to consider the other factors in the origin of conceptual capacities. In the Kantian framework, it is the understanding that accounts for the origin of not only the pure concepts of the understanding, the categories, but also, in a slightly different way, the origin of ordinary empirical concepts which he says are "grounded in empirical intuition" (B 64). My main objection is that his notion of the understanding, however rich it may be in other respects, is not rich enough to account for the development of conceptual capacities and hence for the development of knowledge. As with traditional rationalist and empiricist epistemologies, the problem with Kant's account is that concept formation is conceived of as a purely internal activity of the conceptualizing subject. Thus, on the other hand, in simply assuming the active nature of the understanding, he sees no need to bring seriously into account the subject's overt physical action. On the other hand, an even more serious defect is that he does not take into consideration the communal or intersubjective nature of concepts upon which the objectivity of knowledge depends. P. F. Strawson beautifully summarizes this defect in commenting on the 'considerable limitation" under which Kant's treatment of objectivity is managed:

> He [Kant] nowhere depends upon, or even refers to, the factor on which Wittgenstein, for example, insists so strongly: the *social* character of our concepts, the links between thought and speech, speech and communication, communication and social communities.[4]

Strawson does not explicitly refer here to Wittgenstein's notion of forms of life nor, indeed, does he pursue the problem further himself. Had he pursued it in the Wittgensteinian terms alluded to in this brief passage, the notion of forms of life would undoubtedly have played a major role in a constructive account of objectivity in conceptual development.

In opposition to Kant's essentially abstractionist account of the origin and derivation of concepts,[5] I should like to suggest the view that concepts arise through the coordination of sensory and actional capacities in conjunction with an increasing participation in communal or intersubjective forms of life. This statement encapsulates a complex developmental view of concept formation and knowledge which will take the balance of this article even to sketch. I shall begin with a partial account of what is meant by the term 'forms of life' and explain how this notion must be involved in our understanding of the concept of objectivity. Immediately thereafter I shall turn to a discussion of how the developing actional capacities of the young child play an essential part in the development of his conceptual capacities or his conceptual scheme. In claiming that all three factors—the three "foundations" of knowledge—are jointly involved in the development of objective knowledge, I hope to avoid the irreconcilable subjectivity inherent in a Kantian account and, for that matter, in those provided by his rationalist and empiricist predecessors.

It is widely recognized that the notion 'forms of life' is one of the central notions in Wittgenstein's later philosophy. Although the term appears five times in his *Philosophical Investigations*,[6] it is never defined or explicated. This has led to extensive debate over what it could mean and even whether such a notion could be made sufficiently precise to be of any value at all. Hence it is at some risk that I invoke this notion to serve my purposes. The three most revealing occurrences of the term in the *Investigations* are as follows:

Here the term "language-*game*" is meant to bring into prominence the fact that the speaking of language is part of an activity, or of a form of life. (§ 23)

"So you are saying that human agreement decides what is true and what is false?"—It is what human beings *say* that is true and false; and they agree in the *language* they use. That is not agreement in opinions but in form of life. (§ 241)

What has to be accepted, the given, is—so one could say—*forms of life*. (p. 226)

In an extremely well-research article, John Hunter has proposed what he calls an "organic account" of forms of life which he summarizes thus:

> . . . the sense I am suggesting for it ['form of life'] is more like 'something typical of a living being': typical in the sense of being very broadly in the same class as the growth or nutrition of living organisms, or as the organic complexity which enables them to propel themselves about, or to react in complicated ways to their environment.[7]

Hunter devotes much of his article to defending the claim that "Wittgenstein did hold an 'organic view', or something like it",[8] which I would not dispute and which, incidentally, has interesting parallels with Piaget's organicism. As he recognizes, however, it is a further matter whether his "organic view" is what Wittgenstein meant by 'form of life'. I cannot see that Hunter has provided a persuasive argument that this is what Wittgenstein meant, primarily because the organic view fails to bring in the communal and interpersonal dimension of human life that I would regard as an essential feature of Wittgenstein's notion. On Hunter's account, a form of life is something exhibited solely by an individual, whereas I take Wittgenstein to have intended the notion to capture the idea of something that people in community actively engage in during the course of their lives together. It is quite clear that in each of the contexts in which the term appears, Wittgenstein is talking about communal as opposed to purely individual activities: language, mathematics, human agreement, etc. If this is not the idea he intended to capture by this term, then some other term would have to be invented to refer to the interpersonal dimension of human life which figures so prominently in Wittgenstein's later philosophy, as the quotation from Strawson so aptly indicates.

On my interpretation, Wittgenstein intended the term 'form of life' to encapsulate the notion of very broad types of human activities and practices which have a certain purpose, regularity, and internal coherence, and which have a history. As such, forms of life constitute the tacitly agreed upon ways of doing things within a social community, agreed upon in order that there be some semblance of order to social living. The notion of 'a practice' is important here. As Rush Rhees puts it in a different context, "A practice refers to a way of living in which many people are engaged. We could observe a habit in an individual man, but not a 'practice'."[9] A practice, in the sense I am using the term, is something that would have a history of occurrence within a community. Thus, speaking a language, wearing clothes, raising a family, educating children, and worshipping, would be examples of practices which manifest themselves in the daily lives of people engaged in joint activities and enterprises whose origins, though perhaps obscure, go well back into cultural heritage. In a sense they have become part of the fabric of their lives. In general, a form of life will involve a number of distinguishable but related practices, and one form of life may well overlap other forms of life since the practices and activities that go to make up a form of life may also be involved in other forms of life. Speaking a language is one such practice that occurs in most forms of life. Perhaps its pervasiveness was what led Wittgenstein to say, "And to imagine a language means to imagine a form of life" (§ 19), though he did not mean by this that speaking a language was itself a form of life. (See the first of the three quotations above.)

While it may be difficult to specify sharp bounds for any particular form of life, this does not detract from its usefulness in highlighting the interpersonal nature of human activities and the mutual understandings that they must contain. Thus, in spite of its vagueness, and perhaps because of its broad generality, the notion of forms of life—or something like it—must play an important role in any epistemology, for it is in forms of life that we can find, so to speak, the source of objectivity in human knowledge, and not in some Platonic ideal world of forms or in a universal innate structure of the human mind. Wittgenstein may have been alluding to this role for forms of life when he said: "What must be accepted, the given, is . . . forms of life." To suggest that forms of life are a given, that they have to be accepted, does not imply, however, that they are forever fixed and unchanging. Forms of life may alter, if slowly, because human practices evolve as new needs and interests make themselves felt. In the general context of the *Investigations*, a plausible interpretation of what Wittgenstein might have meant in referring to forms of life as "the given" is that forms of life constitute the background against which all objective understanding of the world must be reflected, in the sense that the system of concepts by which we make the world intelligible to ourselves and which we invoke in communicating with others about the world has its roots in, and thus derives its sense from, forms of life.

Insofar as there may be alterations in forms of life, the consequent conceptual changes that may occur must nonetheless be understood against a background for the then evolving forms of life which may appear static except in retrospect. Thus if our knowledge or understanding of the world is to be objective, as opposed to purely personal or subjective (if such an "understanding" is possible), we must employ, in thought as much as in communication, a set of concepts the meaning of which is shared with other people. This sharing could come about only through mutual participation, in some sense, in shared forms of life. Thus, forms of life have to be "accepted." The reasons they have to be accepted is that to reject them, or to fail to participate in them, effectively precludes the possibility of interpersonal communication about the world. This in turn precludes the possibility of objective knowledge of the world, since without communication not only could knowledge never be shared but it could never be known that what, as an individual, one takes to be knowledge actually meets the public standards for objective knowledge.

On this matter Wittgenstein makes a very revealing remark in the paragraph immediately following the second of the above three quotations on forms of life: "If language is to be a means of communication, there must be agreement not only in definitions [read 'concepts'] but also . . . in judgments" (§ 242). At a deeper level than judgments, what must be involved, (i.e., presupposed) is "agreement in form of life" (§ 241), and this would entail, I have claimed, participation or engagement in the activities and practices that constitute the relevant form of life. While it might be possible (if plausible) to suggest that we are all born with a common set of concepts, the acid test of the objectivity of those concepts and hence the objectivity of our knowledge would be whether in the application of these concepts there can be agreement in the judgments we make. This suggests, not that there will always be agreement in judgments but rather that implicit in the forms of life that provide, in Hamlyn's words, "a necessary underpinning that exists over the application of concepts . . . "[10] are the norms and criteria which determine whether our application of concepts is objective and which in turn make possible the assessment of our judgments as 'true' or 'false', 'successful' or 'unsuccessful'. To summarize this argument: the objectivity of knowledge entails the objectivity of the concepts by which we structure that knowledge; the objectivity of concepts presupposes agreement in the application of concepts in judgments which in turn presupposes participation in forms of life.

By now it might be wondered how all this pertains to the knowledge of a developing child. In fact it is all highly pertinent to our problem. If we accept Piaget's claim about the epistemological egocentrism of the very young child and (as he does) interpret this to mean that the young child is incapable of having an objective understanding of the world, the way is now open to specify the conditions which must obtain if the child is to develop objective knowledge. Since, as I have just been arguing, the objectivity of knowledge is logically bound to the objectivity of our concepts and if, as I shall argue in a moment, we cannot assume that objective conceptual capacities are innate, it would follow that the development of objectivity is logically bound up with the development of objective conceptual capacities. And, as I shall also be arguing, this development could occur only through participation in forms of life. Thus to the extent that a child can engage in forms of life, to that extent is it at least possible for him to develop objective conceptual capacities. But participation in the activities and practices that constitute a form of life is itself dependent on an individual's actional and sensory capacities. Insofar as these are limited, so too will be the possibilities of his developing conceptual capacities. It is to this problem that I must now turn in order to bring out more of the story of the conditions under which objective knowledge can arise.

In the earliest days and weeks after birth, the infant child's actional capacities are severely limited. The behavior he exhibits is little more than reflex responses to internal and external stimulation and semi-reflex activities such as grasping, crying, sucking, and more or less random limb and eye movements. Given that the criteria by which we judge whether and to what extent an individual has conceptual capacities are behavior criteria— verbal and nonverbal—there are two possible ways of interpreting this fact as it pertains to the question of the newborn child's conceptual capacities and hence capacity for knowledge. On the one hand it could be claimed that conceptual capacities are innately present in the newborn child, but that he is simply incapable of using or manifesting those capacities until his motor and actional capacities (including those necessary for speech) develop through maturation and practice. Nonetheless, so the argument goes, we must postulate the existence of innate conceptual capacities in order to explain the very remarkable speed with which the child is later able to acquire his capacity for action, language, and knowledge. On the other hand, it could be claimed that the newborn child lacks conceptual capacities altogether and is therefore incapable of having objective knowledge of the world because, as I should want to put it, he is incapable of conceptually structuring the world in order to establish knowledge relationships between himself and objects of knowledge.

The first alternative must be rejected on two counts. First, as already implied, if we look for behavioral evidence of conceptual functioning we find none. Second, to postulate the existence of innate conceptual capacities in order to explain later conceptual functioning makes philosophically unnecessary and unwarranted assumptions about the "mind" of the young child. Even Noam Chomsky, perhaps the leading contemporary proponent of a strong innateness hypothesis, has not produced any philosophically persuasive arguments to justify such a hypothesis. Although Chomsky's primary concern is with language capacity, for which he postulates an innate knowledge of a language or innate "linguistic competence",[11] he makes it reasonably clear that he supports a traditional rationalist conception of knowledge acquisition at least in principle if not in detail.[12] His usual arguments for the innateness of linguistic competence revolve largely around the claim that the ease with which a child acquires his language could not be explained without the innateness hypothesis, given the shortness of a child's experience combined with the supposed paucity and degeneracy of his linguistic environment. But once this given is exploded, as several commentators have been quick to do, there is little left of the innateness hypothesis on the linguistic plane, much less on a more pervasive epistemological level.

At most, what could justifiably be claimed is that there is an innate potentiality for conceptual and linguistic capacities present in the biological makeup of the newborn human organism, just as there is an innate potentiality for actional capacities. In neither case is this potentiality manifest at birth; but because actional and conceptual capacities are so closely linked, they must develop jointly out of that innate potentiality, or so I should want to argue. This very weak innatism simply recognizes that in the unique neurological/biological structure of the newborn human—its central nervous system and its bodily structure—there exists a potential for actional, conceptual, and linguistic capacity that may not be present in any other known species. But this is far less than Chomsky would require for his notion of an "innate schematism" or an "innate knowledge of a language." It would equally be far less than his favored predecessors, Descartes and Leibniz, would mean by innate ideas and innate principles. If not, there could be little argument between Chomsky and a developmentalist such as Piaget, whose rejection of innatism or "nativism" in its rationalist epistemological context is well known. Indeed, this weak form of innatism (if it may be called such) is not only acceptable to a developmental account but, I should think, would be required by it: development must start from something.

In arguing against an innateness hypothesis, I have at the same time been starting an argument in favor of a developmentalist alternative. The remainder of my case against innatism and the development of a case for development can best proceed by means of a concrete example of childhood knowledge. The example—that of a child's ability to tie his shoelaces—is meant to be representative of a broad range of practical knowledge that could properly be attributed to children, depending on the particular knowledge in question, from about the age of two onward.

It seems to me totally implausible to suggest that a five-year-old child's ability to tie his shoelaces—his knowledge of tying his shoelaces—is in any sense prefigured in an innate structure of the mind or brain of a newborn child. It is obvious that the child is quite incapable of tying his shoelaces for the first few years of his life. What is at least necessary by way of development from those actional capacities mentioned earlier as being present at birth is the coordination of his sight and touch, his sensory capacities, with his hand movements and the development of manipulative skills with his hands and fingers such that he is able to do with shoelaces what is necessary to make a bow knot. This latter manipulative skill develops not only through growth and physical development of the muscles but through the development of a whole range of simpler skills at manipulation which serve as the building blocks, so to speak, for the more complex manipulative skill of tying shoelaces. But along with the coordination of sensory capacities with the development of the actional capacities involved in tying shoelaces, an equally important factor has to be brought into the picture to account for the child's knowledge, and that is his learning what it is to tie shoelaces. This is something a child could learn only from other people, since he must learn not merely the most efficient ways of manipulating the laces, but what counts as a correct as opposed to an incorrect tying of the knot. This learning requires his participation in a form of life in which people wear shoes with laces to be tied in certain accepted ways. This form of life is of course very complex, involving much else as well, but by the time a child is physically able to tie his shoelaces he already has a fairly well-developed understanding of the essential features of this form of life.

The point here is that his actional knowledge of tying his shoelaces involves all three factors jointly. If it is implausible to suggest that his manipulative skills are prefigured at birth, it is totally mistaken to suggest that the third factor, his participation in forms of life, could be innate since it involves something outside the individual, namely, the community of shoelace tiers. In a case such as this, there should be no hesitation in attributing knowledge to the five-year-old in the full sense of that term. And by 'knowledge' here I mean not only the actional ability of tying the laces but also a well-developed conception of what it is to tie shoelaces, what its purpose is in a society of shoe wearers, and what are the accepted criteria for getting the job done correctly. This means that the child would have to have acquired, to some degree or other, a fairly wide range of interconnected concepts of a relatively simple kind—simple relative to the complexity, say, of scientific or mathematical concepts that he may later acquire. To say that the child has this knowledge is not, however, to suggest that the set of concepts he does have need be fully developed or fully elaborated. It is only to suggest that they are sufficiently developed to justify this particular attribution of knowledge. For as Hamlyn puts it:

> To have a concept is not an all-or-none affair; there are degrees of understanding and degrees of complexity of what is understood. Conceptual development is as much as anything an initiation into a web of understanding which may be more or less involuted at any given time.[13]

Thus if there can be degrees of understanding and degrees of conceptual capacity, there can equally be degrees of objectivity to the knowledge we are justified in attributing to the developing child. While we could not attribute a knowledge of how to tie his shoelaces to a two-year-old, given his limited actional capacities and his limited participation in the appropriate forms of life, we could attribute this knowledge to a normal five-year-old, assuming that he can actually perform the operation and given especially his relatively much fuller participation in that form of life. In general, knowledge attributions can properly be made only in accordance with the criteria appropriate to the particular knowledge being attributed. These criteria are determined by what concepts would normally be necessary if a person is to structure the world in order to establish knowledge relationships that would meet the objective standards for that knowledge. Whether a person, child or adult, has the requisite concepts will depend on what goes into acquiring those concepts, that is, what actional capacities, what sensory capacities, what forms of life, and what other concepts are logically presupposed in having those concepts, whatever the particular procedures he happened to go through in acquiring them. Thus, to the extent that a child has developed a conceptual capacity vis-à-vis a certain type of knowledge, even though the concepts involved may become more fully elaborated with greater experience, to that extent would it be possible for him to have objective knowledge of that type.

In the foregoing example, I did not specifically mention the role of language in the conceptual development that must occur. In the development of nearly all—some might say all—concepts, language will play a crucial role from the age of about eighteen months onward when a child begins to speak. In the case of all of our more complex concepts, language plays not merely a crucial but an essential role in view of their dependence on what Piaget calls the symbolic function. To account for even the philosophical aspects of the role of language in concept development would be an immense task which I cannot even begin here. Nonetheless, in concluding this article I want to say something about the development of language capacity—a type of actional capacity—as it relates to the developmentalist theory of knowledge that I have been sketching.

Against the background of Chomsky's innateness hypothesis, we might again ask what, in the case of language capacity, might be present at birth. At the very least, in a greater or lesser degree of physical development, the normal child has a unique grouping of biological structures which are necessary for there to be a language capacity at all. In particular, it has a brain of certain complexity, auditory mechanisms, musculature, voice box, tongue, incipient teeth, etc. If we wish to consider these structures to be "innate," so be it. They constitute the biological basis for an "innate potentiality" for language capacity. What is clearly lacking at birth, among other things, is an ability to make the articulate sounds that constitute the phonemes of a language. But from the relatively undifferentiated and incoherent noises the newborn child can make, this actional capacity develops over the first years into fairly well-differentiated and coherent sound makings. While this story is undoubtedly very complicated, by most accounts a major factor is imitation of the sounds of language made by older members of the linguistic community.[14] Imitation, however, requires the coordination of hearing (and perhaps sight) with the child's sound-making capacities. This coordination of sensory and actional capacities necessary for imitation is apparently not present at birth but must go through a process of development, which must surely cast doubt on an innateness hypothesis.

Even if we were to fill in all of the psycholinguistic details of how the young child's sensory and actional capacities do develop jointly in acquiring a language capacity over the first four or five years of life, this could only tell part of what is conceptually necessary for a child to have a language capacity as opposed to mere sound-making capacities of a very specific kind. For in order to acquire a knowledge of a language (in an ordinary sense, not Chomsky's technical sense), a child must come to understand quite a bit about the complex role that language plays in communication among individuals as well as be able to use language in communication himself. This is something that could not be present at birth since it can arise only through a gradually increasing participation in the form of life of a language-using community. The process by which this understanding takes shape is, of course, started for a child by his parents almost immediately after birth, but his own participation in this form of life awaits the increasing coordination and development of his sensory and actional capacities. Nonetheless, it is only through social interaction, his own engagement with others, that the child could come to have an understanding of the communicative function of language, which is its primary function, and thereby have an objective "knowledge of a language." On this matter, Vygotsky was closer to the mark than Piaget in regarding the child's earliest attempts at speech as essentially social and communicative in nature[15] rather than "egocentric" as Piaget regarded them, at least in his early work. How speech relates to thought and how language relates to the acquisition of conceptual capacities is, as I have suggested, a matter for further investigation beyond what can be done here. Vygotsky's empirical investigations and, more interestingly, his conceptual model as sketched in his 1934 book, *Thought and Language*, would in my estimation provide a most fruitful starting point which I believe is quite compatible with the type of approach I have been advocating in this article. My very limited purpose in raising the issue of language capacity was simply to show how its development would fit into my threefold developmental scheme of sensory capacities, actional capacities, and, not least, forms of life, thereby hoping to avoid making the unnecessary assumptions about innate linguistic capacities that are made in Chomsky's innateness hypothesis.

3. Conclusion

I have now completed my sketch for a developmental theory of knowledge. It is clearly only a beginning, a beginning which I hope can provide a framework from within which some of the serious questions about children's knowledge can be raised. Some of these questions were noted at the end of Section 1 and in my introduction, but I have not attempted to answer them because they properly require detailed investigations which would take me beyond the limited scope of this article. Such investigations would have to involve an examination of the empirical research, and more significantly the theoretical assumptions, of developmental psychology. I have already mentioned the fruitfulness of looking at Vygotsky's work on the relation between thought and language. It would be equally worthwhile to investigate the extent to which Piaget's equilibration or autoregulatory model (assimilation-accommodation-equilibrium) of conceptual development can be meshed with the three "foundations" framework that I have been advancing. Piaget has often been criticized for not taking sufficiently into account the interpersonal nature of concepts in his theory of conceptual development. If this criticism is justified, as I suspect it is, it may well be that the equilibrium model would have to be significantly modified in such a way that it could give proper place to the notion of forms of life as an essential factor in conceptual development and hence in children's acquisition of objective knowledge. This, of course, is only one of the many problems that are in need of philosophical investigation.

It is quite evident that one of the major concerns in the education of children must be their acquisition of an objective conceptual repertoire through which they will be able to structure the world in the process of coming to know it. Developmental psychology has taken this concern seriously. It must equally become a concern for philosophy. It has been an implicit aim of this article to show that this concern can be pursued only within the context of a developmental epistemology. If my sketch for a developmental theory of knowledge has any merit at all, I should hope that at least it would stimulate philosophers, psychologists, and educators jointly to pursue matters that should be of mutual interest in the field of conceptual development and knowledge acquisition in childhood.

NOTES

1. Theodore Mischel, ed., *Cognitive Development and Epistemology* (New York: Academic Press, 1971). On the matter of the respective roles of philosophy and psychology in accounting for the development of knowledge, the articles by Hamlyn, Toulmin, Mischel, and Taylor are particularly helpful.

2. In recent philosophy the idea of 'foundations of knowledge' has come into disrepute insofar as it is connected with the search for certainty that characterized traditional rationalism and empiricism. It will be apparent that my use of the term has nothing to do with that quest. The foundations of knowledge as I conceive of them are, however, to be understood as the joint bases upon which an individual builds his knowledge.

3. Immanuel Kant, *Critique of Pure Reason*, trans. by Norman Kemp Smith (London: Macmillan, 1961). References contained in the text are to the second edition of the *Critique* (e.g., B 29).

4. P. F. Strawson, *The Bounds of Sense: An Essay on Kant's Critique of Pure Reason* (London: Methuen, 1966), p. 151.

5. See H. J. Paton, *Kant's Metaphysic of Experience* (London: George Allen & Unwin, 1936), pp. 198–200 and pp. 249–251, on Kant's abstractionist account of concept formation.

6. Ludwig Wittgenstein, *Philosophical Investigations,* trans. by G. E. M. Anscombe (Oxford: Basil Blackwell, 1963). References contained in the text are to section numbers in Part 1 and to page numbers in Part 2.

7. J. F. M. Hunter, " 'Forms of Life', in Wittgenstein's *Philosophical Investigations"*E. D. Klemke, ed., *Essays on Wittgenstein* (Urbana: University of Illinois Press, 1971), p. 278.

8. Ibid., p. 286.

9. Rush Rhees, "Questions on Logical Inference," in Godfrey Vesey, ed., *Understanding Wittgenstein* (Ithaca: Cornell University Press, 1974), p. 46.

10. D. W. Hamlyn, "Objectivity," in R. F. Dearden, P. H. Hirst, and R. S. Peters, eds., *Education and the Development of Reason* (London: Routledge & Kegan Paul, 1972), p. 256. I am far more indebted to Hamlyn's discussions of objectivity than this brief quotation would indicate. See also his *The Theory of Knowledge* (London: Macmillan, 1970), chap. 3 (d) "Concepts and Criteria" and chap. 5 (e) "Facts and Objectivity," as well as his contribution to the Mischel volume, op. cit., especially pp. 8–10.

11. Noam Chomsky, *Language and Mind* (New York: Harcourt Brace Jovanovich, 1972), p. 31. Other terms that occur frequently are: 'innate universal grammar' (p. 192) and 'innate schematism' (p. 159).

12. Noam Chomsky, "Recent Contributions to the Theory of Innate Ideas" in Stephen P. Stich, ed., *Innate Ideas* (Berkeley: University of California Press, 1975), p. 129. See also *Language and Mind,* passim.

13. D. W. Hamlyn, "Epistemology and Conceptual Development" in Mischel, ed., op. cit., p. 10.

14. See Vygotsky's interesting comments on Yerkes's conjecture that the reason that chimpanzees do not develop speech is that they "have no tendency to imitate sounds. Their mimicry is almost entirely dependent on optical stimuli." Lev S. Vygotsky, *Thought and Language,* edited and translated by E. Hanfmann and G. Vakar (Cambridge: M.I.T. Press, 1962), pp. 39 ff.

15. Ibid., p. 19.

⋘ 4 ⋙

CAN CHILDREN DEAL WITH
METAPHYSICAL ISSUES?

⋘ DAVID L. NORTON

University of Delaware

On the Concrete Origin of Ultimate Metaphysical Questions in Childhood

Contrary to the effusions of sentimentality, the unspoiled curiosity of children does not make them model scientists, nor does children's capacity for pure wonder make them the original metaphysicians.

What in principle distinguishes the curiosity of the child from that of the scientist is the intervening recognition that everything can't be questioned at once. Scientific curiosity is rigorously selective. To question one thing, it must take its stand upon others. At the same time this stand, to be itself scientific, must be hypothetical, not categorical and dogmatic. It is the hypothesis that constricts scientific curiosity, making of it directed inquiry.

By contrast, native childhood curiosity is unselective and is thereby in a perpetual condition of distraction. Ortega y Gasset terms this condition *alteración* and invites us to study it in monkeys at the zoo. "If we can remain still for a time in passive contemplation of the simian scene," he says, "one of its characteristics will presently, and as if spontaneously, stand out and come to us like a ray of light. This is that the infernal little beasts are constantly alert, perpetually uneasy, looking and listening for all the signals that reach them from their surroundings, forever intent on their environment . . . . [I]t is the objects and events in its environment which govern the animal's life, which pull and push it about like a marionette. It does not rule its life, it does not live from *itself*, but is always intent on what is happening outside it, on all that is *other* than itself . . . . The animal is pure *alteración*. It cannot be within itself, Hence when things cease to threaten it or caress it; when they give it a holiday; in short, when what is *other* ceases to move it and manage it, the poor animal has virtually to stop existing, that is, it goes to sleep."[1]

The hypothesis is precisely the self-management of curiosity, transforming perpetual distraction into the power of sustained attention capable of arriving at answers and furnishing the marks by which answers will be recognized when they are arrived at. As dependence, childhood is not capable of self-management. This means that the hypotheses by which the curiosity of childhood begins to acquire discipline must be furnished to it by others who are categorically different from children, namely by adults. The learning this affords is not science but the education of dependents. What distinguishes science is not the desire to know but the capacity to find out, and this capacity "spoils" curiosity, from the sentimental viewpoint, by rendering it no longer spontaneous but disciplined.

Similarly childhood's capacity for unspoiled wonder is categorically different from the wonder which was identified by the fathers of Western philosophy, the ancient Greeks, as the distinctive philosophical capacity.[2] Certainly great metaphysics exhibits the ability to regard with wonder what the world takes for settled matter of fact. But what is there meant by wonder is conclusively beyond the capacities of childhood, for childhood has yet to learn what the world takes for settled matter of fact. What the Greeks meant by philosophical wonder—*thaumázein*—originates reflexively in wonder at oneself and thereby signifies the metaphysical distinctiveness of human being as problematic being, a kind of being which originally appears as a problem to itself. But the Greeks clearly recognized that such awareness is beyond the capacity of childhood in virtue of childhood's dependence. Such awareness, and with it the capacity for philosophical wonder, must await the stage of adolescence.

Trusting that sentimentalism has been put to rest, I turn to a thesis that at first sight may seem to outstrip galloping sentimentality at attributing wisdom to children. For I believe and will here argue that the very loftiest and seemingly most abstract questions of classical metaphysics arise concretely in children between the ages of four and seven. For present purposes I will limit myself to three such questions, each of which has at one time or another claimed priority in classical metaphysics. The first is the paradox of being and nonbeing; the second is the question of the contingency of existence; and the third is the question of appearance and reality. If my thesis holds up, it has significant implications for the nature of childhood and the kind of care it requires. And it also speaks to the kind of enterprise philosophy is, for it suggests that the great questions of classical metaphysics are not sophisticated conceptual mistakes. They arise as questions before the conceptual sophistication to which they are ascribed. They appear in primary experience as concrete testimony to the human condition, and when the discipline of metaphysics subsequently undertakes to conceptualize and analyse them, it engages in an activity of Platonic "recollection" (*anamnesis*).

Around the age of five, children typically exhibit curiosity about their own origins. It begins with the child's question, "Where did I come from?" to which the ordinary reply is, "From Mother's tummy." This satisfies the questioner for at best a week before provoking the followup, "But how did I get in Mummy's tummy?" The response here is apt to be something rather vague about seeds and eggs, but from it the child learns of the necessary participation of Daddy. Again this suffices only briefly before producing in the child the question, "But where would I be if you and Daddy had never met?" And this question is not answered satisfactorily, for no satisfactory answer exists. What the child here confronts is the paradoxical thought of his own prior nonbeing. Western philosophy's first great specialist in this paradox was Parmenides, who concluded, "About nothing, nothing can be said."[4] This is unsatisfactory because in so saying, Parmenides contradicted himself.

In our time two influential philosophers, otherwise divergent, have agreed that one's own nonbeing cannot be conceived and is therefore to be dismissed as a pseudo-problem. The two philosophers are Jean-Paul Sartre and Ludwig Wittgenstein.[5] Both men invoke highly sophisticated conceptual mistakes to account for the genesis of pseudo-problems, but the concrete appearance of the paradox of nonbeing in midchildhood disallows such an account. It also suggests that the word "abstract," as a term of opprobrium, may more appropriately be applied to systems of thought which dismiss profound and universal problems of humanity as pseudo-problems. Where such dismissal reflects distaste for problems for which demonstrative solution cannot be found, the distaste will recognizably be directed at the kind of being which human being is, namely problematic being. The problems which comprise the very problematicity of human being are not to be solved but expressed.[6]

The problem of the contingency of existence is expressed by Leibniz as the question, "Why is there something rather than nothing?"[7] But it did not originate in the mind of the mature metaphysician, having arisen antecedently in the minds of children. What Sartre terms the "fragility" of existence is intuited by the child with regard to his own existence in the circumstances noted above. But it does not end there; it rapidly spreads as a corrosive throughout the whole existence. "I might not exist" introduces the hypothetical mode of thought, and it becomes possible to substitute something else for everything that exists. "Why the situation in which I now find myself (let us say sitting on a sunny hillside) instead of some other?" The child remembers that yesterday it was rainy and he was confined indoors. From his experience of "otherwise" he supposes that all that is might be otherwise, which implies the nonexistence of all that is. This leads to the question, "Why *anything*?" I believe the intuitive apprehension of the child goes this far, although I cannot be certain. But I am sure that it goes as far as the perfectly general apprehension concerning anything that exists, that such existence is precarious. It is this intuition which underlies the highly exaggerated but entirely characteristic fear of separation which besets midchildhood. In this stage the child lies awake at night when his parents are out, wholly unsure that they will return. His apprehension is not logical from the standpoint of experience, for his parents have thus far always returned. The child's separation anxiety is also likely to be aroused by his own sleep and by the sleep of his parents. I know of one case in which a mother who liked to take a Sunday afternoon nap regularly had her eyelids lifted open by her five-year-old and met the question, "Are you in there?"

If the separation phobia is unreasonable by the standard of empirical probabilities, it is a distinctly accurate expression of the child's perception of his situation. This situation appears in the conjunction of two recognitions. The first is the child's recognition of his own dependence upon persons who are responsible for him, and the second is his recognition of the fragility of all existence. It is this latter intuition that I want to stress here, for it is the concrete origin of the metaphysical question, "Why is there something, rather than nothing?" By keeping this intuition of childhood in mind we gain a new perspective on philosophy's persistent discomfort with the modality of existence, a discomfort which is suggested, for example, by Sartre's declaration that existence is "*de trop*,"[8] or by Santayana's observation that "Existence is accordingly not only doubtful to the sceptic, but odious to the logician. It seems to him a truly monstrous excrescence and superfluity in being, since anything existent is more than the description of it, having suffered an unintelligible emphasis or materialization to fall upon it, which is logically inane and morally comic."[9]

A third great metaphysical question whose locus can be traced to childhood is the question of appearance and reality. Its philosophical *locus classicus* is certainly Plato's famous allegory of the cave in Book 7 of the *Republic*, though it had been very active previously, having instigated the work of the Milesians and Parmenides. It is commonly thought to have originated in the recognition of the deceptiveness of the senses concerning the nature of the world. Attention to childhood locates its origin elsewhere, however, for there is but one kind of being that is capable of fundamental deception, namely human being. Misrepresentation cannot be ascribed to the tiger, the tree, or the stone, for each of these things is bound by the law of identity to itself as just what it is. In their cases we are often enough deceived, yet they do not deceive us; we deceive ourselves by hasty generalization which further observation would modify or disallow. Similarly, our senses do not deceive us, for the data they provide does not come with meaning attached but awaits the meaning we ascribe to it. The stick in the water does not deceive us, for it says nothing about the stick out of the water. To one who has knowledge of the ways of water and light, it is not a stick which appears bent but a stick-in-water. And while the atomic structure of matter is not apparent to the unaided eye, there is no deception on the part of matter, for surface and depth are poles of a continuum along which inference may confidently travel.

In the case of man, inference cannot travel confidently between appearance and reality because between them lies the slip-plane of human freedom. Uniquely in the case of man, identity is not conferred but must instead be won. The nature of man is problematic and duplicitous, and it is in man that the problem of appearance and reality arises.

The duplicity of others is beyond detection[10] because what we mean by their reality—their subjective immediacy—is accessible only by inference from appearances. One can attribute duplicity to others, but because duplicity is a relation between two terms, to experience duplicity one must experience both terms, and this is possible only in one's own case. In short, the concrete experience that is the foundation of the great metaphysical question of appearance and reality is the experience of oneself lying. The child's discovery of his capacity to deceive is very evident because it delights him beyond measure. He exercises it at every opportunity, manufactures more opportunities, and carries on his experiments, if need be, by lying to himself. Here is abundant evidence that lying in childhood begins sportively and not in utilitarian fashion to advance the child's interests or to thwart the interests of others. This means that the lying of the child as it originates is to be categorically distinguished from the lying to which moral imperatives apply. By his lying the child is acquainting himself with a profound human characteristic, the characteristic out of which the struggle for human dignity and personal integrity arise. In the words of Socrates's prayer, "Beloved Pan, and all ye other gods who haunt this place, give me beauty in the inward soul, and may the outward and inward man be at one."[11]

Having argued that the great metaphysical questions are traceable in their origins to the intuition of childhood, let me reemphasize that this in no sense represents children as metaphysicians. Nor is the difference a commensurable one such as, for example, a difference between vagueness and clarity in the conceptualization of a problem or between lack and possession of methods for dealing with a problem. The difference lies in the radical transformation of life that occurs between childhood and adulthood, at the time when, as the Greeks liked to say, "the young man's beard begins to grow." For there is one metaphysical problem which does not arise in childhood: the problem of personal identity. It cannot arise in childhood because childhood is the stage of dependence, and the intrusion of this problem is the birth of autonomy. The problem of personal identity is at bottom metaphysical, for it is the manifestation of human being in its distinctiveness as problematic being. Carl G. Jung has identified childhood as the stage of life when the individual is a problem exclusively for others. Very well, adolescence begins in the recognition by the individual that he is his own first problem. It is the instantiation of human being as being which is a problem to itself. And it is the beginning of self-responsibility, for the problem which each individual is to himself can be "solved" only by himself.

In my belief it is characteristic of the great questions of classical metaphysicians that they arise from and express the problematicity of human being. They express this problematicity in their original appearance to the intuition of childhood. But, as with dependence, childhood needs to believe that the problems which it thus apprehends are not its problems, which is to say children need to believe that these problems have solutions which are known to adults, or to God. What the self-responsibility of later life signifies is that to these problems each individual is required to find his own "solution." There can be no objectively demonstrable solution to the ultimate metaphysical questions, not because they are pseudo-problems but because they express the problematicity of human being. By terminating this problematicity, objectively demonstrable solutions would mark the extinction of human being.

When the history of classical metaphysics is regarded in this light, it suffers no shame for its failure to provide final answers for the questions it poses. Instead it deserves the utmost respect for the integrity with which it expresses the human condition. These problems are not to be solved in the demonstrative sense but lived with, and metaphysics affords alternative strategies of living. Its problems are therefore not "philosophical" in the narrowly professional meaning that the word has acquired in the twentieth century. They are philosophical in the profound sense in which human life is obliged to be philosophical by the problematicity of its being. As American pragmatism has insisted to its credit everyone is obliged to be more or less of a philosopher, and professional philosophy serves not professional philosophers exclusively but in principle everyone. The question is not whether an individual is a philosopher but whether he philosophizes in better fashion or worse. One studies philosophy not to learn "the answers," but in order to improve oneself at doing philosophy. Concerning the great metaphysical questions, the only philosophy of ultimate worth to the individual is his own.

The kind of "solution" of which the great metaphysical questions are susceptible is not that kind of objectively conclusive answer which eliminates the problem as a problem. It consists rather in taking a stand and living out its entailments. The task is to take one's stand intelligently, in clear knowledge of alternatives and of their presuppositions and implications. One's stand does not objectively eradicate the question as a question, but lends consistency and identity to the life of the individual and enables other questions to be asked and answered. "Idealism," "materialism," "pragmatism," and "existentialism" are terms which point to some of the stands that have been taken. They cannot be verified or falsified. What can be said of the individual who intelligently so stands is, in Michael Oakeshott's admirably chosen words, "He was an interesting experiment."[12]

"Taking a stand" in the meaning given to it here expresses the autonomy of the individual and is therefore impossible for children, who, as dependents, are dependent on stands taken by others. For this reason the metaphysical questions that appear to the intuition of children are in a certain sense the enemy of childhood, asking of it what it cannot give. If we recognize that childhood has its own autonomous requirements and opportunities to be fulfilled, then we will see in this the need of childhood to be protected from anachronistic demands such as the metaphysical question. Protection here takes the form of the assurance that these questions, which he knows he cannot answer, can be answered by higher authority, and therefore do not fall to the responsibility of the child. But parents cannot long pose as such authority, for the child readily discerns parental uncertainty and confusion in the face of these questions. Here the idea of trust in God offers itself as the means to preserve childhood from anachronistic demands that will jeopardize childhood as such. On the heels of a century of secularization, it is well to be mindful of Erik Erikson's warning that parents "who are proud to be without religion whose children cannot afford their being without it."[13] From the developmental standpoint, however, equal protection can be afforded by what Bergson termed the "shadowy presence" which is sensed by every child as an authority behind its parents and teachers and which is in fact society.[14] This authority has the advantage that the child will recognize it for what it is by growing into it and becoming part of it. It thus exhibits truth to the recognition that the dependence of childhood is *provisional* dependence, and, correspondingly, authority over childhood is provisional authority whose purpose is to foster autonomy and self-responsibility.

I will conclude with a few words directed to the question, "Should children be taught philosophy?" As I hope the last paragraph has made clear, my thesis that ultimate metaphysical questions arise in the intuition of childhood does not in the least imply that metaphysics should be taught to children. To the question, "Should children be taught philosophy?" the answer implied in the foregoing is, "Not directly." Philosophy presupposes the autonomy of the philosopher, and to attempt to teach it to children would be to commit a fallacy of anachronism. But notice that in the very broadest sense, an education designed to enable childhood to fulfill itself as childhood is a training for philosophy. For if philosophy presupposes autonomy, and autonomy itself has certain developmental conditions, then fulfilling those conditions is preparation for philosophy.

The approach suggested here is indirect but is, I think, the right one. An enduring tenet of developmentalism, going back in its early expression to the Hindu Vedas but enunciated no less today by Erik Erikson and Lawrence Kohlberg, is that fulfillment of the requirements of prior stages of life is the primary condition of entrance upon the next one. In this light we supply the conditions of autonomy—and philosophy—by doing our best to see that childhood is fulfilled as childhood. I do not think we are presently very successful at this. We need to know a great deal more than we do about the intrinsic requirements of childhood—its own internal values, virtues, and obligations. And we must want—and place the education of children in the hands of persons who want—childhood to be itself. To want the fulfillment of others along with oneself is love in the classical meaning; it is *eros.*

Philosophy, as I have been using the term, is thinking about ultimate questions—questions which are by their nature insusceptible of demonstrative solution—for the purpose of arriving at a productive stance with respect to them. I have argued that children are incapable of doing philosophy as thus understood because philosophy presupposes the autonomy of the philosopher, while childhood is dependence. I should emphasize that there is no argument here against teaching children the techniques that are associated with philosophy such as clear thinking, informal logic, and the beginnings of formal logic. As distinguished from metaphysics and ethics, for example, early learning in logic consists entirely in conforming to wholly authoritative rules, and such learning is consistent with childhood dependence. Moreover the education of children is in good part a process of enculturation, and every culture embodies a common sense which implies a *stand* concerning ultimate ethical and metaphysical questions. It follows that children will, explicitly or implicitly, be taught a distinctive metaphysical and ethical stance. They will explicitly be taught a moral code, for example, and every moral code implies an ethical stance. All such knowledge can be taught by processes of inculcation, and does not presuppose the autonomy of learners. But it is not "philosophy" as I am using the term. And if the aim is to encourage true philosophizing in its season, the stances thus taught must be taught in such a way as to conduce to their own eventual critical examination. They must not be taught as exclusive and even sacred truth, examination of which is eternally prohibited by ultimate and unquestionable authority.

NOTES

1. Jose Ortega y Gasset, *Man and People*, trans. by Willard R. Trask (New York: W. W. Norton & Co., 1957), pp. 16–17, 19.

2. Aristotle, *Metaphysics*, 982b, 12–13. "For it is owing to their wonder (*thaumázein*) that men both now begin and at first began to philosophize."

3. In Aristotle the attainment to wonder presupposes three prior levels of developed capacities. See David Ross, *Aristotle* (New York: Barnes & Noble University Paperbacks, 1964), p. 154. This implies that the wonder associated by Aristotle with philosophy is not childhood's aboriginal wonder. My contention that philosophical wonder originates in reflexive wonder at oneself is, as far as I know, nowhere directly affirmed by the Greeks, but it is clearly implied by them.

The great Greek imperative inscribed on the temple of Apollo at Delphi, "Know thyself," (*gnothi seauton*), implies the prior appearance of the self as a problem of knowledge, that is, something to be wondered at. The true priority ascribed to man by Greek *humanism* is not metaphysical or moral. Man is not held to be the first thing in the universe in regard to being or goodness. He is held to be his own first problem, upon the solution of which depends his success with all other problems. The *locus classicus* of the recognition of man as fundamentally a problem to himself is Plato's image of the soul as chariot, charioteer, and two opposed horses (*Phaedrus* 246). Philosophical wonder is the attitude in which the self encounters itself as its own first problem. But for the Greeks this encounter cannot occur in childhood. This is indicated in Aristotle, for example, by his advice that the whole of the *Nichomachean Ethics* is not applicable to children, who are "not yet capable of such acts" (*NE* 1100a).

4. Paremenides, Diels Fragment ⅝4.

5. Jean-Paul Sartre, *Being and Nothingness*, trans. by Hazel E. Barnes (New York: Philosophical Library, 1956), part 4, chapt. 1, IIe. And Ludwig Wittgenstein, *Tractatus Logico-Philosophicus*, trans. by D. F. Pears and B. F. McGuiness (London: Routledge & Kegan Paul, 1961), 6.4311.

6. This has been profoundly recognized and ably expressed by Michael Oakeshott, who argues that the ultimate problem of human being is its freedom. The problem is not to be solved but is rather to be enjoyed as the problem it is through the exercise of strategies which it affords. The task, Oakeshott says, is "to make it yield a satisfaction of its own, independent of the chancy and intermittent satisfaction of chosen actions achieving their imagined and wished-for outcomes; the disposition to recognize imagining, deliberating, wanting, choosing, and acting not as costs incurred in seeking enjoyments but as themselves enjoyments, the exercise of a gratifying self-determination or personal autonomy." Michael Oakeshott, *On Human Conduct* (Oxford: Clarendon Press, 1975), p. 236.

It may seem strange at first sight to accuse Sartre of distaste for the fundamental problem that human being is, for it is precisely Sartre who in our time has taught that human being "is what it is not, and is not what it is". But it is also Sartre who insists that this problematic being, in distaste of itself, "envies inkwells" and longs otherwise (in good faith) to be another kind of being entirely, namely God. I only suggest here that what Sartre thus offers as universal characteristics of human being are exhibited in himself.

7. G. W. Leibniz, *Principles of Nature and of Grace, Founded on Reason*, in Robert Latta, trans. & ed., *Leibniz, The Monadology and Other Philosophical Writings* (Oxford: Oxford University Press, 1898), p. 415.

8. Jean-Paul Sartre, *Nausea*, trans. by Lloyd Alexander (London: New Directions, 1949), pp. 172–173. Sartre, *Being and Nothingness*, p. lxviii.

9. George Santayana, *Scepticism and Animal Faith* (New York: Dover Publications, 1955), p. 48.

10. Strictly speaking I must qualify this by saying that duplicity is beyond detection in others *by children*. Elsewhere I have argued that persons have immediate access to subjective content of others by "participatory enactment" (David L. Norton, *Personal Destinies: A Philosophy of Ethical Individualism* [Princeton University Press, 1976], chap. 8. But I show there that participatory enactment has conditions which cannot be met in childhood.

11. *Phaedrus* 279.

12. Oakeshott, *On Human Conduct*. Regrettably I cannot relocate the page.

13. Erik H. Erikson, *Childhood and Society*, 2nd ed. (New York: W. W. Norton, 1963), p. 251.

14. Henri Bergson, *The Two Sources of Morality and Religion*, trans. by R. Ashley Audra and Cloudesley Brereton (Garden City: Doubleday Anchor Books, n.d.), p. 9.

⋝§ MICHAEL GILLESPIE

University of Nebraska, Omaha

Metaphysics and Children

Metaphysical questions and reflections upon them are, it is often said, extremely abstract and abstruse. For much of the public, I think, it is metaphysics that is vaguely conjured up when it is imagined just what it is that philosophers do. Yet, introduce almost anyone to what philosophers have meant by metaphysics, and they find they are already metaphysicians, for what the philosophers were talking about was their "worldview," or "ultimate beliefs," or basic convictions. Thus, while philosophers have been singularly abstract about metaphysical questions, they have actually, it turns out, been dealing with issues that prove important for almost anyone. In fact, most philosophers have insisted that this is the case.

In this paper, I will discuss how such questions might also arise in childhood. Philosophers, for their part, have usually stuck to what Husserl called "adult, wakeful" experience, perhaps understanding childhood as a kind of sleep. But if childhood is a kind of sleep (or dream) it is one from which we never quite awaken. Thus, recognizing the down-to-earth significance that many people attach to metaphysical convictions, philosophers have also been very concerned about ways in which our beliefs about what there is are developed, especially in relation to the study of the possibilities for a good (or better) society. Moreover, it has often been a subtheme of philosophy that the capacities and relationships that make for full and adult lives are themselves philosophical or are enhanced by philosophy. It is the latter that I will deal with here: the possibility that philosophical questioning may prove valuable to anyone. This possibility has again been put before us in a very practical way by advocates of philosophy in the classroom who wish to see philosophical thinking embedded in formal education.

My topic, then, is metaphysical questioning in childhood and the role it might play in education. I assume this question to be separable from that of the role of metaphysical notions used in the justification of educational

This paper was written in connection with a grant from the National Endowment for the Humanities.

practice, though my comments may have implications there as well. My goal is to further the discussion of a topic that is immensely complex. I have my own suggestions about how we ought to conceive metaphysical questioning in childhood, but the reader should not expect a theory of stages. I have no particular cut-off point in mind for an age when such questioning begins and certainly no set stage at which the development of metaphysical questioning is accomplished or completed. Further, I shall assume, when it comes to considering educational practice, that education ought, in part at least, to encourage critical reasoning. That is, it ought in some way to include critical examination of presuppositions, of evidence and inference, and of the implications of various subject matters for practical life and personal belief.

2

It certainly seems that children engage in metaphysical questioning, whether in the form of explicit questions, tentative (or not so tentative) statements, or the looks of perplexity or recognition they display at poignant moments. Many of the questions parents and teachers find disconcerting because, as is notorious with metaphysical questions, they are difficult to specify and difficult to answer even if they should be specified. To a child who proposes the question "What is time?" what does one answer? Or, how can one be sure that that really is the intent and not, say, "What time is it?" or "How do clocks work?" and so on? Thus, children's seeming to engage in metaphysical questioning does not get us very far, for there remain many questions about the nature of such questioning and how it is to be responded to. And these problems are only intensified if we also ask what it might mean to include treatments of such questions in formal education. I shall not attempt to "prove" that children engage in such questioning, however; I trust that, provided there is an adequate view of such activity, anyone can confirm it for himself or herself.

In order to explore this problem further, let us begin by imagining two opposing and truculently stated views. These views will be recognized by most readers familiar with recent debates about education and its practices, although I have written them as though they applied themselves to the topic of metaphysical questioning in children only. My aim here is not to take sides (I believe the debate to be somewhat misguided) but to elicit certain basic concerns that ought to be included in any conception of metaphysical questioning in children. I tend to think of these as (A), the "professional academic" viewpoint and (B), the "childhood is everything" viewpoint, though readers will no doubt be able to supply their own personae.

A: Metaphysics in the classroom! What next? "Moral education" and all its attendant confusions is bad enough, but metaphysics is too much. I teach metaphysics in the university, and it is one of the most abstract and difficult subjects. There is problem enough in getting university age students to discuss these issues sensibly, let alone talking of introducing them to young children.

Granted, it *sounds* as if children ask metaphysical questions, but do they? Is it not the case that much of what sounds "profound" and "metaphysical" in the mouths of children is a confusion of language or a request for factual information? It is usually the adult, who supplies the content and meaning, for whom the child's utterances seem original and penetrating. But the child does not see it that way. To raise truly metaphysical questions, one must be capable of a degree of abstraction of which children are incapable. Thus, it is a confusion to speak of metaphysical questions at this level, because the term itself already means something else as defined by the philosophers who have used it. Finally, however, even if we were to grant that children in some sense do ask metaphysical questions, that would not justify the inclusion of such things in schools. It is clear that children do not have access to ways of thinking properly about such issues. Why not leave that area of experience *out* of the schools and to the universities?

B. Metaphysics in the classroom! Finally! At long last someone has realized that children are continually asking metaphysical questions. True, children's queries are not usually recognized for what they are, but that is because adults assume children are incapable of asking about such things. Or, the adults feel challenged and threatened and put off the questions until a later day. They feel challenged and threatened to realize that children can ask such profound questions spontaneously, when they have no ready "answers." Children can still imagine, and this capacity for imagination is what is most expressed in their reality questions. Our usual response has been to "train" children into established views of matters of fact and accepted views of reality. Then, at some later date, we may offer them an opportunity to study different views of reality—but by that time, their own questioning has stopped and the relation of philosophy to their own lives is negligible. The truth is that children are actually better at asking these questions, and even better at finding solutions. We should listen to them. We ought to do everything we can to encourage discussion of reality questions in the schools.

We could carry out the description of these two views in the form of a debate. Doing so with an eye to verisimilitude, we would soon have A proclaiming B a sentimentalist and B asserting that A is a snob, then A saying that B is opposed to vigorous learning and B declaring A opposed to creativity; and on and on. Fortunately, that sort of extended description is not needed here. Not that the expression of such views is pointless. In certain contexts, they are attempts to sway us toward ways of conceiving of childhood and education or to modify our general attitudes concerning directions of educational reform. Still, even granting that the opposition between such views may be false dichotomy once we move from the level of general attitudes to specifics, we may still learn from the opposition some very real concerns that need to be taken into account by any conception of children's metaphysical questioning. Let me proceed with some comments on these viewpoints.

For one thing, from these views we learn to take care not to rush to judgment about what *are* metaphysical questions. A is certainly correct to warn us that not all that sounds metaphysical is so. A lot may depend upon the interpreter. On the other hand, from B we learn that this can work two ways; the interpreter who is convinced that no such questioning goes on may miss it when it does occur.

The two views of what counts as metaphysical questioning each go too far. A suggests that children do not ask genuinely metaphysical because A means the questions as they are formulated in universities. (One version of this argument can be dispensed with. It amounts to the claim that only trained specialists—"professionals"—should be allowed to talk about certain topics. This amounts to defense of turf and throws little light on metaphysical questionings.) But there is a central point to be gleaned from A's position. If we are to conceive metaphysical questioning as being in some way broader than it is often presented in universities, we must nonetheless come up with a conception that is recognizably metaphysical. That is why, even if it is too narrow, the proponent of position A is justifiably concerned not to allow anything and everything to count as metaphysics. Against B, in other words, it is quite correct to insist that not all "reality questions" are metaphysical; virtually any questions, and nearly any part of school curricula, can be formulated so that they deal with "realities," but to identify that with metaphysics does not satisfactorily classify anything.

If A's view is too narrow in claiming that to be metaphysical, questioning must arise in a certain way, it is also too narrow in claiming that metaphysical questioning demands certain techniques through which the questions are conceptualized. It may be that there are good reasons for dealing with metaphysical issues through an analysis of the major attempts to resolve them—for example, by considering major writers in the history of philosophy or by discussing "possible worlds" arguments, employing modal logic, hypotheses about the status of scientific objects, and so on. It does not follow that to discuss such things just *is* metaphysics, for this would be to fail to distinguish the motivation for these proposed solutions, namely, a questioning prior to proposals for solutions.

On the other hand, position B is too extreme in suggesting that children are somehow adept not only at questioning but at proposing insightful views. Children may, for example, engage in metaphysical questioning at a level at which they are capable; but to recognize that fact, we needn't also claim that they are accomplished at it or that their views are "better" than those of adults. Position A is incorrect, but it correctly warns us to be more rigorous in recognizing the limits of children's questioning.

There is an ambiguity in the recommendations of both A and B for how the metaphysical might be included in educational institutions and practices. A, for example, seems to want to deny the genuineness of metaphysical questioning in children but concludes that, in any case, schools ought to leave such topics alone. B, on the other side, seems to want to affirm the spontaneous occurrence of children's metaphysical questioning yet concludes that we ought to intervene to encourage it. It may be that I have been unfair in my characterization, but it seems to me that the views do often take these turns. Positions like B are often particularly unclear about the connection between the claim that children do do something and the conclusion that that something should be "taught." In any case, this ambiguity results because this is really a separate question, namely, what ought to be the response of educational institutions and practices to the question at hand.

Finally, there is the problem of imagination raised by B. Presumably the claim is that encouragement of the capacity to imagine is in part encouragement to consider different "realities." But is this then to be assumed to be metaphysical? It does not seem always so at least. This raises the whole difficulty of tracking the ways of legends and fairy tales (which nowadays are of course not limited to oral traditions and books.) My own conviction is that often metaphysical questioning among children does have a lot to do with imagination, but not in the wholesale way implied by B.

3

The problem we are left with is to formulate a view of "metaphysical questioning" that captures the sort of thing children engage in but is also relevant to educational practice. I will suggest that we think of a metaphysical dimension of experience rather than of particular questionings or particular contents of questions that are metaphysical. There are some more or less typical notions that present themselves as metaphysical: questions about the nature of time, the existence of God, and so on. But such instances may not be the best model for children's questioning. We should, I think, emphasize the questioning activity and its intents, the ways that metaphysical questionings insinuate themselves into many experiences, and understand the more or less typical cases as instances of this broader activity.

Generally speaking, metaphysical questioning, although it can take many forms, asks after the being-status of something or the nature of ultimate generalities that describe all there is. (In addition, many would include under metaphysics what might be called one's settled view of things or overall ways of looking at the world, though the latter would obviously include many factors in addition to the metaphysical.) By "questioning after the being-status of something", I mean the sort of questioning that occurs when a child asks "Are people in my dreams real?" or "Is my mind the same as my brain?" What is asked is what sort of beings there are, or whether those in question really are. Notice that the questions imply a reference to the reality of *other* things: when children ask about dreams it is perhaps because they are vivid, yet there is something that leads one to doubt their status—one wakes up. They are not real like some other experiences, or what is experienced seems to have a different status. So we have a questioning—are dreams real in *some* sense? If so, there are different kinds of beings. Similarly with questions about minds: if minds are in some sense realities, they are different from bodies, so there must be at least two kinds of beings. Such questions are what philosophers call ontological questions.

Questioning after ultimate generalities is what are often call cosmological questions, and these take the form, "Is everything so-and-so?" "Is everything like the things we can see?" The emphasis here is on the "everything," so that cosmological quuestions also include questions of ultimate origins ("Was everything always here before there were people?"), and for that reason overlap with some religious questions ("Did God make the world just like it is now?"). What is asked often in cosmological questions is whether there are any truly general statements that we can make about everything taken together.

Finally, there are people's settled views of the world, their overall frameworks for what counts as real. This is perhaps not actually a separate notion, for it may cover the same ground as ontology and cosmology. It is worth emphasizing for all that because it comes closest to what many people think of when they consider what the philosophers call metaphysics. In addition, including this allows us to emphasize that the metaphysical may be interconnected with other aspects of one's overall view. For example, metaphysical convictions are often tied to moral convictions, of one's general view of society or of human nature.

Now if these can be accepted as characterizations of genuinely metaphysical questioning, it makes initial sense to say that children do ask such questions. But we notice also that to make this claim we must emphasize metaphysical questioning, rather than particular forms of the questions or attempts to formulate conclusions. That is, metaphysical questioning can occur in children in a fairly concrete way that does not employ the degree of abstraction commonly supposed by more advanced treatments of these questions. The questioning activity is an exploration of *this* subject, situation, experience and so on, insofar as the object, situation, or experience elicits significance to be explored. Such questioning precedes attempts at cognitive theses, and the experience of the world out of which it arises need not be itself cognitive.

Let us say, then, that the metaphysical is (or can be) a dimension of experience for children. A given experience can call forth a questioning attitude that explores the significance of that experience through what above were called ontological and cosmological meanings. More generally, each of the so-called areas of philosophy, such as epistemology, moral theory and aesthetics, can be said to refer to dimensions of experience. By a dimension, then, I mean to suggest that any experience can have that sort of significance (metaphysical, moral, aesthetic, and so on), while no experience need be thought of as having only that significance. Whether in a particular case an experience or situation is interrogated by means of one or another dimension will depend upon the situation and the level of experience and cultural background of the child. Philosophers have always hoped, whether they are considering adult or childhood experience, that an enhancement of these dimensions can be achieved through practice and reflection.

Seen in this way, metaphysical questioning is not questioning about certain "kinds" of objects, nor is it formulable as a certain sort of proposition. In this sense, the metaphysical dimension is not limited to certain sorts of cognitive dilemmas, even though these might often play a role. Rather, we must say that such interrogation of the world could occur during what we would call emotive experiences, perceptual experiences, uses of imagination, and soon.

The experience of the death of a person (or pet), can give rise to strong emotional responses. But often these call forth other thoughts—for example, the idea that in some way that other being lives on in some way. Many of the ways human beings gain in self-awareness can also lead to such questioning—for instance, the many questions children may ask about the differences between themselves, other people, and things. I would also include here the perhaps silent perceptual exploration of the world—that is, the wonderful moments when a child contemplates certain preferred objects as though finding in them models for excellent seeing and touching.

Now it might be objected that these are not really metaphysical since there is actually no overall view of things or generalized doubt. The child, it will be said, will soon find out that the significance attached to these experiences does not hold. Perhaps. A child particularly moved by music may ask whether sounds are "real." Maybe later he or she will learn about sound waves and how they are propagated in an elastic medium. That is not the question here. For the child, it may not be a scientific question. It may turn out that the child is asking whether the music, the performance heard, is real, a question about which philosophers have never come to agreement. Let us say then that the spontaneous occurrence of such questioning can be identified as metaphysical if it functions that way, that is, if it functions as an asking after the being-status of "objects" or ultimate generalities which are taken to be a possible significance of what is experienced. From the adult point of view, the questioning may not appear to be metaphysical because, having a much greater fund of experience, the adult may see immediately that the child's formulation or exploration is dealing with what, for example, is not ultimately general at all. Or, the child may divide things up into what we know he or she will soon come to see are not really different sorts of beings at all. Yet the fact remains that for the child, for that developing view of the world, the questioning may function as metaphysical.

Furthermore, the child's relation to this questioning may be more or less fleeting, more or less urgent. It is particularly important to notice this, because such questions can be taken by adults to possess ultimate importance. But for children they often take the form of momentary entertainments soon forgotten, playful explorations of language, enticing attempts at generalizations, "fun things to think about," and so on. In short, children are often not as interested as adults (or professional philosophers) in maintaining the "truth" of statements or conclusions about the metaphysical questioning in which they engage. That does not mean it is unimportant, only that final conclusions often may not be the main issue.

Finally there may be, from time to time, relations of affinity between two or more of the philosophical dimensions of experience. The most direct way for this to occur is for the metaphysical significance of one of the other dimensions to be questioned. At a particular point in time or for a particular child, for example, moral considerations may seem to harbor a metaphysical significance, perhaps a sort of rudimentary version of Kant's claim that "the moral law within" is of ultimate importance. For another child, it may be more usual to explore what there is through aesthetic considerations, while for yet another it may be that cognitive puzzles are what seem persistently fascinating. In short, different cognitive styles may be (at least in part) attributable to different ways of (more or less indirectly) exploring metaphysical questions.

By affinity I also mean relations of coherence between the metaphysical dimension and other dimensions. For example, it seems that certain metaphysical views have an affinity for certain moral views—they fit together. Philosophers have always had difficulty in showing such connections (it is the problem of coherence taken in a broader sense than logical consistency), but such general fits are often important. This is especially so of negative instances—for example, felt tensions between different conclusions one reaches. One may, for example, tend to believe that science has shown everything to be matter while also tending to believe that (in the moral dimension) there is always more to persons than their material being. Many people live with such divergences all the time, but they also can be cause for concern. What I am suggesting is that something like this may happen at times to children too and lead to metaphysical questioning. Perhaps an enthusiastic and admired teacher says, "For me, the characters in books are *real*," and the child senses a conflict.

What I have been trying to suggest with this notion of the metaphysical as a dimension of childhood experience is a way to relate to children so that we can recognize when it occurs without committing ourselves to the view that children are always raising metaphysical questions. It should also tell us something about how to respond. First, it is clear that many times adults do not spend enough time finding out what the intent of the questioning is. To get at it, the adult too must assume a questioning attitude. Second, this sort of questioning is often not a question-and-answer situation; what is wanted is not an answer so much as suggestions about further ways to go on thinking. This does not mean that we are dealing with something that is nonrational. Questioning is itself rational activity, as is the attempt to connect broader significance with a particular experience.

4

Let me now turn from the question of how to understand the occasion of metaphysical questioning in children to the question of the use of such topics in the classroom. As I wish to maintain that it would be worthwhile to make this inclusion, I will consider an objection that might be made.

The objection runs something like this:

Even if children can be understood to engage in metaphysical questioning, that does not mean that discussions of metaphysical topics should be included in the classroom. There has been recently a movement to take care to build into educational practice more and more that is accessible to the questioning of children. In many ways this has had good results for teaching techniques. But for the general principle that we may often proceed better (teach better) by beginning from questions and experiences that children have, it does not follow (as some seem to assume) that whatever children experience and question ought to be made part of school curricula. Schools are not all of children's lives, nor ought schools to concern themselves with everything that may occur to children—especially with regard to metaphysical questions, upon which children may exercise their imaginations and which may involve very private beliefs. Why not leave children alone, leave them to their own ways of development?

Now much in this position seems correct, and it certainly does not follow that metaphysics should be taught simply because children can engage in metaphysical questioning. A good deal of what may be concluded about this, however, has to do with how the questioning arises and just what is to be taught here.

Thus far, I have spoken of metaphysical questioning from the perspective of how it might arise in a child's ordinary experience. Such questioning we could call "spontaneous," since it may occur without urging and on the occasion of experiences not already marked out as having metaphysical significance. In addition, I have left open the possibility that this questioning could at times be silent or private or both—a sort of interrogative exploration of emotion or perception, for example. But such is not always the case. Usually, there is an exchange with other people, attempts to express thoughts or to formulate questions, or to elicit the opinions of friends, family members, or teachers. We need not always assume that such questioning arises out of privacy. Many children have the experience, for example, of beginning to reflect about beginnings and endings, or of God's existence, because of what they have heard from their peers and adults.

Once we emphasize the intersubjective aspect of childhood experience, however, we need to take into account other ways in which metaphysical questioning may arise. The fact is that children are also presented with many theses about the nature of things that are highly charged with metaphysical meaning. Religious doctrines provide one sort of example, but theses are also urged regarding human nature, the existence of evil, overall views of history, and many others. Television provides a weekly fare of speculations and dramatically presented hypotheses about strange realities. Sometimes these are clearly perceived as fantasy by children (and are hence assimilated to an already active fantasy life full of myth and legend), but not always, as is evidenced by how often children bring up things such as beliefs in strange powers, quasi-religious forces and so on in discussion of scientific topics in school. As the children get older, this sort of thing occurs less and less frequently, but is this because they have outgrown a fantasy, or because they have learned to make their metaphysical concerns more private? I suggest that very often the latter is what happens. We must not forget that in our society there are millions of young people who are apparently not too clear about the difference between science and metaphysical conclusions, children who believe in astrology, for example.

In addition, it is clear that we need not appeal to the mysterious as the only manner in which metaphysical theses are urged upon children and young people. Many of the occasions for metaphysical questioning occur in the schools, where so many children of various backgrounds and family beliefs are placed together. Because of this, many occasions for the recognition of alternative belief-systems arise. Just as important, the curriculum of schools provides such occasions. One common example is the question of the reality of numbers, but there is much more. Questions that aim at understanding the presuppositions of virtually any area of the curriculum can have at least some metaphysical impact. I have been impressed with

how often very young children attempt to form vast generalizations—
"Everything is like that"—on the basis of what must appear to organizers of
curricula as very specialized areas. In addition, there are many theses
presented in schools that are basically metaphysical (ontological). For example, there is a strong dose of individualism—I mean a doctrine about
the individual isolation of human persons—set forth in textbooks and
urged by teachers. There are views of history (especially as applied to the
United States) that are nothing if not metaphysical. No one familiar with
metaphysical theories can read science texts and fail to notice metaphysical
assertions and presuppositions. The point should be clear—it is not a
question of "introducing" metaphysical themes, or providing occasions for
the metaphysical to arise. They are there already. The question is rather
how they will be handled.

Children then, are placed in many situations in which questions may
arise in one of the philosophical dimensions of experience. Metaphysics is
one of these. Instead of perceiving such instances of questioning as breaks
in the curriculum, we ought to recognize that such explorations are often
signs of intellectual aliveness and openness. Moreover, if one of our aims
in education is to encourage critical thinking, then we ought to consider
how our ways of dealing with these dimensions might be enhanced.

But there is another sense of "introduce" that is more relevant. That is,
a type of problem or issue for discussion; even if it is of a sort that arises
already, may be "introduced" if the teached is aware of that sort of thing,
or steers the discussion in that direction, or arranges topics so that that sort
of problem is more likely to arise. It is in this sense that metaphysical
questioning (and philosophical discussions generally) should become a part
of educational practice.

It seems clear that to deal with these questionings more effectively, the
approach should not be to introduce courses in various philosophical subject matters. This follows from our discussion of the philosophical dimensions of experience. If, for example, one were to conclude that it would be
worthwhile to attempt to enhance awareness of felt relationships, various
forms of arts, expressions of culture in artifacts (the aesthetic dimension),
the best way to do this is not to introduce a philosophical course in
aesthetic theory. Earlier I used the phrase "practice and reflections" in my
description, and it is practice that counts most here. Philosophical questions are important only where something else is important. They do not
come first. But they don't come after either—they arise "integral to." The
same is true of metaphysical issues: they arise integral to other knowledges

and experiences, and the best way of handling them is not to have a course on metaphysical theories.

It seems clear that much could be done in the area of teacher training that would produce valuable results in the classroom. The greater development of understanding of how presuppositions and reasoning are similar and different in different parts of the curriculum would be one such result. Connections between what is studied in school and personal belief may be another. A recognition that others may reach different conclusions on metaphysical questions and have different world views and yet be "rational" (this recognition leads to respect for the rights of others) may be another possible result. [1]

5

Let me conclude with two comments—one practical and one theoretical.

I have been discussing metaphysical questioning by children and in the classroom. Along the way I have been critical of dismissing such questioning as being private beliefs and decisions. And I have urged that discussion of such issues should occur in an atmosphere of critical reasoning. But there is another side to this. These may be considered private matters not out of a lack of understanding or a wish to discourage inquiry but because these are thought to be public issues too controversial for the classroom. Once one begins to think of the metaphysical side of questions, it is surprising how many of the "fundamental" criticisms of education are actually metaphysical. This is certainly the case in disputes about the implications of evolutionary theory in biology. My own suggestion has been that such problems should actually be a reason for *including* metaphysical questions so that children may begin to recognize the difference, say, between reasoning on the basis of scientific evidence and speculating about the possible metaphysical significance of a scientific view. Will this argument be convincing in practice? How much of education should be thought of as socialization into the metaphysical habits of the community? If there is no one set of beliefs that characterize the community, are there some metaphysical questions that still should not be discussed in the classroom? Religious questions? These problems go far beyond the scope of this paper, but they are becoming more and more urgent and need to be dealt with by philosophers and educators together. I hope what I have said about the metaphysical dimension of experience will be useful in that effort.

Finally, I think there needs to be much more thought given to how the metaphysical dimension relates to other dimensions. Without going into detail, let me suggest that the various theories of stage development with regard to morality might be questioned concerning their metaphysical assumptions. While these theories are usually seen as purely cognitive, is it not the case that the description of the "stages" contain ontological elements? In moral development, do not metaphysical views influence what one is likely to accept in one's morality? Are certain views of what it means to be a "person" better than others? Is that not in part a metaphysical question?

The hegemony of epistemology in modern thought has perhaps made it imperative to explore "cognitive development" or "genetic epistemology" without regard to questions children may raise and conclusions they may reach concerning what there is. Yet with all the emphasis on the interaction of child and environment and the interconnectedness of various aspects of experience, it would be odd indeed if metaphysical questioning did not play a role.

NOTES

1. See Matthew Lipman, Ann Margaret Sharp, and Frederick S. Oscanyan, *Philosophy in the Classroom* (Upper Montclair, N.J.: 1977). This book contains a much more extensive and convincing treatment of the benefits of philosophical thinking in the classroom than I can go into here.

ೆई 5 ಿಀ

CAN CHILDREN DO

MORAL PHILOSOPHY?

ೆई JOSEPH FLAY

Pennsylvania State University

Is Ethics for Children Moral?

The question of this essay is directed not at the morals of children and the method of their assimilation but at the teaching of principles and techniques for decision-making in moral situations. It concerns teaching ethics in the sense of the difference between teleological and deontological ethics, between utility principles and principles of duty. It is a question of discussing the meaning of 'good' and 'right' and 'ought.' It is a question of teaching ethics as understood in departments of philosophy in colleges and universities. This last remark does not refer to any particular pedagogical techniques such as those used in institutions of higher learning. Methods used in teaching of ethics to the child are irrelevant to my arguments, for I am addressing the content of ethics, the development of the power to make ethical distinctions and apply ethical principles, which can then be used by children in their own moral experience.

I will argue that teaching ethics to children is immoral in a sense that I shall stipulate. My main argument has two elements, the first oriented to the kind of perspective the child has on the world, the second to a structural feature of that world. In relation to both, I am limiting myself to the child and the world in our present American situation, although I would not *a priori* rule out the applicability of my analysis to other cultures and times. It is clear to me, however, for reasons that will become evident, that what I address is not a universal phenomenon. Thus I would not claim to be making an analysis that pertains to human nature, the human condition, or anything of the sort.

In the first part of the paper, I shall offer an analysis of the perspective of the child as it applies to questions of morality and of value in general. This will involve, of course, discussing some central aspects of the social matrix, chosen for their relevance to the values of the individual. In the second section, I will discuss a structural feature of that social matrix, its centrifugal character, to show how moral situations or situations demanding value decisions are affected. In each of these two sections I will lay some ground for the criticism of the teaching of ethics to children. In the third part I will summarize my criticisms of the teaching of ethics to children and bring together the objections that have emerged from the two previous sections.

1

We are all, I suppose, familiar with the crises of becoming an adult, the confusion and sense of alienation that comes when we have made the move away from the family to make our own way in the world. On the one hand, there is a kind of exhilaration at the new-found freedom and responsibility; on the other hand, there is a sense of being unprepared, of not really knowing what to do or how to handle the situation despite the facade we erect in the presence of others. And so we are driven by forces of fear or confusion and of determination or confidence to forge a life for ourselves. In the past several decades there has been an acute recognition of this time of crisis in our culture and attempts have been made to remedy it. Under the assumption that it is caused by lack of education or preparation for the moment of release into the world, many have sought to begin in elementary and secondary education the development of a capacity to cope intelligently with the moral problems of today's multiform and technological society.

There is good reason to think that this is what should be done. For untold centuries in other places, such education has been given through the apparatus of a traditional society, through *rites de passage* and indoctrination and training by elders. In our nontraditionalist society this is not possible; no one is formally initiated into our society, and there are no set traditions that dominate our lives in any holistic way. In addition, elders more often than not are only grandparents, who are sometimes visited but are not part of the immediate family. In the place of the traditional extended family and the *rites de passage*, we have a system of schools, public and private, which brings the children of many unrelated families together, educates them in the technical and social characteristics of our world, and, in a rather weak but still present ritual, passes them through the several "grades" of their education. Where, better than in these schools, should the moral education of children take place? And where, better than in these schools, should they be prepared for the crisis of passage into active adulthood?

The answer to the first question immediately becomes rather complicated; for indoctrination into morals and mores is proscribed in the school system.[1] For reasons I will give in the second part of this paper, it is not possible to teach morals, that is, some specific moral code. So what was an important part of formal and informal education in the traditionalist societies cannot find a place in our school system. But the other question, properly answered, is one which can be addressed; for it might involve only the attempt to develop mental capacities, and there is a great respect for teaching people how to think, but not what to think.

Prima facie, this sounds like a most reasonable proposal. To stand against it would seem to be reactionary, or worse, romantic, or perhaps even cruel and insensitive. Why should a human being be deprived of a chance to enter adulthood without the trauma that now accompanies the transition from school to society, from home to the outside world? And since all too often today the home that is to be left behind has been the scene of trauma and sorrow, why should not enlightened, reasonable people, who have developed their abilities as teachers, take it upon themselves to lighten the sometimes inhuman burden placed upon the shoulders of the child by accident of birth or environment? To have the tools to help and not to use them would surely be socially and humanly irresponsible.

If the situation were this simple and straightforward, I would have no choice but to agree with those who would teach ethics to children— indeed, the sooner, the better. Unfortunately, there is a character to that first decade or so of a person's life that complicates matters.[2] In order to bring this into focus, I shall remind the reader of two philosophical passages from authors very unlike each other in most things. The first will be Aristotle, the second Simone de Beauvoir.

Aristotle, at the outset of his *Nicomachean Ethics*, remarks that it is inappropriate for youth to study ethics. After beginning chapter 3 of book 1 with a discussion of the variability of matters concerning morals and the consequent lack of sound premises from which to argue, Aristotle concludes that precision in ethics cannot be expected to the degree that it is found in mathematics. He begins by recognizing the manifold of opinion and by insisting that we must settle for conclusions that are for the most part, but not always, true. Then he notes that youth are not proper hearers of lectures on the science of politics (that is, on *politikē*, which includes what we would call ethics). His reasoning is interesting, so I will quote the passage in full:

> Each man judges well the things he knows, and of these he is a good judge. And so the man who has been educated in a subject is a good judge of that subject, and the man who has received an all-round education is a good judge in general. Hence a young man is not a proper hearer of lectures on the science of politics; for he is inexperienced in the actions that occur in life, but the discussions of the science of politics start from these and are about these; and, further, since he tends to follow his passions, his study will be vain and unprofitable, because the end aimed at is not knowledge, but action. And it makes no difference whether he is young in years or youthful in character; the defect does not depend on time, but on his living and pursuing each successive object, as passion directs. For to such persons, as to the incontinent, knowledge brings no profit; but to those who desire and act in accordance with a rational principle knowledge about such matters will be of great benefit.[3]

Most notice has been given to the second reason discussed in this passage, namely, the tendency of youth to follow their passions and the need for a time when the firm desire to follow the dictates of reason guides the individual. As important as this reason might be, it is only one of two reasons. The other rests upon the fact about social life which I discussed before quoting Aristotle and which he himself more thoroughly articulates in the passage leading up to his judgment about youth. One is a good judge only of that which one knows, and it is difficult to come to know about morals and problems of socio-political existence since, at best, they cannot be exactly formulated as, for instance, mathematics can be. So the raw material of ethics is not something that can be learned from a book or a teacher or even from reason but must be learned from experience. This is why being inexperienced in life is such a critical matter.

It would follow from this that the study of ethics presupposes two things:

(1) that the individual has adequate experience in life, and (2) that the individual is no longer governed on the whole by passion and whim but by a desire to act according to some rational principles. The first involves experience of the multiformity and qualitative heterogeneity of life, the second a desire to come to terms with the first and to bring order to the variety. Without the experience, the discussion of ethics has little or no relevance to the real content of life; without the desire for rationality, the principles and distinctions of ethics will have no relevance.

If we take a purely historical perspective, it becomes evident that Aristotle's thought must be used with great care in our own contemporary situation. Between the *polis* and the modern nation state there are such great differences that few if any parallels in principles are evident. It is true that Athenian and other Greek peoples had experienced great upheavals and the disintegration, first of traditional tribal life, then of the polis itself; thus far, some parallel could be made with our own times of change. But I think that arguments to the contrary win the day, for there was then nothing comparable to the "civil society" into which we all enter upon leaving our youth. The economic, social, and political structure was radically different.

But I am not interested in simply applying Aristotle's principles to our day. He is not to be taken here as an authority but as a careful and independent observer of the human condition who, together with others, may offer some insight into our problem. As I now turn to a contemporary of our own, we will see some marked differences in observation. But I hope to show that from the rationalist Aristotle, and the existentialist de Beauvoir, some common inferences may be drawn which will throw light on the relationship between children and the study of ethics.

De Beauvoir, in her *Ethics of Ambiguity*, addresses the human condition in light of the insights of the existentialist experience and thought. While her main concern is to give an analysis of moral judgment and moral life for those who have already left childhood behind, she has some penetrating observations on the situation for children and into the transition from childhood to adulthood and moral independence. Again, I shall quote extensively to provide a background:

> The child's situation is characterized by his finding himself cast into a universe which he has not helped to establish, which has been fashioned without him, and which appears to him as an absolute to which he can only submit. In his eyes, human inventions, words, customs, and values are given facts, as inevitable as the sky and trees. This means

that the world in which he lives is a serious world, since the characteristic of the spirit of seriousness is to consider values as ready-made things. That does not mean that the child himself is serious. On the contrary, he is allowed to play, to expand his existence freely. In his child's circle he feels that he can passionately pursue and joyfully attain goals which he has set up for himself . . . . The real world is that of adults where he is allowed only to respect and obey. The naïve victim of the mirage of the for-others, he believes in the *being* of his parents and teachers. He takes them for the divinities which they vainly try to be and whose appearance they like to borrow before his ingenuous eyes. Rewards, punishments, prizes, words of praise or blame instill in him the conviction that there exist a good and an evil which like a sun and a moon exist as ends in themselves. In his universe of definite and substantial things, beneath the sovereign eyes of grownup persons, he thinks that he too has *being* in a definite and substantial way. He is a good little boy or a scamp; he enjoys being it. If something deep inside him belies his conviction, he conceals this imperfection. He consoles himself for an inconsistency which he attributes to his young age by pinning his hopes on the future. Later on he too will become a big, imposing statue.[4]

If we allow for some cross-cultural differences (perhaps one cannot be a scamp in the second half of the twentieth century in the United States, and perhaps the parents and teachers mentioned here are instead sometimes other adults or "the street people" who confront children in our cities), the image is appropriate. The point is that the child lives in a world governed by those who are beyond him in power and whose values he takes up as a given. It is a world of authority in which values are assimilated through enculturation and not derived through thought and decision. It is a perception of the world which may from time to time bother the child, but on the whole a perception which is accepted for truth, however good or bad the experience might be. The "gods" rule.

But also allowing for cultural differences, this is not unlike the world painted by Aristotle. In his terms, de Beauvoir's child lacks the experience of life, lives in a world in which "the important things" happen to others and in which his own passions still rule his daily round of activities. But de Beauvoir then adds a stunning description of the passage to adulthood.

The fact is that it is very rare for the infantile world to maintain itself beyond adolescence. From childhood on, flaws begin to be revealed in it. With astonishment, revolt and disrespect the child little by little asks himself, "Why must I act that way? What good is it? And what will happen if I act in another way?" He discovers his subjectivity; he discovers that of others. And when he arrives at the age of adolescence he begins to vacillate because he notices the contradictions among adults as well as their hesitations and weaknesses. Men stop appearing as if they were gods, and at the same time the adolescent discovers the human character of the reality about him. Language, customs, ethics, and values have their source in these uncertain creatures. The moment has come when he too is going to be called upon to participate in this operation; his acts weigh upon the earth as much as those of other men. He will have to choose and decide. It is comprehensible that it is hard for him to live this moment of his history, and this is doubtless the deepest reason for the crisis of adolescence; the individual must at last assume his subjectivity.[5]

However spread out over time it might be, and however slowly or quickly in coming it might be, the moment of the recognition of the multiformity and qualitative variety of values and experience is consummated only when the serious world of adults that has enclosed the individual cracks, and he emerges from the egg. It is in fact the second birth that tribal and traditionalist societies have always claimed it to be, but that we largely ignore. It is the point at which the desire for order is forced upon the individual; for the individual is now responsible for all of those "serious" affairs which had seemed to be the sole concern of others.

De Beauvoir in fact here gives an anatomy of those presuppositions that Aristotle demanded be met before ethics could profitably be studied. The experience in life has slowly accumulated, but in an other-worldly form. Now, at the moment of fissure, the real and authentic nature of the "serious world" becomes inescapable: I am responsible for it. But in addition to this, she has also said something significant concerning those years dismissed by Aristotle as simply insufficient for the task at hand. If de Beauvoir and Aristotle are correct, then the following sort of picture of the child emerges. The child lives in a world governed largely by authority, be it the authority of adults in general or that of parents, teachers, religious leaders, or older adolescents. In the games and pastimes of children, they do have a certain degree of autonomy, at least while immersed in the activity itself. Yet even there, the authority impinges, for there is always the question whether the children are permitted to do what they are doing. Within that "autonomous" life, however, they are governed by imagination and what we might generally call their "passions." It is true that there is some degree of initiation into the world of seriousness through play imitation and through what is learned in the schools and absorbed from observing adults; but until the authoritarian structures crack and show the true fallible nature of that serious world, the morals and values of the child have their source in that serious, external world.

2

If we now examine that world itself more closely, a picture emerges which would seem strongly to support—even demand—ethics for children. That world is one of competing values and morals. The family, the church, the schools, various adults with which the child comes into contact on a personal level, other youth who have already left the shelter of the serious world, and many other "institutions"—all bring to the view of the child a different set of values. And they are often in whole or in part incompatible sets, for pluralism is a highly valued characteristic of our society (at least when we look at it objectively). 'Freedom' is the word for this characteristic, but we can also describe the society as centrifugal in nature: the various institutions and the roles people play in participating in those institutions are oriented to many different directions. If we look at the individual and the values his different roles embrace, they are seen to pull him in different directions. And it is expected of the individual that he or she will participate in the society in a number of different ways in order to be fulfilled completely.

But while this variety and multifaceted life characterizes our sense of freedom, it is also the source of conflict and alienation. One's job or profession usually competes with family values (even though the former makes possible the fruitful life of the family). One's occupational role often involves values and demands actions that run counter to the values and activities of the family. And the same is true of other institutions and roles in which a single person participates. The religious, aesthetic, practical, political, cultural, and other values sometimes exclude and sometimes are even destructive of each other. Yet each individual embraces several if not all of these systems. I characterize this society as centrifugal since, although for the most part the individual holds himself or herself together, there is a constant pull away from a consistent center that would unify and coordinate all of the various factors.

In contrast to this centrifugal structure is the centripetal structure of a traditionalist society in which the religious (or something functioning like the religious) holds the rationale and meaningfulness of all other institutions and roles. Everything is centered and explained in a consistent manner and the values and demands of the various roles are consistent with each other and for the most part supportive of each other. But such a society is looked upon by us as repressive or as lacking freedom, a society in which the authoritarianism of the serious world of the child is continued beyond into the world of adults themselves. Instead of the adults, various gods or ancestors or some other removed authority sets the values and demands of life. Fragmentation is avoided at the cost of what those in the centrifugal society consider freedom. On the other hand, the latter insist on their freedom, at the cost of fragmentation.

I do not wish here to argue for or against the present centrifugal society; I only want to note that it exists and that it bears on the question of teaching ethics to children.

The question can now be put in the following way: Should we or should we not allow the child to come into that fragmented world without being "armed" with ethics? Should the serious world be allowed to break of its own weight, however deceptive it might be? And deceptive it is; for that world in which values are mutually exclusive of each other, a world in which the child looks upon as the serious world of adults (playing gods) is not the lofty, logical, stable source for values, but a world in which there is in fact no set, universal criterion for value at all.

What I have said thus far, again, seems to be evidence that the proposal made in the beginning—that it is the duty of the schools to teach children how to think about morals so that they can confront this alienated and alienating world properly—should be taken up without hesitation. Otherwise the child is simply thrown out into that world and left to fend for himself or herself. Otherwise we unconsciously perpetuate a deception. Further reflection will reveal that the matter is not so simple.

3

Given the analysis thus far, my objections to the teaching of ethics to children can be formulated in two ways. From the perspective of the child, the world is constituted by the authority of adults and is supposed not to be problematic. To introduce ethics before that world inevitably shatters is to do violence to the development of the child. The shattering of the world is not a rational thing but at least borders on the irrational and in some cases is a violent event. This is in keeping with the overall irrational, because contradictory, nature of that world itself. The introduction of ethics is the introduction of rationality, something alien to the process of that serious world in itself. There is a time, Aristotle argued, at which commitment to rationality becomes proper; there is a time for the birth of the *need* to make individual sense of things and to grapple with the real problems of the real world. To introduce ethics to children brings this change before the need actually arises in the mind of the person.

Perhaps this point could be made by an appeal to an event which happens in several different poems and novels of Nikos Kazantzakis. In one version, in the novel *Zorba the Greek*, the story is related by the main character as he contemplates the nature of the future and of the intuitive wrong in knowing the future:

> I remembered one morning when I discovered a cocoon in the bark of a tree, just as the butterfly was making a hole in its case and preparing to come out. I waited a while, but it was too long appearing and I was impatient. I bent over it and breathed on it to warm it. I warmed it as quickly as I could and the miracle began to happen before my eyes, faster than life. The case opened, the butterfly started slowly to crawl out and I shall never forget my horror when I saw how its wings were folded back and crumpled; the wretched butterfly tried with its whole trembling body to unfold them. Bending over it, I tried to help it with my breath. In vain. It needed to be hatched out patiently and the unfolding of the wings should be a gradual process in the sun. Now it was too late. My breath had forced the butterfly to appear, all crumpled, before its time. It struggled desperately and, a few seconds later, died in the palm of my hand.[6]

This appeal to nature is not a conservative appeal to remain passive in the face of natural laws. Kazantzakis is too steeped in Nietzsche and Bergson and Marx to champion such a cause. Rather it is a recognition that in our activity of creating and shaping our world, there are conditions of *appropriateness*, necessary conditions that must be present if one's creation is to be fruitful. The ancient Greek notion of "kairos" is still alive in this modern Greek poet, and it is to that notion that I am appealing in my claim that ethics should not be taught to children. If philosophy has ever come close to that wisdom it pursues, it was in this concept of 'kairos', appropriate time, and its consequences for human affairs.

The second way in which my point can be made is to put it more directly in the context of the problem of fragmentation in this centrifugal society. The very argument for ethics for children—or at least one of the strongest arguments, namely, that children must be prepared to cope with the fragmented world which lies hidden behind the authority of the adult world—is in fact an argument against introducing ethics. For the introduction of ethics before a felt need demands it is the first introduction of fragmentation in an explicit way. It is one thing to be able to question the authority of one's authorities on matters of theoretical or technical knowledge as a result of one's schooling. A parent or an older person, although perhaps stung by the clear evidence that the child has surpassed him in knowledge of technical facts and theories about nature and society, can usually harbor some degree of pride that the child has learned, reflecting in a positive manner one's association with the child. But a challenge, backed by reason, in the area of values and morals is quite a different matter. While in the former case nothing ultimate has been challenged, in the case of values and morals it has. In the realm of the axiological, important things are at stake, things which give a unique texture to the fabric of life. Values are the weave of our lives.

The parent or older peer or teacher or clergyman can easily confront the differences in values between himself and others when the serious world begins to crack for the child and the child brings the challenge of one authority to another authority. Authority confronts authority, and the fundamentally irrational structure of the world continues. In the face of this, the child begins to grasp the arbitrariness and relativity of the adult world and begins to develop the need to escape from the cocoon. In this process the questions arise on their own, before reason slowly takes form.

When it is not a matter of confronting one authority with another's values, however, but one of confronting an authority with reason and a rational questioning of that authority, then authority is up against something over which it cannot prevail. At that moment, the child's psyche is fragmented in a radical manner; for one power, reason, now stands to challenge all authority simultaneously, and that power is in the hands of the child. The fragmentation is radical because no authority, as authority, can identify itself with reason when reason is the hammer used to smash authority. Every value system, no matter how sound, is vulnerable to the attack of the skeptic.

One might ask what difference it makes whether reason enters after the world of adult authority breaks down or reason is itself the cause of the disintegration. The difference is critical. In the former case reason and rational decision making slowly fills up the cracks in the wall or, to appeal to the Kazantzakis story again, reason and rational decision making slowly and gently and naturally come to play a part in the world. Reason is in this case constructive, building out of the ruins of the authoritative serious world. But in the other case, reason becomes a destructive weapon, finding the whole of the authoritative edifice fair game for its awesome power. Reason becomes, necessarily, a tool in an adversary relationship, mobilized into full employment before the time is ready for it. The result must be skepticism and cynicism, since the question "Why?" meant wholly seriously and not in a game as it often is with children, can shatter even the best and highest values and morals. The ultimate in fragmentation—a fragmentation that threatens, in the name of freedom, to break that centrifugal force that makes freedom an actual and meaningful quality in life—is cynicism and the subsequent boredom and alienation that follow and accompany it.[7]

Fragmentation is therefore increased by the introduction of reason into morals before the time when reason is demanded by the natural collapse of the authoritative, serious world. To deliberately engineer the collapse and cause the fragmentation (albeit in an act intended to bring a kind of unity to the life of the child) is morally indefensible because it leads to cynicism, boredom, and alienation. However "scientifically based" this human engineering, behavior modification, or values clarification might be, it comes to the same thing: an act of breathing warmth on the cocoon and the crumpled wings and death of the butterfly which follow. To allow the deceptive serious world to destroy itself—and thereby to allow the deception and irrationality to continue—seems to me morally preferable.

My answer to the question posed in the title of this essay then, is that moral education, in the sense I have described, is immoral when the students are children for whom the serious world has not fallen. I think it is immoral because the introduction of reason into the value decisions of those still under the influence of the authoritative world of the adult causes a fragmentation of the child's existence that is more destructive than the fragmentation that in fact exists in the world shaped by the adults. The child becomes cynical of that world in which he must exist eventually because he has not yet naturally become aware of the true nature of that world of authorities. Put in a more positive manner, the introduction of reason into morals should be *in response to a felt need* brought about by contact with that world, rather than *as an initiative to cause* that world to crumble.

The sense of 'kairos' is crucial here. But there is no clear criterion by which to determine appropriateness, no orderly scale by which we can determine the kairos. In the present age, governed by manipulation rather than by participation, teachers and intellectuals tend to be engineers at heart, bent on creating under the name of science a world to suit themselves and their theories. The kairos and life cannot be quantified and thus will elude all scientific treatment. But this "defect" does not change its importance, and does not efface the wrong done when it is ignored.

NOTES

1. This is true for all public schools and for many private ones. The exceptions, in some church-affiliated schools, will not affect my argument.
2. There is, of course, nothing exact about the period specified here. When childhood ends is a relative matter and presents a problem only to the "engineer" I shall be addressing at the end of this essay.
3. Aristotle, *Nicomachean Ethics*, 1095a2—a13.
4. Simone de Beauvoir, *The Ethics of Ambiguity*, translated by Bernard Frechtman (New York: The Citadel Press, 1962), pp. 35–36.
5. Ibid., pp. 38–39.
6. Nikos Kazantzakis, *Zorba the Greek*, translated by Carl Wildman (New York: Ballantine Books, 1964), pp. 138–39.
7. An excellent example of this can be found in Matthew Lipman's story for fifth-graders, *Harry Stottlemeier's Discovery*, when religious and parental authority are faced with rational discussion of the grounds for religious objections to the salute to the flag. In the context of the story fragmentation occurs, not simply out of a clash of authorities but on the basis of the moral questions being entertained by the children. In this sequence, the state of affairs does not go as far as I have suggested, but the radicality of the fragmentation is clearly evidenced. See Matthew Lipman, *Harry Stottlemeier's Discovery* (Upper Montclair, N.J.: The Institute for Advancement of Philosophy for Children, 1974).

CLYDE EVANS

University of Massachusetts, Boston

The Feasibility of Moral Education

I have worked as a philosopher, with students from kindergarten through the twelfth grade. In this paper, I will consider specifically elementary school students—mostly in the third and fourth grades. I will try to provide sufficient details to give some idea of my procedure, the dynamics among the children, and the overall feel and excitement of the sessions. I will then discuss those features of the sessions that I take to be of philosophical importance. In closing, I shall say a few words about the significance of such work for philosophy in general.

I was invited to Hillside Elementary School, Hastings-on-Hudson, New York, to work with children there on issues related to values, morals, responsibility, decision making, and the like. This immediately limited my scope as a philosopher to ethical and moral issues. My procedure was as follows: I would ask the class of twenty to twenty-five students to sit on the floor before a movie screen. I then would show them a short filmstrip—*First Things*, produced by Guidance Associates of Pleasantville, New York. Each strip told a story of a child about their own age and dealt with an issue that they could both understand and care about—telling the truth, keeping promises, fairness, obeying rules, property rights. Each story deliberately left the child at the end of the film with a dilemma.

After the film, I would sit with the children on the floor and get a few initial gut reactions about what they thought the child in the film should do. In every case, opinion was divided—sometimes with a few undecideds. I was careful to elicit some comments from children on each side of the issue, complete with reasons for their choices. This insured that everyone realized that there was another point of view, and that there were reasons for holding such a view. Then I suggested that each group separate, talk it over, and try to come up with the best reasons they could for deciding as they did.

If some were still undecided, I had them remain with me to articulate their indecision, confusion, and ambivalence. This helped them to see as clearly as possible just what the issues were and what alternatives existed. When I felt that they all had a sufficiently clear understanding of the pros and cons of each alternative, that they all felt the sharpness of the two horns of the dilemma, I recommended that they join each of the other groups' deliberations and discussion in order to see what kinds of reasons each summoned in support of its position. I also assured the students that suspending judgment is perfectly legitimate if neither side is decisively convincing.

I then visited each of the groups, more or less to monitor the discussion. I was not an active participant, for I wanted them to talk to each other. My primary objective at this point was to prevent them from devising imaginative ways in which to avoid the dilemma. I wanted to keep them from modifying the facts of the situation, offering compromises, or pulling things out of the air. Without becoming totally unrealistic, I wanted them to be forced to decide that particular case, even if they felt the choice to be between undesirable alternatives. I insisted on this because I believe that the important factor is neither which particular decision is reached nor which of the specified alternatives are chosen. Rather, what is of paramount importance is the process by which the decision is made.

Finally, we all gathered again in a circle, with each group trying to persuade the other group, and any remaining fencesitters of the righteousness of its cause. At this point I was mainly a referee. I tried to maintain some kind of controlled warfare. The important task at this point was to prevent the students from presenting position papers completely unrelated to the dialogue of the moment and to get them to respond to what had just been said. We would continue for a while. I explained briefly about why there was no second part to the film divulging the answer, and why in some cases they themselves had to determine the outcome. Then we would adjourn.

To give you some idea of the feel of these sessions, I would like to relate some of the responses. In one of the filmstrips, a girl is taken to a carnival by her father. It is her seventh birthday, and he has promised her that she can choose any five rides. But as they approach the gate, he discovers that he has forgotten his wallet. This is the last day of the carnival, and it is too far to go home and return before it closes. He counts the change in his pocket and tells his daughter that he has enough to pay the entrance fee; they could go inside and look at the exhibits and parades, but there would not be enough left over for the rides; *or*, she could lie about her age, say that she was six instead of seven, and get in for half-price, and then they would have enough left for the rides. Then he dumps the problem in her lap, telling her that she must decide for herself what she should do. They walk to the entrance gate. The father says, "Two tickets please." The ticket seller says, "One adult and, let's see young lady, how old are you?" The film ends and the children watching it are asked what they would do in such a situation.

As expected, the children divided into those who would lie and those who would tell the truth. But the reasons for doing both varied greatly. Some of the reasons given for lying: I waited all year for this day; I only just turned seven *that day*; it's the last day of the carnival and I won't get another chance; it won't hurt anybody; it's only a few cents, not a lot of money; it wasn't my fault that my father forgot his wallet; no one will know; the carnival is probably cheating people anyway, so it's all right to cheat them back; the manager is probably mean.

Some reasons given for telling the truth: it's wrong to lie; I would feel so bad about lying that I could not enjoy the rides anyway; my conscience would bother me and I would not be able to sleep at night; my father would never be able to trust me again; I might get caught; this would lead you to become a habitual liar; if everyone lied whenever they pleased, then no one could every believe anyone else; it would not be fair to the carnival which deserves to make a profit; if everyone cheated the carnival, it might go bankrupt and then no one would have a carnival to attend; it would not be fair to all the other seven year olds who paid the full fare.

Thus while there were only two courses of action chosen, there was a multitude of different reasons given for choosing one course rather than the other. I belive this is an extremely significant feature of these sessions. It helps the students to see that the objective is not merely to decide whether to lie or to tell the truth; the objective is not merely to get the right answer. More is required: the either/or decision must be grounded on particular reasons. In our sessions, the young people begin to see that what is of paramount importance is the strength of the connection between the reasons given and the decision made. They get to see their classmates choose exactly the same course of action, reach exactly the same conclusion for (what they take to be) completely indefensible reasons. For example, Margie decides to tell the truth because it would be unfair to the other seven year olds. Walter also chooses to tell the truth, but his reasons for doing so (you might get caught) are completely unpersuasive to Margie. I cannot overemphasize how important I think this aspect of the experience to be.

Unsurprisingly, not all the children's reasons and comments were as to the point as those cited above. A fair amount of energy and ingenuity went into thinking of ways to solve the whole problem. The tries ranged from fairly ridiculous (tell the truth, pay full fare, and then you would probably find some money lying around on the ground once you got in) to absolutely brilliant (tell the truth, then find some little old man inside the carnival and tell him the whole story; he would then give out the money for the rides, because old men will do anything for little kids.)

This sort of evasion was rare, however. The children generally took the entire enterprise seriously. There was the expected amount of playing around: "We have more on our side"; "All the girls are on the other side" (this actually happened once); "You can't even climb a tree"; "You've never even been on a boat"; "What do *you* know?"; and the like. But for the most part, the students did deal and traffic in reasons. They tried to convince by giving reasons—both for why they were right and why the others were wrong.

A quick story will help to show why I have such confidence in the (general) seriousness of the children. During one discussion of the carnival dilemma, we had a case of persuasion. It was a girl who, at one point in the discussion, said that lying would not be fair to all the other seven-year-olds who had paid full fare. A boy on the other side had never thought of that; and when he did, it was enough to make him change his decision. He decided then and there that telling the truth was the best thing to do. So he moved over to join the truth-tellers. This kind of reversal did not happen often, but it happened more than once. These incidents and others like them convinced me that not only were the children considering reasons but that they also were sincerely and seriously attending to the remarks of their classmates. It was truly a dialogue.

Almost always the students would insist that I give my position on the dilemma. I would always postpone my answer until they had all expressed their own positions and justifications and had heard from their classmates. Then I would give my personal decision, admit it if I felt uneasy about it, and explain why that position was most convincing to me. I would make clear that this was just my own resolution of the dilemma and that each of them, having the same evidence as I, might legitimately disagree with me—for *reasons* that they were in a position to give. When I came out for one of the two sides, it was natural that some of the members of the agreeing group felt vindicated in their judgment and took my decision as a sign that they had "won." But on one occasion, before the last word of my confession had died out, a girl from the losing side animatedly yelled at her opponents, "But that doesn't make it right!" *Success!*

What Does All This Have to Do with Philosophy?

At this point you may well be thinking that this all sounds like great fun but wondering what it has to do with philosophy. First, in these sessions the students learned nothing about Lucretius, Aquinas, or Wittgenstein. If there really was any philosophy present, it could not have been philosophy in the sense of the thought of major philosophical figures. Second, we did not study or follow the development and evolution of philosophical thought on a particular issue. So again, if there was any philosophy in our activity, it was not philosophy in the sense of an ongoing dialogue or conversation continued through the ages. Third, we did not discuss free will, mind/body dualism, the nature of knowledge, or logical necessity. So we could not have "done" philosophy in the sense of studying germinal problems that have recurred again and again in mankind's attempt to make sense of the universe. Finally, we did not engage in any discussions about what philosophy really is, or what philosophy can and cannot do: its limits. We did not do the kind of philosophy that is primarily concerned with meta-issues rather than the issues themselves.

So what did we do that was philosophical? There were three aspects of these sessions that I believe to be philosophically important. I believe further that these three features justify calling our activity philosophical—if only on a rudimentary level. I will call these features philosophical commitments, philosophical skills, and (substantive) philosophical issues.

Philosophical Commitments

First, I think that sessions such as ours introduce the students to philosophical commitments. These are the commitments that make philosophical discourse possible. Whenever people seriously seek to resolve a dilemma or to think their way through a problem, there are certain procedural principles to which they must be committed. I think this is always true, but it is especially true when it is a social enterprise, when several people are involved. Then, things must be done in a certain way, certain criteria must be established and observed and certain attitudes must be adopted toward the endeavor itself. These are, in short, the commitments necessary to make a philosophical discussion go. Let us look at them briefly.

1. There is the commitment to impartiality and objectivity. The idea here is simply that during their deliberations students should not give undue weight to any particular person or interest, *unless* there are relevant reasons for doing so. This means they will give *due* (not necessarily equal) consideration to every proposal made, to every issue uncovered, to every objection raised—as much objectivity as they can muster. They will also not give undue weight to their own positions merely because they are their own. Students should not give any more weight to a suggestion made by their best friends than to any other, nor any less to one made by their worst enemy, nor any special consideration to one made by the teacher. This commitment is necessary in order to insure that all sides of the issue are considered and that no viewpoint or position is prematurely screened out by any sort of biased preselection.

This guarantee is required by the very nature of the enterprise: in philosophical inquiry we seek to arrive at the best understanding obtainable on a particular issue. In order to do so, we must attend to all considerations that are significant for this issue. We will usually decide that some points are less significant than others, that can only be done after they have been given due consideration. Such fair consideration is all the commitment requires.

This commitment is not limited to philosophical enterprise: my endeavor with the children requires such a commitment. For our objective is to understand the nature of the dilemma, see clearly the several issues involved, and arrive at the best resolution of that dilemma. Such an endeavor requires the same kind of comprehensive, thorough, consideration demanded in philosophy, and hence it requires the same commitment of the children that is demanded of philosophers.

2. There is the commitment to consider only relevant criteria. This is important because it is quite possible to be perfectly impartial and objective while considering points completely irrelevant. But it does keep participants aware that such distinction can be made and inclined to try to make it. Deciding which considerations are the relevant ones can be exceedingly difficult. Obviously the context of a given situation will influence a given case. For instance, a girl wants to join an all-boys little league baseball team and the decision is left to the players. The fact that she is the best shortstop in the neighborhood seems to be a relevant consideration in deciding to accept her on the team. An equally relevant consideration leading to rejecting her might be her having asthma. In this case, the fact that she is a girl seems irrelevant to the required decision. In a different issue, for example, casting the role of Ophelia in *Hamlet*, her being a girl seems decidedly relevant, (today if not in Shakespeare's day).

These are fairly easy cases. My point is simply that if the participants in this social enterprise seek to arrive at the best possible understanding of the problem and the best possible resolution of the dilemma, the nature of the enterprise demands that they be committed to considering only those criteria that are significant and relevant to the issues at hand. So again the commitment required of the children is identical to that required of philosophers.

3. Participants must be committed to consistency. That is, they must strive to make their thought and statements at one time compatible with those of another time. This is necessary if the discussion as a whole is to be comprehensible, if the different parts are to fit together, and if there is to

be any cumulative progress toward the objective. This means that it is not acceptable or appropriate to make a statement patently contradictory to any of one's previous statements. In practice this also means that if students raise objections to a classmate's point, they must be willing to apply the same criteria consistently to themselves. To fail to do so would be special pleading, another form of inconsistency.

4. Participants must be comprehensive in their thinking. This means that they must strive to apply the above principles to every aspect of their endeavor. They cannot adopt the critical attitude in some areas of consideration and ignore it in others. There can be no sacred preserves beyond the reach, a priori, of the critical approach. They must be willing, at least in principle, to subject to critical scrutiny everything that may arise during the course of the inquiry. This is necessary in order for the students to protect themselves against uncritically making assumptions, or accepting statements or claims into their considerations that could be shown upon examination to be unwarrantable. This safeguard can operate only if everything is subject to examination.

5. Participants must be committed to respecting each other person in the discussion as a possible source of valuable information, relevant considerations, and persuasive arguments. This is so because, if the prime objective is to arrive at the best possible solution, then it is at least secondary (and at most irrelevant) from what source that solution comes. This means that the student will consider each participant as an equal member of the group, a peer, and a partner in the search. Even if a student does not like a classmate, he or she must still be open to at least the possibility that the disliked person might say something important. Hence, no one can automatically be tuned out.

6. Finally, participants must be committed to the search for reasons, defensible reasons, as the basis upon which to make their decisions and determine their behavior. If this were not so, there would be no sense in jointly discussing reasons in the first place. The students must strive to make decisions not solely on the basis of personal whim or caprice, or according to what friends do, or on impuslve, or by prevailing opinion, or because of what the teacher thinks or says. The student will strive to decide on the merits of the case that is made for or against a particular position.

These commitments are absolutely necessary for any social enterprise in which a group of people try to think their way through an issue. These commitments are prerequisites for any philosophical discourse or inquiry: anyone who seriously engages in the study of philosophy or in the activity of philosophizing must presuppose such things. Philosophical inquiry and discourse could not proceed, would not be possible, without commitments to such principles by the participants. This is true of philosophy at every level, from the most sophisticated to the most elementary. Clearly, it is just as true of the discussions I had with the children concerning what they would do in the given situations. It was just as necessary for these principles to be operative in those discussions as in professional philosophical journals.

As I have just indicated, this aspect regarding commitments is not, properly speaking, philosophical. It is what might be called pre-philosophical, as it precedes any actual philosophizing. I do not think it is crucial to decide here, once and for all, the exact position of this aspect, as long as we understand, first, that these commitments are absolutely necessary for any philosophical discourse to take place, and second, that students can come to form such commitments simply by being immersed in such an activity. I attempted to facilitate the formation of such commitments, not by teaching them or talking about them, but by creating a situation, an atmosphere, in which the students could experience these commitments at work and see their efficacy. I never said a single word about "philosophical commitments" or "philosophical presuppositions." This would have been futile; fortunately it was also unnecessary. I simply engaged the children in a discussion that required for its very existence the presence and operation of such philosophical commitments. I feel that these discussions were just as philosophical as any other which requires these same philosophical commitments from its participants.

Philosophical Skills

The second aspect of these sessions that I want to discuss has to do with what can be called philosophical skills. The commitments that we have just considered are more akin to a philosophical outlook or attitude. I have in mind now the particular skills, the tools that can be used by persons who have such a philosophical attitude. These are the skills necessary for rational inquiry and critical analysis. I believe that sessions like mine with children can help them to acquire such skills, because, again, such a discussion demands the use of such skills—whether they are being used well or poorly, deliberately or unknowingly, systematically or haphazardly. Reasoning processes are taking place at each point of the discussion. All that is required is to make the students more consciously aware of the processes in which they are already engaged.

Thus by directing more attention to the process itself, we could help the children to see that there are some skills that would be valuable to have for effective discussion. We could also help them to understand and develop such skills. They could come to see that it is very helpful to be able to clarify and analyze a complex issue by separating and distinguishing its various parts; distinguish an exposition from an argument; separate the conclusion of an argument from its supporting reasons; distinguish inductive from deductive arguments; determine when an argument is a good one; recognize the common fallacies (and even understand why they are fallacious); understand how language can be used to distort, oversimplify, distract, and so forth. Such sessions involve the use of such skills and thus provide an opening to discuss and further pursue them. The thoroughness or sophistication with which such skills are treated will depend upon the children involved, but even at younger ages it is possible, I have found, to develop some understanding of and facility with these skills.

I think this aspect of such work with children deserves to be called philosophical because it involves developing philosophical tools and skills. It is totally analogous to the way in which budding philosophers develop and sharpen their philosophical tools. The sophistication of the tools themselves is obviously quite different in the two cases, but the basic idea of mastering those skills required by the task at hand is exactly the same.

Let now now give three examples to show the use of these skills. I will describe how they appeared in our sessions. Then I will mention an instance from the history of philosophy in which the same feature is present.

First, let us consider a particular skill. During these sessions, students can develop the capacity to trace out the implications of a given position or claim, that is, to see what follows from it. Sometimes this will lead them to see that the implications of one of their positions are incompatible with the implications of another of their positions. To the degree that these implications are inconsistent with each other, to that degree both positions cannot be maintained at the same time. In one of our dilemmas, a girl wants to climb a tree to save a kitten's life and she also wants to keep her word to her father to stop climbing trees. She is committed to keeping a promise and also to preserving life. These two positions are in conflict.

It is extremely enlightening for students to see that the two positions are mutually exclusive and there is no way around it. Since they cannot act upon both positions at once, they must choose one and sacrifice the other. And this is precisely the remedy we would offer John Locke for some of the problems in his epistemology. Locke wanted to maintain both: (1) that we have knowledge only of ideas and (2) that the primary qualities in objects resemble our ideas of them. But we cannot maintain both. By (1) we can know only our ideas of primary qualities; thus we could never, in principle, know anything else about them to which our ideas of them could be compared for resemblance. Hence we cannot have both (1) and (2). This is a concrete example of how one of the skills developed in these sessions is exactly the kind useful for more conventional philosophical inquiry and analysis. (If these examples are obviously not perfectly analogous, they share one important feature, the necessity of recognizing irreconcilable conflict between two positions.)

Second, let us consider one of the philosophical commitments, say, the commitment to consistency. Some of the students said it was all right to lie at the carnival because only a few cents were involved, not a lot of money. The implication is that it is the smallness of the amount of money involved that allows an untruth to be acceptable. Some others said that if everyone lied, the carnival would lose money and might possibly go bankrupt. Why? Because if everyone lied, then the total amount of money would be large. Some of the students responded to this argument by saying that even so it was still all right to lie because the carnival was probably cheating you anyway. Now, though this response *prima facie* deserves as much consideration as any other, it is not an appropriate response from the first group of students who said that lying was all right because only a little money was involved. For those students to maintain the acceptability of lying even when this instance fails on their own criterion (the amount of money involved) is to be patently inconsistent. They would be applying a criterion in one case and refusing to apply it where it is equally applicable in another.

It will be noticed that the force of this analysis depends on how the first group of students used the criterion of the amount of money involved. If this criterion was being used in a utilitarian way in which the prime consideration was the consequences to the carnival, then my analysis is correct: the students cannot make the second response. This is because the consequences of lying when everyone was lying are no longer negligible. To state it another way, the first justificatory rationale was that the consequences to the carnival were negligible because the difference between full price and half price for a single person was negligible. On this basis, the first group of students can approve of the act of one person lying but they cannot approve of the act of everyone lying, because the first instance meets their criterion where the second instance does not. To approve of the second instance would be not to apply their own criterion in that case.

Suppose, however, that this criterion was never intended to concern consequences. Suppose instead that it was meant to be merely a determining factor in ascertaining the moral fitness of a particular act by a given individual. Then the students can maintain their position. For then, even supposing that everyone was to lie, the act could still be approved since the amount of money is brought into consideration only with respect to each individual decision where, by assumption, the amount is always small. In fact, in our discussion, the students intended the criterion to be used in the first sense.

A comparable philosophical episode involves John Locke and Bishop Berkeley. Recall how Berkeley chastised Locke for assuming the causes of our ideas, namely, material objects. Then Berkeley did exactly the same thing himself when he assumed (postulated) the cause of our ideas, namely, spirits.

Finally, consider an example that combines both the use of particular skills and the operation of one of the commitments. In the carnival dilemma one of the boys felt that the child in the film should tell the truth. Why? because lying in this case would lead one to become a habitual liar, and the first thing you know, you'd be lying all the time. Other students countered by saying that this was just one little lie; it's not as if you lie all the time; and just because you lie this once doesn't mean you'll start lying all the time. With just a bit more sophistication, they could have pointed out, in addition, that the first boy was using a version of the slippery slope argument which, without further support, is always fallacious on the face of it.

The first boy then provided further support. He said that lying is just like pollution. To say that it's only one little lie is like saying it's only one little candy wrapper. But all the little candy wrappers add up. The first thing you know you have a big pollution problem. Likewise, the first thing you know you'll have a big lying problem. Again, a student who had begun to develop these skills could have easily pointed out that this was an obvious argument from analogy—which, of course, is also fallacious without further support. (Awareness of this fallacy is not something we need only when reading Letters to the Editor. Aristotle used this argument in the Nicomachean Ethics in discussing whether a person could choose to be just. And Hume criticized such an argument in his Critique of Natural Religion, while dealing with the Argument from Design. In both cases, facility with particular skills would have greatly increased the sophistication of the exchanges. It is not merely the ability to use jargon that I am after here, for in the first case, the students did make the proper response even though they never used the words *slippery slope*. I want to help the students understand why their response was the proper one (why that argument is fallacious) and to help them learn to spot such arguments more readily.

In the second instance, it will not be surprising when I report that none of the students pointed out that it was an argument from analogy. But the responses they did make will indicate the particular philosophical commitment that was operative. They gave two replies, both of which were *ad hominem* attacks upon the speaker, one for each side of the analogy: "You throw candy wrappers on the ground too" and "You lie too." Clearly the virtue of the speaker is an inappropriate consideration in determining the merit of an argument. In fact, the arguments were lousy, but not because their maker was a litter-bug and a liar. Any knowledge the students had of his character as a litter-bug or liar should not have prevented them from considering impartially whatever arguments he proposed. Hence the operation of the commitment to impartiality. A comparable episode from the history of philosophy again involves Locke. In book 1 of his *Essay*, Locke seeks to show why the theory of innate ideas is indefensible. In addition to giving particular arguments against that philosophical position, he also makes some disparaging remarks about the proponents of such a theory. Such *ad hominem* attacks were just as inappropriate for Locke as for my children.

For both the philosophical commitments and the philosophical skills, we see that our discussion sessions lead to the development in the children of exactly the kinds of attitudes and skills required of practicing philosophers and which have actually been manifested by real-life philosophers in real-life philosophical episodes.

Philosophical Issues

The third and final notable aspect of these sessions has to do with substantive philosophical issues. The point is simply this: in dealing with seemingly straightforward, everyday kinds of issues, the students find themselves almost immediately entangled in traditional philosophical problems. Lurking just below the surface of everyday issues lie substantive philosophical questions. The great lesson to be learned from such sessions is that any serious, nonsuperficial consideration of many everyday issues inherently involves the same kind of philosophy that we have always associated with names like Plato, Aristotle, and Russell; the same questions discussed by them; the same skills used by them in trying to make sense of it all.

After the carnival situation discussed above, the children began by merely trying to decide whether or not to lie at the ticket office. But how should they decide? What are the grounds on which they should make up their minds? Some attempted to decide on the basis of what they thought would be the fair thing to do. But this required some attention to what fairness is, or at least demanded some criteria for determining fairness in this case. And this easily lead on to the problem of justice, with which philosophers have grappled since Socrates. So the children were quickly involved with an old philosophical chestnut.

Some children tried to decide on the basis of a fundamental principle like lying is wrong (always, everywhere, and for everyone). Some philosophers also have tried to ground their judgments on fundamental principles. We think immediately of the categorical imperatives of Immanuel Kant. Some students made their decision on the basis of how they felt about the rightness or wrongness of the act. If they felt it was all right to lie in this case, then they would do just that. Some philosophers (such as Hume) have maintained that this is a perfectly acceptable position, for in the end, that is all there is: our feelings of approval or disapproval for particular actions. The "morality' of an act consists in nothing more. Other students apparently decided, more simply, on the basis of what they personally would get out of it. If a given course of action seemed likely to benefit them, then it was right. (Compare some versions of egoism, such as that in Plato's *Republic.*) Finally, some students decided on the basis of how their decision would affect the others involved for better or worse. Many philosophers (such as Bentham and Mill) have espoused just this kind of utilitarianism.

The students themselves raised these philosophical issues during the course of their discussion, and at least hinted at the philosophical positions by which to deal with them. It is clear that this activity confronted the children with substantive philosophical issues—the level was rudimentary, to be sure, but the philosophical issues were genuine. This consideration alone, I feel, would justify calling such activities philosophical.

It might be objected at this point that I still have not shown that such sessions with children are truly philosophical. Their features are characteristic of any kind of rational discussion. I have shown that they contain features that are necessary for philosophy but not that their presence justifies calling the activity philosophy. My response is simply that this objection is correct. I never intended to show that anything about these sessions belonged exclusively within the realm of philosophy. I attempted merely to isolate certain significant features of the sessions themselves and then indicated that these features do indeed (not to say, necessarily) occur in genuine philosophical activity.

This distinction parallels the one I made while working with the children themselves. I did not attempt to bring philosophy—in all its full-blown tradition, diversity, power—to the children. Rather I attempted to lead the children toward philosophy. The important thing was not whether what we did satisfied all the canons of true philosophy, but whether what we did had enough in common with true philosophical activity to begin leading the children toward the goal of becoming more and more philosophical.

After saying all this, I would like to state that I am not so sure there actually is any important distinction between philosophical discussion and plain, ordinary, rational discussion. A case can be made that there is a philosophical character to any rational discussion and that philosophical discussion is only an ordinary rational discussion pursued with more than ordinary tenacity, sophistication, discipline, and zeal.

If anyone is inclined to deny the title philosophy to such activities, there is a very unpleasant consequence to be faced. Consider the three features discussed above, especially the last one. If what took place with the children was not philosophy, then neither is a large part of what takes place on occasions which are generally accounted to be instances (though maybe not paradigm instances) of the real thing. I refer to freshman introductory classes, graduate seminars, professional association meetings, any occasion when two philosophers talk shop. Leaving aside the degree of sophistication involved in the different cases above and the variations in social contexts, these activities are all essentially the same. To deny the title philosophy to one would deny it to all. To grant it to some requires us to grant it to all, however we distinguish between them on the basis of nonessential degrees of sophistication.

Indeed, denying my children's sessions the dignity of philosophy would mean that much of what takes place in the world of philosophy would be judged not really to be philosophy at all. This result could be taken, not as an unpleasant consequence but as a welcome realization that instances of true philosophy are truly few and far between. While such a response is possible, however, it would entail such a restrictive notion of philosophy that nothing I could ever do with children would, in principle, satisfy it.

Conclusion

What we have seen is nothing more than an ordinary group of people, in this case children, attempting to think their way through an issue that has significance for them. Many implications follow from such an activity that are worthy of note. We have discussed three particular features especially that are noteworthy for philosophy and all it stands for.

We have seen that certain skills are necessary to the success of such an activity, and participation offers a perfect opportunity to develop them. Some of the skills involved are analysis, clarification, argumentation, and basic clear thinking without which people could never think their way through anything. Mastery of these skills is important because they are precisely the skills required of philosophers.

By far the most important features of this social activity were those that we called 'philosophical commitment' and 'philosophical issues.' We saw that the very nature of such an activity required certain philosophical commitments of its participants—exactly the same commitments required of philosophers. Since few, if any, of these students will become philosophers, it is just as significant that these commitments are also the ones required of anyone engaged in any rational inquiry into any problem of any nature. Hence we arrive at the vital realization that such activity helps students to develop that outlook or attitude that they must have if they are to ever think their way through anything whatever.

Finally—and this is the most important point for philosophy—we saw that the students began by talking about a practical, everyday kind of decision and ended by considering hard-core philosophical issues—all in the natural course of the discussion. Merely by the serious, sustained pursuit of some understanding of this practical issue, the students found themselves—not led by me—unavoidably confronting real, substantive philosophical problems. From this they must get a sense that philosophy is neither something grafted on to situations or curricula nor is it a luxury item that can be ignored or omitted by everyone but philosophers. Rather, philosophy is essentially and inherently a part of the total picture and can be ignored only at the price of settling for a superficial, shallow investigation. They will see that even in everyday, concrete, practical concerns, they are unavoidably driven to consider the underlying philosophical substratum and thus see that there is the philosophical dimension to even the most practical problems.

I believe that this necessary link between the practical, everyday kinds of things we see and do and philosophical musings is both the glory and the hope of philosophy. There will probably always be some who enjoy philosophical inquiry simply for its own sake and are drawn to it for that reason alone ("philosophy is its own reward"). But most, I think, will come to philosophy because they discover that they must in order to answer some of the questions that arise in their everyday normal existence.

That was my route. I did not begin by seeking philosophy; I was driven to philosophy. I wanted to understand certain things: I wanted to make sense out of what I saw; I wanted to think my way through certain issues. Time and time again I discovered that I needed philosophy in order to achieve my goals. To be sure, the questions that prompted my journey were not related to the price of admission to a carnival. They were questions like: What makes the world tick? Why does the physical world work the way it does? Why do some people suffer in poverty while others do not? why is our society structured the way it is? Why is there a law against this and not against that? Why do schools teach this particular subject, and why do they teach it in this way? Just what is it that schools are trying to accomplish? How can we tell whether a given statement is well-grounded or just superstitious nonsense? Questions like these were what led me inevitably into the realm of philosophy.

I would like to see philosophy once again thought of as everybody's business and not just the preserve of a privileged few. I would like to see it again known that even ordinary persons can engage in philosophy—even if only at a rudimentary level. Indeed they cannot avoid doing so, whether or not they realize what they are doing. If this were to happen, philosophy would lose its image as the esoteric pasttime of a few erudite minds. It could again be seen as something that has relevance for anyone, as something that has significance for ordinary people living ordinary lives. Then we could begin to direct our energies to finding ways to let philosophy enrich those lives—whether the lives of nine-year-olds trying to decide whether or not to rip off the carnival or the lives of ninety-year-olds trying to cope with the problems of uselessness, leisure, and loneliness. Philosophy can help to bring more meaning into the lives of those who pursue and embrace it. I want to help make that happen.

ᴥᔓ 6 ᣞᴥ

WHAT SHOULD SOCIAL
PHILOSOPHY BE FOR
CHILDREN?

ᴥᔓ JANE ROLAND MARTIN

University of Massachusetts, Boston

Moral Autonomy and Political Education

In recent years our schools have shown renewed interest in moral education. Children discuss moral dilemmas, clarify values, and imagine what they would do if adrift in an overcrowded lifeboat, their teachers intending thereby that they will become autonomous moral agents. The importance of the goal of autonomy should not be underestimated. But it is a mistake to assume, as many people apparently do, that education for autonomy can be divorced from social and political education. Whether or not their supporters realize it, programs that purport to be politically neutral while fostering autonomy in fact do provide children with a social and political education in autonomy in which the received customs, institutions, and doctrines of society are never questioned, in which no effort is made to introduce children to viable alternatives, in which the injustices of the existing order are taken as given; it is an education that breeds unthinking acceptance of the status quo.

The social and political education our children receive ought not to be one in mindless conservatism. So that it will not be, programs intended to foster autonomy must at the very least also try to develop in children a sense of justice (and injustice) and what in this essay I will call openmindedness. To do this, rather than ignore social and political contexts as they tend to do now, they must confront them honestly. Philosophy for children can contribute to this confrontation. In the last two sections of this essay I will outline some of the values philosophy can have for the kind of social and political education that should accompany an education for autonomy. I will begin by discussing autonomy as a goal of education. I will then show that education for it inevitably carries with it a social and political education. I will go on to argue that autonomy must be combined with a sense of justice and openmindedness and that these are appropriate goals for children to attain.

1. Autonomy as a Goal of Education

In the early 1960s Stanley Milgram carried out a group of experimental studies at Yale University.[1] They were variations on a theme. A naïve subject was led to believe that the experimenter was investigating the effects of punishment on learning. This subject was designated "teacher" and was told to administer a learning test to a "learner"—someone in the next room whom the naïve subject saw being strapped into a chair with electrodes attached to his wrists. The "teacher" sat before an impressive shock generator and was told to give an electric shock to the "learner" each time the "learner" missed an item on the learning test, the shocks to be increased 15 volts at each miss. Actually the "teacher," not the "learner," was the focus of the studies. The "learner" was an actor who, according to a prearranged schedule, missed words and cried with pain as the "teacher" increased the voltage.

The point of Milgram's obedience studies was to see how far a person will proceed when ordered to inflict pain on a protesting victim. At what point will people refuse to obey the orders of the experimenter? Will they refuse to participate in the experiment once they realize they are to administer shocks? Will they refuse after the first moans from the learner? Surely all will refuse once the "learner" starts protesting vehemently.

Milgram's results disturbed him and everyone else. It had been predicted that virtually all naïve subjects would refuse to obey the experimenter, if not initially then at 150 volts when the victim first demanded to be freed; that only one to two percent would proceed to the end and administer what they thought was 450 volts. In fact, in half the studies Milgram carried out, a majority of naïve subjects obeyed till the end and in only three studies did a majority of subjects refuse to go beyond 150 volts.

Many questions have been raised about Milgram's methodology and about the generalizability of his results, questions I cannot begin to do justice to here. Fortunately I do not have to. Granted that his sample was small and the laboratory setting of each experiment not a replica of real life, still his findings are only too consistent with our observations of real life. The psychiatrists, professors, university students, and middle class adults who predicted the refusal by virtually all subjects to obey an authority at the expense of a victim did so before My Lai and Watergate.

Actually, Milgram's results should not have surprised anyone who had taken a long hard look at contemporary American schooling. But in 1960–1963, when the studies were carried out, perhaps few of us had done this. The writings of the radical school reformers portraying the hidden curriculum of our public school classrooms came later.[2] Frederick Wiseman's film *High School*, in which episode upon episode reveals conformity and obedience to authority being instilled in young people, was yet to be made. I do not mean to suggest that our schools are solely responsible for the behavior of Milgram's naïve subjects. Church and home, Little League and Cub Scouts all have hidden curricula in which obedience to authority plays a significant role. Yet surely schooling is a contributory cause of the blind obedience to authority we deplore in real life as in the laboratory. The Declaration of Independence and the American Revolution may loom large in the formal social studies curriculum of our schools, but obedience to authority holds sway in their hidden curriculum.

When buttressed by Milgram's findings, the events of the 1970s point up the importance of individual autonomy as an educational goal. If we are not to be robots, mechanically doing what we are told to do, we must be educated for autonomous thought and action. Programs in moral education designed to develop autonomy deserve our congratulations. Yet what exactly is it they are trying to achieve?

Unfortunately there is no more agreement about the nature of autonomy than there is about anything else in education. Two dominant views of it can be rejected out of hand, however: one because it makes autonomy a trivial goal and the other because it makes it an impossible goal.[3]

As autonomy is sometimes characterized, we are all autonomous simply by virtue of being human: our very humanity makes us responsible for what we do and do not do, for what we believe and do not believe. On this view we are all autonomous all the time. But if we are autonomous no matter what we do or how we do it, we need no education to achieve autonomy. Autonomy in this sense cannot be taken seriously as a goal of education, for it is something we all have independently of being educated.

A conception of autonomy as complete and utter self-determination is also irrelevant. On this view we are autonomous only if all our thoughts and actions are independent of all outside control or even influence. Education is indeed essential for autonomy in this sense for if we have not mastered the Three R's, the intellectual disciplines, and a great deal more, we must depend on others, and if we depend on others then we are not entirely self-determined. But autonomy as an educational goal is not therefore vindicated. For autonomy to be a goal of education, it must be something that can be achieved. Absolute self-determination is not possible. We cannot even be completely self-determined with respect to some things some of the time, let alone with respect to all things all of the time.

Absolute self-determination requires deliberation, and that in turn requires having beliefs about oneself and the world. Yet on this second conception of autonomy, you cannot get those beliefs from books, encyclopedias or scholarly journals. Absolute self-determination requires that you do your own research; otherwise your beliefs will be influenced by others. However, original research itself rests on information supplied by others— information about the field under study, experimental methods and research design, the tools being used. And even if this were not so—even if you could find out what you wanted to know by yourself starting from scratch—the education you get that enables you to do original research necessarily involves outside influences.

Neither a trivial nor an impossible conception of autonomy has relevance for education. To be an educational goal, autonomy must be something we can achieve, something which we do not, however, all have without being educated.

A third characterization of autonomy fits these requirements. An autonomous person, on this view, is self-governed or directed without being absolutely self-determined. One who is self-directed makes up his or her own mind about what to believe and what to do, but freedom from all outside control or influence is not necessary, for it is not the source of a person's beliefs or actions that makes him or her self-directed but rather the fact that the person adopts them on the basis of reflection and choice.

Autonomy in this third sense requires education. It is not something we all possess simply by virtue of being human: we must learn to deliberate and to act on the basis of our deliberations. It is impossible, however, to deliberate about everything; indeed, if all our actions had to be self-directed, we would be too busy deliberating about what to do ever to do anything. Thus autonomy as self-direction but not self-determination is an appropriate goal of education only if we conceive of an autonomous person not as one whose every act is autonomous but as one who acts autonomously when it matters.[4]

2. The Inevitability of Social and Political Education

Programs designed to foster individual autonomy are not usually thought to be ventures in social and political education. However, education for autonomy cannot be divorced from either kind of education because actions are not performed in a vacuum. In trying to develop autonomy, teachers may not focus on the social and political background of action, but there will invariably be such a background. To ignore it is to take it for granted, to treat it as a given in the situation. To do this consistently is to contribute to the development of an unquestioning, uncritical acceptance of that background.

Even the moral dilemmas that are constructed so that children will get practice in decision-making presuppose some socio-political background.[5] Should the girl whose father forgot to bring enough money lie about her age in order to get into the carnival, or should she tell the truth? Should the child who borrowed the sled without permission and accidentally broke it confess or not? In the interests of developing individual autonomy, it seems natural to concentrate on the immediate problem of what the imaginary child should do here and now and to ignore the background in relation to which a moral dilemma exists. Yet there are important questions to raise about the backgrounds of these moral dilemmas. Why does the carnival charge admission? Why do its prices go up as a person's age does? Why are sleds made so badly that they break when a child uses them? Why should one have to get permission in order to use a sled? In ignoring the socio-political background of action, including the practices of private property and capitalistic enterprise which lurk behind many of the moral dilemmas used in classrooms, critical questioning of that background is blocked. Children may learn to make up their own minds about what to do in problematic situations, but they will also learn to accept as unproblematic the practices and institutions in which they personal problems arise.

The activities of open classrooms also presuppose a socio-political background that typically is ignored. I speak of open classrooms here because the open education movement—the movement exemplified by the British infant schools that Joseph Featherstone has described so vividly and are characterized in detail in a number of anthologies[6]—takes seriously the goal of individual autonomy: "independence" and "initiative" have been its catchwords; children in open classrooms are encouraged throughout their school day to think for themselves and act on their own. As is well known, open classrooms introduce children to a host of activities. In them, for example, children role-play at banking, store, post office, and keeping house. They also bake cookies, weave, make block prints, publish magazines and newspapers, dramatize stories, and work with wood. In "real life" these activities take place against a socio-political background, one which in open classrooms is censored. Storekeeping in the classroom will involve the exchange of goods for money and even the writing of advertisements; it will not involve price fixing or deceptive marketing practices. Housekeeping will involve reading to baby, cleaning, and cooking, not rats and roaches. Banking will involve writing checks and deposit slips and keeping accounts, not foreign investments and high interest rates.

Typically, the activities in which children in open classrooms engage are idealizations: store running without the profit motive, post office without bureaucracy, housekeeping without desperation.[7] And because they are, criticism of them as they occur in "real life" is once again blocked. Furthermore, their incorporation into open classrooms in idealized form lends them respectability and legitimacy. Thus children in open classrooms do not merely miss out on opportunities to learn the skills of social criticism; they come to accept these activities as ones in which they will some day engage in earnest: to accept not simply the ideal forms but the "real life" activities themselves complete with socio-political background.

If avoidance of socio-political contexts breeds unthinking acceptance of existing institutions and practices, perhaps education for autonomy can remain separate from social and political education by acknowledging such contexts while taking a neutral stance toward them. Yet what would constitute neutrality in this instance? We have seen that to ignore the socio-political background of action is not to be neutral at all. To draw attention to that background without drawing attention to its injustices and without encouraging questioning and criticism of it is not to be neutral either but once more to treat it as a given—something to be accepted uncritically. However, to draw attention to its injustices and to encourage questioning and criticism of it is to foster traits that are part and parcel of a social and political education.

It seems paradoxical to accuse education for autonomy of breeding uncritical acceptance of the status quo. Is not an autonomous agent one who makes up his or her own mind about what to think and what to do? Is it not then impossible for a person to be autonomous and to accept the status quo unthinkingly? Must we not conclude that any education for autonomy that does breed this trait necessarily fails in that it does not develop autonomous agents? The air of paradox disappears once we recall that an autonomous agent is not one who makes up his or her own mind about everything and that autonomy is necessarily exercised selectively. It is quite possible, therefore, to be autonomous yet never to exercise one's autonomy in relation to socio-political issues: it is possible, in other words, to accept the existing order unthinkingly even while making up one's own mind about things aesthetic and scientific, theological, and practical.

We must also realize that it is possible to exercise autonomy about things social and political without ever entertaining serious alternatives to the way things are. Autonomy involves decision and choice which in turn involve alternatives. But if the options considered in making up one's own mind are commonplace or implausible and not at all diverse, no matter. Thus, even if an education for autonomy draws attention to the social and political background of action and encourages students to make up their own minds about it, unless it actively encourages questioning and criticism and the perception of viable alternatives, it will carry with it a social and political education in acceptance of the way things are. It will do so because our decisions and choices are limited by the alternatives we perceive and our perceptions are themselves schooled by habit, custom, and expectation. We cannot adopt a practice that never occurs to us. An education for autonomy which does not train our perception of alternatives will leave us seeing only the old familiar practices of the existing order as viable options and hence accepting them. That acceptance may not be unthinking, but it will be uncritical.

3. Openmindedness and a Sense of Justice

The choice facing those who want to educate children to be autonomous is not between providing them with a social and political education and refraining from doing so; it is between providing one or another kind of social and political education. Attempts to refrain actually constitute an education in uncritical acceptance of the status quo. Mindless conservatism is the hidden curriculum, if you will, of an education for autonomy that tries to be nonpolitical. It is a hidden curriculum which ought to be abolished—on the one hand because the status quo of our society is an unjust one and ought not to be accepted and on the other hand because no status quo, not even a completely desirable one, ought to be accepted uncritically. To abolish that hidden curriculum and to replace it with a full-fledged open and above-board social and political education, education for autonomy must be combined with an education that at the very least develops in children a sense of justice and the complex trait of openmindedness. By a sense of justice, I mean the ability to *perceive* injustice where it exists and to *feel* as well as to *believe* it to be wrong. Openmindedness requires a more extended explanation.

In *On Liberty* John Stuart Mill presented the classic argument against believing doctrine merely *as* doctrine and conforming to custom merely *as* custom.[8] One who does anything because it is custom makes no choice, he said, and gains no practice in discerning or desiring what is best. One who believes anything because it is received doctrine holds it as dead dogma, not living truth. Mill argued against the suppression of ideas by government or society on the grounds that the ideas we take to be true may in fact be false. Because we are fallible, our certainty is not absolute certainty; thus to silence an opinion may be to silence truth. Moreover, even if the opinion we silence is false, Mill said, it might contain a portion of truth. And if it does not—if received opinion is the whole truth, it will be held in the manner of prejudice and its meaning enfeebled or lost unless it is vigorously and earnestly contested.

But Mill's thesis was not simply that no doctrine should be stifled, important as that is. It had a positive component too, namely that there should be free and open discussion of competing doctrines, the doctrines to be presented when possible by those who believe them. For although understanding requires that we know the grounds of the opinions we hold, it is not enough for us to be told those grounds: the other side of the case must be known to us and it must be presented in its most plausible and persuasive form.

Most readers of *On Liberty* know only chapter 2, which is devoted to freedom of thought and discussion. In chapter 3 Mill turned to action, and it is there that he condemned conformity to custom merely as custom. Unity of action is no more desirable than unity of opinion. Accepted custom may not in fact dictate the best way to live. Thus just as we should not merely permit but actually welcome different opinions and their clashes, so we should not merely tolerate but welcome different "experiments of living." Mill was a pluralist where thought and action are concerned, but he was not a relativist. Received doctrine may not be true and accepted custom may not be best, but it does not follow that all doctrines and customs are equally good. We can never have absolute certainty but one doctrine can still have more warrant than another and one lifestyle can have more practical proof. His point was that both warrant and practical proof themselves require a full, free, open discussion of alternative doctrines and life styles.

On Liberty is considered a political, not an educational, tract, yet its arguments have immediate application to education. Can we hold opinions in the way Mill thought we should if we do not learn to? Will we be open to unfamiliar doctrines and lifestyles if we have no exposure to them from an early age? And will we act on choice rather than merely in accordance with custom if we are given no practice? The prospects for the openmindedness for which Mill argued so eloquently and convincingly are dim unless those who educate children introduce them to a wide range of ideas and lifestyles and challenge them to think critically about them.

Open education deserves to be called open on many counts: its classroom space, time schedule, human relationships, and methods of teaching and learning. But open education is not to be equated with education for open minds. To be sure, open education places high value on imagination, curiosity, and independence, all of which would seem to contribute to openmindedness. In open classrooms, however, these traits are typically divorced from contexts in which true openmindedness would develop. Imagination is fostered through engaging in the arts—painting, drama, writing—and through "messing about in science."[9] This latter is a clear break with traditional classrooms where, if imagination is encouraged at all, it is thought to be the sole province of the arts. But were the development of open minds a goal of open education, imagination would surely be harnessed also to social criticism. It is not. Nor are curiosity and independence.

When education for openmindedness is added to education for autonomy, children will be encouraged to question the very customs and institutions and doctrines that an education for autonomy per se takes as given. They will be introduced to alternatives to accepted thought and action; they will be expected to think critically not just about which action to take here and now, but about the socio-political background of such action; in sum, they will begin to develop into social critics. When education for a sense of justice is added to this, they will begin to be able to use their skills of social criticism in humane ways. This does not mean that they will grow up to reject existing institutions and practices. One who is openminded will not accept custom simply because it is custom but he or she may nonetheless accept it. The difference between education for autonomy and for openminded autonomy is that the latter breeds a critical attitude toward the existing order and the realization that there can be viable alternatives to it, whereas the former does not.

4. Mill's Mistake

Despite his fear of interference by state and society with the liberty of the individual, Mill advocated compulsory education. He did so on the grounds that every human being should have an education "fitting him to perform his part well in life toward others and toward himself."[10] Yet even as he maintained that education is essential to the exercise of liberty, Mill worried that it would foster conformity and docility, not freedom and diversity. Thus he opposed the establishment of a public school system, saying:

> A general State education is a mere contrivance for molding people to be exactly like one another; and as the mold in which it casts them is that which pleases the predominant power in the government—whether this be a monarch, a priesthood, an aristocracy, or the majority of the existing generation—in proportion as it is efficient and successful, it establishes a despotism over the mind, leading by natural tendency to one over the body.[11]

The compulsory education for which Mill argued would be enforced not through compulsory school attendance but through a system of yearly examinations. Despotism over the mind would be avoided by limiting the examinations, and hence the compulsory education itself, to languages and their use, to facts and to positive science—in other words to those areas of study he believed to be value-free.

The kind of person Mill wanted us all to be combines autonomy with both openmindedness and a sense of justice.[12] But will we have these qualities if we receive no education in them? Mill seems to have assumed that if the three R's and such fields as history, languages, and the sciences are learned, the rest will take care of themselves. Perhaps they will if you live in the home of a John Mill. If you do not, provision must be made for an education in them. Mill left education to parents because he did not trust the state. Yet if the state, given the chance, will impose its values on the young, will not parents impose theirs? Narrowness, the unthinking adherence to custom, tradition, and received doctrine are what Mill wanted to eradicate. It was naïve of him to suppose that an early education for all in value-free subjects would do the job.[13]

Today we still make Mill's mistake. Those of us who say we value openmindedness do not dream of fostering it until a student embarks on a college education and then only if that education is in the liberal arts. Do we fear that a young person will not know how to handle openmindedness if he or she should achieve it? Or do we assume that it is something only a college student can achieve? Surely we know better than to suppose that in our society we will all become openminded, autonomous individuals simply through osmosis.

A *New York Times* article on the liberal arts quoted the president of Princeton University whose words echo Mill. A liberal education, said Mr. Bowen, "ought to serve a genuinely 'liberating' function—it should help to foster a critical independence and to free us from our own forms of slavery, from the parochialisms of our time and place and station."[14] True enough, but if we must wait for our college to liberate us from unthinking acceptance of received custom and doctrine, those of us who cannot afford a college education or who do not qualify for one academically will never be liberated. Openmindedness should be a property of each one of us, not simply of the rich and the academically motivated.

Perhaps, however, we cannot learn to be openminded until we have mastered the three R's and the standard secondary school subjects; perhaps college must liberate us—even if many of us are thereby denied liberation—because openmindedness has academic prerequisites. It cannot be doubted that openmindedness is a complex trait involving a mix of skills, attitudes, and perceptions. We must first of all see—that is, be aware of—alternative customs, institutions, doctrines. But seeing is not enough: we must become acquainted with them—not just as curiosities but as viable options. We must also get sufficient distance from familiar customs, institutions, and doctrines so that we can criticize them. In addition, we must have skills of social criticism that we are willing and able to use both in relation to our own practices and to the alternatives we perceive, lest we substitute unthinking romantic attachment to new practices for our unthinking habitual attachment to received ones. Openmindedness requires all of this and when as a goal of education it is joined to autonomy it requires more, namely that its component skills, attitudes, and perceptions be harnessed to action, for a person who combines autonomy and openmindedness will not simply be an armchair social critic. Nonetheless, despite its complexity, openmindedness can be fostered while the three R's and the standard school subjects are being taught. It is not necessary to wait until they have been mastered.

If the goal of openminded autonomy is not impossible for young people to attain, perhaps it is unsuitable for them. Granted that its development does not have to wait until college, perhaps openmindedness ought not to be fostered in children. Must not children be initiated into the established practices and doctrines of their own society? Can they receive a proper initiation if they are exposed at an early age to a wide range of alternatives, if they are encouraged to criticize the very institutions within which they are learning to move comfortably? Will not too early an education in openmindedness and autonomy prevent adequate socialization, alienating children not merely from their society but from their own families?

The argument that initiation must precede education for openmindedness because the latter would otherwise prevent socialization and result instead in alienation begs the question. It assumes that openmindedness is not and should not itself be an established practice of the society into which the child is initiated. However, we never socialize a child into all the practices of our society; from some—murder, rape and many others— we try to shield them. Thus, selection accompanies initiation—selection based on what we deem to be important and valuable. The argument prejudges this process of selection by assuming that openmindedness is not one of the societal practices into which we should socialize the young. If we assume instead that openmindedness is a practice into which children should be initiated, the argument for delay becomes an argument for haste, and the spectre of alienation disappears.

The spectre of alienation haunts us because we take for granted that the perception of alternatives and the criticism of received customs, institutions, and doctrines will set the child apart from other members of the society and from society's dominant institutions. But if other members also perceive alternatives and engage in social criticism, the child who receives an early education in openmindedness will not be set apart from them. And if it is accepted practice to get sufficient distance from received customs, institutions, and doctrines to criticize them and to entertain alternatives to them, the child need not be alienated from society's institutions. Provided that a society in which openmindedness is established practice allows for diversity in thought and action and has methods by which its members can change its institutions and doctrines, an early education in openmindedness will not prevent socialization or make alienation all but inevitable.

We can educate children for openmindedness and we should. We should also foster in them a sense of justice, for we cannot assume that this will take care of itself, either. Schools do educate children in justice to the extent that they stress fairness in games, grades, and punishments. But children are not normally made sensitive to social injustice; indeed, its existence is seldom made known to them and when it is, it is done in a way that engages neither feeling nor emotion. Are children too frail and tender to be introduced to social injustice in ways that will make it meaningful to them? Must we protect them from the world's evils until they are of age? A paternalistic approach ignores the fact that many children are themselves the victims of social injustice; for schools to ignore what these children experience every day constitutes neglect, not protection. But if those who have experienced social injustice first hand cannot be protected from it, one wonders if those who have not experienced it should be so protected.

It has been said that John F. Kennedy discovered poverty in West Virginia when he campaigned there in the presidential primary. I take this to mean that, in West Virginia, Kennedy saw poverty from the standpoint of the victim for the first time in his life. Surely he knew before he went to West Virginia that poverty existed; surely he had heard that it did. I have always thought the story did Kennedy credit: he discovered poverty later than he should have, to be sure, but he did discover it, and if we are to believe the story, his sense of justice was thereby enlarged. But while doing him credit, the story is perhaps the most damning I have ever heard about American education. Why did it take him so long to discover poverty? Given the circumstances of his birth, no one could have expected him to see poverty from the standpoint of the victim in the natural course of events. If he was to gain this view from "within," opportunities had to be provided in the course of his formal education. Evidently they were not.

5. Philosophy as "Language" and "Literature"

In a fascinating discussion of university education, Michael Oakeshott distinguishes between a "language," by which he means a manner of thinking, and a "literature," by which he means what has been said in a "language."[15] It is the distinction between poetic thinking and a poem, or between scientific thinking and the theories resulting from it. Not every school subject is amenable to Oakeshott's distinction: a mechanical skill such as handwriting or punctuation or typing does not have this dual aspect; neither does a language such as French. The distinction applies to the intellectual disciplines of which philosophy is one, and it can help us determine the contribution philosophy can make to the social and political education of children.

Oakeshott believes that an education in "languages" belongs in the university, that manners of thinking constitute the heart of a liberal education. On the other hand, the school years, he says, are the time to acquire a stock of ideas, a store of information; they are the time for learning without necessarily understanding or knowing how to use what is learned. For Oakeshott, philosophy for children—if he were to countenance it at all— would be the study of philosophy as a "literature": a study of facts and theories, the point being to accumulate them rather than to gain from them an understanding of oneself and the world or the ability to apply them to the solution of present problems. Drill and memorization would be appropriate ways of teaching philosophy to children. And if children came to view the "literature" of philosophy as dogma it would not matter; when they arrived in the university and studied philosophy as a "language" the tentative status of its "literature" would be revealed.

An Oakeshottian approach to philosophy for children is grim. We should realize, however, that the study of "literatures" with a view simply to the accumulation of information to be used in some distant future characterizes most school education today. Despite John Dewey, despite the curriculum development programs of the late 1950s and early 1960s that stressed inquiry and learning with understanding, despite the radical school reformers of more recent vintage, our schools typically present science and math, history and geography, as Oakeshott would have them do. Whether they would approach philosophy in an unOakeshottian manner is a real question. But those of us who believe that philosophy can have value for children had better try to make sure that they would, for if an Oakeshottian approach to philosophy for children is adopted, I can see no good reason for teaching it to children.

In their book *Philosophy in the Classroom*, Lipman, Sharp, and Oscanyan list many of the values philosophy can have for children: to name just a few, it can contribute to their reasoning ability, their moral development, their self-understanding.[16] But neither these, the other values they cite, nor the contribution philosophy can make to a full-fledged social and political education will be realized if Oakeshott's approach to philosophy is taken. For their realization philosophy must be viewed as a "language,"[17] not as a "literature." Lipman, Sharp, and Oscanyan clearly do recognize

that the values they attribute to philosophy attach to a "language" view of
it. So do the other pioneers in this field.[18] I warn against an Oakeshottian
approach not as a present danger but as a future one—as a danger once
philosophy has become an accepted part of the elementary and secondary
school curriculum.

The manner of thinking that is philosophy has many facets. One of its
most important is questioning, in particular questioning what in daily life
and in the sciences and humanities is normally taken for granted. Such
questioning is central to openmindedness. Yet we must not assume that
children will learn to ask fundamental questions about received customs,
institutions, and doctrines when philosophical questioning is stressed in the
classroom. If children are not encouraged to question the socio-political
background of thought and action, they will take it for granted even while
learning to ask what is truth, beauty, and knowledge.

In *Philosophy in the Classroom* Lipman, Sharp, and Oscanyan stress the
question-raising aspect of philosophical thinking; indeed, they go so far as
to suggest that philosophy and children are made for one another because
both are forever asking questions.[19] In their chapter on moral education,
moreover, they speak of equipping children to think for themselves "so that
they can creatively renew the society in which they live when the situation
demands it . . . ."[20] It would seem that they endorse an education for
openmindedness as well as for autonomy and conceive of philosophy as
contributing to both. Yet in Lipman's novels, *Harry Stottlemeier's Discovery* and *Lisa*, the vehicles through which they would have us teach philosophy to children, fundamental social and political questioning seldom,
if ever, occurs.[21] Harry Stottlemeier corrects his neighbor's logic when she
tells his mother that since Mrs. Bates talks about helping the poor and all
those radicals keep saying we ought to help the poor, Mrs. Bates is a
radical, but neither he nor his mother questions the institution of poverty.[22] Harry and his friends complain about school and have a fascinating discussion about the purpose of education, but no one questions
schooling itself.[23] The newspaper for which Lisa's father works folds and
that very night he dies of a heart attack. Lisa and her friend discuss death,
but they never question the institutions of capitalism and sexism that make
the loss of a job so devastating for a man.[24]

The most dramatic episode in *Harry* concerns a boy who on religious
grounds refuses to salute the flag in school.[25] Again the children have a
fascinating discussion, this time about whether or not the boy should be
forced to salute the flag. No one, however, questions the practice of salut-

ing the flag and its underlying nationalism; no one asks if the school principal or the state has a right to dictate behavior in this way; no one asks if disobedience to laws or rules is ever justified.

Lisa contains an even more telling episode.[26] The older brother of Harry's black classmate Luther mentions that although he does his job as well as everyone else, they get promoted and he does not. Harry suggests that he find a lawyer because there must be *some* law the boss is breaking, but Luther and the brother demur on the grounds that to do so would be asking for trouble. Not one of the three boys raises serious questions about the institution of racial discrimination or the power relationship between a boss and a worker. Instead Luther's brother says, "Let me tell you something. *I* decide what's right for me, and I hope Luther here'll have the good sense to decide what's right for him. Nobody can tell me what girls to go with, or what job to choose, or what motorcycles to buy, or what magazines to read . . . ."[27] He does not realize—and neither do Harry and Luther and neither will the junior high school readers of the novel—that in failing to question and think critically about the socio-political background of action, he is removing it from the sphere of autonomous action even while extolling individual autonomy.

Unlike most disciplines, philosophy deals not just in what is, but in what could and should be. Thus the consideration of alternatives is another important facet of philosophical thinking, one that is stressed by Lipman, Sharp, and Oscanyan. Now the consideration of alternatives is central to openmindedness. Yet once again we should not take things for granted. We should not suppose that when children are encouraged by a philosophy program to construct alternatives, they will automatically do so in relation to established customs, institutions, and doctrines. As long as the socio-political background of action is ignored—as in effect it is in both *Harry* and *Lisa*—children will no more entertain alternatives to it than they will raise questions about it. Asking questions and envisioning alternatives are skills that require practice. The authors of *Philosophy in the Classroom* realize this. What they perhaps do not realize is that the contexts in which practice is provided really do matter: skills such as these can no doubt be *acquired* through practice in a limited range of contexts, but once acquired it is highly unlikely that they will be *exercised* in contexts in which they were not practiced, let alone in contexts to which the skills were always made to seem inapplicable.

Openmindedness involves not just questioning received customs, institutions, and doctrines and entertaining alternatives to them but also critically examining both the received and the unfamiliar. Since reasoned criticism is a central aspect of philosophical thinking, it is not surprising to find Lipman, Sharp, and Oscanyan stressing it, or to discover that Harry and Lisa and their friends frequently engage in it. Still, acquiring the skills of reasoned criticism is one thing and applying those skills in the social and political domain is quite another. Too many philosophers, who reveal themselves to be masters of reasoned criticism when the topic is the existence of material objects or the problem of evil, do not even think to use their skills in relation to basic social and political institutions and practices. An education for openmindedness must provide practice not just in reasoned criticism—or, if you will, critical thinking—but in *social* criticism. Such practice is not provided by *Harry* and *Lisa*. The fictional children carry on philosophical discussions in the way it is hoped the real children will. If the characters in these novels are indeed intended as role models for the children who read them, it is significant that the fictional children never do engage in social criticism.

6. The Limits of Philosophy

I cite *Philosophy in the Classroom* and Lipman's novels *Harry Stottlemeier's Discovery* and *Lisa* here because when taken together they constitute a major, systematic effort in the field of philosophy for children—one I greatly admire. My criticism of the program is one with my criticism of other programs that hope to foster autonomy while at the same time ignoring the socio-political background of action—it carries with its education for thinking for oneself a social and political education in uncritical conservatism. To be sure, that program is less ostrichlike concerning social and political issues than many others which make autonomy their goal: episodes involving racial and sex discrimination do occur in *Harry* and *Lisa*. However, these issues are handled in ways that tend to obscure the fact that they are social and political. I mentioned above that when Luther's older brother intimates that he as encountered racial discrimination at work, the boys evade the topic. Similarly when Lisa, who has joined a ball game with the boys, is denied her turn at bat, the children do not forthrightly discuss the issue of sexism; rather, they latch onto the more abstract issue of the distinction between the notions of 'fair' and 'right'.[28] I have the feeling that in so doing the children in the novels reflect the behavior of real life philosophers, but this does not change the nature of the social and political education that the young people who read *Harry* and *Lisa* will receive.

The kind of social and political education that should accompany education for autonomy is one that harnesses thinking for oneself to social criticism and this is something *Harry* and *Lisa* do not provide their readers. An education for social criticism is not an education for nihilism. An accomplished social critic seeks out the good as well as the bad in customs, institutions, and doctrines and is constructive, not merely negative. When children are taught to be social critics, we should not expect them to accept our social order unthinkingly, but we should not fear that they will destroy it. But of course the kind of social and political education children should receive is not one in social criticism alone. In openmindedness, social criticism combines with the consideration of a wide range of alternatives and with sympathetic understanding of both the familiar and the unfamiliar. Moreover, openmindedness must itself be combined with a sense of justice.

Justice has traditionally been an object of philosophical thinking and inquiry, and the literature of philosophy has significant things to say about it. But the study of philosophy, whether as "language" or as "literature," will not instill a sense of justice in children any more than it will instill benevolent or aesthetic sensibility. To learn to recognize injustice, it is not enough to read and talk about it in the abstract. We must be confronted with it. I do not mean that we will not recognize injustice unless we experience it ourselves, but rather that we must be introduced to concrete instances of it whether through firsthand experience or through literature, history, journalism, and the like. Similarly, to come to feel strongly about injustice, a theoretical study of it will not do. Immediate, vivid experience is needed. That experience can be vicarious; what matters is that it engage the emotions.

Philosophy as a "language" has a significant contribution to make to the kind of social and political education children should have, but we must not glorify the power of philosophy. Under the right conditions its study can help children acquire skills of social criticism, but social criticism requires a grasp of social facts and theories that are beyond the province of philosophy. Its study can also encourage children to consider alternatives, but to envision plausible alternatives to received customs, institutions, and doctrines, a grasp of those which in other times and places have constituted the established order is demanded, so that once again the boundaries of philosophy must be exceeded. Even the questioning of things normally taken for granted requires the educator to move beyond philosophy, for in order to ask worthwhile questions, some knowledge of received customs, institutions, and doctrines is necessary.

Philosophy is an unusual discipline in that its manner of thinking is so generally applicable and its substantive concerns are so varied. But there are some aspects of social and political education that no discipline can provide, and other aspects that can be provided only by disciplines other than philosophy. In this respect, social and political education is no different from moral education. There is a touching episode in *Lisa* in which Lisa's friend consoles her after the death of her father.[29] Consolation is part of moral education, but philosophy as a "language" or a "literature" has little to contribute to it. To do justice to moral or to social and political education, we must be prepared to go beyond philosophy.

Purists will object: philosophy for children must maintain the integrity of the discipline of philosophy, they will say. But the purist's objection must be overruled, for its conception of philosophy for children is scarcely more palatable than an Oakeshottian one. To extrapolate from a disciplinary conception of other school subjects,[30] a disciplinary conception of philosophy for children will view philosophy as a "language" but will place heavy emphasis on philosophy as a "literature" as well. Drill, memorization, and rote learning will be rejected, but the learning, which is to be done with understanding, will be the learning of the structure of philosophy: the basic ideas of the discipline, its fundamental concepts and ways of thinking will be the objects of learning. Presumably, mastery of the discipline will enable students to understand themselves and the world, but such understanding will be expected to take care of itself. The teacher of philosophy must concentrate on transmitting a grasp of the discipline of philosophy, not that discipline's applications.

A disciplinary conception of philosophy for children would have us teach philosophy for itself, not for its contributions to social and political education, not for its contributions to moral education, not even for its contributions to critical thinking. It shares with an Oakeshottian conception the untenable assumption that children have nothing better to do than accumulate knowledge that may some day have application in their own lives, although they may never realize it because its applications are not made known to them. Truly, the integrity of the discipline of philosophy should not be of prime concern when philosophy is taught to children. Rather we should view the discipline of philosophy as a resource from which we select those aspects of philosophical thinking that can contribute, albeit in a limited way, to the social and political and moral education of children.

NOTES

1. Stanley Milgram, *Obedience to Authority* (New York: Harper & Row, 1974).
2. See, for example, the original publication dates of the selections reprinted in Ronald and Beatrice Gross, eds., *Radical School Reform* (New York: Simon & Schuster, 1969).
3. The discussion which follows borrows from Kurt Baier, "Moral Autonomy as an Aim of Moral Education" in Glenn Langford and D. J. O'Connor, eds., *New Essays in the Philosophy of Education* (London: Routledge & Kegan Paul, 1973), pp. 96–114, without adopting Baier's conclusions.
4. On this last point see R. F. Dearden, "Autonomy and Education" in R. F. Dearden, P. H. Hirst and R. S. Peters, eds., *Education and Reason* (London: Routledge & Kegan Paul, 1975), pp. 58–75.
5. See, for example, *First Things and the Adolescent Experience*, Guidance Associates, Pleasantville, N.Y. See also Clyde Evans, "Facing Up to Values," *Teacher*, December, 1974.
6. Joseph Featherstone, "The British Infant Schools" in Gross and Gross, *Radical School Reform*, pp. 195–205; Charles H. Rathbone, ed., *Open Education* (New York: Citation Press, 1971); Ewald B. Nyquist and Gene R. Hawes, eds., *Open Education* (New York: Bantam Books, 1972); Charles E. Silberman, ed., *The Open Classroom Reader* (New York: Vintage Books, 1973).
7. Such idealization is not an essential characteristic of open classrooms, however. The activities children engage in could be relatively uncensored or, if censored from the standpoint of participation in them, children could still be shown them in uncensored form.
8. John Stuart Mill, *On Liberty* (Indianapolis: The Library of Liberal Arts, 1956).
9. David Hawkins' phrase. See his "Messing About in Science," *Science and Children*, February 1965.
10. Mill, *On Liberty*, p. 128.
11. Ibid., p. 129.
12. And with benevolence too.
13. It may also have been naïve of Mill to suppose that an education in "facts and positive science exclusively," even if possible, would be value-free.
14. Gene I. Maeroff, "The Liberal Arts Degree and Its Real Value," *The New York Times*, Sunday, June 12, 1977, p. 9E.
15. Michael Oakeshott, "The Study of 'Politics' in a University," in Jane R. Martin, ed., *Readings in the Philosophy of Education: A Study of Curriculum* (Boston: Allyn & Bacon, 1970), pp. 39–64. Oakeshott does not discuss philosophy for children. The views on that topic that I attribute to him here follow from his general remarks.
16. Matthew Lipman, Ann Margaret Sharp, and Frederick S. Oscanyan, *Philosophy in the Classroom* (Upper Montclair, N.J.: The Institute for the Advancement of Philosophy for Children, 1977).
17. Or perhaps as "languages." Note that when philosophy for children is viewed as a "language" it should not be assumed that what has been said in the "language" of philosophy must be ignored, that children cannot be introduced to great works of philosophy or to standard philosophical doctrines. It does mean, however, that those works and doctrines will be revealed for what they are, namely products of a particular way of thinking, and that they will be introduced less for themselves than for the illumination they throw on philosophy as a "language" and on the problems with which that "language" grapples. A philosophy as "language" approach does not mean either that a university education in philosophy must

view philosophy as a "literature." Oakeshott seems to assume that each kind of education takes a unique view of its subjects, but this need not be so. If philosophy for children is viewed as a "language," philosophy in the university can be viewed as a "language" or a "literature" or both.

18. For example, Gareth B. Matthews, "On Talking Philosophy with Children," *Royal Institute of Philosophy* Lecture, November 28, 1975; Clyde Evans, reprinted in Chapters 5 and 11, as well as in his *Critical Thinking and Reasoning: A Handbook for Teachers* (Albany: University of the State of New York, 1976), Introduction.

19. *Philosophy in the Classroom*, p. 7.

20. Ibid., p. 142.

21. Matthew Lipman, *Harry Stottlemeier's Discovery* (Upper Montclair, N.J.: The Institute for the Advancement of Philosophy for Children, Rev. Ed., 1974); *Lisa* (Upper Montclair, N.J.: The Institute for the Advancement of Philosophy for Children, 1976).

22. Lipman, *Harry Stottlemeier's Discovery*, p. 4.

23. Ibid., pp. 21–25. This episode is cited by Lipman, Sharp, and Oscanyan, *Philosophy in the Classroom*, p. 142, as an instance in which criticism initiates philosophical discussion. My point, however, is that the discussion the children in *Harry* have falls short of achieving the fundamental questioning for which philosophy is known.

24. Lipman, *Lisa*, pp. 98–100.

25. Lipman, *Harry Stottlemeier's Discovery*, chaps. 9, 10.

26. Lipman, *Lisa*, pp. 23–25.

27. Ibid., p. 24.

28. Ibid., pp. 19–23.

29. Ibid., pp. 98–100.

30. See, for example, Jerome S. Bruner, *The Process of Education* (Cambridge, Mass.: Harvard University Press, 1961); R. F. Dearden, *The Philosophy of Primary Education* (London: Routledge & Kegan Paul, 1968); see Jane R. Martin, "The Disciplines and the Curriculum" in *Readings in the Philosophy of Education: A Study of Curriculum*, pp. 65–86, for a critique of this view.

᠊ᢒ§ LOUIS I. KATZNER

Bowling Green University

Social Philosophy and Children

Whatever else we may be, human beings are social animals. We live and work together, and our lives are at least in part defined by the myriad of relationships we have with others. Social philosophy involves philosophically scrutinizing the issues that arise because we are social beings. First and foremost, these are issues about how we should live—that is, issues of value. The basic question is: What rules, procedures, and so forth, should govern the interaction between us? To answer this question (and the numerous questions it spawns) involves examining the fundamental concepts of rights, sovereignty, justice, the individual, society, and freedom. In other words, the goal of social philosophy is to develop a rational way of dealing with the issues and problems that emerge from the fact that human beings live in society. The methodology used in pursuit of this goal involves analyzing both the most basic concepts of social living and the relationships between them.

Let us assume that social philosophy is a worthwhile enterprise, one that merits the expenditure of time and energy. But why, one might ask, social philosophy *for children?* Although the value of social philosophy *about children* (the philosophical scrutiny of the social relationships that pervade the lives of children) follows directly from the importance of social philosophy and children's status as human beings, the value of social philosophy for children does not. Why indeed should children engage in philosophical scrutiny of social issues themselves? The question requires further examination.

One possible answer is that if children are going to be introduced to philosophy, social philosophy is an ideal starting point. This is because the problems and issues of social philosophy pervade the child's life; they are issues that are both real and will not go away. Every child is concerned with questions such as: (1) Why can adults do whatever they want but I cannot? (2) How come my older brothers and sisters get all sorts of privileges that I do not? (3) Why is it that whenever my teacher and I have a disagreement I end up getting punished? (4) Why are people allowed to be so cruel to animals? And so on. All of these questions raise very fundamental issues of social philosophy.

Consider the difference between these kinds of philosophical issues and some others—for instance, the problem of other minds. I do not doubt for a moment that many children can really be turned on to the problem of other minds. Presented in the proper way, this issue both challenges the intellect and stimulates the imagination in all sorts of directions. Nor do I doubt that no matter how well the issue is introduced, there will be a significant number of children who will take a "Ho-hum, who cares?" attitude to it. This is because the problem of other minds is remote from their lives.

The problems of social philosophy, on the other hand, when raised in the context of the day-to-day problems that children have in living, will seldom if ever elicit the "Ho-hum" response. Even those youngsters who are slow to accept intellectual challenges or unwilling to use their imaginations will usually rise to the occasion. This is because they have a real stake in the issues being raised. It really matters to children that their siblings get privileges that they do not. Those who are eager to respond to challenges to their intellect and imagination may well achieve a philosophically more sophisticated appreciation of the issues being raised, but, on the other hand, children are more likely to accept such challenges when they really care about the issue at hand.

Unfortunately, the same features of social philosophy that make it an ideal area for introducing children to philosophy—its reality and immediacy—also create problems for both the youngsters and their mentors. Force-feeding social philosophy to youngsters before they are ready for it can do harm. Forcing children to question assumptions that they are not ready to question or undermining beliefs so as to leave youngsters with nothing to believe in can be damaging both to their intellectual and emotional development. It can be argued that it is precisely because children find the issues of social philosophy to be real and immediate that those issues should be for adults only.

It seems to me that there are two responses to this argument. First, no matter how damaging social philosophy may be to the intellectual and emotional development of children, it cannot be any worse than some of the things already being done to them. I find it hard to imagine that anything can be more damaging to children's development than the ways in which we have woven racism and sexism into our public institutions, including the schools themselves. This does not mean that social philosophy for children is justified even if it is damaging to their intellectual and emotional development. It merely indicates that (1) what is and is not damaging is often both complicated and unclear and (2) if we are really concerned about the intellectual and emotional development of our children, we should give current practices the same critical examination as we do new proposals.

The other difficulty with the argument is that the problems cited are not unique to social philosophy. They arise in other areas as well. Take history, for example. There are undoubtedly some youngsters who are not ready to face the gory reality of war, the inhumanity of slavery, or the bold realities of political in-fighting. Does this mean that we should not teach about war, slavery, and politics? Of course not! Does it mean that we should distort reality by presenting these things in an antiseptic way that would shield youngsters from the harsh realities of life? I hope not! After all, it would be a strange American history course that paid no attention to war, slavery, and politics. The subject matter requires that these things be addressed, the developmental needs of youngsters notwithstanding. The most hat can be done, if American history is going to be taught, is to be sensitive and supportive to the needs of those youngsters who find it unsettling.

But social philosophy has no set ground that must be covered. The philosopher's concern is to identify and examine the underlying assumptions of our beliefs. The basic tenet in this undertaking is that no assumptions are sacred. But this does not mean that one is not doing philosophy unless *all* the assumptions that underlie a given belief or claim are identified and carefully examined. Only the most rigorous philosophical investigations do this. Philosophizing is taking place even when only some of the assumptions are identified and only some of those are critically examined.

This suggests that in social philosophy one can usually sidestep issues that students are not ready for without compromising the nature of the beast. Suppose it becomes clear that some youngsters base some of their beliefs about society on what they take to be the revealed word of God; and they are simply not ready intellectually or emotionally to question the existence of God. This in no way precludes having those youngsters address their beliefs about society philosophically. Helping them to see how their beliefs rest on assumptions about God, and that these assumptions are not shared by everyone, is philosophical progress in itself. If the group is ready to question the existence of God, so be it. If they are not, encourage them to think about other arguments that could be given for their beliefs. This is often of more value philosophically than getting embroiled in a discussion of whether God exists and, if so, exactly what God has commanded us to do (especially with people who are not ready to consider such things).

In sum, the risk presented to the intellectual and emotional development of children by social philosophy would seem to be no greater than that presented by the study of more common things such as history. Moreover, because of the kind of discipline it is, social philosophy permits the risks to be minimized. The mentor who listens to children and is sensitive to the intellectual and emotional needs expressed through what they say can do much to guide the discussion in philosophically fruitful directions without either putting the youngsters at risk or compromising the nature of philosophy. On the other hand, the mentor who insists that certain issues must be discussed and certain beliefs must be challenged, no matter what, may well produce some undesirable consequences for the children's intellectual and emotional development.

The introduction of social philosophy for children may also create risks for the mentors in a way that some of the more antiseptic areas of philosophy may not, and other disciplines do not. Any time a group of youngsters imbued with the philosophical spirit is encouraged to examine the social dimensions of their lives, they are bound to ask questions such as: (1) Why are we required to go to school? (2) Why don't we have a say in determining what goes on at school? (3) Do adults really know what is best for us? In short, they are bound to raise the issue of children's rights in many of its various forms.

This is because, to a large extent, such issues are what social philosophy is all about. This is not true of history, nor of the more antiseptic areas of philosophy. Consider once again the problem of other minds. Although it is true that once one has stimulated the intellects and imaginations of youngsters by introducing this problem, they may very well insist upon addressing what is of concern to them—social issues. But this is a derivative result rather than an immediate one. In itself, the problem of other minds does not hold the same threat to mentors as that posed by social philosophy.

The burden this places on the children's mentor is clear. Although the philosophical spirit is not compromised when mentors skillfully steer a discussion away from issues that children are not ready to discuss, it is indeed compromised when they refuse to discuss issues that children want to examine—when, for example, an exasperated mentor answers "Because that's the way it is!" or "Because I say so!" to the persistent question, "How come you have the right to tell me what to do?" Because of the question it begs, this response betrays the "no holds barred" nature of philosophy. In effect, it tells youngsters, "It is all right to question some things but not others."

To see this more graphically, imagine a teacher who introduces his or her students to social philosophy. As the youngsters get the hang of what is going on, troublesome questions arise: (1) Why can't we decide what goes on in school? (2) Why shouldn't we evaluate the teachers the way they evaluate us? (3) Why do we get grades? And so on. It is the skillful teacher indeed who can help the students to tease out the assumptions of the various answers that can be given to their questions and to see what can be said for and against them. Failure to do this effectively will simply reinforce the antischool feelings that many youngsters have and contribute to the erosion of the teacher's effectiveness. On the other hand, doing it effectively will help many students gain a better understanding of the value of going to school.

Thus we see that although social philosophy is an ideal point of entry for children into the world of philosophy, there are risks involved. Moreover, the argument presented so far has two important defects. First, the argument for social philosophy for children has been based upon the assumed desirability of philosophy for children. Second, the advantages of social philosophy for children cited so far are at least in part offset by the risks involved. The argument needs to be made more rigorous.

To this end, let us examine three social concepts that are constantly recurring themes of the child's life: justice or fairness, evaluation, and authority. Careful examination of these concepts will reveal both how central they are to youngsters' lives and what can be gained by having children explore them philosophically.

There is no doubt that youngsters are concerned with justice or fairness. This concern is most often voiced in the plaintive cry, "That's not fair!" Let us begin by sketching a specific situation in which this cry might be heard, and then analyze the different things it might mean.

Imagine a particularly rough day at school. The children have been very antsy. Note passing has reached a fever pitch, and it appears that a spitball war is about to break out. The teacher, in a last ditch effort to preserve the slightest semblance of order, reacts to the firing of the first spitball with a vengence. "Okay, that's it. There will be no recess today—for anyone." The class groans. Many of the youngsters mutter, "That's not fair!" and you can bet that the teacher's unfairness will be one of the major topics of conversation for the remainder of the week.

When the youngsters in the class say, "That's not fair!" they mean several different things. Some may mean that they do not like the teacher's action. They like recess and don't want to miss it. In other words, when anything happens that they do not like, it's unfair. Others may have in mind the idea that the teacher should not punish innocent people. It's one thing to require the culprit to miss recess: after all, he or she did something wrong. But to make the people who did not throw spitballs miss recess— that is just not fair. Still others may mean that throwing spitballs is not the kind of thing they should have to miss recess for. Spitballing is too minor an offense to warrant such a drastic measure. Perhaps cussing out the teacher would justify it. But a mere spitball, never!

The teacher, on the other hand, would have very different things running through her mind. She might be thinking that the class had it coming. They had been antsy and inattentive all day, and she was just giving them what they deserved. Or she might be regretting that she acted unfairly while feeling that she had to do something to quell the incipient revolution. Sometimes justice must be sacrificed to the cause of classroom management. Or she might not be thinking of self-justification at all. She might simply be feeling better for having vented her rage.

All of this is merely to set the stage. It suggests that children (and teachers) do have a sense of justice and that issues of justice arise daily in their lives. The purpose of paying philosophical attention to the concept of justice is to clarify and refine this sense of justice. It is to help the children to see what justice is and what it is not, what can be said in its name and what cannot.

The first thing to notice is that the youngsters who call unfair anything they do not like do not have a fully developed sense of justice or fairness. This is because fairness is at heart a relational notion—one is treated fairly or unfairly only insofar as the way one is treated is being compared with the way others are treated. This is not to say that these youngsters do not have a legitimate gripe; maybe they do and maybe they don't. It merely is misleading to express that gripe in terms of fairness. The issue of justice or fairness arises only if they claim that they are being treated wrongly *in relation to how others are being treated.*

Those who understand the unfairness of the teacher's action to lie in the punishment of the innocent do have a full-blown concept of fairness. Their basic idea is that people should be treated similarly or differently depending upon the relevant differences between them. If there are no relevant differences, people should be treated the same; and if there are relevant differences they should be treated in direct proportion to them. This is what is called the formal principle of justice—treat equals equally and treat those who are different in direct proportion to the differences between them. This formal principle is the bare bones of the concept of justice—it is what all concepts of justice have in common. However, it does not take us very far until we specify the basis of equality—what is relevant to considerations of justice and what is not.

In other words, the bigot who takes race as the basis of equality and inequality and then in a fully consistent manner treats all blacks one way (as unworthy of respect) and all whites another (as worthy of respect) is acting in a *formally* just way. The dispute with such an individual is not over the formal dimensions of justice but rather over the view that race is relevant to the way human beings should be treated. In contrast, the teacher who has a rule that all students who fail to do their homework must make up the work during recess but then exempts a few select individuals is acting in a *formally* unjust way. This is because the teacher asserts that doing or not doing one's homework is relevant to having recess but then is inconsistent in the application of this rule.

The claim of those who object to punishing the innocent members of the class is that what is relevant to punishment is being guilty—that those who are guilty may deserve punishment whereas those who are innocent certainly are not. Their concern is not simply with the teacher's failure to treat equals equally. They believe that the teacher has failed to take into account a relevant difference. The teacher has treated all students the same whereas they believe that all innocent students should be treated one way and all guilty ones another. The discussion in this case would have to focus on the question of what is relevant to punishing people.

The last group of students, those who feel that missing recess is too extreme a response to the throwing of spitballs, are not questioning the appropriateness of treating both innocent and guilty students in the same way. Their concern is that the punishment does not fit the crime. They allow that throwing spitballs may warrant a reaction from the teacher that not throwing spitballs does not, that there is a relevant difference between the two modes of behavior. However, the response of cancelling recess is out of proportion to the severity of the behavior. At issue in this race is the relative severity of throwing spitballs and missing recess respectively.

The teacher's view of the situation calls attention to other aspects of the concept of justice. If the teacher thinks she has given her students what they deserve for being antsy and inattentive all day, then she perceives the situation very differently from the way her students do. They think that recess has been cancelled because of the spitball incident. In the teacher's mind, the spitball incident, although the *occasion* of her action, is not what *justifies* it. From this perspective the issue must be recast to include the antsiness and lack of attention of the students and whether or not this justifies cancelling recess.

Viewed from the second perspective the teacher may bring to the situation, things get even more interesting. The teacher may acknowledge that she has acted unfairly or unjustly but justify this by appealing to the more important goal of classroom management. At issue here is not the unfairness of what the teacher has done but whether or not unfairness can be justified by other ends. Thus what needs to be discussed is the relative importance of classroom management and fairness, and whether there are ways to achieve the former without sacrificing the latter.

Notice what has happened. We began with a seemingly simple situation and, through clarification and refinement that comes from philosophical probing, have come to see that it is really not so simple after all. We have seen that the claim of unfairness may mean several things and that, depending on which of these things are meant, different issues are being raised. Moreover, it should be clear that people who raise the different issues generated by our hypothetical situation will talk right past each other unless they come to see what each other means by 'fair'. It is only at this point that real communication can begin and rational resolution of the dispute becomes possible.

We have also seen that claims of justice or fairness involve, when unpacked, the giving of reasons, the citation and justification of relevant similarities and differences. Thus philosophical discussions of justice exemplify the importance of reason giving in the social dimensions of our lives. They also serve as a paradigm of rational discourse, helping to demonstrate the importance of insisting that reasons be given for the assertions one makes.

What happens if the need for reason giving is not stressed in this way? Two things. First, very often when reasons are not provided, children will supply their own, much to the misfortune of everyone involved. Second, the failure to stress the value of reason giving, especially in the area of social concerns, renders children easy prey to the twin evils of dogmatism and skepticism. Let us consider each of these problems in turn.

All of us are familiar with the way that children (and many adults, for that matter) supply their own reasons when none are provided. This occurs with alarming regularity when children are evaluated. Be it their eating habits, their school work, their art work, or what have you, youngsters are constantly being evaluated by adults. When the reasons for these evaluations (the standards or criteria being used) are not provided in a way that those evaluated can understand, they supply their own account of what is happening—an account usually aimed at preserving their own self-respect rather than at bringing out what the evaluator has in mind.

An excellent example of this is the giving of grades. When children's school work is evaluated below their expectations, they often say, "Well I guess I didn't give the teacher what he wanted." If this simply means, "I didn't do what the teacher asked me to do," there is no problem. But more often it means, "I did what I was asked to do but the teacher must have had a *hidden agenda* that I failed to meet." This is unfortunate. Even more unfortunate, however, is the reaction: "I got a bad grade. It must be that the teacher does not like me." It is easy to see how children, in the absence of an intelligible explanation of a low grade, can reach this conclusion.

They think they have done well. No one *shows* them that they have not. Hence it must be that the teacher has something against them.

Of course, this conclusion does not follow. But the point is that as long as students think it does, or as long as they think that they are being graded on the basis of hidden agendas, they will not benefit from the grades they get. They will spend their time and energy either trying to psyche out hidden agendas or working at being liked by their teacher. In either case, they will fail to get the message that low grades should convey—that they need to work harder at learning the things they are being evaluated on.

How can this misunderstanding be avoided? It would be silly to say that social philosophy for children is a cure-all, but it is at least a step (if not a long stride) in the right direction. Evaluation is both a prevailing concern of youngsters and an important issue of social philosophy. Youngsters who have been turned on to social issues philosophically are bound to find themselves wondering whether some evaluations can be said to be better than others. They will necessarily come face to face with the question, What is the basis for evaluations? They will come to see that evaluations should be based upon criteria, and that the test of any evaluation is the adequacy of the criteria on which it is based. They will also see that although it is often difficult to choose between competing criteria, some, such as basing grades upon one's like or dislike of a person, are totally unacceptable.

This will not totally allay children's fears, but it should serve to point them in the right direction. Coupled with the teacher's giving reasons for the grades handed out, it should help focus the youngsters' attention on the criteria being used rather than on supposed hidden agendas or the likes and dislikes of the teacher. It will even lead the more sophisticated students to question the adequacy of the criteria. Whatever problems this may create for the teacher, and there are sure to be some, it is a far better consequence than having students totally misunderstand the nature of evaluation and as a result seek to improve their grades by doing things that in no way will improve how much they learn.

The second unfortunate consequence of the failure to demonstrate to children the importance of reason giving is that it renders them easy prey to the twin evils of dogmatism and skepticism. This problem is often manifested in the thinking of adults when they attempt to deal with social issues. As we have seen, these are open issues—they do not have incontrovertibly correct solutions.

Many find this kind of uncertainty unsettling. When faced with it, some turn to dogmatism. They base their social judgments on principles of faith that they refuse to question. One possibility is to base them on a religious creed. Another is to base them on faith in the judgments of another (for example, the ruler is always right) or others (the majority is always right). This renders social judgments empirically verifiable. If, one assumes that the majority is always right, then the way to resolve social issues is simply to take a poll.

Another typical reaction to the ultimate uncertainty of social judgments is to flee in the opposite direction. Rather than assuming that someone (or something) else is the unquestionable judge of correctness, some reserve this position for each individual. This produces the "It's all a matter of opinion" syndrome. Since there are no incontrovertibly right answers, people can believe *whatever* they want. Each person defines what is correct for himself or herself.

Both of these reactions to the open nature of philosophical issues are antithetical to the philosophical spirit. The turn to dogmatism is unacceptable because it rejects one of the fundamental tenets of the philosophical perspective, that all assumptions are open to question. The philosopher recognizes that nothing can be said or done without making assumptions, yet at the same time insists that no assumptions are sacred. Indeed, what tends to separate philosophy from other disciplines is that while the latter make assumptions and never look back, the former aims at teasing out and critically assessing the underlying assumptions.

The turn to skepticism is equally unacceptable, albeit for different reasons. It does not follow that because there are no incontrovertibly right answers, individuals can believe whatever they please. An opinion that contains a contradiction must be rejected. An opinion that has some reasons offered in support of it (albeit not incontrovertible ones) must be accepted over an opinion merely asserted *ad hoc*. This is not to deny the possibility that the latter may turn out to be the correct answer after all (just as it turned out that the sun rather than the earth is the center of our solar system.) But the rules of rational thought require that we decide between competing ideas on the basis of the reasons given in support of them. Nor is it to deny that some competing opinions may end up in a dead heat—that what can be said for and against each of them balances out and so there is no way of choosing between them. It is only to say that some opinions are better than others and what distinguishes the more acceptable from the less acceptable is the body of reasons marshalled for and against them.

This problem most clearly manifests itself in the lives of children in the guise of what we call the authority syndrome. The conflict between their own freedom and the authority of others is perhaps the most dominant theme of a child's life. For the most part it is the adult (parent, teacher, policeman) who calls the shots and it is the child who toes the line. Even when it comes to children's relationships with their peers, the spectre of adult authority is never far removed. There is almost always someone around to break up a fight or veto the deal—in short, to exercise authority.

This authority syndrome is not limited to children's behavior. It pervades their entire lives. This is in part because children learn many things before they are capable of understanding (or at least before we are capable of teaching them) the whys of those things. Hence it is commonplace for a child to answer "Because I read it in a book' or "Because the dictionary says so" when asked Why? It is only the more sophisticated children who realize that reading something in a book does not make it so, that things should be written because they are so. This is not meant to suggest that children lack philosophical curiosity. Indeed, quite to the contrary, if anything they have too much—witness the parent who, at wits' end because of the onslaught of Whys from his or her child, finally voices an exasperated "Because I say so!" in order to shut off the questions. The point is that the authority syndrome plays an important role in every aspect of the child's life. Indeed one of the most important functions of education is to enable the youngster to distinguish appropriate from inappropriate bases of authority.

This can readily be seen by looking at science education. Its goal is not only to get youngsters to understand the scientific facts that govern our lives but also to help them understand the method by which these facts are discovered. Even if they do not replicate the experiments whose results are reported in their science books, they should know that the truth of these facts depends on such experiments and not on the author's say-so. Once children come to understand this, they perceive the book, the discipline, and the teacher in a very different light.

But what happens if youngsters fail to understand it? Either they fall into the dogmatism of "It's true because so-and-so says so" or else, when faced with the spectre of conflicting authorities, they resort to the skepticism of "It's all a matter of opinion". Moreover, many children who place their faith in an authority fall directly into skepticism whenever that faith is shaken. This is not surprising when one realizes that the dogmatist and skeptic share a lack of understanding of the real basis and nature of their beliefs.

Nowhere is this fall of authority more evident than in the child's relationship with his or her parents. Children, at least at a young age, think their parents are infallible. When they try to come to realize that this is not so, all hell breaks loose. Many slide directly from the dogmatism of viewing their parents as the source of incontrovertible truth to the skepticism of believing *whatever* they want. There is usually no room in their thinking for a middle ground—a ground where beliefs are based on reasons even though incontrovertible answers cannot be found. It is precisely this ground that philosophical deliberation illuminates, thus providing an alternative to the twin evils of dogmatism and skepticism.

The argument could go on. We could look at other social concepts—rights, autonomy, society, and the like—to see how children can benefit from examining them philosophically. But it is not necessary. We have already seen enough. Social philosophy is an ideal entry point for children into philosophy. There are risks involved—ones that can be greatly minimized by a skillful teacher. But the benefits that can accrue from having children scrutinize philosophically concepts such as justice, evaluation, and authority clearly justifies taking these risks.

❧ 7 ❧

CAN CHILDREN
VIEW SCIENCE
PHILOSOPHICALLY?

❧ MARTIN TAMNY

City College of New York

Children And The Philosophy of Science

The continuing revision of both our beliefs and the conceptual schemes in which we fit them is the chief element of the intellectual life of man. But it must be admitted that no matter how actively we may pursue the truth in our later years, the time of most profound and frequent change in our beliefs and schemes is the period of childhood. It is then that we proceed from the booming, buzzing madness of our initial perceptions to the so-called common-sense view of a world of causally connected physical objects.

The years of childhood are among the most studied periods of human life. Studies, however, have usually been a part of developmental psychology and thus have approached the problem from the specific standpoint of psychological theory. What I wish to do here is to examine the elements of that growth through the traditional notions of the philosophy of science and to ask whether we can view the child's intellectual growth as the utilization of a scientific method capable of encompassing the limited experience of the child.

To be more specific, I wish to investigate whether notions like hypothesis formation, testability, prediction, and the distinction between description and explanation are applicable to children in the same way they are applicable to the scientist and, further, whether children are or can be critically aware of these concepts themselves. In a sense, then, I will be asking whether the child has a "scientific" approach to the world. I hope that this will shed light on our conception of the intellectual life of the child as well as on the philosophy of science.

Prediction and Explanation

A scientific prediction is the description of some expected future event either on the basis of a generalization from past experience or as the logical consequence of some theory or law in conjunction with a set of initial conditions.

It is clear from the above that not only scientists make scientific predictions. It was claimed by David Hume that the psychological foundation of prediction—expectation—is to be found in our propensity to associate certain ideas that arise from constantly conjoined impressions. Thus the notion of prediction grows out of the psychological soil of expectation in childhood and intensifies as we continue to stock our mind with ideas.

It is a common experience with very young children that they evidently lose interest in an object the moment it is removed from their perceptual field. For the very young, out of sight is not only out of mind but apparently also out of existence. This infantile Berkelianism is best observed when one shows a child an object that arrests its attention; when the object is then placed behind one's back, the child suddenly shows a distinct lack of interest. With older, non-Berkelian infants there will be continued interest, usually manifested in an attempt to see the object behind one's back.

Perhaps our most primitive predictions are related to our early beliefs in the continued existence of unobserved objects. Such beliefs are more metaphysical than scientific, since unobserved objects are not things we observe, but empirical elements do enter into these beliefs. My belief in the continued existence of the fire in the hearth during my absence from the room is at least partially manifested in my expectation—my willingness to predict—that as much wood will have been consumed when I enter the room as would have been consumed had I never left it, and had I seen the fire burning throughout the interval.

Within these and other early expectations lies the constitution of the normal. The abnormal, the unusual, the anomaly *are* the unexpected. The unexpected can become one with our normal experience in two ways. The first is through experience itself. Children who are at first frightened by the moon's odd behavior in following them about, come to think of this as normal when they perceive that the moon always follows them. The second is through explanations that can incorporate the unusual into children's experience. This can be done by telling them something that would have led them to expect the occurrence had they only known it earlier.

When children become discontented with applying only the first way and use it instead as the ground on which to postulate a something that leads them to expect the occurrence of the "anomaly," they have begun to behave scientifically.

To begin is not, however, to finish, and not all hypothesis-makers are scientists. It is also necessary that the hypothesis be testable before we allow that its maker is proceeding scientifically. Does anything in childhood act as a pressure toward the formulation of *testable* hypothesis? I think not, unless it be competition with other children. Children dislike being wrong almost as much as do adults. The untestable hypothesis guarantees not being shown wrong, which is as good as being right to children and Popperians. When competing, however, the situation changes, for then being right is no better than someone else's being wrong. For comparisons to be meaningful, what is needed is testability.

It is questionable whether children are critically aware of the notions of hypothesis formation and testability, but to the degree that these concepts ground children's approach to the world it should be fairly easy to elicit them through philosophical discussion.

That at times considerations of these concepts do come to the fore among children is evidenced by the following conversation between my children, Mark and Tara.

Mark: That's my dime!

Tara: No, it's mine, give it to me!

Mark: Oh, yeah? What's the year on it?

Tara: I don't know.

Mark: See, I told you it wasn't yours.

Tara: I'll bet you don't know the dates on *your* money.

The requirements of evidence to substantiate a claim and the criteria that such evidence must meet are being discussed here and it is easy to see how much more might be elicited by someone trained in philosophical techniques.

Explanation and Description

What science explains is not phenomena but phenomena-as-described.

Any given occurrence or circumstance is susceptible to an indefinitely large number of descriptions. A particular science will seek to delimit such descriptions to those that are relevant to that science. Mechanics, for instance, utilizes concepts such as mass, position, and velocity, while excluding concepts like color, consciousness, and motive.

What does "relevant" mean in this context? I would suggest that it means that the concepts are just those that figure in the explanations provided by current theories. In the process of learning a given science, one is taught both what these relevant concepts are and how to apply them. In this way the language of description grows up out of the language of explanation. Science, then, does not explain phenomena in all their multifarious aspects but explains them only insofar as they are described within the language of description deemed appropriate to that science.

If this account is correct, we are confronted with the problem of determining which came first, the language of description or the language of explanation.

Since we cannot explain what we do not first pick out of our experience, and since such selection appears to be a linguistic process, the answer we seem forced to is that description comes first. But these descriptions are quickly modified as the explanations we offer begin to alter our view of the world.

Og and Charlie sit in their cave while flashes of light cross the sky and earth-shattering crashes force them to shout their descriptions of lightning and thunder to each other. Og suggests that this must be going on because the gods are angry and Charlie nods his head in assent. When a month later Charlie enters the cave in the midst of another thunderstorm and Og asks him what is happening outside, Charlie answers, "The gods are angry again." Charlie and Og are now using their explanatory concepts to describe, and presumably they are unaware of the change.

Children begin language acquisition as inventory-takers, learning which words go with which objects. The fact that the same name is applied to an object when it returns after a period of being unobserved confirms children in their early metaphysical theory regarding the spatio-temporal continuity of the objects of their perception. Indeed even these early descriptive terms may well be viewed as being the products of the concepts that we have even earlier begun to apply to explain the world.

Examples of descriptive revisions based on changes in our explanatory schemes are easy to come by. The animism of early childhood that leads us to describe all things as alive or dead, as feeling pain or not, and so on, gives way to the dualism that leads us to describe things as living or nonliving (not dead, but rather as never alive), as sentient or nonsentient.

That these childhood conceptual revisions and their attendant changes in our language of description take place is, I believe, widely accepted. What is in dispute is whether these changes are evolutionary or revolutionary. In considering this question, one must be careful to distinguish between evolutionary and revolutionary in the psychological and logical sense. I think that the work of Piaget has convinced most of us that there is an evolutionary psychological development shared by most children, but it has not been shown that the child's intellectual view of the world at one stage in his or her life logically follows from that of an earlier stage. In short, it is quite consistent that children's psychological development be evolutionary while at the same time their intellectual "development" consists of a series of conceptual revolutions. I cannot settle the question whether evolution or revolution wins the day here, any more than I can settle the question as it arises in the contemporary philosophy of science, but I can point to an item of *prima facia* evidence for the revolutionary approach. We seem unable as adults ever to make animistic explanations and descriptions plausible, despite our having once viewed the world that way. It is very much as if our conceptual revisions have altered our concepts to the point that we can never recapture our earlier world with any vivacity. This *prima facia* evidence for the revolutionary view may well be only that, but the evolutionist must at least take it into account.

The fact that children do, from time to time, change conceptual schemes much as scientists do, from time to time, change their theories does not mean that the grounds for doing so is the same in both cases. It is not at all clear that there are any rational grounds at work in children when they do so; in fact, it seems more likely that psycho-sociological factors are what cause them to change their schemes.[1] Science, on the other hand, has traditionally been thought of as *the* rational methodology and thus an area where changes are not made without *good* reasons. The good reasons traditionally offered for rejecting one theory and adopting another are the failure of the first to explain certain specific occurrences (this is often, though not always, thought of as disconfirmation) and the success of the second in dealing with those specific occurrences as well as a shared success in all other areas.

This traditional view is now, however, under attack from various quarters.[2] Historical arguments are usually adduced to show that the traditional view does not apply to actual cases of theory replacement, and it is usually maintained that a large number of nonrational (I carp at "irrational") factors often figure in such replacements. These nonrational features are usually claimed to be psycho-social in character—for example, peer pressures as exerted by scientific societies and their journals. On this view children are perhaps more than proto-scientists.

This is not to say, however, that children cannot become aware of what would or would not constitute rational grounds for theory replacements or even whether there can be such grounds. Indeed, the years when such conceptual shifts are a common element of our lives may well be the best time to be made aware of these problems as alive and trenchant issues.

Explanation and Theoretical Entities

A theoretical entity is an object that is in no way an item of our experience but whose supposed existence leads to the explanation of occurrences that do lie in the realm of our experience. Do children have recourse to theoretical entities in coming to terms with the world?

Theoretical entities are usually thought to be constitutive of the gross objects of our experience and to make those objects systematically different from their appearances. Thus positing that all gross objects are made up of a class of theoretical entities called atoms that we are told are mostly empty space, leads us to think of, say, a table, in a somewhat new way—one that departs significantly from our experience of the table.

Children learn very early to think of the world, or at least of items in it, as different from their experience of them. Very early in life the space of visual experience and the space of tactile experience becomes correlated, with the result that we distinguish apparent size from actual size. Thus at an early age we learn that it is the accepted view that objects do not grow in size as they approach us—they only appear to do so. Quite soon even the appearance of doing so ends. That the sun is likely to be quite a bit larger than the thumbnail on my outstretched hand is understood almost as soon as it is noted that they appear the same size. Just *how* much larger the sun is is perhaps never grasped. Children also learn the distorting effects of water quite early—the bent drinking straw precedes the bent oar. All of which is meant to show merely that children are not naïve realists; experience teaches very early that seeing is not always believing, but experience teaches us this without dissuading us from believing that seeing is still our primary source of knowledge.

It is to be noted, however, that as unnaïve about perception as children may be, their reality differs only in a piecemeal way from the way the world appears to them. There doesn't seem to be the systematic schism (spanned though it may be by bridge principles) between appearance and reality that characterizes modern science.

Indeed the child's world may be furnished with monsters, ghosts, and spirits of various kinds. Such concepts may even be invoked to explain certain occurrences, but they share with the imaginary friends of childhood a transitory existence that makes them at best a *deus ex machina* rather than something comparable to the theoretical entities of scientific explanation.

Objectivity

Scientific objectivity has often been analyzed as involving a kind of inter-subjectivity in which the views of any given scientist are to be compared with those of other scientists and to be left open to reexamination. Any results reported by a scientist that cannot be reproduced by colleagues are ignored. Science is thus a social enterprise that is dependent on a scientific community in an essential way. The possibility of such a community fulfilling its function of intersubjective testing is dependent on the ability of its members to communicate with one another. This in turn is possible only if a commonly understood terminology exists. Thus objectivity is dependent on the ability of the practitioners of science to agree on a set of commonly understood concepts. Communication is, however, far more complicated than the mere use of commonly agreed upon concepts. One must be able to talk about new things as well, and often one must use old terms in new ways to accomplish this. Making other people understand talk of new things is a complex activity involving a good deal of social sophistication, a sophistication that children apparently lack.

Robert M. Krauss of Columbia University and Sam Glucksberg of Princeton University conducted a series of experiments in which two subjects were each given a sheet of nonrepresentational but noncomplex figures.[3] The two subjects were placed on either side of a screen and the first was asked to describe the figures on his sheet to the second. The second subject's task was to identify on his sheet the figures being described. Adults found this an extremely easy task and scored perfectly. Children had great difficulty. In communicating about the figures, their descriptions were more personal and seemed to exhibit a lack of awareness of any possible difficulties the hearer might encounter. This was epitomized in an exchange between two four-year-olds. After the first child had finished his description, the second child, on the other side of the screen, asked, "Is this it?" To which the first child responded, "No."[4]

To whatever degree children may approach the world in a scientific manner, the linguistic requirements of objectivity are not met. The degree of language sophistication needed is apparently not achieved before late adolescence. The features of the child's intellectual concern with the world may resemble a scientific approach on an individual basis but insofar as the interactions required for objectivity are lacking, it fails to be science.

Conclusion

The conclusions that we have reached are perhaps not very surprising, for none of us believed at the outset that children are scientists writ small, but I think that the path to our conclusion has gone past some interesting features. We have found reason to believe that on an individual basis children do approach the world in ways that resemble science in important respects. One might feel moved, if it weren't so unnecessary, to recommend childhood as a first step toward learning the scientific approach.

On the other side, our inquiry has, I think, shown us some interesting consequences of the "nonrationalist" view of science, principally that under such a view scientists become children writ large. We have seen enough to know that this is not true, although perhaps it is not as false as we might first have thought.

The similarities in the ways that children and scientists come to terms with the world issue in an extremely interesting consequence for teachers of philosophy, namely, that children and scientists are probably the groups best suited to benefit from the study of the philosophy of science. They are dealing with similar conceptual problems and that through rather similar means. It is true that children labor as individuals while scientists work as a community, but this does not interfere with the susceptibility of their thought to philosophical analysis and it is indeed itself a topic for philosophical consideration.

We currently teach the philosophy of science to undergraduates who are science majors. The issues in the philosophy of science lack vividness for them, for they are both too early and too late. No longer children, they are not yet scientists.

NOTES

1. Neurological factors are also at work here, but one is forced to admit them only as necessary conditions for the changes and not as sufficient ones. It is true that a child cannot employ logical categories before he or she has reached a certain level of neurological development but, once that level of development has been reached, there is no need to employ them.

2. For examples of these nonrationalist positions see Thomas S. Kuhn, *The Structure of Scientific Revolutions*, second edition enlarged (Chicago: University of Chicago Press, 1970), and Paul Feyerabend, *Against Method* (London: NLB, 1975).

3. See Robert M. Krauss and Sam Glucksberg, "Social and Nonsocial Speech," *Scientific American* 236 (February 1977): 100–105.

4. Ibid., p. 103.

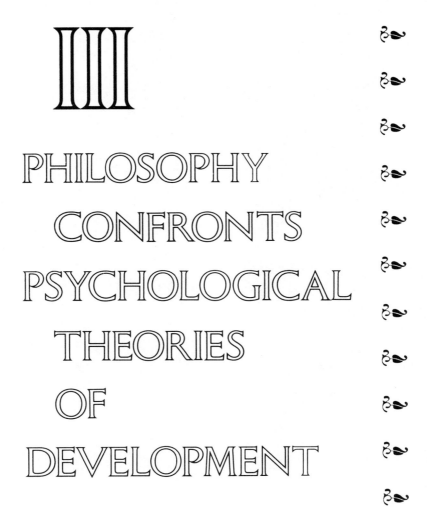

III

PHILOSOPHY
CONFRONTS
PSYCHOLOGICAL
THEORIES
OF
DEVELOPMENT

INTRODUCTION

Once it is acknowledged that children are persons with the capacity to reason, their conduct becomes understandable in terms of their reasons for doing what they do, and not merely in terms of their drives, motives or impulses. And once reasons come into the picture, philosophy becomes relevant to the comprehension of childhood. But this sets the stage for a confrontation between philosophy and psychology over the proper approach to be employed in the realm of moral education. The two selections that are contained within this section sketch out objections which some contemporary philosophers have had with regard to a purely psychological analysis of children's thinking and moral behavior.

These articles are critiques of the work of Jean Piaget and Lawrence Kohlberg. Piaget's work in child psychology, cognitive and developmental psychology has had an enormous influence on twentieth-century thought, and it must be acknowledged that his is one of the most enlightened and liberating views of children that science has yet produced. Despite his rather idiosyncratic notion of what comprises logical development, Piaget has constructed an impressive theory of the growth of cognitive competence in childhood. Kohlberg, on the other hand, has advanced a theory of moral development in children which, from a philosophical point of view, is highly dubious if not pernicious.

Development of Children's Thought

Piaget's early article, "Children's Philosophies," deals specifically with his interpetations of the philosophical thought of children.[1] Moreover, it reveals the affinities found by Piaget between the thought of children and the thought of pre-Socratic thinkers. Children's philosophies, for Piaget, are not coordinated systems of speculative thought. Rather, they are reflective tendencies that issue in unsystematic and uncodified remarks on the nature of things. Piaget gives the impression that children's thought represents a less mature type of cognition than scientific thought, and one is left to conclude that, for Piaget, adult scientific thought is tantamount to truth.

Piaget identifies three aspects of the philosophical thought of children. These features, which appear concurrently and gradually yield to "rational and mechanical explanation," he calls "realism," "animism," and "artificialism." Although the first two of these terms have familiar meanings, Piaget gives them his own particular definitions.

By "realism," Piaget means an orientation in which nothing is taken as inner or subjective. Since consciousness of self is slow to develop, small children make no distinction between thinking subjects and non-thinking objects; to the child, thought is not distinct from material activity. In realism, moreover, the symbol and the thing signified are confused: all thought is symbolic, and for children, symbols remain linked with the things they refer to, as when a child conceives the word "sun" to be part of the sun itself.

Children are "animists" to the extent that they are realists. If in realism there is no distinct thinking subject, in animism, nothing is inanimate, everything is alive and active. Piaget resists Durkheim's suggestion that child animism is more make-believe than real, although he offers no way to distinguish the one from the other. The child gradually withdraws the attribution of life and feeling, first from the periphery of his world, and then from things closer to hand. Psychic activity comes to be reserved for plants and animals, then for animals alone. Children cease to be animists when, between ages eight and ten, according to Piaget, they become conscious of "the existence of thought and its inwardness."

Finally, "artificialism." "For the child, man made nature," Piaget asserts of children of Western culture, although different experiences might lead children in other settings to reply differently to questions about the origins of things. The children in Piaget's studies define everything "by its use," and so they apparently assume that nature is made by man to the extent that it seems to be made *for* man, by omniscient, all-powerful, eternal adults. At a later stage, Piaget finds children saying that things are made by other things, thus more closely approximating the notion of causality. They conceive "the various objects of nature as issuing one from another without so much as stopping to consider whether they are living."

A number of contemporary philosophers who have read this article and others by Piaget have been less than satisfied by the assumptions which permeate his approach to the intellectual processes of children. One such expression of philosophical dismay is to be found in the comments of Maurice Merleau-Ponty on Piaget's procedures.[2] Merleau-Ponty recognizes that the characteristic Piagetian attribution of spontaneity to the child (but not to the adult) is evidence of a very curious presupposition on Piaget's part (p. 55.) If by spontaneous Piaget means that the child's behavior is unreflective, it is difficult to see how he knows this to be so. Moreover, Merleau-Ponty claims that Piaget's general conception of childhood is "provisional, and hence negative" (p. 56). Piaget sees maturation as an upward ascent toward objectivity and truth and away from subjectivity and egocentricism. Merleau-Ponty objects to this, arguing that in respect to expressiveness of subjectivity, the language of children and the language of adults are much more similar than Piaget is willing to concede. Indeed, Merleau-Ponty wonders whether passing from childhood to adulthood may be not an enrichment but an impoverishment, although he resists attributing any such unequivocal superiority to the experience of the child. He points out that "language acquisition is co-extensive with the very exercise of language" (p. 53); therefore, we have no right to assume on the basis of this criterion alone that adults possess fully what children are in the process of acquiring.

Difficulties with Piagetian Stage Theory

Merleau-Ponty suggests that the stage theory typical of developmental psychology may be, for all its correctness on certain points, profoundly wrong on others. For example, is stage theory appropriate to artistic activity? Young children throughout the world manifest an easy mastery of color and composition, which they lose around adolescence, and which most of them never regain. If artistic prowess, rather than scientific knowledge, were the paradigm to which children's thought was compared, might we not have a very different picture of the transition from childhood to adulthood?

The article in this section by Gareth Matthews continues the critique of Piaget, and underscores Merleau-Ponty's argument by observing that we frequently treat children's painting condescendingly. We suggest that it is something they are *trying* to do, when in fact, it is something they are actually doing, and often doing far better than they will do as adults. Could we not be similarly condescending with regard to children's philosophical views? We generally consider their views incorrect; are there correct philosophical views? Granted that adults possess more information, are they any less puzzled about the nature of things than children are? And if children are sometimes infuriatingly sure about things we know to be problematic, are there not times when they must be exasperated by our confidence about things they perceive to be ambiguous or thoroughly mysterious? Children are socially inexperienced and lacking in information about the world in general, but it hardly follows that their philosophical judgments lack insight or sensitivity or depth.

Matthews perceives a number of limitations in Piaget's approach. For one thing, he questions the tendency in Piaget to emphasize typical childhood responses and to ignore the atypical; Matthews finds the atypical responses to be philosophically the most interesting. Again, he wonders about Piaget's tendency to see growing up as a series of successive approximations to conceptual adequacy. Piaget speaks condescendingly of children's early realism, a stage in which their views are in many ways similar to behaviorism. The implication is that behaviorism is merely a primitive stage of psychology and that, as Matthews says, "behaviorists and identity theorists are retarded children." Matthews concludes that Piaget's theory rests upon certain presuppositions which philosophers are bound to question. If these presuppositions are seen as uncertain, many of the interpretations that Piaget puts on the evidence become dubious.

Kohlberg and Moral Stage Theory

Inspired by Jean Piaget, Lawrence Kohlberg has in recent years sought to develop "a typological scheme describing general structures and forms of moral thought." Kohlberg claims that there are three levels of moral thinking in children, with two stages at each level. The levels are distinguished as preconventional, conventional and postconventional. Moral responses on the first level are oriented towards fear of punishment and satisfaction of need. This gives way to the conforming behavior of the conventional level where the concern is with maintaining and justifying social order. It is only at the post-conventional level that there is "a major thrust towards autonomous moral principles," such as "the principle of justice." In other words, Kohlberg contends that moral growth is in the direction of an ultimate stage of ethical maturity in which moral judgments are deduced from universal moral principles.

If we examine the history of philosophical inquiry, we cannot help noting that it is consistently dialogical and pluralistic. This has been conspicuously true of ethics. Among the many theories of ethics that have been espoused, some have been deductive while others have not. To identify ethical inquiry itself as deductive would be an egregious category-mistake, but it is a mistake Kohlberg clearly commits. Those who would like to see children encouraged to think philosophically about ethical issues can in no way accept a view of ethics as a closed and finished system towards which children seek to make their way. If ethics is inquiry, it must be inquiry at every period of childhood, for at even the earliest periods, children can offer reasons for their opinions and preferences, and even at the latest periods of maturity, the philosophically oriented individual will acknowledge a constant, on-going search for improved criteria in the making of moral judgments.

The moral education of children must aim at helping children become increasingly capable of thinking for themselves about moral issues. To convert some empirical data about how children *do* make choices into an educational system as to how they *should* make choices based upon principles which are taken to be a priori and final makes sense in terms of neither philosophy nor education. Kohlberg, who often admiringly invokes the educational theory of John Dewey as justifying his own approach, has somehow failed to see how contrary that developmental approach is to Dewey's view. Dewey writes:

> There is a conception of education which professes to be based upon the idea of development. But it takes back with one hand what it proffers with the other. Development is conceived not as continuous growing, but as the unfolding of latent powers toward a definite goal. The goal is conceived of as completion, perfection. Life at any stage short of attainment of this goal is merely an unfolding toward it.
>
> The conception that growth and progress are just approximations to a final unchanging goal is the last infirmity of the mind in its transition from a static to a dynamic understanding of life. It simulates the style of the latter. It pays the tribute of speaking much of development, process, progress. But all of these operations are conceived to be merely transitional; they lack meaning on their own account. They possess significance only as movements *toward* something away from what is now going on. Since growth is just movement toward a completed being, the final ideal is immobile. An abstract and indefinite future is in control with all which that connotes in depreciation of present power and opportunity.[3]

To put forward one person's moral outlook, or one school of ethical theory, as the ultimate moral philosophy is exactly the sort of thing to which Dewey is objecting. Dewey's notion of growth as a constantly increasing capacity for growth itself is wholly incompatible with any stage theory of moral development.

The foregoing criticisms of Kohlberg are spelled out in more detail by Joseph Margolis in the second article of this section. Without presenting a moral theory of his own, Margolis attempts to show that the internal structure of Kohlberg's thought is inconsistent, and that the practical consequences, where not merely trivial, could well be pernicious. Margolis perceives a danger in Kohlberg's effort to reduce all morality to the principle of justice and to disparage all ethical positions other than his own. So provincial an approach in ethics could, if translated into moral curricula, amount to indoctrination, implies Margolis. Although Kohlberg deplores the educational procedures in totalitarian countries, Margolis suggests that a collectivist society might not find the Kohlberg approach incompatible with its own educational aims.

Other penetrating and disquieting questions raised by Margolis include: How can Kohlberg reconcile his assertion that the nature of morality is formal with his favoring certain particular contents (such as human life) when they come into conflict with his moral principles? How can Kohlberg say that moral stages can be identified as higher or lower, but that the persons in such stages are not to be so identified? Doesn't Kohlberg vacillate between asserting that moral judgments tend to exhibit formal properties and asserting that such judgments are defined solely by those properties? Isn't universalizability either a vacuous or a trivial criterion for determining the highest stage of moral development, since it can merely prescribe that all human beings are to be treated as equals but does not specify in just what moral ways this is to be done?

To Margolis, an essential weakness of Kohlberg's thesis is that he misunderstands the nature of philosophy, in particular, of moral philosophy. Every moral philosophy is an effort to take everything into account and to see the moral life as a whole. In seeing some of these moral positions as clumsy, immature stumblings towards the one true position, Kohlberg manifests his misunderstanding of the philosophical enterprise. When Kohlberg claims that Bentham should be viewed as a Stage Two moral thinker and Durkheim as a Stage Four, Margolis replies "Bentham's advocacy of utilitarianism does not entail his *incapacity* to have subscribed to any other coherent thesis, but his *conviction* regarding the validity of all the competing views he was capable of understanding."

No one can deny the legitimacy of empirical studies which seek to chart the changes that occur in people's moral attitudes. But to convert the results of these studies into educational programs represents a step with regard to which society should have the most serious reservations.

NOTES

1. Jean Piaget, "Children's Philosophies," in A *Handbook of Child Psychology*, edited by Carl Murchison (Worcester, Massachusetts: Clark University Press, 1931), pp. 377–391.
2. Maurice Merleau-Ponty, *Consciousness and the Acquisition of Language*, translated by Hugh J. Silverman (Evanston: Northwestern University Press, 1973).
3. John Dewey, *Democracy and Education*, (New York: Macmillan Company, 1916; Free Press, 1966), pp. 56–57.

✥ 8 ✥

CRITIQUES OF

STAGE THEORY

✥ GARETH MATTHEWS

University of Massachusetts, Amherst

On Talking Philosophy With Children

When our oldest daughter, Sarah, was four years old, the family kitten, Fluffy, contracted fleas. There ensued a primitive ritual of flea extermination that touched off the following discussion.

> Sarah: "Daddy, how did Fluffy get fleas?"
> Me: "Oh, I suspect she was playing with a cat that already had fleas. The fleas on *that* cat jumped off onto Fluffy."
> Sarah (after a moment's reflection): "And how did *that* cat get fleas?"
> Me (warming to the regress): "Oh, probably from another cat."
> Sarah (impatiently now): "But Daddy, it can't go on and on like that forever. The only thing that goes on and on like that forever is numbers."

This brief exchange gave me a new respect for the cosmological argument—and a new respect for my daughter. I have since come to think that archetypically philosophical reasoning is not at all unusual in children, even in young children (and even among children of nonphilosophers).

Consider another example. In an appendix to Susan Isaacs's book, *Intel-*

Lecture given to the Royal Institute of Philosophy, February 13, 1976, and printed here with the permission of the Director.

lectual Growth in Young Children (New York, 1930), there is recorded, without special comment, this anecdote:

> Some question of fact arose between James and his father, and James said, "I *know* it is!" His father replied, "But perhaps you might be wrong!" Denis [4 years, 7 months] then joined in, saying, "But if he knows, he can't be wrong! *Thinking's* sometimes wrong, but knowing's always right!" (p. 355)

Denis's remark is playful, but profound. To say what makes it playful and what makes it profound is a task worthy of the best efforts of a very clever philosopher. The Denis in you and me is what makes that effort worthwhile.

In offering these two examples of philosophical exchange, I mean to suggest that *some* children *some*times very naturally ask questions, and make comments, that professional philosophers have no trouble recognizing as genuinely philosophical. My suggestion, if correct, is important to anyone who wants to understand children; it is equally important to anyone who wants to understand philosophy.

Consider for a moment the second claim. The fact that philosophy makes its first curricular appearance very late in one's academic life—for most people not until college or university—suggests that philosophy is either a "super-discipline," something one can't even get started with until one has already mastered more basic disciplines, or else that philosophy is some kind of perversion that takes hold of people late in their intellectual lives—in, as one might say, their intellectual senility. (Both these views of philosophy have their advocates.) But if the actual impulse to do philosophy, as contrasted with the opportunity to pursue philosophy academically, comes very early to some members of the human race, then perhaps philosophy is both more natural and more basic to the life of the human mind than has been hitherto appreciated.

My first point—the idea that it is important in understanding children to know that some children naturally do philosophy—is even more obvious. We know (don't we?) that some children have natural artistic impulses. We may not be very clear about what responsibility this fact lays upon us as parents or teachers. No doubt one should try to have some respect for the work of aspiring young artists. And one shouldn't be preoccupied with the question, "But what is it you are trying to paint?" Children's art, as we know, is not to be condescended to.

And so it should be with a child's effort to reflect philosophically upon language and the world; that effort should not be condescended to either. The child brings neither sophisticated techniques of reasoning nor firm habits of intellectual discipline to the asking of philosophical questions. But in not having yet been socialized to ignore philosophical perplexities, the child brings to philosophical reflection an enviable freshness and spontaneity. Children can give us adults new eyes to see with. By the time they get to college, they have been conditioned to reject as queer and misbegotten interests and worries that were once as natural to some of them as making music or playing games—and quite as much a part of being human.

At this point in the exposition of my ideas on children and philosophy, someone usually speaks up and asks whether what I am trying to say is not very much like what Jean Piaget presents in his books on cognitive development in children. This response is a natural one. It gives me opportunity to lay out my views concerning the work of perhaps the most important living cognitive psychologist. I shall therefore pretend that someone has now asked me about Piaget. I shall direct the rest of my discussion to him and to one of his works in particular.

Piaget has devoted his spectacularly successful academic life to research and writing on the intellectual development of children. Some of his work has been devoted to the study of the earliest moves an infant makes toward concept formation, but Piaget has concerned himself with later developments as well. In one of his early books, *The Child's Conception of the World* (London, 1929), he takes up a catalogue of obviously philosophical questions ('What is thinking?' 'What is the relation between a word and its meaning?' 'What are dreams and where are they located?' 'What things are alive and what things conscious?' and tries out these questions on youngsters from the ages of five to twelve. One might reasonably hope to learn from this book how to talk philosophy with children.

Piaget's general technique for charting intellectual development is to map three or four stages of progressive sophistication in mastering a concept, and then to show that whereas most children of age so-and-so are at Stage One, by the time those same children are of age such-and-such they will, most of them, have reached Stage Two, and so on.

This procedure raises an initial worry. Is it reasonable to suppose that children (or anyone else) will make, as a matter of standard or normal maturation, well-marked progress in the handling of genuinely philosophical questions? The answer would seem to be No. And the reasons are many. For one thing it is notoriously difficult, some would say impossible, to agree on what counts as progress in philosophy. For another, philosophical progress, marked by any plausible yardstick, is not a standard development among people in any age group, whether 5 to 12, 25 to 65, or what have you.

There is another worry. Piaget proposes to validate his claims about developmental stages by finding patterns of response repeated in case after case. The very repetition is to be something of a guarantee that the thinking of children really does develop in this fashion. As a result of this procedure, the unusual response gets discounted as an unreliable indicator of the ways in which children think. "The only valid criteria," Piaget writes, ". . . are based on multiplicity of results and on the comparison of individual reactions" (p. 7). But, of course, it is the deviant response that is most likely to be philosophically interesting. The standard response will be, in general, an unthinking and unthought-out product of socialization, whereas the nonconforming response is much more likely to be the fruit of honest reflection. Yet Piaget will have the nonconforming response discounted and eliminated from his "results" on methodological grounds.

There is yet a further worry. Piaget aims to arrive at what he takes to be a child's convictions. He distinguishes answers and comments that reveal convictions from those which constitute what he calls mere "romancing." Romancing, he explains, is "inventing an answer in which [one] does not really believe, or in which [one] believes merely by force of saying it" (p. 10). Piaget makes clear in a variety of ways that he has little interest in, or appreciation for, romancing. "One would like to be able to rule out romancing," he says gravely, "with the same severity as [the answer intended simply to please the questioner]" (p. 10). (At this point the soft outline of the friendly Swiss psychologist, puffing reflectively on his curved-stem pipe, hardens perceptibly into the stern features of the no-nonsense schoolmaster and disciplinarian.) It seems most likely that the philosophically interesting comments a child makes will not so much express the child's settled convictions as explore a conceptual connection or even make a conceptual joke. Thus the most interesting and intriguing philosophical comments are likely to count for Piaget as mere romancing. Let me give an example.

Roughly two years ago I decided to take my (then) six-year-old son to a college orchestra concert. My son was about to begin cello lessons. I thought to plunk him down on the front row next to the cello section of the orchestra and say, "That instrument is what you are going to play."

When we arrived at the hall where the concert was to be played we found it dark; the concert had been cancelled. Disappointed, we climbed back into the car to return home. When we got the car started for the return trip, I discovered that a red warning light on the dashboard stayed lit. My son, sensing that I was worried about something, asked me what was the matter. I explained the function of the warning light, how its staying on was supposed to tell us that the generator wasn't producing enough electricity to keep the battery charged and how we might soon be without lights, etc. My son reflected a moment and then piped up, "Maybe its lying!" (An obvious case of romancing!) I picked up his gauntlet. "I told you there was going to be a concert tonight," I said; "I read in the newspaper that there would be one. But there was no concert. Did I lie to you?"

"No," he said slowly, "the newspaper lied." (More romancing!)

Well, we had something to discuss for the trip home. Slowly and carefully we analyzed the concept of lieing. Eventually, after several missteps, we came to the conclusion that to lie you must intend to deceive someone else and so you must yourself know that what you are saying is false. (I deliberately ignored the philosophically problematic notion of self-deception—lieing to oneself.) "Do you think," I asked triumphantly as we put the car in the garage, "that the light might have *known* that what it was telling us was false?"

"No."

"Why not?"

"It hasn't got a brain."

I was pleased. Then came the parting shot.

"Okay, it wasn't lieing," agreed my son; "but maybe it was just teasing."

That last move was a good one. Analyzing the concept of teasing would put off bedtime indefinitely. I was tempted to go on, but not quite strongly enough. Instead of analyzing the concept of teasing with my young philosopher I heartlessly hustled him off to bed.

No exchange like this one turns up in Piaget's book. What Piaget says about romancing suggests that he would have discouraged a discussion in this style. My point is that in discouraging it one discourages philosophy.

So what does Piaget count as progress in concept formation? And how does he think it can be detected? Let us take as an example the subject of Piaget's first chapter, "The Notion of Thought." Here he outlines his procedure:

The technique is briefly as follows. The child is asked: "Do you know what it means to think of something? When you are here and you think of your house, or when you think of the holidays, or of your mother, you are thinking of something." And then when the child has understood: "Well then, what is it you think with?" If, as seldom happens, he has not grasped the idea, the matter must be further explained: "When you walk, you walk with the feet; well then, when you think, what do you think with?" Whatever the answer may be the meaning behind the words is what matters. Finally comes the question, supposing it were possible to open a person's head without his dying, could you see a thought, or touch it, or feel it with the finger, etc. Naturally, these last questions, which are suggestive, must be kept to the end, that is to say till the moment when the child cannot be made to say anything more of itself. (pp. 37–38)

Piaget claims to detect in the developing child three stages of sophistication, thus:

During [the first] stage children believe that thinking is "with the mouth." Thought is identified with the voice. Nothing takes place in the head or in the body. . . . There is nothing subjective in the act of thinking. The average age for children of this stage is 6.

The second stage is marked by adult influences. The child has learned that we think with the head, sometimes it even alludes to the "brain." . . . this type of answer is always found about the age of 8. But more important is the continuity existing between the first and second stages. Indeed, thought is often looked on·as a voice inside the head, or in the neck, which shows the persistence of the influence of the child's previous convictions. Finally, there is the way in which the child materialises thought: thought is made of air, or of blood, or it is a ball, etc.

The third stage, the average age of which is 11–12, shows thought no longer materialised. (pp. 38–39)

Anyone familiar with classical theories of thinking will be able to link them up with Piaget's three stages. The idea that thinking is inner speech is, of course, to be found in Plato, for example in this passage from the *Theaetetus*:

Socrates: Do you accept my description of the process of thinking?
Theaetetus: How do you describe it?
Socrates: As a discourse that the mind carries on with itself about any subject it is considering. You must take this explanation as coming from an ignoramus [someone stuck at Stage One!]; but I have a notion that, when the mind is thinking, it is simply talking to itself, asking questions and answering them, and saying Yes or No. When it reaches

a decision—which may come slowly or in a sudden rush—when doubt is over and the two voices affirm the same thing, then we call that its 'judgment'. So I should describe thinking as discourse, and judgment as a statement pronounced, not aloud to someone else, but silently to oneself. (189E–190A, Cornford translation)

Plato's theory has been revived and modified in modern times. The analogical theory of judgment in P.T. Geach's *Mental Acts* (London, 1957) is one modern version. Quite a different version, but in fact one much more in line with Piaget's Stage-One theory, is to be found in the writings of the American behaviorist psychologist, J. B. Watson. According to Watson's theory, children are conditioned to inhibit their vocal speech by adults who are tired of hearing endless infant chatter. In response to admonitions to keep quiet, children first mumble and finally so inhibit their speech that they make no audible sound or movement of the lips. All they do is to move the muscles of their mouth and throat. This inhibited, or subvocal, speech, says Watson, is thinking. (See, for example, J. B. Watson, *Behaviorism* (New York, 1970), chapter 10.)

Corresponding to Piaget's Second Stage are various materialistic theories of thinking, including what is these days called the "Identity Theory." Thought is not considered to be "made of air, or of blood," or to be a ball, but the identity theorist certainly "materialises thought" when she or he supposes mental events to be identical with brain events. To judge from the space devoted to the defense and the criticism of the identity theory in current philosophy journals, this kind of account offers the most exciting contemporary approach to the old problem of what thinking is.

Finally, the Third Stage in Piaget's classification corresponds to classical dualistic theories, especially imagistic accounts to be found in the empiricist tradition. Perhaps the long and fascinating chapter called "The Stream of Thought" in William James's *The Principles of Psychology* (New York, 1950) gives the fullest and most vivid exposition of this sort of view.

One might, of course, question whether Piaget's sample or his method of conducting research justifies his conclusion that children naturally develop ideas about thinking in this particular sequence. But supposing that we were satisfied with those aspects of Piaget's research, the notion of progress built into Piaget's methodology is still worth worrying about.

It is characteristic of the First Stage, says Piaget, for the child to think "there is nothing subjective in the act of thinking" (p. 38). Piaget makes clear that, in his view, this is a deficiency in the child's notion of thought, a deficiency to be corrected at a later stage.

Again, concerning the First Stage Piaget says this:

> In treating of the development of the notion of thought, we may regard as primitive the child's conviction that it thinks with the mouth. The notion of thinking, as soon as it appears, becomes confused with that of voice, that is to say with words, either spoken or heard. (p. 44)

The implication seems to be that a philosopher like Geach who tries to develop an account of thinking as inner speech is retarded, or unnaturally arrested, in his intellectual development. All the more so if that philosopher or psychologist (I have J. B. Watson in mind here) persists in supposing, even *insists* on supposing, that there is "nothing subjective in the act of thinking."

Identity theorists have at least progressed beyond the First Stage. But, to judge from Piaget's schedule of natural development, their progress is also unnaturally arrested.

"Hold on!" you may protest; "this is all melodramatic and overdrawn. Piaget does not claim that a normal six-year-old child holds, say, a behavioristic theory of thinking, whereas an eight-year-old standardly holds an identity theory and a twelve-year-old a dualistic theory. Piaget doesn't suppose that any of these children has developed, or would even understand, a *theory* of what thinking is. It's just that when you ask a six-year-old the question 'What do you think with?' you can expect to get the answer, 'With my mouth'—whereas two years later you can expect the answer 'With my head' or 'With my brain' etc.

It is no doubt true that Piaget does not attribute theories of thinking to his children subjects. To speak of someone as accepting such-and-such a theory is to suggest that that person has well-worked-out answers to a range of questions concerning the subject of the theory. Piaget expects that his subjects will often be stumped by simple questions about thinking and that their answers will sometimes be incoherent.

So Piaget doesn't really suppose that his subjects subscribe to theories such as behaviorism, dualism, materialism, etc. On the other hand, it isn't right either to say that he simply collects and tabulates responses to such questions as "What do you think with?' (at age so-and-so such-and-such a percentage of the respondents in the sample answered 'With the mouth'). Piaget is interested in the child's *conception* of the world, and thus in the child's *conception* of what thought is. We are to go behind the child's words to what these words reveal about the child's conceptual world. Granted, it may be too grandiose to suggest that the child has a *theory* of what a thought is; but Piaget certainly supposes that the child has, even at age six, a concept of thinking (after all, Piaget's first chapter is called "The Notion of Thought").

Piaget makes all this reasonably clear in the following passage from his opening, methodological chapter:

> . . . an attempt must be made to strip the answers of their verbal element. There is certainly present to the child a whole world of thought, incapable of formulation and made up of images and motor schemas combined. Out of it issue, at least partially, ideas of force, life, weight, etc., and the relations of objects amongst themselves are penetrated with these indefinable associations. When the child is questioned he translates his thought into words, but these words are necessarily inadequate. . . . (p. 27)

So it is the child's conceptual world, to which the child's own words are "necessarily inadequate," that Piaget is interested in. And so it is conceptions of thought, for example, that Piaget means to be dealing with. The sequence of conceptions of thought he claims to find in children from ages 5 to 12 parallels, as we discover, a list of classical theories of thinking. We thus return to our initial embarrassment. Can it be that Piaget supposes a behaviorist to be someone whose conception of thought never advanced beyond Stage One (etc.)? Or does he suppose that a behaviorist, say, first makes progress through childhood and adolescence and then, in adult life, regresses to Stage One?

One might try to get Piaget out of this embarrassment by playing down the idea of progress. Perhaps all Piaget means to point out is that conceptions of thinking, dreaming, meaning, life, etc., change in identifiable patterns. Perhaps Piaget is not committed to viewing this sequence as a line of progress. If not, then perhaps there is no embarrassment after all in finding an adult, even a learned philosopher or psychologist, who takes a view of thinking that corresponds to that of a 6-year-old, or an 8-year-old.

Unfortunately this way out of embarrassment does not fit the text. Piaget makes clear throughout *The Child's Conception of the World* that the story of conceptual change he tells is a story of successively closer approximation to adequacy. The following quotations from a chapter summarizing his discussions of the child's concepts of thinking, meaning and dreaming make that clear:

> In the first three chapters we tried to show that the distinction between thought and the external world is not innate in the child but is only

gradually evolved and built up by a slow process. One result of this is of primary importance to the study of causality, namely that the child is a realist and that its progress consists in ridding itself of this initial realism. In fact, during the primitive stages, since the child is not yet conscious of his subjectivity, all reality appears to be of one unvaried type by reason of the confusion between the data of the external world and those of the internal. Reality is impregnated with self and thought is conceived as belonging to the category of physical matter. (pp. 166–167)

As I read these words, there beats in on me the words of my teacher, W. V. Quine, spoken to me when I was a graduate student. We were discussing whether the element of what philosophers call "intentionality"—that hallmark of the "inner" and the nonphysical—could be eliminated from reports of what someone is thinking. I was skeptical, Quine was insistent: "Let's face it, Matthews," he said earnestly, "it's one world and it's a *physical* world." Back to Piaget.

There are thus two forms of egocentricity, the first logical and the second ontological. Just as the child makes his own truth, so he makes his own reality; he feels the resistance of matter no more than he feels the difficulty of giving proofs. He states without proof and he commands without limit. Magic on the ontological plane, and conviction without proof on the logical. . . . At the root both of magic and of conviction without proof lie the same egocentric illusions, namely, confusion between one's own thought and that of others and confusion between the self and the external world. (pp. 167–168)

Pretty clearly Piaget has not left us any good way of getting him out of the embarrassment of suggesting that behaviorists and identity theorists are retarded children.

There is something else unsettling about these last remarks taken from Piaget. Taken seriously, they suggest that it would be folly to try to talk philosophy with a child. They suggest that a child develops a conception of the world insensible to the legitimate constraints of logic and experience. The unspoken assumption is that only the adult is properly respectful of logic and experience. If Piaget's pessimism about children is warranted, then I was naive at the beginning of this paper to suggest that some children naturally think philosophically. Thinking unguided by the constraints of logic and experience can hardly be philosophical thinking.

In honesty I must say that Piaget's own questions and comments in *The Child's Conception of the World* hardly show him to be a paragon of rationality or a repository of philosophical acumen. After giving a bumbling and confused interrogatory concerned with empty names, for example, Piaget makes this comment:

> This inability to dissociate names from things is very curious. The following observation, involving the same idea, we owe to a colleague, Dr. Naville. A little girl of 9 asked: "Daddy, is there really God?" The father answered that it wasn't very certain, to which the child retorted: "There must be really, because he has a name!" (pp. 66–67)

Piaget makes clear that he regards this "curious" inability to dissociate names from things as nothing more interesting than an irrational and illogical perversity characteristic of young children. To a philosopher Piaget's own judgment is singularly perverse. Perhaps no topic has been more thoroughly discussed in recent philosophy than the topic of empty names—or better, and more broadly, nondenoting singular terms. Countless articles have concerned themselves with whether either 'The present King of France is bald' or 'The present King of France is not bald' is true, given that there is no present King of France. And a whole new family of logics (called "free logics") has been invented to allow for the occurrence in true sentences of empty names like 'Pegasus' and, if atheism be true, 'God'. In standard, or "non-free," logics an argument analogous to (though not identical with) that given by Dr. Naville's 9-year-old friend would be valid.

As is doubtless clear by now, I myself have no sympathy for Piaget's low estimate of the rationality of young children. I have had many a good discussion with them myself. I find some of them more openminded and more responsive to evidence and to logic than are some of their elders.

To see that some children can hold their own philosophically with Piaget one need look no further than some of the interrogatories given in his own book. Many of these exchanges are quoted in such an abbreviated form that it is hard to base much upon them. But some are reported at length. Here, for example, is a fascinating exchange with an eight-year-old that Piaget gives in his chapter on dreams (chapter 3):

> FAV (8) belongs to a class whose teacher follows the excellent practice of giving each child an "observation notebook," in which the child notes down each day, with or without the help of drawings, an event he has personally observed outside school. One morning Fav noted down, as always, spontaneously: "I dreamt that the devil wanted to boil me," and he accompanied the observation with a drawing, of which we give a

reproduction: on the left Fav is seen in bed, in the centre is the devil, and on the right Fav stands, in his nightshirt, in front of the devil who is about to boil him. Our attention was called to this drawing and we sought out Fav. His drawing illustrates very clearly the meaning of child realism: the dream is beside the bed, before the eyes of the dreamer who watches it. Fav, moreover, is in his nightshirt in the dream, as if the devil had pulled him out of bed.

The following are the observations we made: Concerning the origin of dreams, Fav has passed the beliefs of the first stage. Like Schi he knows that the dream comes from thought: "What is a dream?—*It is a thought.*—Where does it come from?—*When you see something and then you think of it.*—Do we make the dream ourselves?—*Yes.*—Does it come from outside?—*No.*" Fav also knows that we think "*with the brain, with our intelligence.*" Further, Fav, like Schi and all the children of this stage, knows that he alone can see his dream; neither we nor anyone else could have seen the dream of the devil in Fav's room. But what he has not understood is the internal nature of the dream: "Whilst you are dreaming, where is the dream?—*In front of the eyes.*— Where?—*When you are in bed, in front of your eyes.*—Where, quite near?—*No in the room.*" We pointed to Fav's portrait of himself which we have marked II, "What is that?—*That's me.*—Which is most real of you, this (I) or that (II)?—*In the dream* (pointing to II).—Is this one anything (II)?—*Yes, it's me. It was specially my eyes which stayed there* (pointing to I), *to see* (I)—How were your eyes there?—*I was there altogether, but specially my eyes.*—And the rest of you?—*It was there too* (in the bed).—How could that be?—*There was two of me. I was in my bed and I was looking on all the time.*—With the eyes open or shut?—*Shut, because I was asleep.*" A moment later it seemed as if Fav had understood the internal nature of the dream: "When you are asleep, is the dream in you or are you in the dream?—*The dream is in us, because it's we who see the dream.*—Is it inside the head or outside?—*In the head.*—Just now you said outside, what does that mean?—*You can't see the dream on the eyes.*—Where is the dream?—*In front of the eyes.*—Is there really anything in front of the eyes?—*Yes.*—What?— *The dream.*" Fav thus realises there is something internal about the dream, he knows the dream's appearance of externality to be illusion ("you can't see the dream on the eyes"), and yet he admits that for the illusion to be there, there must really be something in front of him: "Were you really there (pointing to II)?—*Yes, I was there twice over* (I and II).—If I had been there, should I have seen you (II)?—*No.*—What do you mean by 'I was there twice over'?—*When I was in bed I was really there, and then when I was in my dream I was with the devil, and I was really there as well."*

I shall assume that it was Piaget himself who conducted this discussion with Fav. Clearly Piaget's overriding interest in this exchange is to determine whether Fav still has a Second-Stage concept of dreaming or whether he has moved on to Stage Three. Here is how Piaget characterizes these two stages:

> During the second stage (average age 7–8) the child supposes the source of the dream to be in the head, in thought, in the voice, etc., but the dream is in the room, in front of him. Dreaming is with the eyes; it is looking at a picture outside . . . during the third stage (about 9–10), the dream is the product of thought, it takes place inside the head (or in the eyes), and dreaming is by means of thought or else with the eyes, used internally. (p. 91)

I'm not at all sure that I understand the characterization of these two stages. Common to them is supposed to be the idea that the dream is produced internally (whatever that means). The difference is supposed to be that, whereas in the Second Stage a child takes the dream to be "in the room, in front of him," in the Third Stage the child supposes the dream "takes place [not in the room but] inside the head (or in the eyes)."

So the question is, 'Where does Fav think the dream is, in the room or in his head?' Piaget takes the two figures of Fav in the picture to betray an ambivalence on Fav's part; they suggest he is halfway between Stage Two and Stage Three, or so Piaget supposes. For himself, Fav wants to say both these things:

1. Throughout the dream I was in my bed asleep.
2. Throughout the dream I was outside the bed, in the room.

Fav seems to realize that, given certain natural assumptions, these two things are incompatible. In particular, given the assumption that one person can't be in two places at once, Fav can't be at once in bed and out in the room. His solution is to multiply himself—"There was two of me"—"I was there twice over."

Another solution would be to say that the expression 'throughout the dream' in (1) and (2) is ambiguous. If it is taken to mean 'in the whole of the dream' then (2) is true and (1) is false. If it is taken to mean 'for the whole period of time in which I had the dream' then (1) is true and (2) false.

Actually this second solution is not very good. For if one dreams about the very period of time in which one is asleep, then one is again forced to conclude that, say, at 2 A.M. one was both in bed and standing up in the room.

Piaget suggests that his own solution is simply to deny (2) and replace it with something like this:

2*. Throughout the dream I *seemed* to myself to be outside the bed, in the room.

(". . . he knows the dream's appearance of externality to be illusion.")

So far Piaget's move is a good one. But Piaget is so preoccupied with what he calls the "internal nature of the dream" that he puts to Fav the question "When you are asleep, is the dream in you or are you in the dream?" He puts that question to Fav in such a way as to make clear that, in his view,

3. The dream is in Fav

is true, but

4. Fav is in the dream

is false. Fav is happy enough to accept (3), but quite rightly he refuses to give up (4). After all, it was *his* dream and he knows that he was in it.

For my money it is not at all clear in this exchange that Piaget is more logical, or more responsive to evidence, than his eight-year-old interlocutor. Forced to choose, I should give the edge to Fav.

One thing we see in this example is Piaget being given a chance to do some philosophy with a child and passing it by. Perhaps Piaget is not interested in doing philosophy with anybody. Anyway, his only interest in talking with Fav on this occasion seems to be to place Fav somewhere on his scale of dream competence.

To me the most striking thing about this exchange is Piaget's seeming insensitivity to puzzlement. How can anybody ask anybody, adult or child, "Were you in the dream or was the dream in you?" and not succumb to some puzzlement over the naturalness with which any of us (given a dream with analogous content) might answer, "Both—I was in the dream and the dream was in me." Fav is puzzled. Piaget isn't.

Here we have a clue to how Piaget can treat an inner-speech concept of thinking and a materialistic concept of thinking as mere stages in a child's intellectual development. It doesn't occur to him that what he takes to be the adult concept of thought generates problems, or puzzles, or perplexities. Not having treated the "earlier" conceptions reflectively, he is not prepared to treat the so-called "adult" conception reflectively either. And so, from the point of view of his story of intellectual development, it becomes completely mysterious why adults should revert to the concepts of their youth.

In fact, all the concepts Piaget claims to find in children invite philosophical reflection. And it isn't at all obvious as a general thing that the Piagetian Third-Stage concepts will turn out to be the most nearly adequate or satisfactory.

The idea of puzzlement and perplexity brings me to make a final comment. For anyone interested in talking philosophy with a child I propose the following maxim:

Find something to puzzle over with the child.

Ideally, the thing one finds to puzzle over with the child is something one finds freshly puzzling rather than something that has lost some of its air of puzzlement. That way there is more excitement in seeing whether together we can straighten the matter out. Familiar puzzles will do as second-best, provided one can re-create the puzzlement one once felt naturally and directly. To be avoided are puzzles that have gone stale and, of course, puzzles one never found puzzling.

Some people are largely innocent of philosophical puzzlement. For them there is, perhaps, much to learn about the world, but nothing to puzzle over. To judge from *the Child's Conception of the World*, Piaget is one of these innocents. but to someone like me, who still finds puzzling a great many things about thinking, meaning, dreaming, consciousness, life, etc.—all the topics of Piaget's book—a remark of a child's, or a drawing like Fav's, can serve to start a little colloquy in which one tries to reason one's way out of the puzzle.

Here is Fav's drawing. Fav appears in the drawing, as he says, "twice over." In a way it seems quite right that he should. After all, he was there in the bed for the whole time he had the dream and he was also, for the whole dream, outside the bed, standing on the other side of the devil. But can anybody be in two places at once? "Yes," says my (now) eight-year-old son; "you can be in the bedroom and in the house at the same time." "But I don't mean that!" I retort with a mixture of pride and annoyance. "So? what do you mean?" he inquires with an impish grin. We are doing philosophy.

As I said at the beginning, the fact that philosophy can get going with a child in this simple way says something important about philosophy and something important about children. It is something Piaget has missed.

NOTES

1. At Harvard in August 1976, sponsored by the Institute for the Advancement of Philosophy for Children and directed by Matthew Lipman and Ann Margaret Sharp.
2. For more on the medieval account see my "A Medieval Theory of Vision," *Studies in Perception: Interrelations in the History and Philosophy of Science*, P. K. Machamer and R. G. Turnbull, eds., Columbus, Ohio, 1977.
3. *Philosophie als institutionalisierte Navitaet, Philosophisches Jahrbuch* 81 (1974): 139–42.
4. For more on Piaget and philosophical thinking in children, see my "On Talking Philosophy with Children," also printed in this volume.
5. For more on how philosophy shows itself in children's stories see my "Philosophy and Children's Literature," *Metaphilosophy* 7 (1976): 7–16.
6. I have tried to offer some tips on talking philosophy with children in my "Philosophy and the Young Child," *Metaphilosophy*, forthcoming.

ക്ട് JOSEPH MARGOLIS

Temple University

Does Kohlberg Have a Valid Theory of Moral Education?

No one doubts that the moral education of children is a serious matter; some would say, an unavoidable, perhaps even an obligatory, concern of families and communities. Hesitation or doubt here signifies the uncertainties of moral truths. It's all very well to institutionalize an educational program that a homogeneous or doctrinaire or authority-prone society will support with conviction, but if in some sense we mean to base our education on the discovery of the correct principles of moral grooming we are bound to come to terms with obvious counterindications. For a start, these would include: (1) that the biological gifts and dispositions of man are compatible with an endless variety of social arrangements that support competing claims and are, on different specimen views, taken to be both morally valid and invalid; (2) that there are grounds for doubting that moral principles, rules, directives, judgments can be objectively derived from an examination of the biological or sociobiological nature of man; (3) that there may be no consensus on the part of the human race regarding moral principles, rules, directives, judgments except of a purely vacuous sort; (4) that at any given time there are always prominent, compelling, sincerely adopted conceptions of morality and moral education that cannot in principle be reconciled or rendered compatible with one another; (5) that we appear to lack a method for validating moral principles, rules, directives, judgments except relative to higher-order moral commitments that are not themselves validated; (6) that invalidating moral claims at any level of generality, however objectively, does not entail validating competing moral claims. These are persistent worries that are not easily offset. Historically, they are as old as the confidence of such ventures as that of Plato's *Republic*. They are, after all, the dark side of just such an endeavor as Plato's.

In recent years, these pessimistic themes have been systematically challenged, with regard to the moral development and education of children, by Lawrence Kohlberg. In a series of intriguing papers,[1] Kohlberg has sustained a most uncompromising resistence to all forms of moral relativism, morality as social indoctrination, even moral cognitivism—informed by a reasonably thorough familiarity with the most advanced work in moral philosophy; at the same time, he has defended a doctrine of moral universalism in accord with a structuralist view of "cognitive-developmental" phases of the moral life. It would be extraordinary if Kohlberg's theories were valid and adequate. For, if they were, it would be a relatively straightforward matter to institutionalize the educational arrangements in school systems in order to facilitate the "correct" sequence of developmental stages. The general resemblance to Piaget's conception is obvious;[2] Kohlberg acknowledges and exploits it with some adjustment. On the other hand, if he is seriously wrong, then there is good reason to fear that his own recommendations may serve, in a particularly pernicious way, the "hidden curriculum" that he himself inveighs against, that is, whatever is the consequence of construing "moral education as the promotion of collective national discipline."[3] Sympathetic as he is to Durkheim's "functional sociology," Kohlberg recoils from the intended moral neutrality of Durkheim's conception of the function of the classroom.[4] He finds that the "Durkheimian sociology" no less than the Marxist embraced by the Soviet Union leads "logically" to the "rather horrifying innovations" involved in the "use of collective responsibility, collective punishment and reward" in the classroom.[5] Of course, the judgment may be justified on the vindication of Kohlberg's theories. But if Kohlberg is wrong—or at least, if he cannot vindicate theories strong enought to justify the judgment—then it would seem a fair criticism to hold that Kohlberg's own thesis is in effect an instrument of precisely the sort of indoctrination he claims to oppose. Also, whether his own purported moral values or those he opposes are valid or defensible is an entirely fair and independent question. In any case, the possible tendentiousness of Kohlberg's thesis must be noted.

Clearly, the classroom cannot escape providing moral instruction. The authority of the teacher, the impressionability of children, peer-group pressures—all serve to infect even the most innocent-seeming episodes with a decided moral import. More than this, on Kohlberg's view, the moral development of the child is relatively autonomous (though based on social interaction) and corresponds, with some play, to the sequence of intellectual development. If "development [moral or intellectual] [were] defined as the direct internalization of external cultural norms,"[6] then our concern with education would (on the functionalist view) properly focus on promoting collective discipline. But if (on the "cognitive-developmental view," that Kohlberg says he shares with Dewey, G. H. Mead, J. M. Baldwin, and Piaget) "moral stages and their development represent the interaction of the child's structuring tendencies and the structural features of the environment,"[7] then our concern with education properly focuses on providing experiences congruent with and facilitating the "invariant sequence" of the stages of moral development.[8] Only a theory that both denies an objective morality or a "natural" order of moral development and resists collective discipline could (naively) construe the school as the locus in which children are free "to be themselves," in which "all discipline, all direction, all moral training" is renounced.[9] Kohlberg will have none of this and, quite literally, maintains that "we all, even and especially young children, are moral philosophers" (that is, "the child has a morality of his own"[10]): "moral principles are neither external rules taken inward nor natural ego-tendencies of a biological organism, but rather the interactional emergents of social interaction."[11]

Now, Kohlberg explicitly wishes to link the theory of moral education to "just two basic 'disciplines' "—findings regarding the "psychological and sociological facts of moral development" and judgments "based on a philosophically defensible concept of morality."[12] There are, therefore, two distinct lines along which we may question the tenability of Kohlberg's account. For example, Kohlberg says that he defines "morality in terms of the formal character of a moral judgment or a moral point of view, rather than in terms of its content. Impersonality, ideality, universalizability, and pre-emptiveness are among the formal characteristics of a moral judgment."[13] Nevertheless, he also holds, against the potential extremes of a morality devoted to such features—the Kantian is singled out—that "true principles guide us to the obligating elements in the situation, to the concrete human claims there. The case is always higher than the principle, a single human life is worth more than all the principles in philosophy to the mature man."[14] It is difficult to see this contrast other than as a device to support certain favored values from among those that could in principle meet the putatively formal traits of a moral judgment. How else could we deny the moral relevance of the formally correct "claims" and "interests" that particular partisans sincerely support? If formal properties are the mark of the moral, then appeal to favored "content" cannot be relied on; and if the latter is operative, then it may not be possible to show that all moral claims and judgments (even the most "mature"—since presumably the judgment sketched, "a single human life . . . ," is an instance of mature moral sensibility) exhibit the formal traits required. (The nature of the adduced formal traits poses other difficulties, to which we shall return.)

Kohlberg also insists rather emphatically that "moral judgments are not true or false in the cognitive-descriptivist sense."[15] By this, Kohlberg wishes to emphasize that moral judgments have the formal property of being "prescriptive" (or, "categorical")—following the accounts of Kant and R. M. Hare. Presumably, this qualification enables Kohlberg to hold at one and the same time that, although the stages of moral development are "higher" or "lower" than one another—higher in fact in the sense of being "more moral," more "adequate" morally—"there is no valid or final meaning to judging or grading persons as morally better or worse . . . from a moral point of view, the moral worth of all persons is ultimately the same, it is equal."[16]

Here, multiple difficulties arise. For, for one thing, *if* the distinctions made at later stages of moral development are morally better or "more moral" than those at earlier stages, then it would seem impossible to deny that persons may be judged more and more accurately at these later stages as "morally better or worse," *whether judgments are treated descriptively or prescriptively*. And for another, *if* there is not truth or falsity of the matter, then it is unclear how Kohlberg could know, apart from applying the purely formal criteria of moral concern, that "a single human life is worth more than all the principles in philosophy to the mature man." These puzzles point to characteristic difficulties in Kohlberg's account. It needs to be emphasized that these are not merely verbal quibbles, since, on Kohlberg's own view (correctly), the detailing of the putative stages of moral development cannot be defended except in the context of a philosophically valid analysis of what a moral consideration is. In short, *if* Kohlberg is confused about the properties of a moral judgment, then he cannot, as he characteristically does, fall back to *confirming* his own thesis by reference to putative empirical evidence of the invariant moral development of children across all cultural lines. The very status of the evidence is called into question in calling into question Kohlberg's characterization of moral issues.

Let us pursue this a bit further. Kohlberg claims: "moral language and moral action are *sui generis*; they cannot be evaluated except in their own terms. We shall claim, however, that only stage-6 thinking or language is fully moral, that each higher stage is a closer approximation to the characteristic which philosophers such as Hare have taken as defining distinctively moral language."[17] But in the same context (and reasonably), Kohlberg also says: "Moral judgments are judgments about the right and the good of action. Not all judgments of 'good' or 'right' are moral judgments, however; many are judgments of aesthetic, technological, or prudential goodness or rightness. Unlike judgments of prudence or aesthetics, moral judgments tend to be universal, inclusive, consistent, and grounded on objective, impersonal, or ideal grounds. Statements such as 'She's really great! She's beautiful and a good dancer,' or 'The right way to make a Martini is five-to-one,' involve the good and right, but they are not moral judgments since they lack the characteristics of the latter."[18] There is an extraordinary number of confusions hidden in this pair of juxtaposed statements. For one thing, Kohlberg claims that moral judgments both *tend* to exhibit certain formal or quasi-formal properties and are defined *solely in terms of* such properties: they are after all what distinguish the moral from the aesthetic and the prudential. But he cannot have it both ways: if he takes the weaker alternative, then he has simply failed to distinguish the moral from the aesthetic and the prudential, and his intended empirical confirmation rests on a confusion of categories; on the other hand, if he takes the strong alternative, then insofar as pre–stage-6 children make judgments that lack the defining traits of the moral, their responses cannot in principle be used to support his thesis. The dilemma shows very clearly why it is that Kohlberg's own proposal uniting psychosocial and philosophical investigations threatens to undermine the force of his own findings.

Second, on his own admission, Kohlberg has no basis at all for including pre–stage-6 stages as stages of moral development, except the intuition that they are. After all, the use of 'good,' 'right,' 'ought' and the like do not decide the matter. In this respect, it is simply not in the least clear whether Kohlberg's stories about the importance of "links" in Russian moral education or of Heinz's stealing drugs for his sick wife[19] are actually viewed in moral terms by children in pre–stage-6 stages. It's clear enough that Kohlberg views them as morally relevant but what is the evidence, given Kohlberg's own criteria, that the children view them thus? In effect, this is the critical difficulty in Kohlberg's effort to derive the "ought" of adequate moral development from the "is" of its putatively preliminary stages.

Third, the qualifications of the moral that Kohlberg here provides are not entirely formal or quasi-formal; also, some seem to be question-begging or inconsistent with what Kohlberg has said elsewhere. For example, Kohlberg says both the moral judgments are (or tend to be) universal and *grounded on objective, impersonal, or ideal grounds*. But he himself, as we have seen, denies that moral judgments can be true or false or that there are cognitive grounds for determining what is morally required. Again, it's not clear whether appeal to "impersonal" grounds are or are not precisely what Kohlberg inveighed against in insisting—against the application of purely formal criteria—that "a single human life" is worth more than any principles. Again, it's hard to see how "ideal" grounds could fail to reflect the ideological or doctrinal conviction of particular moral partisans. Why, for instance, should "ideal grounds" exclude "the promotion of collective national discipline"? By what formal criteria could it justifiably be excluded?

Fourth, it's not at all clear whether moral judgments or moral behavior are, as Kohlberg insists, *sui generis*. If they are, then the admission that pre–stage-6 thinking only *tends* to exhibit the full properties of *sui generis* moral thinking actually precludes such stages from being instances of moral thinking; and if moral is not *sui generis*, then there is good reason to doubt that there could be *any* such thing as an "invariant sequence" of the stages of moral development—precisely what is most distinctive about Kohlberg's account. In fact, if there are no *sui generis* features that could be introduced serially with developing stages of moral thinking, then, contrary to Kohlberg's own insistence, there probably could not be any way in which to distinguish the stages of *intellectual* (or cognitive) and *moral* stages, whatever they may be. "Maturity of moral judgment," Kohlberg says, "is correlated with cognitive maturity but is clearly distinguishable from it."[20] "The correlations," he adds, "are not one-to-one but of the order that a certain level of cognitive maturity is a necessary but not sufficient condition for a given level of moral judgment."[21] So, the very thesis that there is a structural sequence of moral development paralleling in a way the (alleged) structural sequence of cognitive development presupposes that an independent ordering of the elements of moral development should be formulable. Kohlberg's equivocation on this matter as well as the prospect that moral judgments and moral thinking cannot, on any reasonable basis, be shown to be *sui generis* (or, "autonomous," as Kohlberg says, again following Kant) seriously threatens the entire venture. (This is, of course, still provisional: we must turn in a moment to the details of Kohlberg's account.)

We see, therefore, the intimate bearing of certain philosophical distinctions on the viability of Kohlberg's "cognitive-developmental" or structuralist thesis. Consider, then, a few more distinctions. It is true that Kant first formulated the thesis that moral judgments are *sui generis*; but he did not hold that they were *sui generis* on the same grounds as those favored by Kohlberg (or Hare, whom Kohlberg professes to follow), and it is not clear that Kant would subscribe to the latter.[22] For example, there is a certain telltale equivocation on 'universal' both in Kohlberg and Hare, which, since "universalizability" seems to be the most distinctive trait of the moral, threatens Kohlberg's account directly, threatens to raise doubts about the ready sense in which his account would find favor with "most moral philosophers from Kant to Hare,"[23] and threatens the reliability of "the cultural universality of the sequence of stages that we [that is, Kohlberg and his associates] have found" on the basis of different cultural samples.[24] In one sense, 'universalizability' signifies no more than consistency of linguistic usage: "similar things must be similarly judged under similar circumstances." In another, 'universalizability' is conflated with 'generalizability,' that is, with the thesis that all putative moral distinctions must as such be able to be generalized to hold for all human beings simpliciter. Now, the first sense is simply not a moral distinction: call it a logical or conceptual distinction, but it applies to all discourse insofar as such discourse is coherent. The second *is* a distinctly philosophical claim about moral discourse, which is either trivial—in being tantamount to the first— or dubious. Kohlberg is perhaps not responsible for this confusion; it already appears prominently in Hare's original account.[25] Thus, for example, Kohlberg claims, "these students [that is, conventional college students who say: 'the principle of loyalty to your family comes ahead of obeying the law here' or 'the principle of honesty comes before helping

your wife'] do not wish to universalize the rules [mentioned]."²⁶ Read in
terms of the first sense of 'universalize,' Kohlberg's claim is false: they do
universalize in the sense that they are willing to treat similar cases similarly; they also believe that the cases are circumscribed and that other
considerations take precedence in a larger context of review. Hence, read
in terms of the second sense of 'universalize'—at least, read in one way in
those terms, they do not universalize, simply because they do not believe
that the "rules" given hold for all human beings *qua* human beings
merely, solely as such, or *simpliciter*. But they may well believe that there
are no comparably determinate distinctions that could convincingly hold
for all human beings.

The trouble with the second interpretation is multiple. For one thing, it
would entail that the putative rule, "Loyalty to family comes before obeying the law, sometimes" or "Honesty comes before helping one's wife" *are
not moral prescriptives*, that is, are not even candidates for valid prescriptives. But that is clearly absurd. It would entail that there are *no* prescriptives that apply to human beings in virtue of some office, contract, relationship, or similar qualification; that moral prescriptives apply to human
beings only in virtue of their being human beings. Second, the constraint
may be easily trivialized merely by holding that any putative moral prescriptive of the restricted sort *is* a bona fide prescriptive if it is thought to
obtain for all human beings *in a similar situation*. That of course would
reduce the second sense of 'universalize' to the first, which, as already
remarked, is not even a distinctly moral consideration. The equivocation
dogs Kohlberg's account because he worries a great deal about the difference between "rules" and "principles," seems to want to distinguish them
by considerations of universal scope, and even admits that "we have so far
never encountered a live human being who makes moral judgments in
terms of principle in this sense [that is, in the sense of deriving the judgment in question from principles of universal scope and the facts of the
situation]."²⁷ Small wonder, since it's quite impossible. All morally relevant claims are made in virtue of *some* qualification affecting *some* subset
of the human race. Otherwise, we might all, on a theory of Kohlberg's
sort, be obliged to do all things for all human beings merely as a result of
being human and of there being needs and interests that call for moral
attention. It appears, therefore, that only the trivial and nonmoral sense of
universalizability can have any force; the strong interpretation of the gener-
alizability-condition is, to put the point as mildly as possible, simply implausible. (Kohlberg himself seems not to favor it.)²⁸ But if it is implausible

and if the trivial (first) sense of 'universalize' is the only viable one, then Kohlberg will have failed thus far to pinpoint the *sui generis* nature of moral thinking *and* the formal distinction of moral principles. The least inspection of the other conditions mentioned in passing will show either that they are not distinctive of moral thinking or that they are doubtful qualifications. But that means that Kohlberg lacks a conceptual basis on which to set off moral development from cognitive development, *a fortiori*, to confirm his structuralist claims about the invariant sequence of moral development.

Just how deeply these considerations undermine Kohlberg's account may be seen at a stroke, by attending to his remarks about the nature of justice and the distinction of stage-6 thinking. "Our major and most controversial claim," he admits, "is that the only 'true' (stage 6) moral principle is justice." And what is the nature of justice? "The basic rule of justice," Kohlberg declares, "is distributive equality: treat every man equally."[29] Though he appears to favor John Rawls's account of justice,[30] he confines himself, in the present context, to conceding: "while there is no single accepted principle of justice which orders all these aspects, we generally assume a sphere of human rights in which equality takes priority over the special claims of commutative justice."[31] These remarks suggest the tendentious (however attractive) features of Kohlberg's claims; similar considerations have been brought to bear on Rawl's theory,[32] and it is fair to say that a theory of human rights as opposed to positive rights can only be vacuous.[33] But leaving these quarrels aside, the least reflection will show that Kohlberg's *principle* of justice is not more than the principle of universalizability read in the first sense (above): what the restrictive respects are in which men are to be equally treated *in the morally relevant way* is utterly unaffected by the injunction to treat them equally; the latter injunction is no more than a constraint of coherence and consistence of usage on any cognitively significant discourse; and the additional "specification" of the required equality of human rights (for instance, life, liberty, property, pursuit of happiness, dignity of person, and the like) simply invites all ideologically competing partisans to give whatever determinate interpretation of those vacuous rights they choose to. But *if* the principle of justice is the touchstone of Kohlberg's system, then, on the evidence, it is quite impossible for him to distinguish the sequence of moral development from that of cognitive development; *and* if Stage 1 through Stage 5 thinking is reasonably consistent, *then the principle of justice (Stage 6 thinking) must already be present or implicit in the others*. Without a more satisfactory formulation of the principle of justice, it is quite impossible even to contrast the putative stages of moral development. Hence, Kohlberg's conception of justice amounts to a *reductio* of his own account and enables us to assign an entirely trivial reading to his "argument for justice as the basic moral principle."[34] Kohlberg's chief thesis is that moral thinking is, when fully developed, principled. Nevertheless, he seems unable to say what distinguishes principled thinking—it cannot be universalizability, universal scope, or the having of reasons.

We must remind ourselves of Kohlberg's claims. "From the moral point of view," he says, "form is absolute, the fact-value distinction is absolute, and science and ethics are different."[35] The trouble is that, if the foregoing be conceded, the formal distinction of the moral is uncertain. We may add, now, that Kohlberg has offered no "absolute" distinction between facts and values and that the distinction of science and ethics hangs in the balance. In fact, it is quite reasonable to suppose that the difference between valuational and nonvaluational judgments depends not on the formal or logical features of such judgments but on the semantic properties of relevant predicates—in particular, that valuational predicates are explicable only by reference to norms governing grading and ranking, whereas nonvaluational predicates are explicable in terms of resemblance to standard specimens not assigned such normative standing; and that judgments are moral judgments rather than aesthetic or prudential or similar judgments not because they are prescriptive or action-guiding or categorical but because certain predicates are, on a theory, thought to be morally relevant.[36] Thus, for instance, a statement like "The sun ought to rise tomorrow at 6 A.M." may fairly be regarded as a valuational judgment but also as a factual judgment (facts and values not being distinct species of a common genus), since the implicit claim is that, on the evidence, it is more likely that the sun will rise tomorrow at 6 A.M. than that it will not. and a statement like "St. Francis lived a saintly life" is a moral judgment, since we may appreciate Francis's life in light of the morally relevant distinction of saintliness; it is not, however, prescriptive or action-guiding, since, on the usual view, saintliness involves gifts that no one can deliberately develop or choose.[37]

Once these distinctions are conceded, it's clear that Kohlberg must fall back—for the purpose of sorting moral development—to whatever he is persuaded is the *content* of such development. Here, he cannot hope to rise above the partisan disagreements of just those philosophers whom he rather grandly assigns to particular developmental stages within his schema: Bentham, it turns out, is merely a stage 2 moral thinker; Durkheim, a stage 4.[38] This partisan involvement seems, in fact, to be the upshot of his otherwise rather puzzling reversal of distinctions. "The scientific study of morality," he says, "must include in its scope the functions of morality for the development of the individual and the group. Here the fact-value distinction breaks down in a new way, and we get a Deweyan statement of morality, not as an autonomous absolute, as in the Kantian law or the Platonic good, but as a non-absolute part of the social life of the child, whose welfare is more important than his moral status."[39] It is difficult to understand this maneuver, like the rejection of Soviet collectivism noted earlier, as anything but the advocacy of a favored set of libertarian values. It may well be that we wish to stand for such values, but Kohlberg cannot—any more than Hare or Rawls—extract them from an objective study of the conditions of human existence. This, of course, is precisely the conscientious dilemma of a liberal-minded conception of American education: it pretends to pursue objectively and openly the issue of which moral values to infuse with its program of training, but in its heart it already knows which values must be sustained. Thus, for instance, although he insists, "following Dewey and Piaget," that "the goal of moral education is the stimulation of the 'natural' development of the individual child's own moral judgment and capacities,"[40] and that "the experiences by which children naturally move from stage to stage are nonindoctrinative, that is, they are not experiences of being taught and internalizing specific content,"[41] Kohlberg claims that "the 'official' morality of rights in our society also represents a culturally universal principled stage of moral judgment, so that the teaching of justice is also the stimulation of moral development";[42] and he himself finally offers the example of a certain Friend's Meeting School as the model of "a moral education program" in contrast to the model of "a political education program."[43]

It cannot be denied that there is a developmental sequence that children pass through—for any significant dimension of human sensibility. But to say so is emphatically not to say that the sequence is invariant. The structuralist thesis that Kohlberg subscribes to is not so much disconfirmed as unconfirmable, because it is conceptually muddled and vague. For example, Stages 3 and 4 form what he calls the "conventional level" of moral development. Here is Kohlberg's general characterization:

At this level, maintaining the expectations of the individual's family, group, or nation is perceived as valuable in its own right, regardless of immediate and obvious consequences. The attitude is one not only of *conformity* to personal expectations and social order, but of loyalty to it, of activity *maintaining*, supporting, and justifying the order and of identifying with the persons or groups involved in it.[44]

There is of course a certain abstractness involved in recognizing such social complexes as "groups" or "nations" other than the family. Kohlberg concedes that, for the stages involved, the child not only *conforms* but *intends* to conform, grasps and understands something of the relevant justifying considerations bearing on the interests of such groups. Nevertheless, he insists on contrasting such Stage 3 and 4 sensibility to Stage 6 thinking, in which "Right is defined by the decision of conscience in accord with self-chosen *ethical principles* appealing to logical comprehensiveness, universality, and consistency."[45] No doubt, there are *some* differences registered by the descriptions given. But it is impossible to hold, on the foregoing argument, that Stage 3 and 4 thinking fails to conform to the requirements of universality or universalizability (in the first sense given) any less than Stage 6 thinking. Furthermore, *if* a child is conceded to be able to identify nations and other extremely abstract groups—say, socio-economic classes, ethnic peoples, ecosystems, the population of the earth as opposed to the science fiction populations of other planets—then it is quite impossible to show that a State 3 or 4 child is incapable of considering the values assigned, on some ideology, to the entire human race. But if that is so, then, on Kohlberg's own thesis, it is quite impossible to show that a child's nationalistic orientation is inherently "less moral" or "less adequate morally" than one directed, say, to sacrificing national objectives to the putative utility of all members of the human race: the reason is simply that it is quite possible for a child (or anyone else) to favor nationalistic values against the backdrop of understanding that human beings are also members of one human race. *There is no loss of universality in favoring the interests of one subpopulation of the human race over others, including (in whatever sense may be deemed intelligible) the "interests of the human race" itself.* One has only to be convinced that there are *relevant* differences among given subpopulations. The other Stage 6 criteria, "logical comprehensiveness," "consistency," can hardly be expected to fare any better. Also, a (Stage 6) choice of "conscience" in accord with "principles" is rather unreliable, both because Kohlberg has failed to define 'principle' satisfactorily and because a choice of conscience may well favor social arrangements thought by Kohlberg to obtain at a lower level of development.

This last consideration, in fact, points to the essential weakness of Kohlberg's thesis. For Kohlberg somehow supposes that the content of one's moral doctrine signifies one's stage of moral development along the scale provided. This is the reason Kohlberg treats Bentham as a Stage 2 moral thinker and Durkheim as a Stage 4 moral thinker. What, otherwise, would prevent us from viewing Bentham and Durkheim as fully developed, that is, as capable of understanding all of the cognitively relevant distinctions of moral thinking? On that view, their moral doctrines represent their partisan convictions, having reviewed relevant alternatives, *not* the stage of development at which they have been fixated. Bentham's advocacy of utilitarianism does not entail his incapacity to have subscribed to any other coherent thesis but his conviction regarding the validity of all the competing views he was capable of understanding. It may be the case that children are actually, at one time or another, incapable of understanding one set of distinctions or another, but it is difficult to see how the socially developed convictions of children at one time or another can be supposed, for that reason alone, to entail their incapacity to understand the distinctions favored at another "stage" of development. It looks very much as if Kohlberg has conflated cognitive capacity with doctrinal conviction and training: the regularities he confirms in the development of childhood morality suggest not so much stages toward a "better" morality, construed as cognitive stages of some sort—whether definitely structured with regard to invariances being itself debatable—as cognitive stages not clearly ordered morally (or paralleling such an order in the scheme of moral development), through which a child learns to review and reappraise the doctrinal convictions he has been provided.

From this point of view, it is hopeless to deny that education, moral education in particular, is ideologically oriented; hopeless to deny that the values inculcated are or could be anything but values favored by the very society supporting the public educational system. The puzzles of a so-called democratic education or of an education devoted to so-called pluralistic values are real enough.[46] But what is the use pretending that it is based on a "natural" order of things or that there is an objectively discernible order of increasingly adequate stages of moral development?

Kohlberg does indeed wish to avoid the obviously doctrinaire. As he says, "our 'claims of superiority' for higher stages are not claims for a system of grading the moral worth of individual persons, but are claims for the greater adequacy of one form of moral thinking over another . . . . The general criterion we have used in saying that a higher stage's mode of judgment is more adequate than a lower stage is that of morality itself, not

of conceptions of rationality or sophistication imported from other dom-
ains."[47] But what does this come to? Kohlberg claims that a "deontological" emphasis on duties and rights is superior to a "teleological" emphasis
on aims or ends or on an "approbative" emphasis on personal worth or
virtue;[48] but this has never been demonstrated. Once the conceptual distinctions involved are admitted to have been grasped, how would one hope
to demonstrate that there was a *morally* correct way of ordering such
considerations? Kohlberg has stressed that Stage 6 thinking is principled,
but, as we have already seen, this either means trivializing the distinction
among the various stages; or it means emphasizing that the scope of moral
thinking extends to the entire human race—which is in itself neutral to all
sorts of preferential systems; or it means favoring some substantive doctrine
for the entire human race as such—which is itself tendentious. Again,
Kohlberg links the thesis with the claim that morality is *sui generis.*[49] But,
as we have seen, he means this in a "formalistic" sense which he cannot
effectively provide. Finally, he stresses that his theory assumes a metaethics
according to which moral judgments "are not true or false in the cognitive-
descriptivist sense."[50] But, in deriving the moral "ought" from the "is" of
moral development, he *does* maintain that it is *true* that stage 6 thinking is
morally more developed than any other sort of thinking; also, *if* the vacuity
of the concept of justice and human rights is denied by Kohlberg, then it is
quite impossible for him to deny that *some* substantive findings are validly
derivable from the grounds of Stage 6 thinking. But if so, then he cannot
oppose the "cognitive-descriptivist" thesis. But that is precisely why Kohlberg's theory amounts to the support of a "hidden curriculum." More than
this, it is precisely why every program of moral education—as enlightened
as we can imagine—supports some "hidden curriculum."

NOTES

1. Cf. for instance, Lawrence Kohlberg, "Stages of Moral Development as a Basis for Moral
Education," in C. M. Beck, B. S. Crittenden, and E. V. Sullivan, eds., *Moral Education:
Interdisciplinary Approaches* (Toronto: University of Toronto Press, 1971)—hereafter abbrevi-
ated "Stages" (page references are to the Newman Press edition [1971]); "From Is to Ought:
How to Commit the Naturalistic Fallacy and Get Away with It in the Study of Moral
Development," in Theodore Mischel, ed., *Cognitive Development and Epistemology* (New
York: Academic Press, 1971)—abbreviated "Is"; Lawrence Kohlberg and E. Turiel, *Moraliza-
tion Research, The Cognitive-Developmental Approach* (New York: Holt, Winston, 1971); L.
Kohlberg and E. Turiel, "Developmental Methods in Moral Education," in G. Lesser, ed.,
Psychological Approaches to Teaching (Chicago: Scott, Foresman, 1971). I have confined my
attention essentially to "Stages," since Kohlberg's other discussions—for instance, "Is"—are
remarkably similar even in detail.

2. Cf. Jean Piaget, *The Moral Judgment of the Child*, trans. by Marjorie Gebain (New York; Free Press, 1969).

3. "Stages," p. 28.

4. Cf. Emile Durkheim, *Moral Education: A Study in the Theory and Application of the Sociology of Education*, trans. by Everett K. Wilson and Herman Schnaurer (New York: Free Press, 1961), cited by Kohlberg, "Stages".

5. "Stages," p. 27.

6. Ibid., p. 30.

7. Ibid., p. 42.

8. Ibid., p. 36.

9. Cf. A. S. Neill, *Summerhill: A Radical Approach to Child Rearing* (New York: Hart Publishing Co., 1960), p. 4; cited by Kohlberg, "Stages."

10. Ibid., p. 34.

11. Ibid., p. 55.

12. Ibid., p. 24.

13. Ibid., p. 55.

14. Ibid., p. 61.

15. Ibid., p. 48.

16. Ibid., p. 54.

17. Ibid., p. 54.

18. Ibid., p. 56.

19. Ibid., pp. 27–28, 33.

20. Ibid., p. 45.

21. Ibid., p. 45. Cf. also, "Is," IV.

22. Cf. Immanuel Kant, *Critique of Practical Judgment*; also, R. M. Hare, *The Language of Morals* (Oxford: Clarendon, 1952).

23. "Stages," p. 55.

24. Ibid., p. 38.

25. Cf. Joseph Margolis, *Values and Conduct* (Oxford: Clarendon, 1971), pp. 83–86.

26. "Stages," p. 58.

27. Ibid., pp. 58–59.

28. Ibid., pp. 64–65.

29. Ibid., pp. 62–63.

30. Cf. John Rawls, *A Theory of Justice* (Cambridge: Harvard University Press, 1971).

31. "Stages," p. 63.

32. Cf. Norman Daniels, ed., *Reading Rawls; Critical Studies of "A Theory of Justice"* (New York: Basic Books, 1975).

33. For example, capital punishment, imprisonment, legal forfeit of property, and the like cannot in principle be incompatible with any set of what are usually described as ("inalienable") human rights; cf. Joseph Margolis, *Negativities* (Columbus: Charles Merrill, 1975), chap. 10.

34. "Stages," pp. 65–66.

35. Ibid., p. 70.

36. Margolis, *Negativities*.

37. These are, in fact, clues to the essential weakness of Hare's moral philosophy, which Kohlberg professes to follow; cf. Margolis, *Negativities*, chap. 10.

38. "Stages," p. 66.

39. Ibid., p. 70.

40. Ibid., p. 71.

41. Ibid., p. 72.
42. Ibid., p. 72.
43. Ibid., p. 84.
44. Ibid., p. 87.
45. Ibid., p. 88.
46. Cf. Kurt Baier, "Ethical Pluralism and Moral Education," in Beck et al., *Moral* Education, op. cit.
47. "Is," pp. 214–215.
48. Ibid., p. 214.
49. Ibid., p. 215.
50. Ibid., p. 215.

IV

THE
PHILOSOPHICAL
EDUCATION
OF
THE
CHILD

INTRODUCTION

As a number of contributors to this volume have indicated, children are inclined to raise questions that require philosophical reflection and discussion if they are to be responded to adequately. Indeed, it is children's readiness to engage in such discussion which prompts our belief that children possess a philosophical disposition. Children wonder at the world and they reveal that wonder through the kinds of questioning and exploring that are conventionally associated with philosophical behavior.

But the philosophical disposition of children is no different from any other of their creative tendencies, in the sense that few such tendencies are likely to come to fruition if they are not carefully nurtured and cultivated. Just as children's mathematical or musical or other proclivities need training, guidance and encouragement, so do the philosophical tendencies of children if they are to be brought to expression.

There exists a peculiar affinity between philosophy and education. At the heart of philosophy is interrogation and dialogue; at the heart of this discipline is therefore what is essential to education. The craft of philosophy contains within itself a pedagogy—the need for dialogue, the need for questioning and a method of inquiry—which are essentially characteristic of education in general. This is why education cannot be divorced from philosophy and philosophy cannot be divorced from education. One view of the role philosophy can play in education has been typically expressed by Ernest Nagel:

> philosophers can play a constructive role in the detailed formulation of a central educational objective. That objective, when stated in general terms, is to replace intellectual habits which tend to make men accept and retain unexamined beliefs by intellectual habits that place a premium on responsibly based thought. However, if this general objective is to be realized, the character of cogent reasoning must be set forth clearly, not simply in the abstract but in the context of teaching the concrete materials of various specialized domains of inquiry. In short, I believe that a supreme educational objective can be realized only if both the sciences and the humanities are presented to students not simply as miscellaneous bodies of useful and enlightened information, but as the fruits of a characteristically human method of intelligence. For organizing such presentations, there is needed expert familiarity with the credited outcome of educational research, and expert familiarity with the relevant distinctions and principles of logic. By participating in such a cooperative reorganization of the content of instruction,

philosophy can make what I think is an invaluable contribution to educational practice.[1]

The role of philosophy in education can certainly be no less than what Nagel says it could be, but on the other hand, it certainly could be much more. It is not sufficient for philosophers to reorganize the curriculum in a rational fashion; there remains the task of introducing children to philosophical ideas and encouraging them to reflect upon these ideas in an independent and critical fashion. Both these requirements must be met. It is not enough just to encourage children to think critically. They have to be acquainted with the thoughts of the major thinkers of the past so that they can build upon those thoughts rather than be forced to invent everything for themselves.

When viewed in this more comprehensive fashion, it would be reasonable to expect that the encouragement of children's philosophical thinking would serve to stimulate and improve the entire educational process. Education has both a preparatory function and an intrinsic, consummatory value. It is preparation for life, and at the same time it is an end in itself. In either case philosophy, when integrated into the curriculum, can serve to enhance both the immediate and the instrumental goals of education. By encouraging children to ask questions at every stage of the educational process, the meanings they are searching for can be made available at every stage of the process. Once this occurs, the value of education is no longer postponed until "some day in the future" but can be made present and satisfying within every hour of the child's school day.

This is not to say that philosophy, as valuable as it is in itself, should be introduced into the educational process as just another course, merely for its own sake. A recognition of the affinity between philosophy and education would lead us to realize that once philosophy enters the curriculum, it is likely to permeate children's experience of the whole range of academic disciplines in the school. The questioning of assumptions, the search for broader generalizations, the stimulation of reflection and imagination, the recognition of the importance of giving reasons for beliefs, all of these have a contagiousness about them which can readily be replicated when teaching any discipline.

There are those who see philosophy as primarily critical and appraisive, and who fear that the encouragement of similar attitudes among children can only produce young people who are overly analytical and contentious, and who lack esteem for what is worthwhile in our civilization. But this is a misunderstanding of philosophy, whose function is as much to commend to our attention that which is worthy of appreciation or deserving of commendation as it is to discern those values for which little or no justification can be found. Encouraging children to think philosophically should therefore not be identified with the fostering among children of merely negative attitudes towards all which is traditional or conventional.

The question then arises as to what particular problems are posed by the introduction of philosophy into the elementary school curriculum. The major inconsistency which has to be faced is the way that philosophy must be taught, and the way that instruction is often carried out in many other disciplines. Bruner has argued that any subject can be taught with integrity at any level, and this is true for many subjects—provided that the content of such subjects be suitably reconstructed so as to be understood by children. This is certainly true of philosophy, provided that one realizes that one cannot teach the subject-matter in a didactic manner to children. Some subjects lend themselves more than others to a separation of content and methodology. But philosophy doesn't lend itself at all to that separation. When properly taught, the content and methodology are not readily distinguishable from one another. One cannot properly teach philosophy without to some extent doing philosophy oneself and instigating similar activity on the part of one's students.

Another problem that arises in introducing philosophy into the elementary school curriculum is the issue of what aspect of the existing curriculum should be sacrificed to this new discipline. Teachers will inevitably ask, "Must other subjects be compressed in order to make room for philosophy and if so, what is the justification for doing so?" The justification of any curriculum lies in the educational results that it produces. If a curriculum with philosophy produces better educational results than one without philosophy, then that is the curriculum we should employ. Indeed, if the attainment of educational goals is measurable, then the value of philosophy's contribution to such education will likewise be measurable.

It has been said that teaching is a subversive activity. But perhaps it is more true to say that philosophy is a subversive activity because its methodology is inherently dialogical and open-ended. It thus establishes standards of what education should be, such that conscientious teachers are compelled to unlearn that whey have been doing and to begin to think about the meaning and underlying assumptions of all that they present to their students. When philosophy enters the classroom, it demands of teachers that they engage in continuous reflection upon the methods and curricula they employ. Whether or not teachers have the commitment to education to engage in such ongoing reappraisal of what they do and their reasons for doing so will determine whether or not we are to have philosophy in the classroom.

Four considerations are listed by Oscanyan, in the opening essay in this section, as essential to take into account in teaching children logic. (1) In their earliest use of language, children already demonstrate their ability to reason. "We should view logic teaching as the development of abilities that children already possess, not as bestowing new and unfamiliar skills." (2) Children display different proficiencies with respect to any particular logical competency. (3) Children's reasoning skills are affected by the situations in which they find themselves: some settings are more conducive to reasoning than others. (4) Teachers are responsible for finding hospitable contexts in which the children in their class are disposed to develop their skills in reasoning. Thus the discussion in the classroom of a philosophical novel may be far more conducive to the development of those children's reasoning skills than the didactic presentation of deductive arguments.

That children employ logical reasoning when they use language can be discerned in their response to encouragement and discouragement. Thus, we cannot encourage them to engage in certain forms of behavior nor discourage them from others without assuming their ability to perform rather intricate logical tasks. Suppose that we would like to discourage a child from a certain form of behavior. We tell the child, "if you suck your thumb, you will get buck teeth." What is implied (and presumably mutually understood) is that he would find buck teeth undesirable or even abhorrent. Thus, we are indicating to him a consequence of his actions *which he does not desire*, and he is able to infer that if he does not *want* the consequent, then he should not *perform* the antecedent. The principle here is one that is employed in all conditioning theory: that is, conditioning theory assumes the capacity of a small child to perform the logical operation of inferring that the denial of the antecedent follows from the denial of the consequent.

Oscanyan argues elsewhere in his article for curriculum approaches which present children with models of self-directed intellectual inquiry. By presenting them with models of a wide variety of thinking styles, we encourage them to become aware of the diverse possibilities of reflective conduct. At the same time by showing such inquiry as public and social, we can help children realize what a community of inquiry can be, so that they come to appreciate the fact that the cooperative and social dimensions of reflection are as precious as those that are private and personal.

Oscanyan's paper shows that there can be a fresh and meaningful approach to the teaching of logic to children. The many experiments that have been conducted with the aim of showing that children can learn formal logic have not been at all fruitless. They successfully demonstrated that children can learn to perform logical operations better than children who have not been exposed to the same formal material. But the problem has always been: How does logic become part of the larger educational program? How can it be integrated into the elementary school curriculum? What Oscanyan is saying is that if attention is paid to the logic that is already embedded in children's language itself, as well as to the language of the already existing curriculum, then children can learn logic much more readily and efficiently, so long as they are guided by perceptive and knowledgeable teachers. Thus, to introduce logic into the curriculum does not necessarily involve adding another subject, but it does involve helping children become conscious of the logic that already exists in the present curriculum. Moreover, to facilitate the pupil's becoming conscious of the logical dimension of language, Oscanyan notes the desirability of presenting such logic, as spoken by children themselves, in fictional contexts so that the students in the classroom can identify with such models and endeavor to sharpen their awareness of their own thought processes.

Valuable as the Oscanyan article is, it is no more than the first step in indicating the path that must be taken towards the construction of an effective thinking skills curriculum. Such a curriculum would have to be embedded in the humanistic materials that are representative of our culture. If children can be attuned to the complexities of our language and to the rich heritage of ideas that philosophy can provide, then their own pursuit of meanings in these fictional materials will acquaint them with the employment of language in a logical fashion more effectively than any didactic demonstration of syllogistic reasoning could ever do. This is not to deny that there are times when didactic instruction is essential if one is to understand logic, but such demonstrations have to be performed within the context of children's experience, rather than as seemingly extraneous demonstrations of the teacher's logical virtuosity.

According to David Ecker, children's talk about art should be taken seriously, not simply on the level of art criticism, but on the meta-critical level of philosophical aesthetics as well. He argues that children make significant comments about art, are able to provide reasons for their judgments, and can classify such judgments according to categories of their own devising. It would follow that children's aesthetic opinions are not derived from adult views, but are constitutive of their own original aesthetic theorizing.

If Ecker's interpretations of his empirical studies are correct, one may be led to ask why aesthetics—certainly one of the most esoteric areas of philosophy—would provide so rich a field of exploration with regard to children's philosophical activity. But an answer to this question may not be difficult to discover. Children reflect upon and are often inclined to discuss those experiences which stir them and affect them deeply and directly. But many school subjects are not *directly* experienced. Thus, for example, history is retold: it is related to students by intermediaries. Likewise, much that is included in scientific study is remote from direct experience of the natural world. But works of literature and works of art affect children directly. What is more, children are likely to be more in touch with the creative (as over against the appreciative) aspects of art than are most adults. This lends to their aesthetic comments an undeniable freshness and acuteness.

Talk about art of course is not necessarily philosophical talk about art. Thus the fact that one is a mature artist is not sufficient to guarantee that one's comments about art are philosophical in nature. The situation with children is no different. Children's remarks about art can be considered "critical" when the criteria underlying such remarks can be identified, and "philosophical" when the criteria employed can themselves be subject to discussion. But children's talk about art also bears a philosophical character when they inquire into those meanings of human existence as are to be found in art. Thus the child who asks, "Pretty—what do you mean by that?" is raising a question of criteria, but the answer to that question— revealing the role of "being pretty" in human experience—equally involves the child in a profound pursuit of philosophical understanding.

Perhaps what Ecker has best demonstrated is that children are capable of talking about art in ways as valuable and fascinating as their artistic creations. But this natural inclination of children to discuss what they have created may reveal only the most rudimentary traces of philosophy unless the conversation is guided and encouraged by a philosophically oriented adult. Like any other branch of philosophy, aesthetics flourishes in an educational setting. It is the character of this setting which Wilson seeks to identify.

Wilson's essay is concerned with the question of how to see to it that children experience works of art in an intelligent fashion, so as to avail themselves of the meanings and values that such works have to offer. The appreciation of such works is indispensable—children should not be encouraged to become little pedants who know all about art but don't like it. In addition to liking art, they should be able to express good reasons for their judgments. And finally, the reasons they cite should be the very same reasons which account for their likings and dislikings. In the process of encouraging children to deal intelligently with works of art, we are doing more than sharpening their perceptions: we are in fact heightening their sensibilities and educating their emotions. For in aesthetic education (as in moral education), the cultivation of intelligent emotions is one of the educator's most important goals.

It is with the help of this analogy between aesthetic and ethical education that Wilson can effectively compare the experience of appreciating a work of art with the experience of loving a person. He acknowledges the enormous extent to which, in both cases, we often find ourselves inarticulate when it comes to expressing our reasons for feeling as we do. So often we are not conscious of just what it is that moves us. But whether we are head over heels in love with a person or with a work of art, the situation is quite the same: we want to appreciate what is genuinely there to be appreciated, rather than be victims of our own misperceptions, or enjoy what is there for the wrong reasons, for in either case, we do not educate our sensibilities so as to make them capable of still richer experiences in the future.

One who is engaged in aesthetic education can therefore help children first to care about works of art, Wilson suggests. Then, once they care, the teacher's comments will relate more and more to what the student feels and is moved by. Gradually, the student will learn from the instructor's comments and questions—will learn to care about such problems as the distinction between the sincere and the insincere, the genuine and the fraudulent. Students will come to see that appreciating, like any other form of experiencing, has its own artful and intelligent dimensions, and can be done well or badly. The perceptive teacher, moreover, will pay attention to what children do, how they perform, and not merely to what they say, so as to catch the non-verbal dimension of the child's aesthetic responsiveness.

There is much to applaud in Wilson's approach to aesthetic education. His recognition that the cultivation of attention and care is of primary importance is one which those already engaged in aesthetic education will readily assent to. At the same time, such teachers will probably acknowledge that children's readiness to learn encompasses aesthetics as fully as it does any other area of understanding. Children do not resist discussing why some works of art, particularly works by children of their own age rather than adults' works, might be better than others in some respects and worse than others in other respects. It falls in easily with their eagerness to be able to distinguish generally between the better and the worse. But Wilson is correct in cautioning that even this can become a mere technical proficiency. What matters ultimately, as Leo Stein once remarked, is not that we should be able to distinguish better art from worse art, but that we should be able to live in such ways that it matters to us whether we can distinguish the better from the worse.

The articles dealing with moral education approach the subject from a number of different angles. According to Martin Benjamin there is sufficient likeness between the pursuits of scientific and of moral under-standing to establish the objectivity of moral knowledge, without being absolutistic on the one hand or subjectivistic on the other. Benjamin concludes that such an analogy between science and ethics provides the teacher with a flexible and suitable model for moral education. Diller approaches moral education through literature, through moral discourse, and in terms of a parent-child setting rather than a teacher-student setting. What she seeks to show is that everyday situations between adults and children can have an undercurrent of moral force. If the adult is capable of guiding the discourse in a delicate but understanding fashion, then the pressures of the dialogue can be so directed that the child comes to his own realization of the moral issues involved. Thus the discourse is not an end in itself but a means of developing moral perception so that the child can be in a better position to make a moral judgment. Lipman and Sharp seek to show that moral education cannot be self-sufficient. Benjamin has al-ready made this point by indicating the need for non-moral knowledge in the course of moral education. In similar fashion, Lipman and Sharp contend that the education of moral judgment is an aspect of philosophical inquiry which cannot be isolated from other branches of philosophy. Clyde Evans approaches the question of moral education with respect to its im-pact upon parental values. He seeks to allay the fears some parents have expressed that moral philosophy will undermine such values and undercut parental authority. Evans argues that children who have not undergone experiences of moral searching, questioning and inquiry will hold their values more precariously and with more fragile commitment than those who have carefully considered the alternatives and have made their own judgments after reflection. Richard Hare suggests that the role of the teacher in moral education is to be neutral with regard to substantive issues and unneutral with regard to methodological issues. Scolnicov, on the other hand, feels that such neutrality must be taken very cautiously and in some respects is insufficient. This is because the teacher must convey a serious concern with respect to what he is teaching. In this regard, the teacher must be partial rather than impartial.

Benjamin first argues for the analogy between science and ethics, then acknowledges certain limitations to the analogy, and finally seeks to show the implications of the analogy for moral education. The science-ethics analogy is based upon the similarity Benjamin finds between systems of scientific understanding, where singular perceptual judgments are said to be in equilibrium with theories or principles, and systems of ethics, where individual moral intuitions are supposedly in equilibrium with ethical theories or principles. In each case, the equilibrium is fluid and dynamic, allowing for revision of the less stable components, with constant readjustments taking place all around as each shift or alteration occurs.

If we accept the science-ethics analogy, Benjamin contends, we must admit the fallaciousness of both subjectivism and absolutism in ethics, for we can recognize that the system of ethical understanding possesses an objectivity not fundamentally different from that of scientific understanding. We also realize that subjectivism and absolutism merely exploit certain extreme cases while ignoring the vast plurality of ethical judgments which are not totally subjective and about which there is little unanimity, but which nevertheless can be systematically ordered and understood.

The implications of Benjamin's argument for moral education are these: (1) Once teachers come to see that singular judgments and general principles stand in reflective equilibrium in ethics just as they do in science, they can help their children work to emphasize and improve that equilibrium by bringing ethical theory and ethical practice ever closer together. (2) Teachers can better model morally committed behavior for students, and demonstrate what it is to be a morally integrated person, once they, the teachers, become aware of the logical implications of their own moral positions. (3) Teachers can recognize the need for cultivation of children's moral perception and moral imagination, since this is the only way children can be brought to care about other people's needs and interests. And morality demands that moral judgments take place only when *all things have been considered*. Other people's interests are precisely the kinds of things that are meant by that stipulation. (4) Benjamin reminds us that moral and non-moral awareness can be of mutual value, for familiarity with technical matters can give us valuable insights into moral problems, and moral awareness, in turn, can throw new and important light on otherwise pointless factual information.

Whether Benjamin's portraits of science and ethics—with their striking likeness—will be acceptable to most philosophers is perhaps a somewhat less important question than whether the analogy can play the useful, heuristic role in moral education which he argues it can. Still other questions emerge from a critical reading of Benjamin's article. Are moral intuitions sufficiently similar to scientific observation to justify the parallel status which Benjamin assumes them to have? Does the analogy between ethics and science rest primarily on the fact that both involve rational systematizations of beliefs or would it perhaps be more apt to say it rests on the fact that doing ethics and doing science alike involve the internalization of the principles and methods of inquiry? Moreover, is it possible that the prevalent model of science as a set of activities that develop cumulatively and converge upon an ideal goal is sharply at variance with the tradition of philosophical ethics whose character has been generally dialectical and pluralistic? We have seen that developmental theories which hold that there is a "highest stage of morality" are inevitably interpreted as portraying an ultimate and final paradigm toward which everyone should aspire. In this sense, the "reflective equilibrium" Benjamin speaks of might, in a pedagogical setting, be misinterpreted as urging teachers to aim for some kind of comfortable ethical stasis, despite the fact that Benjamin himself would deplore such a situation.

Diller's paradigm of moral education differs sharply from Benjamin's. Yet the model she sketches, though drawn from a literary source, would seem to embody a great many *desiderata* that Benjamin calls for: ability to engage in inquiry, moral imagination, sensitivity, moral perception, awareness of oneself and awareness of others. It is true that the situation Diller analyzes is not a teacher-student relationship, but a parent-child relationship. And the Salinger passage she analyzes is not a philosophical essay but a work of fiction. Ordinarily, this might be a very hazardous combination. But Diller handles the matter very deftly and, without doing violence to the aesthetic surface of the story, probes beneath that surface so as to get at the underlying network of emotional and moral relationships. It is likely that not many works of literature lend themselves as readily as this work to being demonstration pieces for purposes of moral education. The Salinger story demonstrates the possibility of children and adults conducting a meaningful moral dialogue in which the adult, in this case the mother, takes a responsible role and yet, without being overbearing toward the child, manages to arouse in the child a corresponding sense of moral responsibility. It is likely that both teachers and students could profit from the moral paradigm of Salinger's story as illuminated by Diller's analysis.

If moral education is to be introduced into the schools, one of its emphases will have to be on the enhancement of moral perception. To accomplish this, considerable attention will have to be given to understanding the conditions of dialogue. For Diller this involves directing "Lionel's attention to the moral aspects and relationships of the situation in such a way that he could perceive these as moral for himself." If, through such dialogue, children can be nudged into perceiving for themselves and thinking for themselves, then education will acquire both a philosophical and moral dimension.

The editors of the present collection have included a selection from their book for teachers of elementary school philosophy. While we are not inclined to challenge the content of the selection, which deals with moral education, we must acknowledge the failure to specify the prerequisites for effectively training moral educators, as well as the minimal requirements for a really effective moral education curriculum. There are questions that remain to be answered.

Perhaps the primary importance of Clyde Evans' article on philosophy and parental values is that it serves to clarify what has ordinarily had a tendency to remain rather obscure: the justification to parents of moral education programs in the schools. Evans contends that moral education, when properly conducted, encourages children to become free, autonomous and reasonable individuals. And this, he argues, is just what parents want for their children: to be able to use their own understanding. There is more than an echo here of Kant, exhorting us to emerge from our self-imposed immaturity, cultivate our minds, and dare to think for ourselves:

> A large part of mankind gladly remain minors all their lives, long after nature has freed them from external guidance. They are the reasons why it is so easy for others to set themselves up as guardians. It is so comfortable to be a minor. If I have a book that thinks for me, a pastor who acts as my conscience, a physician who prescribes my diet, and so on—then I have no need to exert myself. I have no need to think, if only I can pay; others will take care of that disagreeable business for me. Those guardians who have kindly taken supervision upon themselves see to it that the overwhelming majority of mankind—among them the

entire fair sex—should consider the step to maturity, not only as hard, but as extremely dangerous. First, these guardians make their domestic cattle stupid and carefully prevent the docile creatures from taking a single step without the leading-strings to which they have fastened them. Then they show them the danger that would threaten them if they should try to walk by themselves. Now this danger is really not very great; after stumbling a few times they would, at last, learn to walk.[2]

Evans assumes that parents do not want their children to be thoughtless, inconsiderate and irresponsible. Quite the contrary: upon reflection, parents will recognize that their fears concerning moral reflection are unfounded, because their morally thoughtful children will not automatically reject parental values, but rather will turn their attention to seeking justification for those very values. Reflective parents will recognize that merely to take one's values and graft them onto the child is not equivalent to the child's internalization of such values. Nor does it equip the child to deal flexibly and effectively with new and changing circumstances for which parental experience may be inadequate.

Evans points out that the entire enterprise of moral education hinges upon the adequate training of teachers. Should an inadequately trained teacher take advantage of an opportunity to indoctrinate or in any way undermine parental values, then it follows that the parents in this instance will likely feel threatened by and hostile towards the moral education program itself. For many parents, what is placed in question is not simply their values, but their status as parents, that is, as parental authorities. Therefore it is necessary to demonstrate to parents that the moral education of their children can be conducted with integrity, and that it can be counted on to supplement—rather than interfere with or countermand—their own efforts to help their children become morally responsible individuals.

In one sense, Evans' article represents an answer to Joseph Flay's contention that moral education is itself immoral because the dependency of children should be preserved intact. But perhaps it would be better to see both positions—that of Evans and that of Flay—as introductory arguments which stand in need of considerable development if the issue they both address is to be adequately formulated and understood. In a pluralistic society, "in which," as Hare says, "nobody has the power to indoctrinate everybody, the only solution is to teach as many people as possible to think as well as possible."

It is Hare's contention that we are faced with a bewildering array of "values, principles, ideologies, ways of life, etc.," and that it is necessary to fit children "to make, *for themselves*, the choices with which they will inevitably be faced." We cannot expect children simply to do whatever we tell them when it comes to questions of value. "Ultimately," says Hare, "children have to make up their own minds." They can do this if we teach them how to think for themselves. This means we must teach children how to think and not merely what to think. If, Hare argues, we can familiarize children with the rules of reasoning so that they will understand what a moral question is and so that they will know what kinds of arguments are legitimate, if we can explore with them the possible answers in light of the facts, then the chances are that they will be able to engage in careful, fair and clear discussion and to reach agreement with others.

A theme which runs through Hare's paper and is alluded to in the preceding paper by Evans as well is the distinction between substantive and methodological values. Thus with respect to the substantive and controversial issues under discussion, a teacher may well remain neutral until the students have internalized the procedures of analysis and discussion to the point where they can accept the teacher's presentation of her own views regarding the substantive issues being discussed. But the teacher need not be neutral on methodological values; on the contrary, Hare is quite emphatic that it is the teacher's role to impose a suitable intellectual discipline in the classroom. Unless teachers insist upon rules of procedure, students will not be encouraged to internalize such rules, and it is only when they do internalize them that students are equipped to think for themselves.

Hare's essay is an eloquent plea for children's intellectual emancipation, and it would be difficult to find a better reasoned argument for just this kind of education. Nevertheless it is desirable that the distinction between methodological and substantive values not be interpreted to mean that one should only cultivate children's logical prowess in moral arguments, while neglecting to turn their attention to those philosophical ideas which have immeasurably enriched our understanding of what it is to be moral beings. Moral education is, at the very least, the cultivation of clear and logical and critical thinking; but it cannot be merely that. Unless it is set in a context that is relevant to children's own experiences, that lights up children's own imaginations and at the same time provides them with a glimpse of the rich array of intellectual alternatives embodied in the philosophical tradition, the kind of value education Hare proposes may well be inadequate.

The last two paragraphs of the Hare essay, dealing as they do with the exemplary role of the teacher in the classroom, relate directly to the content of the Scolnicov article which follows. Scolnicov agrees that the teacher of philosophy must develop in students both facility in critical thinking and profundity of philosophical understanding. He examines with great sensitivity the responsibility of the teacher to facilitate discussion without intruding his or her own views in such a way as to inhibit student participation in the dialogue. While aware that teachers may have to be neutral in other disciplines, Scolnicov nevertheless contends that the notion of neutrality must be taken with great caution insofar as philosophy is concerned. The educational function of teaching philosophy is to bring students to care about truth and rationality. It is essential that teachers reveal that they too have this same concern. This educational function, Scolnicov maintains, is not compatible with full-fledged neutrality on the teacher's part. In this connection, he contrasts the philosophy teacher with the tennis instructor. The latter teaches the student to be in a position to play tennis if the student should ever want to do so. But the philosophy teacher is not saying, "Should you ever want to be rational, here is how to go about it." The philosophy teacher is committed to encouraging the student to *prefer* rationality over irrationality. In this sense, the stance of the philosophy teacher is not a neutral stance. One cannot help hearing in this distinction an echo of Kant: the approach of the tennis instructor is "hypothetical"—students may or may not play the game they have learned. But the approach of the philosophy teacher is "categorical"— students are being shown how they *ought* to live. Nevertheless, readers who are not persuaded of the categorical versus hypothetical distinction in Kant may be equally difficult to persuade with regard to the similar distinction in Scolnicov. Certainly teachers of other disciplines—whether in the sciences, arts or humanities—might contend that they are committed, no less than the philosophy teacher, to taking a stance of commitment to truth and rationality.

There is an irony that is intrinsic to the teaching of philosophy, Scolnicov notes, adding that such teaching "is a kind of balancing art" in which one should reveal neither too much nor too little of one's own views to the student. Yet, he says, this cat-and-mouse approach must present itself as merely a mask, behind which the teacher is in utter earnest. This seriousness is what makes the teaching of philosophy effective in the formation of character, rather than being merely a "whetting of wits for wit's sake."

Perhaps Scolnicov, as well as a number of other contributors to this collection, is suggesting that the question "Why philosophy for children?" cannot be answered by philosophy without circularity. Thus if a person asks, "Why should I be rational?" he is in effect questioning the giving of reasons itself, so that no reason can possibly satisfy him. Under such circumstances, one can only hope, by means of some modelling procedure—by the example one sets in one's teaching—to modify the skeptic's attitude so that he no longer feels it important to pursue that particular line of questioning. In this sense, teachers of philosophy can convey by their stance a serious commitment to rationality and a profound sense of care with respect to both people and ideas. If they succeed in communicating this attitude to their students, then in effect the question "Why philosophy for children?" has been answered. The value of philosophy for children will either be demonstrated in practice in classrooms, and thereby justi- fied—or it will not. But reasoning alone cannot establish such a value.

NOTES

1. Ernest Nagel, "Philosophy in Educational Research," in *Modern Philosophies of Educa- tion,* ed. John Paul Strain (New York: Random House, 1971) p. 244. This article originally appeared in *First Annual Phi Delta Kappa Symposium on Educational Research,* ed. Frank W. Banghart (copyright, 1960).
2. From Immanuel Kant, "What is Enlightenment?" 1784.

◆§ 9 §◆

THE ROLE OF

LOGIC IN

EDUCATION

◆§ FREDERICK S. OSCANYAN

Berea College

Teaching Logic to Children

Can children learn logic at all? The question invites a variety of research projects: pre-tests, learning instruments, control groups, statistical analyses, and such like. Now this approach is not entirely misconceived but there is something quite wrong with it. Here, logic is treated as a group of skills acquired in a highly specialized setting, and there are reasons for doubting whether this is really a sensible way to address the question.

If we will listen to how we speak to children and to how children converse, we will notice a shared presumption that language users are capable of reasoning. Rightly or wrongly, an ability to reason is characteristically associated with linguistic competence, and it is just this which makes the idea of designing special tests to determine whether children can learn logic so wrongheaded. Not only does the specialization run contrary to the broad diversity of settings in which children display linguistic competence but also such tests would have to assume some sort of linguistic competence, at the very least an ability to follow verbal directions. Since an ability to reason is associated with linguistic competence, they would presume what they supposedly test. Properly written and administered, they should be failure proof.

To see how logical ability is associated with linguistic competence, consider the following real-life examples:

1. Paul, a four-year-old, follows his grandmother everywhere during a visit. She goes into the kitchen and lights a fire under a frying pan. Paul walks up to the stove and reaches for the pan. "No, Paul," she says, firmly grasping his wrist. "If you touch that you will get hurt. Burn! Burn!"
2. Jimmy, age five, has been pestering his mother about going out to play. He has been after her for over an hour. "If you don't stop bugging me, I swear I'll never let you go out!"
3. Ellen, age nine, wants to play with her friends without the constant presence of her four-year-old sister, Denise. Ellen to Denise: "You don't do as I say, I'm going to give you a good one! You go on home, y'hear?"
4. Irate father, upon returning home from work and receiving a very negative report on his six-year-old son's behavior during the day: "You better mind your momma! You keep this up, I'm gunna hit you up 'side of the head, boy!"

Each of these utterances has a certain logical form and presupposes an ability to reason. They are also perfectly typical, ordinary ways of speaking to children. The logical form is that of the *conditional* 'if . . . then——'-type sentence: 'If you touch that (*then*) you will get hurt,' 'If you don't stop bugging me (*then*) I'll never let you go out,' '(If) you don't do as I say (*then*) I'm going to give you a good one,' '(If) you keep this up (*then*) I'm going to hit you.' In each case, the ability to reason involves rejecting the consequent in the 'if . . . then——' sentence and then drawing as a conclusion a rejection of the antecedent. For instance, "If you touch that (then) you will get hurt. But you do not want to get hurt. Therefore, you do not touch that." Another example: "(If) you don't do as I say (then) I'm going to give you a good one. But you do not want me to give you a good one. Therefore, you do as I say." The reasoning is in each case practical; it bears on what the children *do*.[1] This is exhibited in the rejection of the consequent, which appeals to the child's wants and desires ("But you do not *want* to get hurt," "But you do not *want* me to give you a good one"). As a result, rejection of the antecedent would not be accurately described as the child thinking to itself: "Therefore, you do not touch that," or "Therefore, you do as I say," but as not touching the pan on the stove, as doing what the older sister says, etc. In these examples, parents, a grandparent, and a sibling assume—as we all typically assume—that these young children are capable of performing a complex piece of reasoning, reasoning which connects desires to actions.

One might want to protest here that these observations prove no such thing, for in each case it is an elder who presumes that the child can do the reasoning, while it is never *shown* that the children go on to reason. However valid such an objection may seem, it is really quite misleading. The examples are not intended to prove the thesis that young children do in fact reason—they are strictly meant to suggest that if we will listen to quite ordinary conversations with and among children, we will notice that an ability to use and understand language is taken to be a sufficient basis for assuming the presence of reasoning skills, and that this applies even to the very young.

Associating reasoning skills with linguistic competence is plausible because perceiving relationships between sentences requires logical thinking. And using and understanding multiple sentences, such as in asking questions and comprehending answers, are early marks of linguistic competence. Once one becomes aware of this, it comes as no surprise to discover that certain basic logical particles (linguistic terms that mark logical relationships, such as 'if', 'then', 'and', 'or') are parts of early coherent sentences. This can easily be substantiated by listening to children speak. Consider the following example of a complex conditional sentence, spoken by a seven-year-old when being urged to give away a used toy (emphases added): "*If* the child won't do something, *and* the grownups force the child to do it, (*then*) that isn't fun for the child." Observations of linguistic usage do not entirely justify associating reasoning with some ability to speak and understand since the objective basis for the association remains obscure, but they do make the connection plausible enough to use it as a working hypothesis in teaching logic to children.[2]

If we assume that there is a close connection between logic and language, between reasoning ability and linguistic ability, what does this tell us about teaching logic to children? Children come to school more or less able to speak and be spoken to; under the language-logic hypothesis, this means that they also reason. This has four specific consequences for teaching logic in school.

First, we should picture logic as something to be elicited from the children rather than derived from a book or series of exercises; thus we should view logic teaching as the development of abilities the children already possess, not as bestowing new and unfamiliar skills. Second, children exhibit varying degrees of linguistic competence; thus we should expect varying degrees of reasoning ability among different children and from the same child day to day. Third, children are more interested in certain linguistic settings and less in others; thus we should expect them similarly to display their abilities to reason in different ways and different contexts. Finally, language has uses in a tremendous variety of situations; thus we should expect a similarly broad number of settings in which reasoning skills can be elicited and improved upon. In sum, successful logic teaching will require a high degree of flexibility—a willingness to search through a variety of settings for optimum learning conditions for a specific class, a particular child.

Taken together, these four points outline essentials for effectively teaching logic to children. But much remains to be said about implementing such a program, and especially the specific reasoning abilities one can seek to develop. Consider one such program, which uses *Harry Stottlemeier's Discovery* and *Lisa* with fifth through eighth graders.[3]

The books present a variety of characters who think and reason in many different ways. In *Harry Stottlemeier's Discovery*, this is accomplished by attributing different sorts of mental acts to the characters, in *Lisa*, by showing children engaged in a number of intelligently organized and directed inquiries. To see how these models of intelligent activities contribute to successful logic teaching, we need to examine them in detail.

The mental acts in *Harry* range from being suddenly aware that one is being looked at to sharing a special insight with a friend, from wondering whether one's grandfather will keep a promise to constructing a rule of formal logic. Those mental acts most commonly performed include thinking about oneself, thinking to oneself, being uncertain, remembering, consciously using a rule, consciously expressing an opinion, inventing an example for a proposed rule, trying to figure something out, wondering (whether, why, how, what), and making a decision. Among the major characters, certain kinds of mental acts, especially logical ones, recur. These suggest dispositions to think in certain ways, that the characters have different *styles of thinking and reasoning*. Those which predominate are wondering, thinking in formal logical patterns, intuitive or hunchlike thinking, seeking and enjoying explanations, being sensitive to the feelings of others, and thinking independently. This is only a partial list of types of mental acts and associated styles of thinking in *Harry*; a very broad mix is presented.

The diversity of styles of reasoning is further illustrated by occasional overlaps. For example, Lisa characteristically reaches conclusions by

means of hunches and sudden insights while Harry's inferences are generally thought out, yet both make snap judgments that turn out to be faulty.
They differ again in that Lisa promptly expresses hers, while Harry's remains implicit until he is eventually led to revise it in the face of new
evidence. Another example: Harry shares with Anne Torgerson an ability
to have insights into others, yet for Harry this depends largely on verbal
clues while Anne's are visual. Thus, while Lisa and Harry do differ in
patterns of thinking, they are in some respects similar, and so too for Harry
and Anne. The lack of any explicit contrast between Lisa and Anne shows
that the matrix of kinds of thinking is not fully articulated, thus leaving
room for the reader to add in his or her own ideas on similarities and
differences between the characters and their thinking styles.

Two distinct types of logic govern this matrix of thinking styles. One,
exhibited through a progressive discovery of explicit rules, is that of formal
deductive logic. This emphasizes the use of formal patterns of inference—
such as govern the conditional, mentioned above—and the importance of
consistency, validity, and coherence for clear thinking. The second logic is
a nonformal "good reasons" approach that emphasizes seeking and assessing reasons for opinions, actions and beliefs, and the importance of using
principles such as impartiality, objectivity, and respect for others in these
searches.[4]

By displaying formal and nonformal logical rules and principles through
this complex matrix of mental acts and thinking styles, the books provide
extensive and varied illustrations of logical thinking. The characters'
speeches and actions thus contribute to three essentials for teaching logic: a
picture of logic as stemming from children, how such logical thinking is
exhibited in varying degrees by different children and by the same child at
different times, and clues to a wide variety of settings in which such
reasoning skills reveal themselves. The thoughts and activities of the fictional children in *Harry* and *Lisa* help serve these three criteria by *direct
modelling*.

By 'direct modelling', I mean to characterize the special way in which
these books bring the reasoning capacities of real students to life. As classroom children read and hear about the characters, fleshing them out on
their own, they imaginatively and in a highly vivid manner *directly experience* the characters' mental acts and styles of thinking. This contrasts sharply with encountering logical thinking secondhand, such as by mem-
orizing rules and applying them to exercises. As reflective thoughtful characters, though thoughtful in differing ways, the fictional children *model*

logical ways of thinking, particularly through their distinctive thinking styles. By providing these models of reasoned thinking, the books elicit logic from their readers. Directly experiencing efforts to think reasonably provokes similar actions on the part of the readers. These are by no means blind imitations—the readers are as likely to disagree as to agree with conclusions the characters reach. Such real instances of logical thinking may only be first approximations to precise reasoned reflection; much may need to be done in order to refine them. But they are all-important raw materials for the teaching of logic.

The numerous mental acts and styles of thinking associated with the diverse characters in *Harry Stottlemeier's Discovery* can thus elicit logical thinking from students. But the teaching of logic not only requires selective attention to certain abilities, it also needs a clear notion of how to encourage and develop those selected. *Harry* and especially *Lisa* meet this requirement by presenting models of *self-directed inquiry*.

There are many examples of self-directed inquiry in *Lisa*. Topics range from Tony's recurring interest in formal logic as a way to understand how to think to Lisa's repeated concern with whether she should eat meats given that she strongly cares for animals. Characters wrestle with how to tell whether or not something is good, situations in which what is right differs from what is fair, the nature of thinking for oneself, whether it is ever right to lie, and whether turnabout is always fair play. Although not all inquiries are resolved, each exemplifies a certain pattern of development: first a puzzle is articulated, next follows imaginative thinking which expands on the topic—typically through a conversation with others—and eventually (though not always) a solution is proposed. The outcome is then compared with the original puzzle, to see whether the need for inquiry has been satisfied. If it has not, another round begins.

Although it would be quite a mistake to view these patterns of inquiry as recipes for automatically producing solutions to problems, they do have a certain organization and are subject to formal and nonformal logical guidelines. In cases where the process of inquiry is relatively well structured, as in Tony's investigations of formal logic, proposed solutions take on the character of hypotheses which are themselves tested in a formal logical fashion. Each test has the form of a conditional: '*If* the hypothesis is true, *then* a certain result is also true,' so that should the proposed result upon examination fail to be true, the hypothesis then must be modified or abandoned. This uses the conditional inference: '*If* hypothesis, *then* result. The result fails. Therefore, as it stands the hypothesis is false.' A good example (*Lisa*, p. 56): Tony and Harry take two sentences they know to be true, combine them in what they take to be the correct logical fashion, and yet get a false conclusion. This leads them to reject the hypothesis that they have accurately described correct combinations of logical sentences and to seek a refinement in their picture of valid logical arrangements.

Although there are only occasional uses of formal guidelines such as the conditional inference, the inquiries in *Harry* and *Lisa* are uniformly subject to nonformal standards of logic. This is most vivid in *Lisa*. Tony's search for a way to understand how to think true thoughts exhibits *objectivity*; he tries to avoid preconceived results and examines relevant implications wherever they happen to lead. For example, while greatly discouraged by the realization that his approach to his topic has led to the need to investigate 256 different logical sentence arrangements, Tony proceeds to examine them one by one (until receiving considerable assistance from an adult). His search is also *relevant*—the considerations brought up in the process of inquiry bear on the problem at hand—for instance, his treatment of the internal structure of logical sentences is consistent both with his view of logical sentence arrangements and with the logical sentence structure discovered earlier (in *Harry*). It shows a real *respect for persons*: Tony repeatedly presents tentative results of his inquiry to others, seeking their comments and advice.

Lisa, puzzled by whether eating meat is consistent with her concern for the welfare of animals, explores the topic with her father and with other children in her class. This leads to a hypothesis, "If I really cared about animals, I wouldn't eat them." She tests this against her own actions: "But I do eat them." So she concludes, "I don't really care about them." Although this test of her hypothesis is formally valid, Lisa is not satisfied with the result. This leads to further inquiries concerning what is fair and what is right, culminating in a decision to try being a vegetarian. Lisa explicitly uses formally structured thinking in this search for a solution to her puzzle, but nonformal logic is equally significant to the inquiry. Her inquiry is *impartial*, it is fair to comments and suggestions from others. For example, when her father asks whether animals have a right to live she admits she doesn't know and, rather than bias the subsequent inquiry by ignoring the issue, she goes out of her way to ask other children for their views. Also, her inquiry is *objective*; Lisa does not hesitate to draw out the implication that she may not really care for animals when her reasoning calls for it, even though she is troubled to do so. Her inquiry, like Tony's, exhibits a strong *respect for persons*—she seeks opinions from others and never rejects a view opposed to her own just because of the person who expresses it. Her inquiry characteristically *searches for further reasons:* "Do animals have rights?" "Are my reasons any good?"

While both formal and nonformal reasonings are essential to the success of Lisa's inquiry, the nonformal component overrides the formal in a special way. While the structural validity of the formal pattern of inquiry is not itself questioned, as mentioned above, she does reject a formally valid conclusion. Comparing this formal logical consequence with the initial puzzle, she eventually finds a good reason for setting the conclusion aside by developing some insight into her own true feelings about animals and the taking of life. Tony's inquiry similarly illustrates how uses of formal logic can reasonably be questioned. Tony discovers that, using valid sentence arrangements, true as well as false conclusions equally well follow from false or absurd sentences. Using formal logical thinking, he first draws the inference that studying patterns of sentence arrangements cannot lead to a sure way to think true thoughts. Later, treating Lisa's remark that "with true premises and correct arrangements, your conclusions are sure to be true" as a good reason for doing so, he sets aside his formal conclusion and looks for a way to tell when given sentences are true in order to be able to reason formally to truths by restricting his uses of valid arrangements to true premises.

These models of intelligent self-directed inquiry contribute to the fourth essential for successfully teaching logic: eliciting and improving specific reasoning skills. Each model inquiry is a sequential development of specific responses to a given question, responses evaluated by formal reasoning techniques and nonformal logical standards. As the fictional children directly model intelligent inquiry, the paths they follow and procedures they use meet standards of good inquiry such as impartiality, objectivity, relevance, and searching for further reasons. And as in the case of the direct modellings of mental acts and styles of thought, modelling such as this does not invite sheer imitation but instead often triggers doubts and questions. It is then up to the teacher to see to it that the real inquiry which follows—concerning the activities of the characters in the book, and ideas they have suggested—elicits and exhibits these same standards of good inquiry, keeping in mind that under the language-logic hypothesis, real students will already share an interest in these standards and have some ability to apply them.

A special feature of the directed inquiries in *Lisa*, which can help contribute to recognition and use of such standards in a real classroom setting, is their *publicity*. Each inquiry includes conversation with others, often in a public space such as a classroom, playground, or sidewalk. And each puzzle at the heart of an inquiry is always, eventually, told to another person. This may be another child (" 'It's something else that puzzles me . . . ' Lisa told him about the incident in the store with her mother. 'My mother thinks that what's right for everybody ought to be right for me, and I think it doesn't make the least bit of difference to everybody else what I choose to wear, but it makes a lot of difference to me. So my point is, regardless of how other people dress, what's right for me is what I think suits me best.' 'But that's clothes!' Harry protested. 'You can't compare the question of whether a dress is right or wrong with whether what I did was right or wrong.' 'Why not?' Lisa wanted to know") or a problem may be described to a number of children ("Luther laughed at Mark's reply. 'I'd have done the same think you did. But still—why is it right to tell the truth sometimes and not other times?' Just then Maria, Fran, Millie and Lisa came out of the school building. Mark told Maria what had happened, while the others listened attentively. Then Luther mentioned how odd it was to hear Mark reply two different ways when asked the very same question"). Some puzzles are described to adults (to parents—"Mark shook his head. 'You're both way off base. I wasn't worried about that particularly. What I wanted to know was, how can you tell when something's good and when it's not? I mean, what counts for good and what counts for bad?' " Millie, to her grandfather—"Am I dumb?" "Grandfather, am I inferior?"). And, occasionally, an adult will introduce a line of inquiry to children (a school principal, to several children—"Why should I believe you when you tell me that all kids can think for themselves? That's what I want to know".)

The puzzles are stated in a matter-of-fact way; the characters share the courage to admit a point of doubt or ignorance. Though at times beset by fears of being thought foolish or stupid, they overcome these concerns, providing clear and effective models of persons willing to risk disclosing their ignorance in order to participate in inquiry that will, it is hoped, lead to what they want to know. While not always sympathetic, the respondents to whom the puzzles are stated usually accept the problems as genuine, and answer as best they can. Together with the courage to admit ignorance, this points to an important dimension to the public character of inquiry: that inquiry itself is social. Not only is the puzzle at its origin to be shared with others, the process of inquiry which follows is an exercise in cooperative thinking.

Another public dimension to inquiries in *Lisa* is that the issues they raise are uniformly *philosophical*, of universal interest and significance. This guarantees that the topics will reach beyond the pages of the book, inviting readers to bring their own experiences and reflections to the written discussions. The public character of the inquiries thus can engage the readers, encourage them to express their own doubts and questions about its topics, and point them toward cooperative reflection in response to these matters of interest.

The models of self-directed inquiry basic to the program which uses *Harry* and *Lisa* thus provide much that is useful for teaching logic to children. But like all models, their uses are limited by the resources and imaginations of those who employ them. As previously mentioned, this means that encouraging the recognition and use of formal logical patterns and nonformal standards of inquiry is highly dependent upon the teacher's efforts to elicit and promote them. Under the language-logic hypothesis, this will require that children learn logic by actively responding to these models, that they actually take part in shared inquiries. The process of inquiry, the evaluation of reasons, can properly be mastered only through repeated public performance.

Formal logic is a very useful and important topic for directed inquiry, but can never take its place. The specific formal logic one chooses to teach should depend upon one's own interests and the likely interests of one's students, just as nonformal inferences chosen to be taught—inductions, analogies, explanations, justifications—should be selected with an eye to similar criteria. But under the working hypothesis that associates reasoning with linguistic competence, one can teach logic to children only by encouraging shared self-directed inquiry in a public space such as a classroom.

NOTES

1. Of course there is also an informative component to each example—that touching pans on a hot stove causes burns, that a mother can be pestered once too often, that older sisters don't always want their younger sisters around, that a father's authority can extend to things done when he's absent. But the main thrust of each utterance is to influence subsequent actions of the child.

2. One might now ask whether it makes any sense at all to construct specialized tests for whether children can learn logic. It certainly does, provided that the tests are designed to examine the validity of associating an ability to reason with linguistic competence. They should seek answers to questions such as: Can a child show linguistic competence yet not be able to reason at all? If a child has linguistic ability, what could prevent it from having logical competence? What would have to be done to such a child in order to keep it from reasoning?

3. Matthew Lipman, *Harry Stottlemeier's Discovery*, Second Edition Revised (Institute for the Advancement of Philosophy for Children, Montclair State College, 1977); Matthew Lipman, *Lisa* (Institute for the Advancement of Philosophy for Children, Montclair State College, 1976).

4. Lipman, et al., *Philosophy in the Classroom* (Institute for the Advancement of Philosophy for Children, Montclair State College, 1976), chap. 7, especially pp. 125–135.

❥ 10 ❦

THE ROLE OF

PHILOSOPHY IN

AESTHETIC EDUCATION

❧ DAVID W. ECKER

New York University

Analyzing Children's Talk about Art

Art is the memory of a vision.
> *Ten-year-old boy*

The professional artist and the young child share, in their inspired moments, a spontaneity, a sureness of touch, a fluency, and an originality that is a wonder to behold. Recognition of this fact—that aspects of the creative process revealed in the art work of children bear a striking resemblance to those of the mature artist—may well be what initially attracts people to the field of art education.

As for myself, I was captivated by the controlled scribbles of three-year-

Reprinted from the *Journal of Aesthetic Education* 7 (No. 1, January 1973): 58–73 with the permission of that journal and the author.

old children, the discriminating figure drawings and clay sculpture of five-year-olds, and the intuitively balanced tempera paintings of six-year-olds. I marveled at pictures that combined both the top and side views of a scene to show significant details, at paintings that abstracted and exaggerated pictorial elements or showed X-ray views of buildings and "fold-over" baseline representations of streets. I remember vividly the performance of an eight-year-old boy who drew a series of monsters and then freely invented stories to go with them. But the sheer inventiveness of the average child's talk about the products of his imagination no less than the seeming miracle of his untrained ability in art is certainly what drew me into the field—initially to wonder, and then to question.

The child's way with line and color, his sense of form, and the expressiveness of his words and gestures demanded an explanation. Is the child innately an artist? If so, there would seem to be little of importance left to teach him. Wouldn't adult instruction and criticism block his creative development? And might he not, therefore, become self-conscious and destructively critical of his own performance? If the answer to these questions is yes, then perhaps the teacher should only note periodically where each child is, jotting that on a chart of characteristic patterns of creative and mental growth, and avoid imposing her aesthetic judgments on the direction of his development. And if the answer is no, it might be more appropriate to evaluate the performance of children according to artistic and aesthetic educational objectives the teacher sets.

As a young teaching assistant in the Saturday morning children's classes in the Albright-Knox Art Gallery in Buffalo and later as an elementary-school art teacher, I was quick enough to learn how to organize lessons and materials that apparently succeeded in stimulating and enhancing creative activity. That is to say, I worked out practical answers to these questions. (I also collected enough contour drawings, finger paintings, murals, collages, hand puppets, potato prints, and junk sculpture to fill a room.) But an understanding of creativity, at least in the sense of having a scientific explanation of how young children are able to do what they do, was beyond me then as it is beyond me now.

Human creativity is surely not beyond human understanding, unless of course one defines it literally as a miracle. However, I do believe that the lack of a powerful explanation of artistic creativity remains the central problem of art education, despite its dormant status as a problem among art educators today. I emphasize the problematic nature of creativity not because I have discovered something new about it but because I want to begin my analysis of children's talk about art in light of the emerging redefinition of the problem of language acquisition now exciting researchers in the fields of psycholinguistics and language-arts education. Certain newly appreciated facts of the child's linguistic ability are in some respects quite similar to phenomena art educators associate with a child's artistic creativity.

Specifically, the ability of children to generate "well formed" utterances according to grammatical rules they cannot state and to produce novel sentences they have never heard has led Noam Chomsky and other linguistic theorists to raise some profound doubts about the commonly held belief that children learn their native language by imitation and about the behaviorist's more refined commitment to the idea that linguistic acquisition and production can be explained entirely by the external stimuli in the child's experience.[1] What I have come to suspect, but will not further explore here, is that educational research which limits itself strictly to observable behavior (whether the creativity studies of the 1950s or the aesthetic preference studies currently under way) may be open to the same fundamental doubts. On the other hand, I believe that research which follows the lead of contemporary linguistics in identifying the underlying *structures* of behavior may reveal children's talk about art to be the second major avenue toward an understanding of their artistic creativity, the first avenue, of course, being the art work itself.

These personal and programmatic remarks are offered to suggest some of the larger issues with which I am concerned. But this paper will be limited to (1) a brief discussion of the need for studies to explore the linguistic aspects of the artistic and aesthetic development of children, (2) a critique of the use of transcripts of teacher-student interaction to exemplify or generate strategies for the teaching of art, (3) an analysis of a sixth-grade lesson in aesthetics, and (4) the identification of "levels" of aesthetic inquiry in this lesson and a restatement of the problems requiring research.

1. Studies of Artistic Development

What importance have reseachers in art education attached to the systematic study of children's talk about art? Generally very little, it would seem. It is interesting that in *Analyzing Children's Drawings*, Rhoda Kellogg's monumental study of over a million drawings of children from two to eight years of age, she makes so few references to what children actually say about their work. One could argue that because her classification of devel-

opmental stages is based on the formal aesthetic properties of these drawings, what children say is scientifically irrelevant. Yet she attempts much
more than a descriptive morphology of child art when she reflects on the
meaning of the art and prescribes the appropriate adult conduct with children in the presence of their work. And in a defense of her theory of "the
visually logical system of child art" against the alleged pictorial bias of
many art educators (Lowenfeld, Gaitskell, and McFee, among others),
Kellogg does mention what she believes to be the "truest response" to the
"Would you tell me about your picture" approach, namely, the response
of the child who said, "This is not a story, it is a picture to look at."[2]

Apart from the question whether this one response is representative of
the universe of statements children make about their art, it should be
obvious that what a child says spontaneously about his art may just as
readily relate a story, if there is one to tell. In either case, he will be
revealing his artistic intentions and the significance he finds in his art. As
to the statement of the child quoted above as a general maxim about the
proper way to view children's art, it would be easy to cite multiple counter-
examples that focus exclusively on the intended subject of a drawing or
painting. Consider only this unsolicited comment made by a four-year-old
girl drawing a bird: "He is my friend, I talk to him, he likes me, then he
hopped about."[3]

In any case, the correct adult response is not at all obvious. What does
one do when the child has set out, on his own, to achieve a specific
objective—whether to depict a scene, illustrate a story, make a design, or
punch holes in the paper with his pencil? Commonsensically, of course,
we might assume that it depends on the situation: the value the child
places on the activity, his sense of failure in reaching his objective and the
consequences of this self-appraisal, and any social or moral constraints the
teacher judges to be applicable to the performance. But Kellogg is ada-
mant. "I believe," she writes, "that teachers should accept everything made
with good grace and should not try to evaluate its worth. No questions
need ever be asked, and comments that teachers make can be restricted to
such constructive ones as 'very interesting,' 'nice colors,' 'I like that,' 'good
work,' 'a nice scribble,' 'pretty,' " and so on.[4]

The inevitable consequence of adult assistance or criticism is, according
to Kellogg, to divert the child from his self-education in art and toward an
effort to please the teacher. She believes that "the child's mind must
develop through the impact of his own scribblings—not through the supervision of adults."[5] Yet the impressive amount of art she has collected over

a twenty-year period cannot by itself justify claims about the outcome of this or that teaching strategy, nor can her descriptive analysis of child art. Scientific confirmation of her pedagogical claims would require that clearly delineated alternative strategies of instruction (or noninstruction) be tested with children under controlled conditions. While descriptive data can be a vital source of fruitful hypotheses, only experimental data can yield generalizations about the relative success of alternative strategies.

The potential scientific value of Kellogg's work lies not in her pedagogical claims, plausible though they may be, but in her systematic classification of child art. The developmental patterns she identifies are grounded in solid empirical data. The initial stage of basic scribbling, and on through the successive stages of placement patterns, emergent diagram shapes, diagrams, combines, aggregates, mandalas, radials, humans, and early pictorialism—all demonstrate the natural capacity of young children to produce spontaneous gestalt constructions with universal characteristics that, initially at least, are independent of culture and adult influence. She explains this development as primarily aesthetic in nature and not reducible to sexual, affective, cognitive, magical, spiritual, or communicative needs. Nor is this development the product of wishes and unconscious conflicts, assertion of the individual will, or such. Thus her analysis challenges theorists of child development such as Freud, Jung, Rank, Piaget, Kris, and Ehrenzweig, and lends support to central aspects of the child-art theories of Franz Cizek and Gustof Britsch, and the more recent theories of Florence Cane, Schaefer-Simmern, Arnheim, and Herbert Read. Not surprisingly, Kellogg also finds the formalist art theories of Clive Bell, Roger Fry, and Ernst Cassirer compatible with her analysis of the development of aesthetic form in children.

Art educators can only speculate, at present, on the possible connections between the development of aesthetic form (the child's "visually logical system") and the development of linguistic form (his syntactical rules), given the basic research of Kellogg, Chomsky, and others. A next step toward such understanding, as I suggested earlier, is a systematic analysis of children's *talk* about art to match Kellogg's analysis of children's art.

Here we must acknowledge the larger problems of formal art education left virtually untouched by Kellogg's work on the biological genesis of child art. Where she leaves off with the "early pictorialism" of the four- to seven-year-olds, the art teacher must begin with instruction calculated ultimately to produce an aesthetically educated young adult skilled in the "criticism of life in the furtherance of humane values," to borrow a phrase from Ralph Smith. For culture does not unfold from within the child; humane values must be passed on from generation to generation. The human animal can neither fully appreciate nor denigrate the social order into which he was born—he cannot contribute to it or change it—without a long apprenticeship. And what impresses many people in the field of art education today is that the perceptive critic as well as the creative artist can provide models of excellence for the older child to emulate.

One of the larger problems, then, is to accomplish the shift from biological to cultural orientation in art activities in the public school without excessive grinding of gears. That is, we must accomplish this shift without consciously working against the best information we have about the innate capacities of youngsters and with an understanding of how artists, critics, and other professionals in the arts actually perform their creative and critical functions.

2. Strategies for Teaching Art

In view of the general lack of knowledge of art education gained through formal experiments, one is all the more impressed by the fact that skillful and sensitive teachers do work out viable and sometimes inspiring classroom practices. A study of what actually goes on in these classrooms will force the researcher interested in children's talk about art to deal with the import of this talk in the context of real-life situations. The most valuable document I know in this regard is *Through Art to Creativity: Art in the Elementary School Program*, Manuel Barkan's analysis of classroom records (both transcriptions of dialogue and sequence-photographs of art activities) of eighteen teachers in nine school systems, kindergarten through sixth grade.

The value Barkan places on close observation and description is made clear in his preface, where he points out that "the theory of good teaching of art can explain the nature of imagination and its significance in the education of children. By itself, however, theoretical explanation does not convey how imaginative children sound, nor does it convey the life-like images of how they behave. Furthermore, it does not transmit the live and moving interchange between good teachers and their children as they strive to enhance the ability to be imaginative."[6] Barkan then proceeds to show us how good teachers act, what they talk about and how they treat children in order to stimulate their imaginative abilities, and how their students, in turn, talk and act.

As we turn the pages of the book, the chronologically ordered photographs and transcripts project a sense of the child's rapidly developing psychomotor and social skills and of his growing awareness of his artistic abilities and aspirations. For example, the differences in level of performance between the children in Miss Lee's kindergarten and those in Mrs. Shrosbree's fourth-grade class are remarkable. The five-year-olds finished their crayoned pictures of Raggedy Ann's adventures in about twenty minutes and were interested in showing and telling about their pictures for ten or twelve minutes. A typical statement may have been provided by Bobby: "Raggedy Ann went to a stranger's house."[7]

In contrast, the nine- to ten-year-olds discussed the aesthetic qualities of Eskimo sculpture, its place of origin, carving materials and techniques, and struggled at length to state the distinction between sculpture and painting. Their talk revealed not only their deepening interest in particulars (the features of the small carved soapstone sculpture of a seal they were examining, for instance) but also an interest in the general concepts of sculpture and painting. Yet their concepts are still very personal and action-oriented. Bonnie said: "Well—ah, a painting is, ah—you use a brush and paper—well, on a piece of paper."[8] And Danny, in response to the teacher's question about "what's really different between a piece of paper and a piece of sculpture," said: "Well, paint. You can't carve in it or anything."

Perhaps the most subtle interaction is between Miss Cupelli (the visiting art teacher) and Bonnie after a discussion on whether feelings are something or nothing. Their last exchange ("Yeah, it's nothing." "It is nothing?") is followed by this statement by Mrs. Shrosbree:

> It would be nice if you would think about the feelings you have, and the things that you love, and the things you want to spend your time with. And then you'll be able to think of something. There's no need to make a sculpture of some things, because if you were going to make them, you'd make the things themselves. And there are other things that you love so much that you can't make, but you get a nice feeling from them. Maybe you could think of something you would enjoy having, and that you would enjoy making. You can also think about the way Eskimos felt about their carvings. Do you remember the man who bought a beautiful seal carving? What did he say? . . . [9]

It is not clear from Barkan's transcript how many of the distinctions implied in these suggestions Bonnie actually grasped. But surely we can assume that the fourth-grade teacher offered her ideas on the objectification of feelings in art because she believed that the children were capable of understanding them.

In his decision to focus on artistic creativity, Barkan could approach only indirectly the problems of teaching for developing art appreciation in children. And what children say about art takes on a different significance when analyzed with this objective in mind. An excellent example of the explicit use of transcripts for this purpose may be found in the book *Children and Their Art* by Gaitskell and Hurwitz.[10] After comparing past and present methods of teaching art appreciation and after offering a model unit of instruction involving both creative and critical activities for sixth-graders, the authors suggest that one way to organize classroom discussion is in four "basic" stages: description, formal analysis, interpretation, and judgment. This critical terminology is derived, in part, from a complete recording of a group critique of Picasso's *Girl before a Mirror*, one of the sessions Edmund Feldman conducted with art teachers in an in-service program of art appreciation.

This first proposal is followed by an excerpt of a discussion led by James Ackerman, the Harvard art historian, with sixth-graders comparing Claude Monet's *Popular Trees* and an Egyptian fresco from the Twelfth Dynasty. This transcript is offered to demonstrate in action the four categories Ackerman considers important in teaching sixth-graders: technique, form, meaning (soon changed to "subject" when he found the children had difficulty grasping this concept), and feeling.

Ackerman's approach is then adapted by Hurwitz to develop a "discovery" method, to lead children to "discover for themselves a system of criticism." The teacher begins by asking the children to identify all the differences they can find in four paintings. As the children proceed, the teacher writes each comment on the blackboard in the appropriate column, as yet undesignated. When the children cannot continue, the teacher writes the names of the categories at the top of each column: Materials, Subject, Meaning, Form, Style.

Hurwitz's method has at least two virtues. First, it encourages children to look at paintings on their own, without being told beforehand what to look for, except in a general way. Thus the teacher avoids placing restrictions on what the children are likely to perceive in the works. Second, this approach no doubt encourages children to talk about many more aspects of an art work than they would ordinarily tend to talk about.

Yet, strictly speaking, by this method the students could be said not to "discover a system of criticism" but to guess, on the inductive evidence of how the *teacher* sorts their comments into columns, what the items in each of those columns have in common (e.g., Materials). An alternate strategy might be for the teacher or students to write down all their remarks on separate slips of paper and pool them. Then the teacher could ask the *students* to group the slips according to what *they* believe are the significant similarities and differences in their statements, generating as many groups as seem required. (This latter approach might properly be called the "creative method of building categories to organize anyone's talk about art.") In any event, it is clear from a study of the Feldman and Ackerman transcripts that the lessons were successful to the degree that the students' output matched the teacher's input, at least with regard to the system of criticism employed.

However one classifies the verbal operations of classroom instruction, it will involve the sorting out of student responses. And if the chief problem is seen as the fashioning of categories of critical talk, the resulting taxonomy will inevitably suggest to teachers that children should attempt to conform to these categories. It is then but a short step to setting up behavioral objectives in art criticism for children, the model for good criticism quite naturally being taken from the best that professional art historians and art critics have to offer. The danger for the researcher, of course, is that he may treat children's transcribed talk as if it were more or less badly written art criticism. When analyzing transcripts, it is easy to forget that the extemporaneous speech of both children and adults is of a radically different character from their written expression.[11]

What is more to the point, when children think creatively their talk is often divergent. And when the teacher gives free rein to student thought, students tend to raise questions—and forward answers—that were they refined and cast in more technical language would have to be identified as sociological, psychological, and philosophical as well as aesthetic inquiry.

Before analyzing a transcript that exhibits this kind of freewheeling inquiry, it should quickly be noted that the analyses reviewed above did not attempt to explore such possibilities, but served much more practical purposes.

3. The Sixth Grade Tackles Aesthetics

The linguistic evidence of creative student thinking I will refer to in this section has been selected from an hour-long discussion of the relationship between theories of art and contemporary realistic and abstract paintings. The discussion was led by Mrs. Bonnie Danson, then a student-teacher.

The utterances of these sixth-graders seem extraordinary when examined one by one, but they do not seem so in the context of the entire discussion. Nor are they much different from the kinds of statements older children make in "open-ended" discussions about art, judging from a number of similar tape recordings I have collected over the years. What is fairly unusual about this classroom discussion, however, is the formal objective set by the teacher: to stimulate students to relate their own concepts of art to the criticism of work they had seen in an exhibition by formally introducing aesthetic theory as a consideration.[12] Here is a précis of the transcript of that discussion, portions of which will be quoted in full below.

Outline of a one-hour taped discussion of the relationship between theories of art and contemporary realistic and abstract paintings; Mrs. Bonnie Danson teacher (T) and discussion leader for sixth-grade students in Whitehall Elementary School, Columbus, Ohio; April 1965; transcription, précis, and notes by D. W. Ecker; Wollensak recorder at 3¾ speed; Tape 6, side 1

	counter		
Time 11:10 A.M.	006	T:	We're going to pick up our discussion of theory this week.
SUBJECT:	018	T:	Each scholar tries to add to the store of knowledge. [Aristotle]
definitions	026	T:	Bob, you said that there must be one theory for all times.
students' examples of relatives and personal experience	139	T:	Another theory says that all people have [artistic] thoughts but only some can put their thoughts down on paper. [Croce]
	159	T:	Theory about art is called aesthetics.
	165	T:	The two theories we have been discussing oppose each other.
unexpected directions: on an art exhibit at a shopping center	232	Bob:	Realistic art is imitation.
	274	Mike:	Why that's, like, personal taste.
	312	Craig:	[That artist] had a one-track mind.
	319	Jeff:	They don't look at pictures; they look at the price.
	339	Karen:	Jeff said Aristotle had a one-track mind.
syllogistic argument	347	Jeff:	A house has a window; a window is a square; a square is a shape; and a shape is modern art.
		T:	Yes, it is in a way.
	364	Bob:	Modern art is mostly thought and thought is not realistic—
		T:	Some people call art intuitive knowledge.

	386	Jeff:	I know I'm an agreeable guy, but I'm not going to agree on everything.
	412	Jeff:	It's possible but not probable that. . . .
	441	T:	We have to define in order to talk about something. . . .
far afield: on the reality of dreams, mirrors, ideas, things, tables, chairs, etc.	481	Class:	[Long argument about what is real]
	526	Walter:	Microphone. . . .
the necessity for defini- tions in an argument	540	T:	[Definition of autism and autistic behavior—not artistic behavior; atheism]
	587	Class:	[Atheism, etc.]
	664	T:	Is an atheist un-American? Can an atheist be a good person?
	721	T:	The end of a rather unsuccessful week, I think. [Said more to herself than to the students]
Time 12:10 P.M.	Bell		

After Mrs. Danson introduces the theory of art as imitation to the class, Bob says, "Realistic art is imitation" (counter 232). Mrs. Danson immediately probes his understanding of the theory by asking whether abstract art would be considered as art by a person holding his theory: "In other words, they [anyone subscribing to the views of Plato and Aristotle] wouldn't agree that abstract art is imitation? Is that what you're saying?" Bob says Yes, but Jeff quickly announces that he has "three things to say. Starting from Aristotle. I don't know why, but I want to contradict him. I think he didn't have an open mind." "He —," Jeff pauses. "His own theory was, all right, it had to be realistic to be art. Well, if he saw something new, he'd just keep this same one-track mind: realistic is art. Then he'd once look at it [abstract art] and he'd think it's disgusting. And he should have an open mind. And, second of all," says Jeff, "when Walter was talking about his mother's painting—he even mentioned, himself, the way she saw it. My sisters and I," says Jeff, launching a detailed example, "we sat in front of a bowl of flowers—the same bowl and everyone saw it—and we painted it with oil, and it came out three different ways. My one sister was real quick in putting it on, and another sister was doing it just right, and the thing turned out real different. But that's the way they saw it. And also —"

After his punch line, "But that's the way they saw it," Jeff is challenged by Mrs. Danson to state the point of telling the class about this experience: "Now what's the point of that, Jeff? That's good, but what's the point of that?" And Jeff constructs a second hypothetical situation (the first being what Aristotle would have done if confronted by an abstract painting) by saying, "Well, you could see a tree right here, straight, and the way *you* see it may be crooked." Jeff then agrees with Mrs. Danson's paraphrase of his point: "In other words, we can't be sure of what is correct imitation" (counter 255).

Jeff later introduces his own analysis of modern art with a syllogism: "A house has a window; a window is a square; a square is a shape; and a shape is modern art" (counter 347). His point here, apparently, is that modern art can be both realistic and abstract at the same time. Following this tour de force the teacher can only add: "Yes, it is in a way." (Earlier—see counter 165—she had stated emphatically that the two theories the class was discussing "oppose each other.") At this juncture Bob offers two premises of his own syllogism: "Modern art is mostly thought and thought is not realistic —" But before he can draw the conclusion that most modern art is not realistic, Mrs. Danson interrupts him with the information that "some people call art intuitive knowledge" (and later mentions Croce by name). Soon Jeff again becomes impatient: "I know I'm an agreeable guy, but I'm not going to agree on everything." Listening to Jeff in the recording, we think: heaven forbid!

In guiding the students in their own theoretical inquiries into the nature of art, Mrs. Danson is clearly more Socratic than dogmatic in her approach. She does not reveal her own theoretical commitments but attempts to keep her contributions to the dialogue either substantively factual or methodologically helpful. Thus it would be reasonable to identify many of these students' arguments as evidence of original thought on their part, even though the typical argument is a response to stimuli provided by the teacher and other students.

The unanticipated directions free inquiry may take is demonstrated by Mike, Craig, Karen, and Jeff in another part of the same discussion (counter 274–312). Jeff had given an example of contradictory aesthetic judgments by two men, one of whom said "That is a beautiful painting of a flower" while the other said "It's bad." Mike attributes their behavior to personal taste. Craig disagrees. "No, it isn't!" he exclaims. "Jeff said his grandfather don't know anything about art. Well, it wouldn't be personal taste; it would be ignorance."

Effectively refereeing this debate, Mrs. Danson says: "In other words, it wasn't his taste because he wasn't even using it; he was just going along with the crowd. Is that what you mean?" Craig accepts this interpretation: "He was just going along with the crowd." But he quickly amplifies the teacher's interpretation of his original statement: "Ya know, his, say, best friend is a millionaire—he says, 'Oh, that's a beautiful painting of a polka-dotted —' " "Zebra?" Karen interjects, getting a laugh from other students. "—circle. And he [Jeff's grandfather] says, 'Oh, yes, that is.' And then —"

In the first instance, we hear Craig draw the inference that ignorance, not personal taste, is the explanation, partly from the alleged fact that Jeff's grandfather didn't know anything about art. In the second instance, Craig invents an example of "going along with the crowd," specifically, a hypothetical situation in which the grandfather accepts an absurd aesthetic judgment because it is made by his best friend who is also a millionaire. Even in the most straightforward "surface" analysis of this short exchange, one must be impressed by the mobility of thought revealed here.

And what are we to say about the remaining dialogue in this part of the discussion? Mrs. Danson then asks: "But Jeff also said that he did think realistic pictures were good. Didn't you?" To which Jeff responds by speculating on how one's mood affects one's interest in abstract and realistic pictures, and consequently, one's judgment: "It's good and it's bad. It depends on what—If you can compare pictures—even though you can't compare—If you have a whole roomful of realistic pictures, maybe you're in the mood for it; but if you are looking at all abstract pictures and you're looking at abstract and somebody [showed you] a realistic picture, the heck with it. You want to see some more abstract —."

Craig interrupts, to advance his personal theory of art by describing two paintings and evaluating them: "You know, I think there's two kinds of art: good art and bad art. And there's compound art and there's plain art. Well, I've seen this—I don't know what the name of it was—it was a modern art—all blue —" Mrs. Danson asks, "Was this the painting of the spaceship you were talking about before?" "Yes," says Craig, "one shade of blue. And I thought it was horrible. And then you go down a little bit," referring to the art exhibit the students had visited, "and there was this other thing. It was sort of striped, lumpy, circles—it had all different things. And I thought it was good. The guy had a change. The man that did this other one about Cape Canaveral, I think it was bad. He had a one-track mind" (counter 312).

It would not be difficult to imagine Jeff setting up a modest psychological experiment to test his claims, after getting instruction on the appropriate research methodology. And Craig seems fully capable of elaborating his theory of art with more practice at criticizing art work he sees.

4. Research Problems

From the foregoing, short as it is, we may conclude that children can think creatively in the kinds of language that might collectively be called aesthetic inquiry. Children not only talk about art but also talk about their talk; they not only criticize art objects and events but also reflect upon the nature of the critical act itself. In fact, when their powers of imagination and curiosity are unrestrained, five levels of inquiry can be identified. If we count art production and appreciation as the first level of inquiry, we find children (1) creating and appreciating art, (2) criticizing it, and (3) challenging or supporting the judgments of others, whether adults or children. Moreover, we find them (4) theorizing about the nature of art and criticism, and (5) analyzing theories and arguments.

We speak here of different *levels* of inquiry in virtue of the fact that language at a "higher level" of inquiry refers to inquiry at a level or levels below it. For example, the fifth level (metatheory) finds its referents in the fourth level (theory), while the third level (metacriticism) finds its referents in the second level (criticism). This fact is basic to aesthetic inquiry because the inquirer—whether researcher, teacher, or student—must convert it to a value or control if he is to solve aesthetic problems. Elsewhere I have called this control the "criterion of referential adequacy."[13] This criterion ensures that inquiry conducted at higher levels ultimately demonstrates its aesthetic significance by empirical confirmation—by returning to the first-level experiences of art production and appreciation. It is precisely this methodological control that distingushes inquiry from historical, sociological, and psychological inquiries.[14]

Unfortunately, it is also precisely this control that is most easily lost in the intellectual excitement of spontaneous and freewheeling discussions in the art room. For the creative talk of children may diverge so widely that aesthetically irrelevant ideas, associations, and conclusions may result from inquiry that is undisciplined from within or without.

Mike, Craig, and Jeff *do* rather consistently refer to their experiences (or hypothetical situations when they feel it would help) in attacking the problems that puzzle them about modern art. But toward the end of the hour-long session, both teacher and students are ranging far afield of the aesthetic domain as they discuss the reality of dreams, mirrors, ideas, tables, and chairs, the necessity for definitions in an argument, autism, and whether an atheist can be a good person. Perhaps this increasing divergence or lack of closure is what prompts Mrs. Danson to say, after the school bell rings and more to herself than to the students: "The end of a rather unsuccessful week, I think."

More than "vertical" control between levels of aesthetic inquiry is required, however. What is also required is that "horizontal" control gained in proportion to the degree of mastery one achieves in methods of inquiry at one or more levels. Creating a painting, judging an exhibition, or theorizing about abstract expressionism involves distinctive methods and techniques. At minimum the teacher should be able to identify and distinguish among (if not demonstrate) the problems, materials, and methods appropriate at all five levels. It goes without saying that the researcher *must* be able to do so if he is to discover the capacity of children for aesthetic inquiry at each level under various conditions and at different ages. But what bears repeating here is that virtually this entire range of linguistic activity has gone uninvestigated in art education.

Specifically, we lack knowledge of child growth and development at all levels of aesthetic inquiry but the first (creation and appreciation). And all levels but the first necessarily involve language as the medium of communication and performance. Thus the acquisition of such knowledge will require a comprehensive classificatory scheme that will discriminate among linguistic activities both vertically and horizontally; that is, between levels and within levels. To be sure, it is difficult to relate key concepts in the literature of aesthetics to instances of children's talk, not because children are incapable of judging, preferring, describing, defining, interpreting, explaining, and so on, but because so many aesthetic concepts are problematic (e.g., the nature and justification of aesthetic judgments). So when the researcher looks for certain of these activities in the classroom, he faces conceptual as well as empirical problems.

I'm sympathetic, therefore, with the metacritical efforts of Edmund Feldman, Ralph Smith, and others to lay out categories to guide teachers and their students in critical performance. But we must remember that Mrs. Danson's students were not only able to criticize art but also ready and eager to test the theories of art and criticism offered them. Perhaps students, teachers, and researchers alike should be prepared—indeed, encouraged—to reflect upon the adequacy of *any* set of categories to do the job assigned to it, which is to say, to work at the theoretical and metatheoretical levels as well as at the critical and metacritical levels of aesthetic inquiry. In any case, to commit ourselves to categories appropriate for understanding or guiding performance at only a single level of aesthetic inquiry is to risk not recognizing talk operating at other levels. We may thereby unintentionally suppress what art educators have long professed to be their chief value and aim: the fullest development of creative potential through art.

But apart from any categories we may devise, we will all undoubtedly continue to wonder at those remarkable displays of creative insight by the young, such as the intuition of the ten-year-old boy who, when asked what art is, said "Art is the memory of a vision."[15]

NOTES

1. Some publications representing important developments in linguistic research are: Noam Chomsky, *Syntactic Structures* (The Hague: Mouton & Cie, 1957); Jerry A. Fodor and Jerrold J. Katz, eds., *The Structure of Language* (Englewood Cliffs, N.J.: Prentice-Hall, 1964); Charles Carpenter Fries, *The Structure of English* (New York: Harcourt, Brace & World, 1952); Jerrold J. Katz and Paul M. Postal, *An Integrated Theory of Linguistic Descriptions* (Cambridge, Mass.: M.I.T. Press, 1964); Robert B. Lees, *The Grammar of English Nominalizations* (Bloomington, Ind.: Research Center in Anthropology, Folklore, and Linguistics, 1960).

2. Rhoda Kellogg, *Analyzing Children's Art* (Palo Alto, Calif.: National Press Books, 1969), p. 156.

3. Betty Lark-Horovitz, Hilda Present Lewis, and Mark Luca, *Understanding Children's Art for Better Teaching* (Columbus, Ohio: Charles E. Merrill, 1967), p. 6.

4. Kellogg, *Analyzing Children's Art*, p. 156.

5. Ibid., p. 143.

6. Manuel Barkan, *Through Art to Creativity* (Boston: Allyn and Bacon, 1960), pp. viii–ix.

7. Ibid., p. 41.

8. Ibid., p. 220.

9. Ibid., p. 223.

10. Charles D. Gaitskell and Al Hurwitz, *Children and Their Art*, 2d ed. (New York: Harcourt, Brace & World, 1970), pp. 422–442.

11. Just how far apart written and spoken language can get may be appreciated by perusing this verbatim transcription of an extemporaneous utterance, said to be representative of those produced at a conference of psychologists and linguists: "As far as I know, no one yet has done the in a way obvious now and interesting problem of doing in a sense a structural frequency study of the alternative syntactical in a given language, say, like English, the alternative possible structures, and how what their hierarchical probability of occurrence structure is." From H. Maclay and C. E. Osgood, "Hesitation Phenomena in Spontaneous English Speech," *Word* 15 (1959): 19–44.

12. Over a four-year period at Ohio State University, my student-teachers and I explored the possibilities of teaching aesthetics and art criticism in the lower grades by analyzing video and audio recordings of the student-teachers' interactions with their students. The lesson plans attached to the transcripts of the lessons had titles of which these are characteristic: "Objective: To Teach Four Six-Year-Olds the Difference between Ordinary and Aesthetic Perception"; "A Lesson in Architecture: Form and Function"; "Lesson on Movement and Degas"; "Introduction to Cubism and the Collage through the Works of Paul Cézanne and Pable Picasso" (seventh grade); "A Discussion of Criticism and Artistic Intention with Eight Eleventh- and Twelfth-Grade Students: A Middle-Class New Neighborhood."

13. See "Justifying Aesthetic Judgments," *Art Education*, 21 (May 1967): 5–8.

14. For a complete analysis of the scope of aesthetic inquiry, see D. W. Ecker and E. F. Kaelin, "The Limits of Aesthetic Inquiry: A Guide to Educational Research," *Philosophical*

Redirection of Educational Research, 71st Yearbook, Part I (Chicago: NSSE, 1972), pp. 258–286.

15. I am indebted to Howard Conant, who related to me this statement made by a student in a New York City elementary school.

⮜§ JOHN WILSON

Oxford University

Education and Aesthetic Appreciation

If (perhaps rashly) we were to consider 'aesthetic education' as a whole, what sort of aims should we have in mind? What sort of pupils would we hope to produce? It seems that there are three things we should *not* count as sufficient for success:

1. We should not be satisfied with pupils who merely *knew* certain facts or could make certain correct judgments about works of art. A pupil might know all the details of the Shakespearean stage and the principles of classical harmony, and be able to say correctly that *Othello* was poignant and the *Eroica* noble (or whatever we want him to say) but if he did not *enjoy* Shakespeare and Beethoven, there would be something missing.

2. We should not be satisfied if he thoroughly enjoyed *Othello* and the *Eroica*, but for the wrong reasons (as we think): if, for instance, he just enjoyed any play with a black hero, or any symphony with some fortissimo passages. We should say that he was not enjoying it for the right reasons.

3. Nor should we be satisfied even by a combination of (1) and (2): that is, if he could *both* quote the 'right reasons' *and* enjoyed the works. For he might still not actually be enjoying them *for* these reasons. It might not be *those* reasons which caused his enjoyment: the reasons might be good, and he might to able to quote them, but they would not be *operative* in him. But it is not clear what we mean by this: though one thing we do not mean, as Wittgenstein points out,[1] is that we want him to be subject to a certain set of causal laws, and to

An earlier version of this article was printed in the *Oxford Review of Education* 3 (no. 2, 1977).

know that he is subject. We ask him "Why do you like the *Eroica?*" and (having learned a lot more experimental psychology than we now know) he says something like "Boys from middle-class backgrounds with strong father-figures, etc., always like such-and-such types of music, of which the *Eroica* is one example." Here we would say that he is strong on psychology but has given no evidence of being educated in relation to works of art.

When we ask this pupil "Why . . . ?" are we asking only for a cause? No, as this example shows. Are we then asking for only a justification? No: for he might offer *a* (satisfactory) justification for liking the *Eroica*, e.g. by repeating what the best critics had said about it, yet we still would not know whether that was *his* reason for liking it. Are we then asking for both a cause and a justification? Wittgenstein is nervous about using 'cause' ("There is a 'Why?' to aesthetic discomfort not a 'cause' to it . . . If I look at a picture and say: 'What's wrong with this?' then it is better to say that my feeling has direction, and not that my feeling has a cause and I don't know what it is."[2] But we want some word to express our desire to know that the pupil's correct remarks about the *Eroica* are (as I put it) *operative*— that he is not just *saying* them because they are true for other people, or because the examiner expects him to.

Perhaps we might put it thus: When he hears and talks about the *Eroica* he sees it in a certain light: there are certain things about it which he perceives and likes: his attention is directed towards it in certain ways. Then what we want to know is whether he really *does* see it rightly, or just says the right things about it; and 'see' here must mean something more than just *knowing that the Eroica* is noble, tragic, or whatever. He must *feel it as* noble, etc. When we ask him "Why . . . ?" we invite him to say what it is about it that he likes. We hope that he will say the "right" things and not the "wrong" ones (e.g. that it reminds him of his Aunt Flossie). But we also want him to be sincere in his self-reporting. (And not only sincere but correct; there is a common view, I think certainly false, that there is no possibility of mistake, incorrect observation, etc., when reporting one's own feelings, intentions, sensations, and so on. But there is: we may not only lie, but also deceive ourselves, fail to note, or forget, just what it was we felt, and many other things.

This is very difficult, because it is easy genuinely to think that one likes X for some reason approved by oneself or by other people, but actually to like it for some quite other reason. Plainly aesthetics is a sphere (morals and religion are others) where unconscious reasons play a very large part; indeed, one might suppose, almost every part in aesthetics—for it is hard to see why there should be *any* specifically aesthetic enjoyment without bringing in some story of unconscious or buried associations or symbols. 'Aesthetic education' is a subsection of the education of the emotions, but a peculiarly baffling one. For we can establish some criteria of appropriateness in non-aesthetic cases: certain things simply *are*, as a matter of fact, dangerous or thwarting, and reasonably or appropriately invite fear or anger. But it is no good trying to say that some works of art just *are* moving, or elegant, or noble—so long as we continue to talk of them *qua* works of art, not *qua* bits of real life. Works of art are mysterious in being at once second-hand, so to speak—removed in some way from the everyday world and demanding the kind of optional withdrawal noted by Hampshire[3]—and yet also immensely powerful and moving. This is (partly) why we find it difficult to decide what sorts of things we want our pupils to say about them, and what sorts of reasons or perceptions we want to operate in our pupils.

Of course (Wittgenstein again)[4] we do not have to insist on our pupils actually *saying* things, or anyway not elaborate things. Their "appreciation" may emerge in other ways. One who appreciates, say, Wagner may show this by various types of behavior: the way he smiles at certain passages, the way he recognizes a leitmotif, the way he waves his hands about, and so on. Or he may just say "Gosh!" or "Wow!" or something at the right time. Indeed with many of the most moving works of art one may feel it very difficult to say anything much—anything, that is, which relates closely to why one is moved. You can talk about the diction and imagery of *Hamlet*, the tempi and fugal constructions of Bach's B Minor Mass, the geometry of the Parthenon, and so on; but if someone says "Very interesting, but what moves you about these works?" what do you reply? It would be easier to say something about an Ovidian elegiac couplet, or a nostalgic little tune, or a nice piece of domestic architecture. Perhaps this is because the scale is smaller, or perhaps it is because the feelings are more specific ('neatness', 'nostalgia', 'elegance'): or perhaps there is some connection between the small-scale and the specific. Anyway, it is not clear how we should really assess our pupils' love and understanding of works of art.

It might be that instead of getting our pupils to say or write things about works of art we should assess their love and understanding of them much better by getting them to *perform* in some way. If you listen to a class of children reading a play, you can tell which ones really understand and like certain bits. It is the boy who speaks "The iron tongue of midnight hath told twelve" in a certain way, the girl who can play Lady Macbeth despite her feminism or Miranda despite her membership of Women's Lib. And a *fortiori* with music. *Saying* something about a Chopin nocturne is very difficult: but we can distinguish easily enough between the performer who appreciates it and the performer who hams it up.

This is perhaps just a special case of a general point of methodology in assessment: behavior (particularly involuntary or semivoluntary symptoms) is in an important sense more direct evidence, and less easy to fake, than anything the subject says about his feelings. Nevertheless we have to consider the latter, at least in principle; for the behavior ('performance') has disadvantages of its own. It may mislead, because the same behavior can often flow from quite different perceptions. You can get a very good or at least a pretty good reading of certain parts by someone who does not really understand the parts at all. We can say, if we like, in some cases, that such a person has some sort of intuitive feel for the part; but obviously the notion of being *educated* involves a higher degree of consciousness than that. The person who misses the ambiguities in 'told' misses something important in "The iron tongue of midnight hath told twelve".

It is striking that we find it much easier to *disallow* certain things that a person says in reply to the question: "Why . . . ?" than to approve such things. We have a fairly firm grasp of *bad* reasons: "Because I like pictures of horses," "Because it's the latest number," etc. We would generalize and say, "These reasons, these ways of seeing, are not relevant to it *as a work of art.*" But then surely we must have some idea of what sorts of reasons *are* relevant. Well, do we? Certainly we can talk about the construction, the rhyme-scheme, the elegance of the plot, etc.: but are these really relevant? They are not what we are moved by; or, at least, that is certainly not the whole story. Anything we can be forced to admit—anything which is in some straightforward sense descriptively or factually verifiable[5]—such as that X rhymes or does not rhyme with Y, or that one poet has a wider vocabulary than another, cuts very little ice when it comes to our expressing what there is about the work that makes us feel as we do feel. Apart from that, what can we say?

What we do say very often takes the form of a series of adjectives like 'poignant', 'elegant', 'striking', 'life-like', 'dainty', 'glorious', 'subtle' and so on. One trouble with these terms is that they are too general, and hence in a sense artificial. Perhaps it is true that some Chopin nocturne and bits of *Lear* are both 'poignant', but they are very different: and if we are asked why *that nocturne* or *that line* moved us, is it an answer to say "Because it's poignant"? There is a temptation to classify when we say that, rather as one might classify musical marches as 'stirring' or some plays as 'tragic': to do the sort of thing some critics do when they say things like "The whole play breathes the spirit of fairyland." Perhaps the play does do this: but we do not necessarily see it so when we watch it, and we do not necessarily *say* to ourselves as we watch, for instance, *Midsummer Night's Dream*, "This is the spirit of fairyland"—or if we do, our attention may well be wandering (perhaps we are already trying to compose our review for tomorrow's paper). The trouble is, we often do not *say anything* to ourselves.

Suppose you value a certain person. I say, "What do you value about him?" You can reply, honestly and correctly, "I value his loyalty and good sense." Now suppose you are in love with someone. I say, "What is there about her which you love, what do you see in her?" Now you might say (as philosophers have condemned aestheticians for saying) "She's beautiful": but what else could you say? Perhaps something like, "When she smiles, my heart turns over," or "In that dress she's so queenly," or "She's like a beautiful flower," or something. But the noteworthy thing is, you often *do not know the answer.* No doubt you can come to discover some 'answers': you notice that you fall in love with tall willowly blondes, and say "I suppose it must be something to do with her being tall and willowly and blonde." But now this is a causal answer: you are not reproducing what goes on in your head or your heart when you see her: you are just inducing.

Being moved by works of art is often more like being in love than like valuing a trusted friend; more like what one may feel about one's native land than like one's rational preferences for Ruritania as a place for a touring holiday. Most of the crucial operations (as also in religious belief) are unconscious—if available to consciousness, available only with difficulty. Nor does this apply only to works of art which move us very deeply or passionately. An elegant dress, a neat couplet, a well-turned vase give us satisfaction ('move' might be too strong here). We can, indeed, sometimes put the satisfaction *sub specie boni alicuius*—being neat, or elegant, or well-turned (rather than glorious, poignant, or whatever)—but that is all we can do. We cannot show the *appropriateness* of our feelings, as we usually can with fear and danger. And this is because the targets or objects of our feelings are in a sense unseen; the *species boni* which moves us, and which may move us appropriately, lies not solely in the notes, words, or bits of paint, but in a relationship between them and parts of our minds of which we are unconscious.

Nor surprisingly, the difficulty of giving 'proper reasons' is particularly apparent in those areas where art-objects are hard to disentangle from life-objects: I mean with cars, clothes, physical attractiveness, the interior decoration of houses, and so on. How on earth, for instance, are we to distinguish clothes or lifestyles that 'really' look nice (*sub specie aeternitatis*, so to speak) from those which commend themselves to us, often semi-consciously, because of their associations with social class, money, status, functionality, current fashion, and so on? What is the relevance (or irrelevance) of time, boredom and the desire for change? Are we to count it as a good aesthetic reason for 'this year's color' or 'this year's model' that it is not like last year's, with which we are bored? These and similar problems arise to some extent with 'high' (or higher) art: there are fashions even in classical music, and many people may imagine that their appreciation of (say) Greek poetry is aesthetically 'pure', when in fact a limited degree of alienness and romance in the language itself may attract them. It is no good saying "Strip it of its associations, and look on it purely as a work of art." For works of art would not affect us at all if it was not for *some* associations, however, deeply buried: the symbols have to be symbols of *something*.

For something like these (too briefly adumbrated) reasons, one might suspect the search for a general class of 'pure' and 'aesthetic' reasons to be vain. As an alternative approach, we might think that the reasons in each case can be derived from the particular set of traditions, conventions, etc., which govern that particular art-form. For instance, suppose we ask what it is to 'appreciate' a really good move in chess (and after all, such moves are often described as 'elegant', 'imaginative', 'creative', 'beautiful', etc.). Well, we might say, surely someone who had any deep understanding of chess (1) could hardly *help* 'appreciating' the merits of the move: and (2) would express this *just by* pointing out (if asked) why it was so good ("Don't you see, it gets his king out of trouble while simultaneously threatening mate in three ways and forking the queen. . . . " and so on). What else could we want from him? The 'appreciation' and the 'reasons' come purely from criteria within the game: rather like 'elegant' solutions by architects to problems posed by stresses and strains, the materials they have available, and so on, such as the flying buttress.

I do not want to deny the importance to 'appreciation' of tradition and convention (and also of the background of ordinary life and language).[6] But the examples above reinforce the difficulty. A flying buttress (most believe) is aesthetically as well as mechanically 'elegant'; one could ima-

gine another mechanically elegant (i.e., cheap, space-saving, etc.) solution, perhaps a skilfully-placed bit of ferro-concrete, which would be very
ugly. Similarly a person might be brought to see that a particular move in
chess solved the player's problems very efficiently (if you like, 'neatly',
'elegantly', 'economically'); but he would not thereby necessarily find himself describing the move as 'beautiful'—or, if he did, 'beautiful' would
mean only 'efficient', 'economical', etc. He would not warm to the move
in the way that a person who loved chess as an art-form would warm to it.
Of course this is a borderline case: we (including the person himself) would
often be hard put to say whether he warmed to something 'aesthetically' or
otherwise. But the borderline does, however roughly, demarcate two real
and different territories.

We may still feel inclined to say that *if* the person really *loved* chess or
was really keen on it for its own sake (rather than as a way of making
money, for instance), then he could not help but 'appreciate' it 'aesthetically' as well as in other ways; so too perhaps with anything one really loves
or is keen on (cricket, equations, places, people). This seems right; but still
leaves us with an inevitable mystery, which is as much to do with the
notion of 'loving something for its own sake' as with 'aesthetics'. Certainly,
if a pupil 'loves' a work or art 'for its own sake', then this *means* both that
he is genuinely and 'aesthetically' moved by it, and that he has 'the right
reasons' for doing so—that is, since he loves it for itself he will understand
it, keep his own personality in the background, appreciate the tradition on
which it rests, and so on. But this does not show what specific aspects of it
actually move him.

This seems something which it is important both to recognize and to
accept as inevitable. To take a parallel: suppose we were trying, by some
means or other, to educate a pupil about love and marriage. Then we
should want him (1) to be able to love some woman or women—that is, to
be genuinely moved, not just to 'go through the motions' as a matter of
convention or other people's expectations: and (2) to appreciate, at the
same time, what women were really like and give due weight to their
qualities, neither misperceiving them for psychological reasons of his own
nor being too much moved by reasons we might think irrelevant to their
merits as mistresses or spouses. But we should recognize and accept that,
underlying all this, there are powerful unconscious symbols and forces
without which the whole business of sexual love would be ultimately
unintelligible. All we can do is to remove any unnecessary blocks or
impediments to these forces, and (perhaps only to a limited extent) sophis-

ticate them: that is, educate our pupils so that they take pleasure in what is real about women rather than what is unreal or irrelevant.

The major work here for philosophers of education (in cooperation with other workers) seems to lie, as so often, in trying to get clear about the *sorts of ways* in which this can be done; and by 'sorts of ways', I do not refer to particular and specific 'methods' (drama, musical appreciation classes, rhythmic dance, etc.). Before we can judge these effectively, we must have an expanded version (so to speak) of the aims: a set of categories which specify certain general tasks or objectives clearly and discretely. This is an immensely difficult business; the few remarks that follow may be less valuable in themselves than as pointing to the enormous gap between any highly generalized philosophical account and the use of specific educational methods.

One might be inclined to say something like this: "There are two things which we demand of our pupils. First, they must clear their minds of whatever makes them see things in a distorted way, or not see them at all: of the different kinds of blocks, demands of the 'fat, relentless ego'[7] and so on, which make them impose their own requirements on a work of art and prevent them from seeing it for what it is. Secondly, they must enter into the world of the work itself, learn about it and enjoy it." This suggests a two-stage process: and very often the situation can be fairly represented thus. A person who refuses even to go to *see* abstract paintings because he insists on imposing naturalistic schemata on all paintings, or will not listen to music because it is composed by Jews or Germans, can hardly even start. By far the most common situation is that people do not even, seriously, *try*.

But, of course, the two demands can also coexist in time, and interact: prejudice and distortion continue to operate while one initiates oneself into a work, and conversely the more one steeps oneself in it the less liable one becomes (or may become) to prejudice and distortion. This is why *time* is essential, and we cannot do this sort of education too quickly: the work of art needs time to sink in, to be accepted as real and existing in its own right. For various reasons, the process cannot be hurried (several reasons contribute to the hopelessness of trying to force certain novels on pupils before they are, as we say, 'ready' for them).[8] This too is like getting to know and love a person.

Most deliberate 'aesthetic education' tries to meet only the demand for intellectual initiation; and much of this is in a way just a device, almost a cheat. We tell pupils to note the rhyme-scheme and vowel-sounds, observe how character X 'develops' in the story, distinguish the voices in a fugue, etc.: or we may even talk to them about the poet's life and times, and dating of Shakespearean plays, the invention of the transverse flute. None of these is really about the work of art as such, about what moves us in confronting it. They are devices to retain the person's attention while the work sinks in. One person's attention to the Moonlight Sonata may be retained by talking about clouds scudding across the sky, another's by talking about the development of sonata form and other such technicalities. When a person is already to some degree in love with a work, *then* the critic who knows it more and loves it better can say helpful things, things more closely relevant to what moves us or may move us when we connect what he says with what we know of the work already.

But by then, half the battle is won. These first stages, the attention-getting devices, may be necessary, though the devices we use might often be queried. If the idea is (rightly) just to get pupils to listen to (read, see, etc.) the work so that it will sink in, then might not this be done in other ways? Perhaps we should get as far, or farther, by just *playing* lots of good music at them, running tapes or films of Shakespeare plays, and so on, and not trying to *teach* them about these works at this stage ('immersing' rather than 'initiating'): or perhaps what we need to know is what makes pupils really like *any* kind of good music (plays, books, poems, pictures, etc.) for almost *any* reason. Given some degree of commitment or love, we have some basis for teaching: not till then.

This is why the first demand, the freedom from prejudice and distortion, seems worth more attention in our education that we usually give it. Clearly there will be many categories here. For example, to make one rough distinction, we can separate the people who cannot tolerate a particular piece of art unless it abides by certain formal rules (poetry that scans, naturalistic painting, music with classical harmonies, jokes that are not puns) from the people who cannot tolerate it unless it has a particular content (happy ending, plenty of blood, clear-cut 'good guys' and 'bad guys'). Most people's approach to many art-forms, I suppose, is dictated by a desire for some naïvely mimetic substitute: in libraries they make straight for various content-categories of books—'horror stories', 'romances', 'crime', 'westerns' (some libraries classify their stock partly thus): in fact this is no doubt true of everybody some of the time. In some leisure moments, perhaps particularly when the real world does not seem very nice and I do not want to make the (enormous) effort of 'appreciating', I just want a 'thriller' or a 'science fiction'; and when I say I want a good one, I do not mean much more than that (1) it should lift me out into a fantasy world and, (2) that it should not be so atrocious that my critical faculties bring me back to earth with a bump. This happens a lot, and why shouldn't it? But it shows that the appreciation of works of art is *very hard work*. Much of the prejudice and distortion, when pupils are confronted with good works of art, will inevitably come from their (various) needs to find substitutes for a chill world. A quite different but equally important part of the educator's job is to discover what aspects of the world seem chill to them, and how they can be sufficiently well-fed in other ways not to need this substitution.

It needs to be stressed that this substitution takes many forms (at some levels of our minds it may always operate), not only a desire to fill the consciousness with sweetness and light or sex and violence. For instance, there are people who very badly need to repeat or reenact to themselves the principle that virtue always triumphs and vice is always punished—perhaps all the more badly because it is obviously not true. So the acceptance of a more subtle world, perhaps that of some Shakespearean or Greek tragedies, is intolerable to them. They must have obvious heroes and out-and-out villains. Or (common among intellectuals) there is the person who cannot really enjoy anything unless it makes severe intellectual demands (Donne, Proust, complex Bach fugues, the 'astringent', 'unsentimental', etc., not "What is love? 'Tis not hereafter", Gould, Siegfried's straighforward horns). Or conversely there is the impatient juice-extractor who can hardly wait till the murder actually happens or the trumpets sound *fortissimo*—to him the build-up is a bore, as if sex did not really start at all until one was actually in a state of orgasm.

These superficial sketches are just to make the point, I hope by now obvious, that we cannot get far with education in this area unless we can identify the particular compulsions our pupils are under. (And, of course, we can detect all or most of them in ourselves.) We may start, indeed, by building on some kind of commitment or love for an art-object; but this is only a start, and we find ourselves almost immediately up against the difficulty that pupils do not really use the 'aesthetic mode' or take an 'aesthetic stance' at all; or anyway, not much. So we ought surely to give pupils a clear and fully conscious grasp of what such a stance is like, in relation to *some* (any) work of art. Plainly we shall be most likely to succeed if we start with very simple and easily 'appreciated' works: but we have to be clear what the criteria of selection are here. The prevailing fashion (at least in some 'progressive' quarters) is to take works which are 'closest to the pupil's own life', or 'immediately relevant to the pupil's own experience'. A lot of these are barely works of art at all, and some are trash; and in any case, what we want is not something which the pupils just like or enjoy for *any* reasons, but something in which it will be easy for them to see the difference between this undifferentiated enjoyment and appreciating the work for its own sake.

One would be inclined to start with works where the importance of form or tradition is very clear: for instance, the limerick or the joke (told well or badly), the strip cartoon, the western film, simple songs. If we concentrate sufficiently on different works which are in some sense 'doing the same thing'—neat or sloppy limericks, boring or dramatic westerns, etc.—the pupils will come to see that the 'same thing' can be 'done' well or badly, and to perceive and differentiate the kind of pleasure which can be gained from a perception of this. Thus most pupils, with very little education, can distinguish between sincerity and cliché, or clarity and vagueness, in a simple love-letter: between those *graffiti* which are amusing and effective, and those which spin out of the author's fantasies in a way quite unregulated by the effect on the reader. There is a range or scale rather than an absolute distinction, of course, in such cases: but this makes it all the more possible to get the pupils to see what it is a scale *of*, to transmit the idea of what it is to produce and enjoy a work *as such*. If one can achieve this even in a single case, the pupil has something to cling on to; he has the *concept* of a work of art, and can know what sort of thing to do with cases which he has not met before.

How far individual pupils can be expected to go in 'appreciation' is another matter. But without wanting to put any predetermined limits in anyone's way, I suspect many cannot go very far. It is not necessarily accident, or lack of (formal) education, or the incompetence of teachers, that makes the higher art-forms a minority taste. It is something which may correlate with intelligence, social class, and the usual variables in orthodox research: but it is more like what they call 'deferring gratification' than anything else. The limiting factor is what we have noticed already: the ability and/or desire to put one's ego in the background, so that one can attend. This limitation makes it all the more important not to renege on our basic task, to give everyone as effective a grasp as we can of *art as such*, not just to get them to 'like' books, music and other things for any old reason: though we may start with that. Educators are not paid just to provide new sources of pleasure.

NOTES

1. L. Wittgenstein, *Lectures and Conversations* (Oxford: Blackwell, 1966), p. 17ff.

2. Ibid., pp. 14–15.

3. Stuart Hampshire, "Logic and Appreciation," in *Aesthetics and Language*, ed. by W. Elton (Oxford: Blackwell, 1954), pp. 162–167.

4. Wittgenstein, *Lectures and Conversations*, p. 7ff.

5. P. F. Strawson, "Aesthetic Appraisal and Works of Art," in *Freedom and Resentment and Other Essays* (London: Methuen, 1974), pp. 184–187.

6. R. W. Beardsmore, *Art and Morality* (London: Routledge, 1971), chaps. 4 and 5.

7. Iris Murdoch, *The Sovereignty of Good* (London: Routledge, 1970), p. 52.

8. Sometimes it is hard to see how one can even *start* the process: "Literature illuminates life only for those to whom books are a necessity. Books are unconvertible assets, to be passed on only to those who possess them already" (Anthony Powell, *The Valley of Bones*).

⋞ 11 ⋟

THE POSSIBILITIES OF

ETHICAL INQUIRY

IN THE SCHOOLS

⋞ MARTIN BENJAMIN

Michigan State University

Moral Knowledge and Moral Education

1. Introduction

A major obstacle to introducing moral education in the schools is a pair of prevailing misconceptions about the cognitive status of ethics. Many people believe that all ethical knowledge is in some sense "absolute" and thus that it must simply be inculcated into students in the most direct and efficient manner. Many other people believe that all ethical knowledge is in some sense "subjective"; from this they infer that one may be able to help students clarify their ethical values but that there is no nonarbitrary way to establish that some ethical values are better than others. Absolutists are opposed to moral education in the schools because they fear that the content of what is taught will be determined by absolutists of another stripe, or by subjectivists. And subjectivists believe that any legitimate moral education must be confined to what is called "values clarification." Anything more substantive, subjectivists fear, can only enter under inadmissible absolutist assumptions.

Each of these positions presupposes that the cognitive status of ethics is radically discontinuous with the cognitive status of other things taught in the schools; for example, science or history. I want to show that this presupposition is incorrect. For, to borrow a metaphor from Wittgenstein, both absolutists and subjectivists suffer from the sort of philosophical "deficiency disease" that is the result of an unbalanced diet of examples. Absolutists dwell on easy cases, subjectivists on difficult ones; but neither group is true to the full range and complexity of the moral domain. Closer attention to the variety of moral phenomena and the similarities between the cognitive status of (reflective) ethical and scientific judgments will reveal that ethics has at least as strong a claim to a place in the curriculum as does science.

In what follows, attention will be drawn to the similarities between the methodology and cognitive status of science and philosophical (rational, critical) ethics. Although important differences between the two will be acknowledged, it will be argued that they do not undermine these fundamental similarities. Perhaps the most important difference is that, unlike the particular sciences, where certain assumptions restrict the range of admissible problems and questions, the frame of reference for ethical inquiry is relatively unrestricted. Thus, the range and complexity of relevant considerations in ethics (where the fundamental question in a given situation is: "All things considered, what ought I to do?") will require us to exercise many different skills and faculties; and as a result these considerations will more often than not outstrip our capacity to comprehend and evaluate them. In such cases one may not know how to choose between two or more alternatives. But even here one can know that a number of other alternatives are unacceptable, although there is no clear way to decide among those remaining. A similar situation, it should be noted, can arise in the practice of medicine; a physician may reject a number of possible treatments for a particular illness on cognitive grounds while being left with two or more possible treatments whose efficacy cannot, at the time, be cognitively distinguished. Yet the occurrence of such cases is not a reason for denying the cognitive status of medical science.

This essay is aimed at parents and teachers who are concerned about the introduction of moral education in the schools in a pluralistic society. If its arguments are clear and sound, it will allay some of the apprehensions of skeptics, provide a firm intellectual foundation for enthusiasts, and, to the extent that it reaches them, reduce the ranks of both 'absolutists' and 'subjectivists'.

2. Moral Knowledge and Scientific Knowledge

In this section I review the similarities between moral and scientific knowledge. I begin by identifying the root of some common misapprehensions which exaggerate their differences. I then present a brief account of the important respects in which their methodology and cognitive status are similar. The section concludes by showing how this account preserves those aspects of the impulses toward absolutism and subjectivism that have something to recommend them.

A. *Some Common Misapprehensions.* Underlying many attempts to demonstrate a radical discontinuity between the methodology and cognitive status of ethics and science are various instances of what Alan Gewirth has identified as the "fallacy of disparateness."[1] One commits this fallacy when, in comparing two fields or subject matters, one compares one of them as it is manifested on one level or one respect with the other as it is manifested on a quite different level or in a quite different respect. Thus, for example, if we base claims to the cognitive decidability of particular scientific controversies by appeal to the criteria employed within a particular science and base claims to the noncognitive status of ethical controversies on the unavailability of clear-cut criteria for readily deciding between opposing ethical framworks, we commit the fallacy of disparateness. For the proper comparisons are between the resolution of controversies *within* a particular science and *within* a particular ethical framework, on the one hand, and between the way we justify a basic scientific paradigm[2] and the way we justify a basic ethical framework, on the other.

Considerations of space do not permit an enumeration of the many instances and forms of this fallacy.[3] One, however, deserves explicit consideration insofar as it is aggravated by common patterns of moral and scientific education. Science education, at least in the earlier years, focuses on standard phenomena that can be explained by well-entrenched lower-level theories. Thus the notion of 'scientific fact' as something deeply rooted and nearly incorrigible soon takes hold in the student's mind. Explicit consideration of moral problems (as opposed to moralizing), on the other hand, usually focuses on tough cases—often cruel dilemmas—that can be resolved, if at all, only by appeal to sophisticated forms of moral reasoning and complex factual considerations. The student, then, is confronted by the contrast between the epistemic status of claims about planetary motion, which serve to introduce him or her to science, and claims about whether a young Frenchman during the Second World War should stay with his dependent mother or join the Free French, a standard problem in introductory courses in ethics.[4] It is therefore understandable that people generalize from such introductions and conclude that scientific judgments have a significantly more firm epistemic status than do moral judgments. Here, once again, we have an instance of the fallacy of disparateness. For if students were to pursue their scientific studies further they would learn that controversies about the nature and ultimate foundations of the particular sciences, as well as certain contemporary controversies within them, are as difficult to resolve as many moral dilemmas; and the debates in science are no less lacking in fervor. Moreover, the natural desire of teachers of ethics to present and discuss particularly knotty cases and complicated current issues like capital punishment and euthanasia often disguises the fact—and it is a fact—that there is little or no disagreement about the majority of moral judgments that, unnoticed, guide our everyday behavior. For nearly every time we keep a promise, resist an opportunity to steal, or contain an impulse to strike a screaming child, our conduct is justified by judgments whose truth most students are not, at least initially, inclined to question.

Finally, we should note that discussions of Sartre's celebrated dilemma of the young Frenchman invariably focus on just two possibilities: should he remain with his dependent mother or seek to make an uncertain contribution to a large and important, but impersonal, cause? Other courses of action are never considered and any suggestion that he follow his father's collaborationist footsteps or go abroad to pursue a lucrative career would be met with either scorn or disbelief. But if this is so, it seems strange that Sartre believes that the case shows, among other things, that "No general ethics can show you what is to be done."[5] For even in this extremely difficult case, "general ethics" has narrowed the possibilities to two; and in most other cases (those that do not generally provide the focus for courses in ethics) "general ethics" can do even better.

B. *Method in Science and Ethics.* Having identified the fallacy of disparateness as a frequent source of misleading comparison, I turn now to a brief account of the important similarities between science and ethics. Readers who are uncomfortable with its lack of detail will, I hope, be able to consult more fully developed versions.[6]

Particular sciences aim at formulating and developing systems of beliefs about the world. They begin with reasonably secure singular judgments rooted in ordinary sense perception. Scientists then try to systematize and explain these singular judgments by devising general principles and theories that relate them to one another and provide a basis for prediction. In addition to providing an important test of adequacy, the predictive power of such general principles and theories allows them to be extended and refined.

In developing particular principles and theories, scientists attempt to do a number of things. First, they try to achieve a better "fit" between the singular judgments in which they have the most confidence and the principles and theories designed to relate and account for them. Second, they endeavor to make their principles and theories more comprehensive. By formulating them in more general or abstract ways, they are often able to bring them to bear on a greater range of singular judgments, thereby extending their explanatory and predictive power. And, third, they attempt to obtain a higher degree of consistency or compatibility both between various theories within a particular science and between various particular sciences.

In attempting to achieve these goals, scientists engage in a dialectical interplay between the singular judgments—new and old, rooted in ordinary sense perception and derived from abstract theory—which might be pictured at the periphery of the scientific map, and the more general principles and theories located closer to the center. When new experience or efforts to achieve higher degrees of "fit," comprehensiveness, consistency or compatibility magnify the discrepancy between singular judgments, on the one hand, and general principles and theories, on the other, something must give. Often, in mature sciences, initial efforts will be aimed at preserving the principles and theories at the expense of singular judgments. In other cases, and especially in more fledgling sciences, it will be the principles and theory that give way.

A standard example of this dialectical process is an historically oversim-
plified version of the shift from the Ptolemaic, geocentric view of the
universe to the Copernican, heliocentric one.[7] The singular judgments
upon which Ptolemaic astronomy was founded were our common sense
observations of the sun and the other heavenly bodies moving about in the
sky. We, as it were, stood in a fixed place while they moved about, and the
problem was to arrive at principles and theories which could adequately
account for and be used to predict these basic "facts." The predisposition to
save the appearances or preserve the facts led geocentric astronomers to
devise principles of planetary motion that became increasingly complicated
and cumbersome. It was not until the sixteenth century that a more fruitful
theory ignited the Copernician Revolution; and the belief that the earth,
like the other planets, revolved around the sun began to induce people to
revise their conception of the "facts." It was, for example, no longer a fact
that the sun rose and set, but rather what appeared to be its rising and
setting was explained by the earth's revolution around the sun and rotation
around its own axis.

Such radical revisions, though not frequent, are understood to be demanded by the aim of science. As A. C. Ewing has observed,

> the object of science is to build up that system which will best account
> for our perceptions and knit the judgments based on them together into
> a consistent whole in which the different parts do not contradict but
> confirm each other. In order to attain the system which of those at our
> disposal will explain our experience best and give us a rationally con-
> nected picture of the world, the sciences and indeed common-sense are
> constrained to reject certain of our perceptions as illusory in order to be
> able consistently to give reality to others.[8]

The Copernican Revolution, then, provides an example of singular judgments being revised in the interests of preserving a theory or principles
which ultimately "explain our experience best and give us a rationally
connected picture of the world." Other examples—such as the rejection of
the phlogiston theory of combustion in the eighteenth century, attributable
in part to firmly grounded singular judgments of an increase in weight in
roasted objects when, according to the theory, there should have been a
decrease—illustrate how theory or principles have given way to singular
judgments.[9]

Thus, even the most secure scientific knowledge is provisional. Continued efforts to achieve a comprehensive, consistent view of the world an-

chored in and confirmed by experience insure that our scientific beliefs can never form a closed and finished system. The possibility of new and unanticipated experience prevents setting our scientific course on automatic pilot. This is not to deny that there is such a thing as scientific knowledge and that it is objective and the sort of thing that ought to be taught in the schools. Properly presented—that is, by helping students *think scientifically* rather than having them simply absorb scientific "facts"- —science is a cornerstone of a child's education. And, I now want to suggest, ethics, properly presented—that is, by helping students to develop skills and sensitivity in *moral thinking* rather than simply reiterating moral "facts" or expressing values—is another educational cornerstone. For there are important similarities in method and structure between (philosophical) ethics and the foregoing conception of science.

Like science, ethics aims at formulating and developing a comprehensive, consistent set of beliefs. Unlike scientific beliefs, however, which are largely descriptive and predictive, moral beliefs are more prescriptive and normative. They are less directly concerned with what is the case and more directly concerned with what ought to be the case. Their principal concern is with the evaluation and regulation of human conduct. Despite these differences, to which I will return in the following section, there are impressive similarities between the methodologies of science and ethics and between the cognitive status of their respective belief systems.

First, like science, ethics does not begin in a vacuum. It starts with those singular judgments in which we have the greatest confidence and would be extremely reluctant to give up. Such singular judgments are the analogue of the singular judgments about the world rooted in sense perception that provide the empirical touchstone for scientific inquiries. An attempt is then made to systematize and justify these singular moral judgments by identifying or formulating a set of principles that together with certain statements about factual circumstances, seem to support them. The process is characterized by the same sort of dialectical interplay between singular judgments and general principles and theories that one finds in scientific inquiry.

This dialectical interplay is governed by a number of aims. As in science, we strive to encompass as much of the relevant domain as possible while still preserving a tolerable "fit" between singular judgments and principles and theories. After initially formulating principles and theories by extracting the implicit rationales from our most secure judgments, we then subject them to further testing and development by extending them to new or old circumstances where our "intuitive" singular judgments give less guidance or are simply nonexistent. As this process continues, adjustments are often made at both ends in the interest of achieving a more coherent and useful overall system. Thus, if we are just beginning to develop an overall system, an otherwise promising principle may be rejected or radically modified if it conflicts with a particularly strong (set of) singular judgment(s). Or, if an application of a fairly well-grounded set of principles in a new context issues in an intuitively unsettling singular judgment, we may, if no further refinement of the principles will mitigate the discrepancy, decide to throw in with the principles and thus dismiss as unfounded our intuitive misgivings about the singular judgment. In proceeding in this manner we are, as Joel Feinberg puts it, "always aiming at the ideal of a comprehensive personal and interpersonal coherence in which singular judgments and general principles stand in a 'reflective equilibrium'."[10]

Feinberg's explicit distinction, in this passage, between two measures of coherence is extremely important for understanding the sense in which it may be said that ethics is both an individual and collective undertaking. As individuals, each of us is concerned to develop his or her ethical framework. Although most of us do not start from scratch, we should be continually subjecting our received singular judgments and principles to critical reflection with the aim of more closely approximating the ideal of a comprehensive personal coherence. But the personal dimension is not the only one that matters; one of the main reasons for engaging in ethical reflection is to arrive at principles for guiding conduct and resolving disagreement. Such principles, if they are to be effective, must be such that the concerned parties are inclined to subscribe and submit their conduct to them. Thus, in developing one's ethical framework, one seeks interpersonal as well as personal comprehensiveness and coherence. The process of putting and maintaining one's singular judgments and general principles in reflective equilibrium must, then, be regulated by what others can reasonably be expected to agree to as well as by what is conducive to maintaining one's own sense of integrity.

All of this has been fairly abstract. Let me therefore present a brief example of the dialectical interplay that can occur between singular judgments and ethical principles. Suppose that after reflecting upon our initial singular judgments about what we ought to do if we come across people in distress whose plight we can easily relieve, we extract the following principle: "If it is in our power to prevent something bad from happening, without thereby sacrificing anything else of moral significance, we ought, morally, to do it."[11] We then, according to the foregoing account, proceed to test this principle be seeing, first, how well it fits with other of our principles and then by extending its application to contexts where our moral intuitions give little guidance. Let us also suppose that the particular singular judgments from which this principle was extracted all concerned aiding those nearby whose plight we could both see and easily do something about. Of course, there may also have been people in other parts of the world in the same distressful condition, but because at the time our principle was formulated, we could neither see nor aid them, it was not considered applicable to them.

In recent years, however, the development of sophisticated forms of communication and transportation have transformed the world into a "global village." The question now is whether widespread famine and malnutrition portrayed on television and the existence of effective international relief and self-help offered by organizations like CARE require most of us in an affluent society to donate fairly large sums of money if we are to be true to the principle just quoted. My aim here is not to settle this substantive issue. Rather it is to illustrate how settling it involves the dialectical interplay between new and old singular judgments, on the one hand, and principles and theories, on the other. For, if we do not want to affirm a singular moral judgment that would require our giving up some measure of comfort in order to send (more) money to organizations like CARE, we shall have to reject or suitably qualify the moral princile; or, alternatively, we may, despite *prima facie* resemblances, try to show that there is a relevant difference between those in distress who live across the street and those who live across the ocean. But if we do not think geographical or national differences are relevant, and if we feel that this moral principle is very strongly grounded and cannot be qualified without weakening the support of singular judgments that appeal strongly to our moral intuitions, we may feel that we are now obligated to dig into our wallets and give more money to overseas relief and self-help than we have in the past. In either case (and the matter is actually more complex than this brief account reveals), the form of our reflection will be remarkably similar to that employed by scientists in relevantly similar situations.

To summarize, there are important similarities between ethical and scientific thinking. Three features shared by both are especially relevant to the relationship between moral knowledge and moral education. First, on this account, ethical as well as scientific knowledge is provisional. It is always possible that new experience or unconsidered possibilities will induce us, in the interests of achieving the most comprehensive and coherent view of things, to revise either singular judgments or principles and theories. Second, it follows from this that our work in science or ethics is never done. There is no flying our course on automatic pilot. An understanding of the method and epistemological foundations of science should leave us open to the possibility of having to make frequent minor and occasional major changes in our world view in the light of new experiences. Similarly, new circumstances or newly recognized implications of established ethical outlooks may force us to make significant revisions in either our received singular judgments or principles (or theories) or both. Third, even though our scientific and ethical frameworks, no matter how highly developed, both fall short of perfection, the least imperfect framework will always be better than none at all. Criticisms of any particular framework are not sufficient for rejecting it unless one can replace it with another that, all things considered, can reasonably be expected to be better.

C. *Absolutism and Subjectivism.* We are now able to explain how both ethical absolutists and subjectivists ground their positions in basic insights only to have them weakened by unwarranted generalization. What gives absolutism its *prima facie* appeal is its emphasizing that in ethics not anything goes. A judgment or principle is not correct, even for a particular person, simply because he or she believes that it is. In developing and certifying our ethical judgments, our efforts must not only strive for personal, but also for interpersonal, coherence and comprehensiveness. And although it does not necessarily happen, under this constraint practically all ethical frameworks turn out to contain certain singular judgments and related principles that are extremely unlikely to be replaced.[12] Thus, for example, the absolutist may stress that no acceptable ethical view can mandate or allow for the torture of children. Where absolutism goes wrong is in extending this insight about certain initial fixed points of ethical reflection to the entire domain of ethical knowledge. In short, absolutists fail to recognize that even our most secure principles do not provide adequate guidance in *all* current situations nor is there any reason to believe that, in their present form, they will be adequate for all new and unforeseen situations. And it is the frank recognition of this limitation that provides both for strong objections to absolutism and the basis for subjectivism.

Where the absolutist centers on, and then overreaches, insights into our most secure singular judgments and principles, the subjectivist centers on, and then similarly overreaches, insights into contexts where our most highly developed ethical views provide little guidance. Subjectivists are disposed to dwell on dilemmas like that posed by Sartre or on particularly difficult issues like capital punishment or those raised by advances in medical knowledge and technology. It is precisely such contexts that fully engage the personal and interpersonal dialectical interplay between singular judgments and principles, the resolution of which may reverberate throughout the entire system. But although such interplay is characterized by great uncertainty, it does not follow that *anything goes*; for the inquiry will have clear, though not fully determinate, boundaries rooted in the overall ethical framework that is, at that time, judged most adequate. Thus, for example, even parties to disputes over capital punishment can agree that, even if justifiable, capital punishment ought not to be deliberately humiliating or torturous.

At the root of both absolutism and subjectivism, then, is a failure to understand the nature of ethical knowledge and the full range of complexity of the moral domain. And, I have suggested, this is in large part attributable to a failure to appreciate the similarities between inquiry and knowledge in science and ethics.

3. Two Important Differences

In stressing similarities between scientific and ethical inquiry, I have naturally emphasized certain cognitive skills and standards. In addition to consistency and comprehensiveness, these include conceptual clarity, drawing relevant distinctions, formulating cogent arguments, continual testing and refining of provisionally held positions, and the like. There are, however, two especially important differences between science and ethics that should be noted.

First, inasmuch as ethics is concerned mainly with the evaluation and regulation of human conduct, it is more directly concerned with what *ought to be* the case than what in fact *is* the case. This means that there will be certain noncontingent connections between certain of our moral principles and judgments and certain of our emotions, attitudes, and dispositions to behave in certain ways. As Brian Crittenden has pointed out:

> Moral concepts and principles form an integral part of the complex human practice of morality. They cannot be learned in abstraction from this context without distortion. . . . [In addition] it is a necessary part of learning such concepts as 'truth telling,' 'lying', 'honesty', 'cheating', 'fairness', 'respect for human life', or 'murder' as *moral* concepts that we

would have attitudes of approval and disapproval, and would experience certain feelings or emotions (e.g., sympathy, disgust, remorse, guilt) toward the actions we are prepared to describe in such moral terms. These affective aspects are not contingently related to our acquisition of a moral concept in the way that certain emotions may come to be associated in an individual's life with such terms as 'snow', 'home', 'autumn', 'red'. A person may know that 'murder' is commonly understood as a moral concept in our society, but he does not possess it as a moral concept himself unless he disapproves of murder, or would feel guilty if he committed murder.[13]

Thus, in ethics there will be as much emphasis on achieving consistency between certain moral principles and judgments, and certain emotions, attitudes, and behavior as there will on achieving consistency simply between principles and judgments.

The second important difference between science and ethics is that, unlike the particular sciences where certain assumptions restrict the range of admissible problems and questions, the frame of reference for ethical inquiry is comparatively unrestricted. The basic question in ethics is '*All things considered*, what ought one to do (in a given situation)?' The thoughtful consideration of all things relevant to a particular moral decision, practical or theoretical, will, it turns out, require the exercise of a number of skills and capacities in addition to those generally considered relevant to scientific inquiry. Among these will be: (1) a highly developed moral imagination grounded upon first-hand or vicarious experience of what it is like to see and undergo things from the standpoint of others; (2) a more or less sophisticated understanding of the historical, psychological, and sociological antecedents of one's own behavior and that of others; and (3) a capacity to resist self-deception by striving to perceive relationships between oneself and others clearly and vividly.

In an illuminating essay, the philosopher-novelist Iris Murdoch has pointed out how a failure to understand the importance of attentive moral perception has led many contemporary philosophers to exaggerate the significance of seemingly intractable moral dilemmas. In so doing, she claims, they provide a misleading picture of ethical choice. For,

I can only choose within the world I can *see*, in the moral sense of 'see' which implies that clear vision is a result of moral imagination and moral effort. There is also of course 'distorted vision' and the word 'reality' here inevitably appears as a normative word. . . . One is often compelled almost automatically by what one *can* see. . . . This does not imply that we are not free, certainly not. But it implies that the exercise of our freedom is a small piecemeal business which goes on all the time and not a grandiose leaping about unimpeded at important moments. The moral life, on this view, is something that goes on continually, not something that is switched off in between the occurrence of explicit moral choices. What happens in between such choices is indeed what is crucial. I would like on the whole to use the word 'attention' as a good word and use some more general term like 'looking' as the neutral word. Of course psychic energy flows, and more readily flows, into building up convincingly coherent but false pictures of the world, complete with systematic vocabulary. . . . Attention is the effort to counteract such states of illusion.[14]

Thus an incapacity or unwillingness to strive for day-in day-out 'attentiveness' in Murdoch's sense is as likely to lead to moral error as an incapacity or unwillingness to work towards the ideal of a systematic, comprehensive, personal and interpersonal coherence of singular moral judgments and principles.

4. Moral Education

There is no doubt that both the preschool years and the continuing influence of the home and other nonscholastic environments have an enormous effect on a child's moral development. But the child's experience in school is also of considerable significance. Thus, if the account I have given of the nature and structure of moral knowledge and reasoning is correct, it is important that it be reflected in the curriculum. The detailed development of such a curriculum is, of course, a large and complex task. In what follows I would like simply to indicate the sorts of things such a curriculum should stress.

First, teachers should be highly skilled in the dialectic of moral reasoning. They should, themselves, always be "aiming at the ideal of a comprehensive personal and interpersonal coherence in which singular judgments and general principles stand in a 'reflective equilibrium'." And, whenever possible and feasible, they should be helping their students, at levels and on topics suitable and meaningful to them, do the same. This means engaging in discussion where emphasis is placed upon consistency, comprehensiveness, conceptual clarity, drawing relevant distinctions, formulating cogent arguments, continual testing and refining of provisionally held positions, and the like. Discussions of this sort could be stimulated both by certain educational materials and by seizing upon everyday disagreements over rules, games, standards of behavior, and so forth.

In addition, teachers should cultivate the child's appreciation of the relationship between certain moral concepts, judgments, and principles and corresponding emotions, attitudes, and behavior. There is, perhaps, no better way to cultivate this form of moral integrity than by example. The teacher or parent who frequently betrays in his or her behavior and attitudes what is extolled in words does repeated damage to the child's developing understanding of the nature of moral concepts and moral commitment. In addition, the teacher should, when appropriate, remind students of the implications of their moral judgments and principles and ask them to reflect on the extent to which their behavior is consistent with them.

Emphasis must also be given to the cultivation of a child's moral perception and imagination. This can be achieved, in part, by helping children become more sensitive observers of themselves and each other. Teachers should be explicitly aware of the reciprocal relationship between self-knowledge and knowledge of others. We learn more about others by learning to recognize in them emotions, attitudes, and patterns of behavior that we have identified in ourselves; and, correspondingly, we gain further knowledge of ourselves by coming to recognize emotions, attitudes, and patterns of behavior that we first identified in others. This process may be furthered by providing children with a *reflective* exposure to literature, drama, and song in the earlier years, supplemented with the study of history and the social sciences in the later ones.

Also to be made clear to the older child is the extent to which many contemporary moral problems can be addressed intelligently only if one has a reasonable amount of nonmoral knowledge. For example, controversies in international relations, biomedical ethics, and technology assessment require familiarity with a number of areas. "Some of this knowledge," notes Michael Scriven, "will be picked up while covering other subjects in the regular curriculum, but much of it is best learned in connection with discussion of the moral issues which hinge on it for reasons of efficiency as well as interest."[15] For many students, then, a focus on moral education will give new meaning and coherence to their acquisition of other knowledge.

5. Conclusion

I have tried to show that both ethical absolutists and ethical subjectivists fail to recognize important similarities between the methods and structure of science and ethics. Stressing these similarities, I have then suggested that if the nature and activity of science is an appropriate subject for the schools, so too is the nature and activity of ethics. Thus we are able to meet the objections to introducing moral education into the schools that are based on certain prevailing misconceptions about the cognitive status of ethics. Moreover, if a course of study along the lines sketched in the previous section can be developed and intelligently integrated into the curriculum, the capacity of children (and the adults they will become) to reach well-grounded agreement on difficult moral issues will be significantly enhanced. Given the many complex and momentous issues that children will one day have to address, no aspect of their education can be regarded as having more importance than that which aims to develop their capacity to reach well-grounded agreement on matters of moral concern.

NOTES

1. Alan Gewirth, "Positive 'Ethics' and Normative 'Science'," *Philosophical Review* 69 (1960): 311–330.
2. The notion of a 'paradigm' figures prominently in Thomas S. Kuhn's well-known *The Structure of Scientific Revolutions*, 2nd ed. (Chicago: University of Chicago Press, 1970). Paradigms are taken by Kuhn "to be universally recognized scientific achievements that for a time provide model problems and solutions to a community of practitioners" (p. viii).
3. In addition to Gewirth, one might see Renford Bambrough, "A Proof of the Objectivity of Morals," *American Journal of Jurisprudence* 14 (1969): 37–54, for more detailed development of this line of argument.
4. Jean-Paul Sartre, *Existentialism and Human Emotions*, trans. by Bernard Frechtman (New York: Philosophical Library, 1947), pp. 24–28.
5. Ibid., p. 28.
6. For this conception of science see, in addition to Kuhn, Nelson Goodman, *Fact, Fiction and Forecast* (Cambridge, Mass.: Harvard University Press, 1955), pp. 65–68; and Willard Van Orman Quine, *From a Logical Point of View*, 2nd ed. rev. (New York: Harper and Row, 1963), pp. 20–46. For the corresponding conception of ethics, see Jerome Schneewind, "Moral Knowledge and Moral Principles," in *Knowledge and Necessity*, Royal Institute of Philosophy Lectures, vol. 3, 1968–69 (London: Macmillan and Co., 1970), pp. 255–262; John Rawls, *A Theory of Justice* (Cambridge, Mass.: Harvard University Press, 1971), pp. 17–22, 46–53, 577–587; and Joel Feinberg, "Justice, Fairness, and Rationality," *Yale Law Journal* 81 (1972): 1018–1021.
7. For more sophisticated and historically accurate versions see, for example, Norwood Russell Hanson, "Copernicus," *Encyclopedia of Philosophy*, 1st ed., 2:219–222; and Arthur B. Millman, "The Plausibility of Research Programs," in F. Suppe and P. D. Asquith, eds., *PSA 1976*, vol. 1 (East Lansing, Mich.: Philosophy of Science Association, 1976), pp. 140–148.
8. A. C. Ewing, *Ethics* (London: English Universities Press, 1953), pp. 1–15.
9. Kuhn, pp. 70–72.

10. Joel Feinberg, *Social Philosophy* (Englewood Cliffs, N.J.: Prentice-Hall, 1973), p. 3. The expression "reflective equilibrium" is from Rawls' *A Theory of Justice.*

11. Peter Singer, "Famine, Affluence, and Morality," *Philosophy and Public Affairs* 1 (1972): 235. This article, together with others exploring this particular problem, has been reprinted in William Aiken and Hugh LaFollette, eds., *World Hunger and Moral Obligation* (Englewood Cliffs, N.J.: Prentice-Hall, 1977).

12. Nonetheless, the absolutist's position might still be overstated inasmuch as even the most secure ethical judgments and principles are not "absolutely" (or unconditionally) true.

13. Brian Crittenden, "A Comment on Cognitive Moral Education," *Phi Delta Kappan* 56 (1975): 696.

14. Iris Murdoch, *The Sovereignty of Good* (New York: Schocken, 1971), p. 37.

15. Michael Scriven, "Cognitive Moral Education," *Phi Delta Kappan* 56 (1975): 692.

~§ ANN DILLER

University of New Hampshire

On a Conception of Moral Teaching

Neither his mother nor the reader knows why yet, although the domestic help may be implicated, but Lionel is running away. He has gotten as far as the dinghy, moored off the end of a pier near the house, when his mother, "Boo Boo," finds him. His mother, on the pier, then conducts a conversation with four-year-old Lionel, in the dinghy. The ensuing conversation forms the climax in J. D. Salinger's short story "Down at the Dinghy."

Salinger's portrayal of this encounter between a mother and her four-year-old son includes a passage that is, I believe, an unusually apt and rich illustration of one form of moral teaching. In the first section of this paper, I want to dissect this passage and examine the features that I see as constituting a moral teaching situation.

To take a single example from fiction, however apt and well drawn, and use it as a paradigm of moral teaching may seem heavyhanded and problematic. It not only does violence to a well-told story, it also presumes a certain generalizability. Although I would not claim that the features found in this example encompass or necessarily characterize all forms of moral teaching, I want to suggest that they are often common characteristics of effective moral teaching, especially with children. And I claim that the example runs true to my own experience and to my observations among parents and teachers concerned with moral education.

1. Gingerly Respect

As I read it, Salinger's passage moves, smoothly and subtly, through a full teaching sequence, without either belaboring or omitting any essential point. Let us look at the passage itself, with Boo Boo still on the pier and Lionel in the dinghy:

> "Well, will you tell me from there why you're running away?" Boo Boo asked. "After you promised me you were all through?"
>
> A pair of underwater goggles lay on the deck of the dinghy, near the stern seat. For answer, Lionel secured the headstrap of the goggles between the big and second toes of his right foot, and, with a deft, brief, leg action, flipped the goggles overboard. They sank at once.
>
> "That's nice. That's constructive," said Boo Boo. "Those belong to your Uncle Webb. Oh, he'll be so delighted." She dragged on her cigarette. "They once belonged to your Uncle Seymour."
>
> "I don't care."
>
> "I see that. I see you don't." Boo Boo said. Her cigarette . . . burned dangerously close to one of her knuckle grooves. Suddenly feeling the heat, she let the cigarette drop to the surface of the lake. Then she took out something from one of her side pockets. It was a package, about the size of a deck of cards, wrapped in white paper and tied with green ribbon. "This is a key chain," she said, feeling the boy's eyes look up at her. "Just like Daddy's. But with a lot more keys on it than Daddy's has. This one has ten keys."
>
> Lionel leaned forward in his seat, letting go the tiller. He held out his hands in catching position. "Throw it?" he asked. "Please?"
>
> "Let's keep our seats a minute, Sunshine. I have a little thinking to do. I *should* throw this key chain in the lake."
>
> Lionel stared up at her with his mouth open. He closed his mouth. "It's mine," he said on a diminishing note of justice.
>
> Boo Boo, looking down at him, shrugged. "I don't care."
>
> Lionel slowly sat back in his seat, watching his mother, and reached behind him for the tiller. His eyes reflected pure perception, as his mother had known they would.
>
> "Here." Boo Boo tossed the package down to him. It landed squarely on his lap.
>
> He looked at it in his lap, picked it off, looked at it in his hand, and

flicked it—sidearm—into the lake. He then immediately looked up at Boo Boo, his eyes filled not with defiance but tears. In another instant his mouth was distorted into a horizontal figure-8, and he was crying mightily.

Boo Boo got to her feet, gingerly, like someone whose foot has gone to sleep in theatre, and lowered herself into the dinghy. In a moment, she was in the stern seat, with the pilot on her lap, and she was rocking him and kissing the back of his neck. . . . [1]

A. *The Query*. His mother's opening question to Lionel is a genuine question. She does not know the answer, Lionel does. It is not a rhetorical question or a testing or diagnosing one. It is appropriate to the situation; indeed, it seems to be the crucial question for understanding and resolving the dilemma.

The phrase " . . . tell me from there. . . . " conveys an acknowledgement of both the physical and psychological differences in perspective. Lionel has his own point-of-view, which may or may not adequately explain his actions but which must, in any case, be counted in an assessment of the situation.

To ask "why" seems to presume, furthermore, that Lionel's perspective includes his reasons (not merely impulses or whims) and that these reasons are of interest, are indeed *the* relevant items, those to be told. Thus Boo Boo's question is directive as well as genuine. She does not ask, in a therapeutic or freewheeling way for just anything Lionel might feel like telling. She does not ask about how it feels to be all by yourself in that dinghy, or where you are piloting your boat, or how's the breeze, or even "What are you doing out there!"

But Boo Boo's question is not only directive, it is morally directive as well; she asks: " . . . why . . . After you promised me. . . . " She states her own moral premise, conveying her sense of moral indignation, of violated expectations which call for an explanation.

Boo Boo's query has set the direction of the conversation and it has focused on the moral aspects of the situation. She has not, however, determined or prejudged the outcome. Lionel is put on the spot, but his spot is not one of trying to guess the "right answer" or to "psyche out" his mother's position or mood. She has not only asked her question, she has also revealed her own initial stance.

The form of Boo Boo's query has both moral and pedagogical validity. Pedagogically, she starts with where Lionel is, recognizing that it is he who must tell her this. Morally, she asks for Lionel's reasons, which should be counted in judging his actions. She is honest in stating her own sense of things, her reasons and her moral premises.

B. *The Reply.* "For answer, Lionel . . . flipped the goggles overboard. They sank. . . . " Lionel replies with a nonverbal act. An act of—what?— of defiance, of frustration, of kicking out at what he cannot manage? The nonverbal message is both clear and unclear—we can empathize with it, we can get a rough sense of his refusal to acquiesce in the direction set by his mother. But the precision of language is missing.

His immature verbal facility plus the emotional weight of moral demands may leave Lionel less articulate than normal. More likely he is not ready yet to say what has upset him. His act may be partly a tangential response to feeling put on the spot. One cannot be certain of its significance for Lionel.

Whatever else, Lionel's act is clearly a reply, an answer which returns the conversation to his mother who accepts it as a reply. She does not press him to speak up or to say what he means. She just moves on from there.

C. *Moral Explanation.* "That's nice. . . . Those belong to . . . he'll be so delighted. . . . " Using low key irony which is presumably her characteristic style, familiar to her son, Boo Boo gently states her evaluative judgment and gives what she sees as the relevant facts. She does *not* explicitly judge or categorize Lionel; she does not recite any rules or maxims; she preaches no sermons and makes no general exhortations or lamentations. She simply tells Lionel about the history of the goggles and their connection with others who matter to her. Boo Boo thus continues to maintain and elaborate on the moral focus—on what affects other persons, on the human consequences of the actions.

D. *Moral Impasse.* Lionel's "I don't care" indicates that, for whatever reasons or causes (private misery, genuine indifference, lack of knowledge or experience), he does not give these facts and consequences the same moral priority that his mother does. It is not that Lionel disputes the facts or challenges his mother's perception. He just refuses to budge.

We have then a moral impasse—a shared situation, with undisputed facts, but disagreement nevertheless over which aspects take moral priority or what is morally decisive. At the moment Lionel's misery seems to take priority for him; but he has not yet given his mother any basis for accepting or even comprehending this from her perspective. He has rather, on a literal level anyway, conveyed a grand indifference. Boo Boo acknowledges ("I see") the impasse, and grants recognition to Lionel's opposition stance. Indeed she appears, at first glance, either to have capitulated or at least to have changed the subject.

E. *Being There.* "Her cigarette . . . burned dangerously close . . . suddenly feeling the heat . . . " Boo Boo's inattention to her cigarette brings out the intensity of her close attention to Lionel and what is going on between them. The immediate situation and Lionel's words and acts are not only what is at issue, they are also where Boo Boo herself is, so much so that she doesn't notice her own cigarette. She is not merely putting in her time, waiting to see what happens; she is putting in herself, being there, a vital part of what is happening.

We do not have Lionel interacting with the universe while his mother merely looks on, classifying or categorizing things. Of course, she is thinking and deliberating over what to do, but not apart from the immediacy of the encounter, not as a cool outsider or an ideal observer. To sustain such a presence is costly: she almost burns herself.

F. *Personal Connection.* Part of what Boo Boo seems to "see" is that Lionel has little or no basis for any personal sympathy with those affected by his action. Furthermore, from a pedagogical standpoint, her student's interest in waning. So she takes a new tack, one which is of immediate personal interest to Lionel. She introduces *his* key chain. Lionel leans forward, engaged positively for the first time in the conversation. Boo Boo now has his full attention and Lionel has a new personal stake in the evolving situation.

G. *Logical Connection and Moral Imperative.* Although the physical focus of attention has shifted to Lionel's key chain, Boo Boo's viewpoint is still moral, as some practical reasoning ("a little thinking") soon demonstrates. She now resorts to an explicit moral imperative ("I should throw . . . "). But notice that it is in the first person. She speaks of what she herself should do, not Lionel. Boo Boo is still sharing her own moral perceptions, she is not mandating for Lionel. She then hits home with a clear logical point, the equivalent "I don't care" that leaves no doubt about either its moral relevance or its logical force. Lionel understands.

Lionel seemed to be sensing the drift of things with his "diminishing note of justice." But he fully comprehends the point only after his mother's "I don't care." Boo Boo seems to be stating the obvious, indeed to be painfully overbearing on an all-too-clear point. Yet for Lionel this comes as a revelation, irrefutable once it has been grasped but only dimly perceived before that. Boo Boo recognizes that Lionel's cognitive, emotional, and moral learning are not separate here, that they require each other. It is both the moral weight and the logical connections that Lionel must see, in combination, that together change the total configuration for him.[2]

H. Moral Perception. Boo Boo has focused Lionel's attention on the morally relevant aspects of the situation in such a way that he can now grasp for himself the human consequences as well as the logical similarities. That's as far as she goes. She now turns the key chain and the situation over to Lionel. His mother does not punish Lionel, she does not act for him or decide for him, she does not manufacture excuses, discount his responsibility, or absolve him from the burden of his new understanding. He must make his own decision, choose for himself what he will do.

Lionel has his key chain. He looks at it, it is still his same old key chain. But, given his new perception, he can no longer see it in the same way. He sees instead the similarity between his key chain and the sunken goggles. Lionel's new moral insight takes over for him; it reconstructs the whole situation, captures his focal attention, and demands an appropriate response on its own terms.

Seeing, perceiving the moral aspects of the situation is an achievement, a discovery of a perspective; in one sense it was there already, a given; in another sense, it is only one of many ways of viewing these events. What Lionel, with his mother's help, comes to see are the moral relationships and connections. Such a way of perceiving does not automatically impose itself on him. His mother teaches it to him, points out what's there, focuses his attention on selected features in a deliberate, carefully chosen fashion.

I. Decision and Action. By tossing his key chain into the lake, Lionel is, in his own way, within the limitations of his powers, taking the loss upon himself. He is accepting responsibility and attempting to bring this particular chain of events to an appropriate end, since he sees no way to remedy or reverse what has already occurred. From an adult point of view there may seem to be better alternatives, such as an attempt to retrieve or replace the goggles. From Lionel's vantage point, within the realm of his experience and knowledge, these are not live alternatives. In any case, there's no perfect, ideal solution.

Furthermore, Lionel is preoccupied with his new insight, the similarity between the key chain and the goggles, which demands his full attention and interferes with any more balanced view that he may be capable of at other times.

J. Crying. Lionel takes what responsibility he can and he cries over what he cannot now do or undo. He has seen there is no painless magical way to stop what has been set in motion. One bother with moral insights and decisions is that they often hurt.

Lionel's crying is also an appropriate outlet for him after what must have been a tense and exhausting sequence of events. If students can become emotionally drained from struggling with mathematics or reading, surely any serious encounters with moral burdens and perceptions require psychic energy and stamina. Lionel's efforts, thwarted by his mother's persistence, to withdraw from facing the situation are some indication of the personal cost of moral engagement. Very few of us can handle concentrated doses of moral dilemmas without resorting to some stratagem of disengagement (sophistry, intellectualizing, precipitous action, dogmatism, etc.). Crying acknowledges rather than glosses the tragic element.

K. Gingerly. Throughout our quoted passage Salinger uses only one adverb, 'gingerly', for modifying Boo Boo's actions. And 'gingerly' does, I think, properly describe the way Boo Boo interacts with Lionel. She speaks and acts with deliberation, taking care, moving cautiously, concentrating, waiting for Lionel to have his turn. She neither violates his personal rights and freedom nor does she absolve him from responsibility for his actions.

Perhaps one of the most difficult and treacherous tasks in moral teaching is to avoid overkill, to avoid overwhelming the student on the one hand and yet to engage the student as a moral being on the other hand. Boo Boo's respect for Lionel's chosen distance and reticence constitute a moral act in itself, an ethical restraint in her confrontation with him. But her imaginative pursuit of the moral issues show a threefold concern: not only (1) for Lionel's present well being, but also (2) for his moral growth, for the educative outcome of this experience; and (3) for the moral issues at stake in the situation. She maintains a delicate balance among all three without allowing any one to override or compromise the others. This in itself can only be accomplished gingerly.

2. Moral Discourse

If we are not mothers with dinghys and four-year-olds, what can we learn about moral teaching from the example of Lionel and Boo Boo? Much of my answer is already contained in the extensive exegesis of Part 1. In this last section I want to reiterate and elaborate on a few points that I find significant or interesting.

First of all, I think the example as a whole shows that beneath its surface simplicity, doing moral teaching is a complex, intricate task. To recognize this complexity and even more, to remember it, is important in its own right. For when we forget about the inherent complications and difficulties, our impatience and inevitable frustrations lead us to oversimplify, to look for quick and easy solutions, or simply to become dismayed and give up.

Indeed many of us have become so aware of the dangers and dilemmas in trying to do moral teaching that we have tended to adopt a noninterventionist stance. We may have seen too many negative results: moral verbalism, intellectualizing, rationalizing, moral rigidity, hypocrisy, and sophistry. Or we may just feel uncomfortable with the role of moral teacher, with its implication of moral superiority akin to self-righteousness. Yet to refuse to engage in moral dialogue, especially when the situation warrants it, is also a moral decision. Boo Boo proceeded gingerly but she nevertheless proceeded.

Boo Boo proceeded to do what? In essence, she directed Lionel's attention to the moral aspects and relationships of the situation in such a way that he could perceive these as moral for himself. She stopped there, leaving Lionel to make his own decisions, to choose *his* course of action. How did she do this? She did it primarily by engaging Lionel in moral discourse.

Moral discourse is only one of many ways of directing attention to moral considerations; some ways are nonverbal and many would not count as teaching. For example, persons often serve, knowingly or unknowingly, as moral models for other people. Children frequently imitate their parents, siblings, and teachers. Movie stars and television personalities are common models (moral and otherwise). Mythical and religious heroes have often been influential models, as, to a lesser extent perhaps, have historical figures and fictional characters. The choices we make, the way we spend our time and money, and our general life style all tend to call attention to our values. But moral discourse is more precise and direct, although not necessarily more effective.

Moral discourse can also take many forms. We sometimes assume that verbal moral teaching must consist of inculcating moral rules and maxims, or systematically studying formal arguments, judging moral dilemmas or assigning moral praise and blame. All of these are, of course, appropriate forms of moral teaching, but they do not exhaust the possibilities.[3] In our passage from Salinger, very little of any of these forms occurred. Moral judgments are low key and minimal, no rules or maxims are stated, praise and blame are withheld, and only two standard moral terms occur ('promise' and 'should'). Yet Boo Boo's perspective and direction is persistently moral throughout the encounter, in the assessments she makes, in the grounds she gives for her point-of-view, in her appeal to moral consequences, reasons, and similarities.

We should not, however, be misled into thinking more explicit moral statements are never necessary or helpful. Although it is a mistake to equate moral learning or moral character with verbal facility in moral matters, explicit moral formulations are often needed. For example, in his campaigns Gandhi made a point of defining and announcing in detail the specific goals, actions, and rules that were to be followed, so that they were an explicit matter of public knowledge.[4] And the formulations that students generate for themselves may be pedagogically powerful regardless of their theoretical adequacy.

The use of standard moral terms (such as 'should', 'ought', 'wrong', 'right', etc.) can be meaningful on a number of counts. First, such terms usually do occur somewhere in a moral discussion. Their occurrence clearly signals the speaker's point-of-view. They also carry the general warning that affirming a moral good or condemning an evil, in principle, means something more than mere intellectual assent. It may signify that, given the appropriate circumstances, we have made a *prima facie* commitment to act accordingly.

But what makes 'moral discourse' moral—or what all the forms have in common—are not the terms or formulae but rather the priority issue, the fact that the decisive questions and considerations are seen as moral ones. However much the specific terms and topics may change (running away, sunken goggles, key chains, etc.), the prevailing point-of-view is still moral.[5]

To engage someone in moral discourse, in any form, does not mean that one is necessarily doing moral teaching. We often have moral discussions among peers, colleagues, or friends where there is no teacher-student relationship in any standard sense.[6] If one is using moral discourse for teaching, one has additional responsibilities and headaches beyond those of a mere participant in moral discussion.

For example, it is the teacher who has to maintain the conditions necessary for ongoing moral discourse. This includes keeping the discussion on target—directing and often redirecting attention to the moral aspects or issues. How one can do this effectively is a difficult practical question, which can ultimately be answered only within the particular situation. But some general considerations may also be applicable; let us look at a couple of these.

Perhaps one reason why moral teaching is so treacherous is that authentic moral dialogue is difficult to sustain.[7] The teacher needs to be at once both honest and cautious in sharing her own sense of moral indignation or delight. She must somehow avoid both moral retreat and self-righteousness. She has to proceed "gingerly."

In a discussion among adults, especially among those in the Socratic tradition who thrive on verbal dispute, hot and heavy argumentation may be part of the appeal in doing moral battle (always, of course, with the expectation that ethical truth will prevail once the smoke has cleared). In teaching situations, this same atmosphere may sometimes work for discussion between students, among peers who see themselves as equals, but it is rarely appropriate between teachers and students or adults and children, because the adult's experience and verbal facility combined with institutionalized power and authority places the student at a decided disadvantage not easily forgotten or overcome.

The advantaged position of the teacher also carries its own inherent dangers. One of these is the danger of prematurely judging either the student or the situation. Genuine dialogue is unpredictable—we may surprise each other, the unexpected may occur. If we move too quickly to classify the situation or to categorize the other person, we close ourselves off from the unexpected, prevent full communication and prejudge, if not predetermine, the outcome.[8]

As teachers, parents, and developmental theorists we are, I think, often prone to underestimate children's moral capacities and perceptions when we might better be providing them with necessary information, pointing out consequences, or clarifying relevant connections. This is not because we adults are necessarily perverse in our judgments of children; it is more likely that we are misled by related nonmoral factors.

The child's limited vocabulary is one such factor. Inaccurate verbal comprehension is a frequent and often humorous experience of childhood.

And Salinger gives us a good example at the end of our "Down at the Dinghy" passage, when Lionel, still crying, now volunteers the reason that he was running away:

> "Sandra—told Mrs. Smell—that Daddy's a big—sloppy—kike."
> Just perceptibly, Boo Boo flinched. . . .
> . . . "That isn't the *worst* that could happen." . . . "Do you know what a kike is. . . . ?"
> . . . "It's one of those things that go up in the air," he said. "With string you hold."[9]

Lionel's experience illustrates how children commonly misunderstand our words and yet still grasp the meanings. Although he confuses "kike" with "kite," Lionel accurately comprehends the thrust and tone of Sandra's remark. He is not mistaken about the hostility. We would do him an injustice to assume that his inability to define a key term in any way diminishes his moral indignation or hurt.

Another way in which we may be misled is that the child's preoccupation with a single newly discovered moral factor may temporarily interfere with any more balanced view of the total situation. In moral learning, as in the acquisition of other skills and knowledge, we must, I think, go through stages of moral clumsiness.[10] What appears after the fact to be a simple straightforward matter must first be grasped, processed, and learned in its own right. So, for example, Lionel must come to see that what he does with someone else's goggles may be similar to what someone does with his key chain, and that the reasons (or lack of them) for so acting ("I don't care") have a bearing on how the situation is assessed.

3. Conclusion-Triviality and Caring

In concluding, I want to deal briefly with two of the possible objections that might be raised to the approach in this paper.

One may object, first, that the issues here of tossing goggles and key chains into a lake are trivial, comparatively harmless and simple, in contrast to the horrors and evils of the "real world." Yes. But an understanding of the continuity of our lives, of the inevitable human consequences of our actions, of what it is like to suffer loss, to feel regret; a comprehension of the morally relevant similarities among persons and their experiences, of the inexorable logic of such connections—these are not trivial; they are the basic stuff, the minimum requirements, for moral sensitivity and reflection.

It is true that we must, from time to time, face life's grand dilemmas, recognizing that in many situations there is no truly right or ideal course left to be taken, that one can only choose what seems least harmful. Such realizations are necessary for moral maturity. But we must also lead our daily lives and avoid contributing unnecessarily to our dilemmas as well as working to resolve them. Furthermore, triviality is difficult to judge. An apparently trivial experience of childhood humiliation or of thoughtless treatment may be far-reaching in its effects, issuing much later in revenge and violence.

Second, one might object that this example from Salinger is simply too far removed from most of our teaching experiences. What if we are not mothers with sons and dinghys, but public school teachers with hundreds of students? Such an objection raises a serious problem, more for moral teaching than for this paper. It may be that unless we can approximate some of the favorable conditions enjoyed by Boo Boo and Lionel, we may be unable to do much if any effective moral teaching outside of families or other close, caring communities. But I also think that, given conducive situations, the general principles and considerations we have discussed may be applicable. There is, however, no claim here that our example illustrates the one, only, or best form of moral teaching. There are many alternatives. Much has been left out here, such as the role of the larger physical and social environment. Our study of this example is merely intended to illuminate one way in which moral discourse can serve a teaching function and aid in moral perception.

NOTES

1. J. D. Salinger, "Down at the Dinghy," *Nine Stories* (Boston: Little, Brown, 1953), pp. 126–128. I borrowed this example from Salinger once before, at the end of my article "Teaching Moral Rules: A Preliminary Analysis," *Philosophy of Education* (1975), pp. 233–241 (hereafter referred to as TMR). In some ways, this present article picks up where that preliminary one left off and the Salinger example forms an appropriate bridge between them.
2. This illustrates how the emphases of emotivists, prescriptivists, and cognitivists are all helpful if taken together; each position can be enlightening as long as it does not claim to be the exclusive or decisive view.
3. Whether or not the student is thereby, or ought to be, acquiring moral rules is a controversial and ambiguous question. If one means by 'rules' explicit formulae of the moral maxim, prescription/proscription variety, then it is fairly easy to say at least whether or not the student can state or recite these. But if one includes elliptic and implicit senses of rule-following, such as are evidenced by a person's tendency to correct his behavior in somewhat consistent fashion, to distinguish right and wrong ways of proceeding, to give moral reasons, and/or to make moral judgments, then the question becomes more interesting, more relevant, and

considerably more difficult. I have dealt with this matter in some detail elsewhere; in "Rules and Moral Education," unpublished doctoral dissertation, Harvard University, 1971; and more briefly in *TMR*.

4. Erik Erikson, *Ghandi's Truth on the Origins of Militant Nonviolence* (New York: Norton, 1969), p. 415.

5. On the question of what makes 'moral discourse' moral discourse, I essentially agree with G. J. Warnock, *The Object of Morality* (London: Methuen, 1973), pp. 125–138; and I want to thank Francis Schrag for bringing Warnock to my attention.

6. In any case, what counts as 'teaching' is problematic, as I have noted and discussed elsewhere (see Ann Diller, "How Strong Is the Case against Teaching," *Philosophy of Education (1973)*, pp. 266–272). In this discussion, a moral teacher is taken to be a person who is helping another person, one somewhat less mature morally, to gain moral insight or understanding; and the teacher has some awareness of or intention to be doing such helping, and s/he does so in a morally acceptable way.

7. An adequate concept of dialogue is crucial to the conception of moral teaching discussed here, but discussion of the conditions for dialogue is beyond our scope. It has already been done extensively and well many times, most notably by Martin Buber.

8. The effect of teachers' expectations on students' performance and achievements has almost become a field of study in its own right since the publication of *Pygmalion in the Classroom* by Robert Rosenthal and Lenore Jacobson (New York: Holt, Rinehart & Winston, 1968). But the general point still holds: namely, that teachers' expectations do have an effect, ranging from horrendous to minimal.

9. Salinger, p. 129.

10. I have elaborated on this point in *TMR*, pp. 236–237.

◄§ MATTHEW LIPMAN AND ANN MARGARET SHARP

Montclair State College

Can Moral Education Be Divorced From Philosophical Education?

1. SETTING THE STAGE FOR MORAL GROWTH

Few teachers today are unaware of the expectation of parents and society that education, in addition to developing basic skills, will also expand the moral dimension of the child's personality. But to do this, a teacher must become a substitute parent, and of course it is no easier for a teacher to be a

This paper appered in slightly different form in *Philosophy in the Classroom* (Upper Montclair, N.J.: IAPC, 1977), pp. 138–172.

surrogate parent than it is for a parent to be a surrogate teacher. In brief, the question of how a teacher is to encourage students to be moral is one of the most perplexing issues in modern education.

Educational theorists have presented the teacher with so broad a spectrum of alternative theories of the moral nature of the child that the extreme views virtually cancel each other out. On the one hand, the child is viewed as a little savage who must be tamed and domesticated; on the other hand, children are seen as little angels with impulses already moral and virtuous, so that all that is necessary is to provide the right environment for them to be themselves. A more reasonable view is that native to the child are innumerable dispositions which, if encouraged, could lead to *any* kind of human behavior, and often do. What is important is that the environment in which the child grows up should be such as to screen out those forms of conduct that do not contribute to growth, while encouraging those that do. This is not the same as the romantic view which holds that all one has to do is to provide the right environment and let children be their "naturally good" selves. In other words, a teacher has a responsibility for screening out those forms of behavior in pupils that are obviously self-destructive, and for screening in those forms that are self-constructive. The teacher may have to decide on the basis of knowledge of individual children just which features of conduct need to be encouraged or discouraged in each individual case. One child may need to be drawn out; another may need to develop more self-control. But the object is to liberate the child's creative powers of thinking and acting and making by developing his or her capabilities in ways that reinforce and strengthen each other rather than block each other or cancel each other out.

Each child is an individual and at the same time each child is part of the class. The teacher must forget neither of these facts. But they are not separate facts. As an individual the child is distinctive and can develop his or her unique powers within the roles to be played in the group. The individual distinctiveness will reveal itself in the difference that he or she makes in the classroom, and *every child in the classroom should make a difference.* Thus, in a sense, the teacher's role is to ensure that each child feels that he or she has the capacity to make a difference and each day acts on that presupposition. Teachers should ask themselves regarding each child in their classroom: "Would the absence of this child make a distinguishable difference in the classroom?" If the answer is "no," then something is definitely wrong with the way that they have conceived their teaching role in relation to that child. To the extent that they have not encouraged that child to be an active seeker of his or her own uniqueness, an active harmonizer of his or her own powers, an active creator of his or her own contributions to the class group, the teacher has fallen short of success.

It may seem harsh to place so much responsibility on the teacher's shoulders, but children cannot be expected to develop a sense of responsibility unless the adults that they are surrounded by, and whom they seek to emulate as models, likewise accept responsibility for what happens in the classroom. In this regard, it is worthwhile to distinguish those things that are responsible merely in the sense of being *causes* from what is responsible in the sense of being *accountable*. Thus, the child's organic impulses and native dispositions play a causal role in his conduct but they cannot be held accountable for his behavior. The child is, of course, accountable for controlling those impulses.

On the other hand, the school environment over which society has control, an environment that encourages or discourages those dispositions, is something for which society can very much be held accountable. To this extent, the moral development of children can be estimated only in relationship to the accountability of the society in which the children find themselves. A society that does not value a school environment conducive to moral growth (and often this is expressed in the amount of money that it is willing to invest in education) is a society that should openly accept its share of blame for the amoral conduct of its children.

Instead of relying on a child's home environment, a setting which might or might not be conducive to moral behavior, the teacher must focus on the kind of environment that can be created in the classroom. The teacher's responsibility is to screen in those kinds of dispositions that lead to children's growth, and to foster interaction between the individual child and the classroom environment as a whole. (That environment includes the teacher as well as the other children.) It is a truism that a child in the classroom who has been treated in the past with condescension and contempt is now likely to treat himself or herself with disrespect. Those who treated this child in this fashion are of course accountable for having done so. But the teacher of a child such as this should accept the responsibility for seeing to it that the child finds an environment that accords respect and support, so as to counteract the treatment of which he or she was a victim in the past. Another child may display a lack of imagination or curiosity, again as a result of a deadening environment or regimen either at home or in school. The responsibility of the teacher is to see that an environment is created for this child that is challenging on a daily basis so as to overcome the numbness and apathy resulting from his former environment. Still another child, perhaps as a result of the home environment where he or she is often the object of aggression, may resort to very aggressive behaviors towards others. It is the teacher's responsibility to make sure that this child is placed in such a setting that there is no need for him or her to engage in aggressive behavior in order to protect or to restore damaged integrity.

It is proverbial that the child who disturbs others is a disturbed child. But this is inadequate because it diagnoses *the child* as pathological rather than *the situation* that produces the behavior. Thus, once the teacher begins to assume responsibility for actively creating environments that are supportive, and lend themselves to the building of self-respect and self-mastery, an essential step has been taken toward engaging in moral education. Unless an environment is created that is conducive to mutual trust and respect for each individual in the classroom, no educational program, neither philosophy for children nor any other, is going to make much of a difference in helping children to become moral individuals.

2. Socialization and Autonomy in Moral Education

Very often, it is taken for granted that children are complex, difficult, unruly, and amoral. One then infers that the child is responsible for the problematic character of moral education, rather than acknowledge that the problem of moral education is complicated by one's own presuppositions about it. But it should be evident that if we better understood just how much autonomy we are willing to accord the child and just how much control we are willing to retain and relinquish—if we better understood and were more honest with ourselves about what kind of persons we want our children to be and what rights they have in exercising choice concerning the kinds of persons they want to be—the moral development of children would be considerably less perplexing.

It is not uncommon to pose the problem of children's moral development in this fashion: either moral education must be construed as a way of getting children to conform to the values and practices of the society in which they find themselves, or education is a way of liberating children from those very values and practices so that they can become free and autonomous individuals. Such a formulation of the problem is unfortunate, because it commits education to the kind of ideological controversy from which education itself should rescue human beings. So to pose the problem of moral growth is to gloss over the many nonconstructive disposi- tions and proclivities of any individual and to gloss over the many suppor- tive and beneficial aspects of human society. Putting these value labels on society and on the individual is counterproductive if our objective is to encourage children to judge for themselves. To think of human individuals as innately good or bad or of society as innately good or bad is to foreclose all possibility of determining through inquiry what is responsible for each situation as it stands and how it can be improved. To the extent that any dogmatic statement about society or the nature of the individual cuts off inquiry, man is reduced to a passive unresponsible spectator rather than an active, involved, and responsible shaper of the society in which he lives.

Moral education worthy of the name necessarily involves acquainting children with what society expects of them. Moreover, it involves enabling children to develop the tools they need in order to assess such expectations critically. As with the parent-child relationship, the society-child relation- ship is fraught with mutual duties and reciprocal rights. It is not education to present these in a one-sided fashion. Some of us think of institutions as themselves repressive and suppose that in a better world we would not suffer from institutions at all. But this is a serious misreading of the situation. The question is not whether to have institutions but rather whether the institu- tions we have are to be organized in a rational and participatory fashion. When they are not, it is correct to say that the individual is at their mercy. When they are, they cease to be coercive and become constructive instru- ments for the achievement of individual concerns and objectives.

Acquainting children with the conduct that society expects of them is only part, although a very important part, of a responsible moral education. It is also necessary that children be equipped to think for themselves so that they can creatively renew the society in which they live when the situation demands it, and so that they can further their own creative growth.

When we say that education of necessity must enable children to de- velop the tools they need to assess society's expectations of them in a critical fashion, we do not mean to imply that the teacher's role is nothing more than the fostering of critical judgments on the part of students. The objective is not to form a classroom of critics but to develop human beings who have the capacity to appraise the world and themselves objectively, as well as the capacity to express themselves fluently and creatively. The forming of a critical attitude is only part of the teacher's role. Students must come to realize that, although being able to stand back and look objectively at the institutions around them is essential, it is not enough. If one is disposed to be critical, one must also try to propose something new and better. This is why dialogue in the classroom is helpful: it brings out the positive and constructive ideas that children are capable of generating as well as their negative ones. A teacher must be able to applaud creative insight when encountering it just as a teacher has to be able to applaud instances of logical reasoning.

A child in the classroom may begin not with a criticism but with an imaginative alternative proposal for how things could be, but without any indication of how it is to be put into practice. Rather than concentrate on the ineffectiveness of such an idea, the teacher should encourage the other children in the classroom to suggest specific ways that the idea might be put into practice.

But what of ideas—creative as they might be—that the teacher judges to be destructive? For example, suppose a child suggests, "Let's get rid of minority X as a first step to a better society." Always, the best source of the answer is the other children in the classroom. If the idea is genuinely unconstructive, then the critical abilities of the other children should spot its deficiencies and point them out. But suppose they don't? Should the teacher intervene? Well, the teacher always has the right to intervene and state his or her own opinion if the circumstances warrant. What is obnoxious is the teacher introducing his or her own opinion before the children have had a chance to respond to the original proposal, thus foreclosing genuine consideration of alternatives. On the other hand, if the teacher feels that the children have been able to develop their own ideas and can hold them in a strong and confident fashion, then that teacher should not feel hesitant about introducing his or her own ideas where the children themselves have failed to bring forth such a point of view. The children should understand that the teacher has temporarily abandoned the role of moderator in order to assume that of coparticipant.

Now let us push the matter a step further. What if, after presenting a point of view, the teacher gets this response: "Well, that's only one point of view and we don't buy it!" It is here that philosophy is unique. Since it is inherently a process of dialogue, it is not under any obligation to come to a particular conclusion at a particular time. The teacher's response could be, "Well, let's talk about it some more tomorrow." Or, "I'll take your views into serious consideration and we can talk about it again."

The substance of what we have been saying is that it is unconstructive for the teacher to put himself or herself in the role of bringing about the child's submission to social values, or to assume the role of encouraging the child's individuality to give way to mindless nonconformity in the area of moral education or any other area. The teacher is a *mediator* between society and the child, not an arbitrator. It is not the teacher's role to adjust the child to society but to educate children in such a fashion that they can eventually shape the society in a way that is more responsive to individual concerns. If society is to continue in a participatory fashion, it is important that educators recognize the plasticity of society as well as that of individuals and the necessity for community self-renewal. Nothing so guarantees the inflexibility of society with respect to individual creativity as teaching children that society is inflexible with respect to individual creativity.

3. Dangerous Dichotomies in Moral Education

Teachers today are bewildered by the overwhelming array of alternatives in moral education. There are purely cognitive approaches, which portray morality as efficient reasoning. Others construe morality as obedience and acceptance of discipline, thereby making it a matter, not of intellectual reasoning, but of character. Still others interpret the child as being naturally virtuous, so that good behavior will naturally ensue if only the emotions are unthwarted and sensitivity to others heightened. What bewilders a teacher is that experience in the classroom indicates that each of these positions has a degree of validity. There is an element of reasoning in moral education, as there is an element of character-building, and as there is an element of emotional liberation and sensitivity training. The problem is not to devise a program that would do any of these things but to do all of them.

If morality were simply a matter of knowing rules and obeying them, then moral education would consist of developing in children a conscientiousness that would permit them to carry out these rules in a happy, unquestioning fashion. But morality is not so simple. It is not clear that there are rules for every situation, nor is it clear that accepting uncritically those rules which might apply contributes to children's development. Consequently, the child must be equipped to cope with situations lacking clear guidelines, situations that nevertheless require one to make choices and to accept responsibility for them.

We have been stressing that, in the area of moral education, the teacher must do much more than acquaint the child with the predominant values and morals of that society. The teacher must involve children in a process that will insure that they learn to think for themselves, that they are trained to read the cues and signs of other people's interests in situations in which they are involved, and that they become aware of their own emotional needs. We do children a disservice if we hold them responsible for behaving in a particular way in a particular situation when we have given them no practice whatsoever that would develop their capacity to deal appropriately with such a situation when it comes up. This is one reason why programs in moral education that emphasize moral *thinking* are insufficient. They fail to develop the patterns of constructive *conduct* that make moral behavior something children can readily engage in when the need arises. Unless such patterns are developed beforehand, each new moral confrontation becomes traumatic for children, because they have not been given preparation in moral practice. Moral education is not just helping children to *know* what to do; they have to be shown how *to do*, and be given practice in *doing* the things that they may choose to do in a moral situation. Without such doing, moral education breaks down. Nowhere so much as in moral education is the bond between theory and practice, knowing and doing, so important—yet nowhere is it so often disregarded.

Children find themselves in various situations during the course of a day. Some of these situations call for action, some do not. But children can hardly know what actions or decisions are called for or appropriate unless they have developed an awareness of the dimensions of each situation, its complexity and its various nuances and subleties. If children can become aware of the requirements a situation places upon them and the opportunities it offers them, they can respond to it appropriately and effectively. We therefore emphasize the importance of calling children's attention to what is involved in the various life situations they face, as a prerequisite to their responding intelligently. Once they grasp the meaning of a situation, they will better know what they want to do.

We can hardly expect children to carry out their response effectively if they have not been able to prepare themselves through various forms of moral practice. We can hardly expect children to be tactful in moral situations where tact is called for if they are unfamiliar with tactful performance. There are situations that call for a young person to encourage another child, to console another child, to express gratitude, to advise, to reconcile. Yet children can be mute and inarticulate and passive with such demands because they have had no practice in performing in these ways, or even in imagining how they might perform. Exercises in moral practice are therefore important supplements to sensitization of the child to the moral aspects of situations.

But it is not enough to criticize the dichotomy between thinking and doing and to recognize the need for both in an effective program of moral education. It is equally necessary to insist upon the indissoluble bond between thinking and feeling. There is little value in instructing a child in what would be universally right to do in a given situation when the child doesn't care about anyone, let alone everyone. It is hard to see how a child who is not interested in other people's feelings can have any sympathy with their needs, or how one who is not in the habit of putting himself or herself in other people's places would be the least bit interested in acting in accordance with moral rules even if they were known and accepted. Moreover, the feelings necessary to moral conduct are not restricted to particular sympathies for this person or that person, since it is equally indispensable that one be sensitive to the entire situation of which one is a part. Such sensitivity may require the most delicate awareness and capacity for discrimination. It involves an ability to appreciate what a situation requires and what might be appropriate to those requirements. It requires the capacity for considering as fully as possible the consequences of one's behavior. Often, what we condemn as immoral behavior may simply be the result of an individual's insensitivity to the character of the situation and lack of capacity for seeing himself or herself in relationship to the whole. The morally inconsiderate person is often one who has failed to take all things into consideration before acting. The tactlessness of a child in the classroom is often due simply to a lack of a sense of proportion, so that individual needs and feelings which should be placed in the context of the needs and feelings of everyone are instead accorded absolute priority.

Now the teacher may ask, "How can I develop this kind of tact and sensitivity in my pupils?" Here is where the heightening of aesthetic perception can lead to a greater moral awareness and sense of proportion. For example, a child may have difficulty picking up cues about what is going on in a meeting or be incapable of seeing how his talents and insights can play a contributory rather than monopolistic role in a certain group. He still continues to view his relations in an egocentric rather than social way. Instead of endlessly moralizing about the need to develop sensitivity, empathy, a feeling for "what is going on" without giving the child any definite tools to develop these traits, involvement in the type of dance activities called kinetics, or the type of musical activity (chime activities, choral activities, group work of one kind or another) which calls for listening to the notes of others and then attempting to play an appropriate sound, often results in the child's beginning to develop the necessary sense of proportion that was formerly lacking.

An assumption frequently made is that the child's intellect is educable but his feelings are not. Human emotions are assumed to be primitive and irrational. One can tame and domesticate them, but one cannot cultivate and refine them, much less use them in cognitive enterprises. They are simply brute forces, and one must use all the wiles and stratagems of one's intellect in order to discipline and control them. This is a very curious view of human emotions. If our desires and feelings were not educable, we would never want better food, better friends, better art, better literature, better communities. The theory of the ineducability of human feelings and desires flies in the face of the fact that people do learn to desire more knowingly and more reasonably. Instead of always pitting intelligence against feelings, an educator should focus upon making desires more intelligent and intellectual experiences more emotional.

To separate the affective and cognitive in moral education is treacherous and mistakes the nature of learning. Our own conception of intelligence is not a "mentalistic" one. We do not see intelligence as something that takes place in the "mind." Rather, intelligence can be displayed in any form of human behavior—in one's acts, in one's artistic creations, and in one's reflections or verbalizations.

Today, when a teacher hears the word 'affective', all sorts of things are suggested. In the realm of affective education, expressing one's feelings, getting things off one's chest, baring one's soul, letting off steam, all seem to be part of the picture. Such an approach implies a patronizing view of human emotions. The image is of a person building up too much emotional pressure and then finding release in some harmless escape. In this way, the emotions are dispersed and the force that they might have provided for the child's constructive activities is lost.

On the other hand, an alternative and equally mischievous view of affective education is that the affective is superior to the cognitive and should be the primary focus of all education, including moral or value education. Such a view has no more to recommend it than its polar opposite just discussed. The school that fails to sharpen children's cognitive skills condemns such children to be helpless to deal with those aspects of life that call for rational analysis. The result is a fatuous dwelling upon affective behavior, with no development of the skills essential to making a difference in one's society or to making an imprint on one's world. If we fail to develop their cognitive skills, it is paradoxical of us to hold children morally responsible for their behavior.

Another dichotomy that underlies many moral education programs is the dichotomy between fact and value. This has often led teachers to believe that somehow value education can be treated as a self-sufficient and autonomous discipline, separated from the different subject areas of the curriculum, and that it is valid to separate "facts" from "values" as though they were two different things, facts being "objective" and values being "subjective."

Thus, we have a time during the days when we explore and clarify values (a personal, subjective enterprise) and other times when we explore and clarify facts (an objective social enterprise.) But the teacher who is compelled to deal with values by themselves in this detached fashion often finds that it is an area of curiously bloodless abstractions, or even worse, an endless discussion of children's demands for "what we want," and "what we desire," rather than of "what matters are really of importance to us."

While we urge that children be given practice in reading aright the individual character and significance of the individual situations in which they happen to find themselves, in no way do we assert that moral values are merely subjective or merely relative in the sense that any response is as right as any other for a given situation. We deplore the fashionable doctrine: "In matters of value, everything is relative; what may be right for you may be wrong for me, and that's the end of it!" To assert this is equivalent to saying that anything goes.

Our stress upon logic and inquiry is meant to counter this subjectivism by giving children some tools they can use to analyze the situations in which they find themselves in order to come to sound and reliable conclusions. Children who have the opportunity to discuss their feelings with one another can proceed to analyze those feelings and understand them more objectively. As they develop habits of thinking carefully and critically, they reach out more systematically for factual evidence and begin to consider alternative ways of acting rather than merely basing their judgments on hearsay, first impressions, or "subjective feelings."

To assume that facts and values are separate is treacherous in its implications for moral education. Given this separation, it is easy to suppose that one can change one's values without a change in the facts of one's situation. But this is an illusion. It is futile for a teacher consciously engaged in moral education to hunt for certain disembodied entities called 'values' or to encourage children to eke out such entities on their own when, in fact, all that is meant by the term 'value' is *a matter which is or should be of importance to the child*. All too often, children encouraged to clarify their values end up talking about their feelings and wants rather than assessing the *objective worth* of what their feelings and wants are about. For example, children may say that they feel much more positive about being in the playground than about being in school. What a philosophical discussion should bring out is what the objective differences are between playgrounds and schools, so that children can assess the importance of each, and determine under what circumstances one is to be preferred to the other. Values should not be identified as a person's desires but as those things that after reflection and inquiry are found to be matters of importance. Thus the process of inquiry moves from a subjective to an objective orientation.

In the perspective of perceptual observation, this round bit of copper is identifiable as a 'fact': in the perspective of economic matters, this same thing is the least valuable of our coins—and is therefore an economic 'value'. That you are now reading this page is a fact. That you find it worthwhile to do so makes reading the page not just a fact but a matter of value. The existence of the apples you consider purchasing is a fact, but the store identifies them as 'fancy' and thereby cites their grade of 'value'. So fact and value are the same thing viewed in different *perspectives*.

For purposes of analysis, we can isolate an order of 'facts' and likewise, for purposes of analysis, we can isolate an order of 'value', but matters that concern us are always at the intersection of those orders. There are not two different things, 'facts' and 'values': there are simply matters that are simultaneously factual and valuational. This is essential for a teacher to understand, because it is the teacher's responsibility to see that children do not disconnect moral ideals from moral behavior. This separation often occurs when children are encouraged to talk about values as if they were independent and self-sufficient entities divorced from the world of fact, instead of talking about courageous behavior, fair behavior, respectful behavior, right behavior, and just behavior in particular situations.

On the other hand, we should not assume that children are incapable of talking *about* morality. That children can analyze moral issues does not exclude their discussing abstract ethical concepts such as 'fairness' or "rightness', since children are able to function on a theoretical as well as on a practical level, and may sometimes prefer to do so.

4. What to Do to Help the Child Know What to Do

The teacher's role is not that of a supplier of values or morals but that of a facilitator and clarifier of the valuing process. The child who comes to realize the uniqueness of many moral situations will be able to discover that no moral rule can be uniformly helpful in determining what to do. Insofar as previous educational experiences have challenged this child to improvise and invent where rules have been lacking, such ingenuity will stand him or her in good stead. However, the appropriateness of children's actions is to a great degree dependent on their understanding of and personal commitment to the valuing process itself. Thus, the fact that a child may have to come up with a new solution in a particular moral situation in no way excuses that child from being concerned about his or her motives, society's expectations, or the probable consequences of the action.

The teacher, in the role of facilitator and clarifier of the valuing process, must introduce children to certain criteria by which to judge whether an action is moral. Such criteria can enable children to reflect on (1) how this action affects them; (2) how it affects the structure of their habits and character; (3) how it affects the direction of their lives; (4) how it affects the other people around them, and (5) how it affects the institutions of the society of which they are a part.

These measures or criteria become the guideposts that the teacher can use to steer the children toward some kind of cumulative understanding of the nature of particular actions.

It is always important to keep in mind that moral situations are not necessarily routines to which routine solutions apply and that moral criteria must be reevaluated constantly and reconstructed to make them relevant to the times. It is this openness to criteria and moral actions themselves that sets the philosophically oriented teacher apart. The realization that often situations are opportunities for innovation (and such innovation could well involve going beyond the call of duty rather than merely living up to it) must always be kept in mind. Thus, it follows that the teacher should concentrate on helping children engage in moral reasoning for themselves and not merely on passing along to those children the values of society or the teacher's own values.

We do not mean to say that every personal moral situation is unique. Situations can have much in common, and when they do, rules that have generally worked in like cases can be expected to work again. What we *are* saying is that the child should be equipped to distinguish like from unlike situations, usual from unique situations, typical from atypical situations. The child should be prepared to confront the different or unprecedented courageously, resourcefully, and imaginatively, rather than try to impose upon the unusual situation a rule that is doomed to fail.

So long as the child cannot distinguish similar situations (to which rules based on past experience may apply) from dissimilar situations (which require that unique solutions be devised), the whole question of the role of rules in moral behavior is moot. The sensitive discrimination of similarities and dissimilarities among situations is of fundamental importance to the child's moral development. The child must be able to take into account a large number of subtle and complex features of situations—their metaphysical, aesthetic, and epistemological as well as their moral aspects—that are present whenever we compare or contrast such situations with one another. We cannot expect to encourage children to respect persons unless we acquaint them with the full implications of the concept of a person, and this requires philosophy. Nor can children be expected to develop an ecological love of nature without some philosophical understanding of what 'nature' is. The same is true of such terms as 'society', 'thing', 'wealth', 'truth', and countless other terms and phrases that we constantly employ but that the child generally has only the most diffuse understanding of. Comprehensiveness is what philosophy in its broad sense tries to provide. More than anything else it is comprehensiveness that moral education—in the traditional sense of rule-inculcation or in the conventional sense of decision-making or value-clarification cannot provide.

5. Imagination and Moral Education

To many people moral reasoning is confined to logical reasoning, that is, to drawing conclusions from premises or from factual evidence. But moral reasoning should not be so narrowly defined. The role of imagination in moral reasoning is of utmost importance.

Of course, this would hardly be so if the solution to moral problems could be worked out in a purely mechanical fashion as one might pose an arithmetical question to a computer and have it display an answer. Very often, wrongdoing is not the result of someone's malice but merely of someone's inability to imagine a constructive or creative approach to a predicament. For example, two decades ago the spread of polio had reached serious proportions and there was considerable anxiety among parents. When it was announced that a polio vaccine had been invented, there was widespread relief. But the Department of Health, Education and Welfare promptly provoked a blast of criticism by confessing that it had ordered only a relatively small number of doses. The Secretary of HEW responded: "Who would have thought that the public demand for polio

vaccine would be so extensive?" For an official in a position of responsibility to make such a remark would seem to represent a failure of moral
imagination, to say the least.

Moral problems are a subclass of human problems in general. It takes
imagination to envisage the various ways in which an existing unsatisfactory situation might be transformed. One has to be able to visualize what
would happen if this were to be done, or that were to be done, or nothing
were to be done at all. In other words, imagination is needed to anticipate
the goals and objectives that a moral individual or a moral community
might seek.

At the same time, it takes imagination to review the alternative ways in
which each of these goals might be achieved. What steps would have to be
taken? What materials would have to be employed? Who would have to be
involved? What must be done first, and then second, and so on? And what
would happen as a result of the employment of each of these alternatives?
It takes a vivid imagination to rehearse all of these possibilities. But insofar
as morality is the planning of conduct, it exhibits very much the characteristics of any successful planning. One can't plan without imagination. One
can't plan a business venture without imagination and one can't plan one's
conduct, if it is to be successful, without imagination. Now it is evident
that the kind of conduct we prefer children to engage in is the kind we
should encourage them to practice. Likewise, it seems plausible to expect
that exercises in moral imagination could very well develop a readiness in
the child for dealing imaginatively and creatively with situations that otherwise the child might find perplexing and bewildering.

Exercises in moral imagination consist of two major varieties; first, those
that involve consideration of different types of means-end relations, and
second, those that involve different types of part-whole relations. Getting
children to practice breaking down a problematic situation into its parts,
then imagining how it could be transformed into an improved alternative, is
a combination of both of these varieties. Children have to be encouraged to
exercise imagination in each of the facets of solving moral problems.

A. *Imagining means-end connections.* Such practice in moral imagination of the means-end variety can be formulated in a cooperative fashion:
for example, one might engage the class in an exercise like this:

1. Imagine someplace you would like to visit. Write it down and exchange papers with your neighbor. Now let your neighbor write down

all the things he or she can think of that you would have to do in order to get to the place you want to go, while you write down all the things your neighbor would have to do in order to get to the place he or she wants to go.

Suppose, for example, your neighbor says she would like to visit her grandparents in a city that is 3,000 miles away, and would like to stay there for a week.

You might write something beginning like this:

First of all, you want to arrange transportation. You may want to go by airplane. So you have to get tickets. Find out how much they will be. Do you have money to buy them? If not, maybe you will have to use a cheaper means of transportation.

Next, you will have to decide what you will need to wear at your grandparents'. You will have to have some kind of luggage to take it in, too. You will have to prepare your clothes, etc., etc.

2. Perform the same exercise, only imagining the following:
   a. What you would like to be someday.
   b. What you would like to do tomorrow.
   c. The kind of "best friend" you'd like to have.
   d. What kind of community you would like to live in.

3. Are there things you have now that you wouldn't want to change at all? Name some of them.
   a. . . . .
   b. . . . .
   c. . . . .

In the first part of this illustration, children are encouraged to think of where they might wish to go as an imaginary exercise. They are then made to see by their neighbors that such wishes are ends that require means for their implementation, and the neighbors spell out these needs. How well the neighbor does in this task will again depend on a capacity to visualize and anticipate the practical aspects of getting something done. Thus, this is an exercise in encouraging children to specify an imaginary end and then requiring them to cooperate in the imaginative construction of the means of achieving such ends.

B. *Part-whole connections.* Similarly, moral imagination requires encouraging children to consider how wholes can be broken down into parts, and how parts can be used to build imaginary wholes. Of course, if the teacher doesn't know how to do this, it will be impossible to transmit the art to a child. For example, suppose you are considering admonishing a child who has been disruptive by sending him to the principal or counselor. A segmental view of this situation would involve your merely directing this admonition to the child. But you can hardly neglect consideration of the larger context of your actions, namely, how will this action be viewed by the class as a whole and how consistent will it be with the remainder of your behavior towards that class? Thus, your action is not just between you and the disruptive child but involves the totality of interrelationships in the classroom.

An example of the part-whole exercise in moral imagination might be the following:

Suppose, (as editor of the school newspaper), someone has suggested to you that you run a contest to see who is the prettiest girl in school. You decide to talk this over with the other editors and one of them points out that this would probably get people to read the newspaper, and that's good. But another editor asks what the effect of this will be on the school community as a whole. Your class can take it from there. The questions that it can raise include: what is meant by pretty? why is the contest limited to girls? how do the losers feel when the contest is over? Is it worth having a contest when so many people might feel badly? Is the kind of competition encouraged by this sort of thing healthy? In other words, one tries to see a particular activity as a part of a larger frame of reference.

Needless to say, one of the most useful ways of stimulating a child's moral imagination is to place him in situations that call for innovative conduct although they are not specifically moral. Discovery-type situations in science classes have this character but even more helpful are dramatic or dance situations in which inventiveness on the part of each participant is encouraged. A ballet, for example, in which one of the dancers comes up with a novel movement can excite the entire group to respond, each in his own way, although what they do does not have to be lacking in composition or coordination. Every time a child paints there is the need to work from parts to wholes and to analyze wholes into parts. The same is true in writing a poem or any other instance of artistic creation. What the teacher concerned about moral imagination must be prepared to do is to help the children relate these instances to one another. The teacher can point out that the heroic deed discussed in a literature or history class was creative; it was an act that took the same kind of imagination as a remarkable innovation in one of the arts. We are not all called on to be heroes, just as few people are great artists, but every moral problem presents a need for some degree of imagination if its reconstruction is to be effective to all concerned.

C. *The role of models in moral imagination.* One of the virtues of the using philosophical fiction in moral education is that one can portray model communities of children. Children reading the novels can identify with the characters, while at the same time, they can provide models of intelligent discussion among children as well as between children and adults.

The novels can also provide models of inquiry, models of cooperation and models of caring, sensitive individuals. What this does for the student is demonstrate the feasibility of such an ideal children's community, where the participants are intellectually and emotionally wholesome, lively, and actively involved. A student having no inkling of the possibility of ever interacting with such comrades in such a situation is deterred from using his own powers of reflection, cooperation, and discussion. One reason that children are often taciturn or reticent, even to the point of being withdrawn, is that they cannot see the feasibility of using their powers in a constructive fashion. They are often creatures of fear, anxiety, and pessimism.

A model community, even though fictional, converts such fears into hope. It lets the child know of the imaginative possibility of a world where people relate to each other in a way that evokes the creative possibilities of each individual. The model therefore stimulates children's moral imagination. They may never have known what they wanted or what they sought. The model helps them to understand their own needs, their own desires. They begin to see that this is how things could be. And they can begin thinking seriously of alternative means that can be explored and examined in an effort to achieve something like the ideal they have now glimpsed.

However, the ideal is not held up for the child to imitate in a docile or uncreative fashion. A young artist wishing to be like Rembrandt would not think that his life task would be the slavish copying of Rembrandt's paintings; he would seek to be true to his own situation in the way that Rembrandt was true to his. To emulate a model is not to imitate it or copy it but to use the model and allow it to stimulate feelings of hope, courage, and belief in oneself that will enable one to live as effectively in one's own unique and creative way as the children in the novel live in theirs. So models are enormously useful for stimulating moral imagination in the child; and in turn constructive feelings and energies are liberated that can be converted into moral activity.

6. *Where to Begin*

Perhaps a word should be said about 'moralizing'. To help children develop morally does not require that, at every possible moment, one points out to students the moral implications of what they are doing. Children have every justification for finding such behavior on the teacher's part difficult to tolerate. From an educational point of view, it is counterproductive, for it sets up a situation in which the child recognizes a patronizing and condescending attitude toward his or her own moral capacities. The child's strategy of self-defense is to seek ways to challenge or test the teacher's interpretation of the situation; and the battle is on.

In order for a moral education program to be adequate, it must enable the child to think reasonably, develop patterns of constructive action, become aware of personal feelings and the feelings of others, develop sensitivity to interpersonal contexts, and acquire a sense of proportion regarding his own needs and aspirations vis-à-vis those of others. Obviously, this is a huge task for any teacher. The teacher may well throw up both hands and say, "This is more than I can do. How can I even begin to go about it?"

The teacher can begin by helping children to develop habits of logical and critical thinking, by encouraging them to engage in philosophical dialogue where they can discuss their opinions and feelings with others and at the same time learn about other people's values and points of view, and by giving them the opportunity to engage in individual and collaborative inquiry where they can appreciate the values of objectivity, impartiality, and comprehensiveness, values that are indigenous to the philosophical enterprise. When children are encouraged to engage in moral practices, allowed more and more responsibility in the classroom, on the playground, and in the schools as a whole, and exposed to all other aspects of philosophy, they gradually can begin to make sense of the moral dimensions of their world.

How much autonomy should a child be given? Neither more nor less than he or she can handle at a given moment. It is up to the teacher constantly to assess and reassess what children are capable of handling, thereby providing an opportunity for them to test and retest their capacities. The word 'responsibility' often has an unpleasant connotation for children, because they associate it with being blamed if they do not do what they are supposed to do. This is a most unfortunate interpretation, because it is only insofar as children are given more and more responsibility for dealing with the conduct of their lives that they acquire any modicum of freedom. The child who thinks of freedom as the opposite of responsibility has bought the same misconception that his parents may have accepted: that freedom is merely getting away with not doing what one is supposed to do. This interpretation, characteristic of immature individuals, equates freedom with license. The misguided child thinks of freedom as not doing what grownups want rather than seeing that freedom resides in doing what one *upon adequate reflection and inquiry* desires to do in a particular situation. However, children can seldom realize this unless they are given more and more opportunities to have some say over their own behavior and to have some input into the decision-making processes of the group to which they belong.

Thus, from the viewpoint of the child, Children's Rights means the child's right to say, "I want more and more responsibility, as I am able to handle it with regard to my own conduct. To deny me the opportunity to discover what is appropriate conduct, to deny me the opportunity to be responsible for myself, is to keep me a perpetual child, dependent on others for setting up the laws and rules of my behavior. It is to deny me that experiential foundation of freedom and responsibility that is essential if I am ever to think for myself about morality." Obviously *the role of the teacher is to gauge the rate and timing of the child's acquisition of this enlarging capacity for assuming responsibility.*

7. Why Moral Education Cannot Be Divorced from Philosophical Education

Now it may be asked "What has all of this to do with philosophy for children? How will philosophy for children accomplish this moral education? How is it different from other methodologies now available to teachers?" In the first place, philosophy provides a regimen for thinking, so that the logical aspects of the moral situation can be dealt with by the child who has learned how to unravel the logical aspects of a situation and to see the need for objectivity, consistency, and comprehensiveness in his or her own approach to such situations. Second, philosophy involves a persistent search for both theoretical and practical alternatives, with the result that the encounter with philosophy generally leads the child to a more open and more flexible attitude toward the possibilities in a given situation. Third, philosophy insists on awareness of the complexity and multidimensionality of human existence and systematically tries to point out this multidimensionality to children so that they can begin to develop a sense of proportion about their own experience. It stresses that a problem situation is seldom merely a moral situation but has metaphysical, aesthetic, epistemological, and other such aspects. Consequently, as the child comes to engage more and more frequently in the practice of considering life situations fully and exhaustively, taking into account their many dimensions instead of treating them superficially, he or she becomes more and more sensitive to the complexity of such situations and the need to take into account as many of their dimensions as possible. Fourth, philosophy for children involves not just reasoning about moral behavior but also devising opportunities to practice being moral. This contrasts with programs that stress decision making or making choices by the child, in that it seeks to prepare children for moral life by developing the competencies that they need in order to do what they choose to do. Exercises in moral practice can give children an opportunity to act out how they would engage in forms of behavior that often have a moral dimension, such as consoling, caring, advising, honoring, sharing, and the like. We cannot expect children to be considerate if we do not give them opportunities to learn what being considerate is, through allowing them to practice engaging in such conduct. Exercises in moral practice are primarily designed to involve the child in doing. We can exhort the child to care and to be considerate, and we can even show the logic of this behavior, but it will avail us very little if the child does not know what actions are consonant with care and concern. *Moreover, it is not that such actions emerge naturally from a caring and concerned individual, but rather that the voluntary performance of such actions tends to develop care and concern in such individuals as perform these actions.*

This insight is very important for the implications it sheds on the role of the teacher in the classroom. Rather than to talk about considerateness, caring, or any other moral virtue, the teacher's role is to set up situations in which children can actively participate in experiences that will reveal to them what considerateness, caring, and other moral characteristics are and what people do who have such feelings, for morality consists not in the feelings themselves but in the conduct that is conjoined to them.

Fifth, we said that a sufficient moral education program would have to develop in the child an awareness of the feelings of others. Philosophy can never be separated from dialogue because philosophy inherently involves questioning, and questioning is an aspect of dialogue. When philosophy for children enters the classroom, the classroom becomes an open forum for all sorts of ideas. But it is not just a brainstorming session where all ideas can be thrown out uncritically. Philosophical discussion leads to acquaintance with the wide diversity of points of views to be found in any group and with the equally broad set of differences among opinions and beliefs. Since offering opinions in a classroom discussion does not pose the demand for competence which is posed when the teacher asks for a correct answer to a question, children find the exchange of opinions and the disclosure of differences in perspective inviting and reassuring rather than threatening.

However, once this reassurance has been established, the teacher must assume responsibility for introducing the criteria of a philosophical discussion (impartiality, comprehensiveness, and consistency) and for making sure that the discussion itself builds and makes a difference for the children. Students will become rightfully impatient if too much irrelevance is tolerated. Similarly, if the discussion does not seem to have a cumulative development, students will become fatigued by it. Moreover, the teacher has to be aware that a discussion leader has to be extremely careful, if it becomes appropriate to endorse a particular opinion voiced by a student, not to close off further discussion and inquiry by such partisanship.

It is the teacher's role to encourage consistency in the presentations of the students, although such encouragement may take different forms. For example, in one case it might be necessary to point out to a student that what he or she is saying does not follow from what was said before by the same student. In another case, where the student's intent was evident but the presentation fumbling, the teacher may offer to restate the position in a more coherent fashion. In short, philosophical discussion, by making children aware of one another's beliefs and points of view and by subjecting such beliefs and opinions to philosophical criteria, leads children to become conscious of one another as thinking and feeling individuals. Without such dialogue, children may sit side by side in classrooms for years without encountering one another as individuals who are, like themselves, striving to make sense of their own experience. One unfortunate consequence of this is that the child often comes to an erroneous conception of knowledge itself, thinking of it as a merely private matter. In contrast, philosophical dialogue leads children to realize that the acquisition of understanding is more often than not a *cooperative* achievement.

8. The Relationship Between Logic and Morality

A crucial aspect of morality may be not so much a person's values taken individually as the relationships that obtain *among* them. The person who has been taught that morality is concerned simply with the particular values held on particular issues will likely fail to see much significance in the point here. Either lying is right or it isn't, he will say. Either stealing is right or it isn't. But these are flagrant cases, lurid cases, about which we have intense anxiety, and it is very difficult for us to discuss them reasonably. Consequently, we may find it very difficult to explain to a child just why we believe that not lying is right or why not stealing is right. Focusing on the act alone is like looking at something through the wrong end of the telescope: suddenly it looks too large, out of all proportion, and no longer in context. When we focus just on the act of lying itself, without envisaging it in its connections with other acts and beliefs, when we consider the act as isolated and out of context, we find that we are talking about an abstraction. Yet we feel so strongly about the act that we cannot think of any other way to deal with it but to insist upon its wrongness more and more vehemently. Unfortunately, this gets us nowhere with the child we are trying to educate morally.

Nothing is easier than to disregard the connections among our values, but in so doing we disregard the basic structure of morality. For example, it is possible to take a large-scale social event culminating in some atrocity and dismember it, isolating into discrete, simple, and morally neutral acts all that preceded it and contributed to it. By breaking a large-scale moral fact into such tiny splinters or fragments, we effectively de-moralize our world. Looking at each action individually, detached from the connections that would reveal its deeper meanings, we see nothing in each such act to condemn or to praise. We refuse to look at how it paves the way for the atrocity and we exonerate it. Needless to say, the same demoralization process can be performed on actions that contribute to magnificent, heroic events, when they are viewed as mere aggregates of disconnected "morally neutral" human actions.

When children want to know about morality, we find it very difficult to answer them effectively, because the matter seems both vast and elusive. We are at a loss for an authority whose credentials they cannot question, and we are likewise at a loss for *unquestionable* ethical principles. Involving the children's consciences seems not to get us very far, and conducting sessions in "value clarification" seems to succeed only in demonstrating our moral wasteland. Nor can we think of good reasons to offer for being honest, respectful of others, and the like, without sounding shallow and superficial. We are sure that there must be a better justification than the one we eventually settle on.

A child whose life has *integrity*—that is, whose thoughts and actions are consistent with one another, will resist performing an action incompatible with the rest of that child's life; in fact the child will be shocked and disgusted by that which is greatly out of line with that child's normal practices. She'll no more need parental injunctions to avoid telling lies than she'll need to be warned repeatedly not to cut herself when handling a bread knife.

We see this in the learning of grammar. Children learn the rules of grammar and the practice of those rules until they become "second nature." One doesn't have to think whether this or that intended statement is correct grammar because one habitually practices correct grammar and deplores grammatical slovenliness. And yet, when on occasion there are good reasons for violating grammatical rules, one may easily do so, for the rules are not rigid and inflexible. So too with moral practice: it should develop consistently and form an integral whole in the case of each individual. The unwarranted violation of that whole, of that consistency and that integrity, should seem to the individual himself as a self-destructive violation of his own integrity and therefore wrong, if morality is to be effective.

Children who come to value their own integrity and who practice honesty as a consistent portion of such integrity, feel lying as a rupture of the self and avoid it much more assiduously than they would if it were simply a matter of fairness (although it may be that too). And children who have learned what reasoning is, so that they can distinguish sound from sloppy reasoning, are not so likely to be deceived about what is or is not compatible with their own integrity or with the basic direction of their lives. It is for this reason that the learning of reasoning is essential to morality. It is not that children who study reasoning are able to use their logical skills to settle quarrels with one another and with their parents, although this may occasionally happen, but that such children have criteria with which to assess what is relevant and what is irrelevant to their interests. They can better judge what fits into the basic scheme of their lives and what doesn't.

We wish to repeat this so as to leave no doubt about our emphasis upon the point. We do not encourage the teaching of reasoning to children because we believe that moral problems are simply disguised logical problems that will yield promptly to logical analysis. Such is the glib premise of cognitivists, and we cannot accept it. What we think important is for adults to encourage children to develop a consistent texture to the fabric of their lives; and children cannot tell what we mean by this until they can appreciate what it is for ideas to be contradictory, or inconsistent or incompatible with one another. A child can have a life of integrity without learning logic, of course, but logic helps him appreciate the difference between what integrates life and what disintegrates it.

We are saying then that children whose lives display wholeness and coherence and integrity are children to whom the distastefulness of, say, a lie, will come as no surprise, insofar as it represents a dismemberment of that integrity. Children whose habits and beliefs have been coherently integrated are the best guardians of their own virtue. If we value virtue in children, we should do everything possible to encourage the development of the integrity of their selves.

At the same time, it must be emphasized that the child who is committed to the practice of honesty will shun lying not only as inconsistent with that practice but as inharmonious with the whole or integrity of that child's life. In this sense, awareness of part-whole relationships is as truly disciplinary in moral education as is awareness of logical consistency.

Thus integrity of one's self is based upon an integrity of praxis—one's thoughts consistent with thoughts and actions, and one's individual acts in line with or compatible with the whole character of one's conduct. Unless such praxis has been built day by day, bit by bit, lesson by lesson, moment by moment, into a tough closely-knit texture, the individual lacks a strong moral base. Such practice is not reducible to a "good reason" for telling the truth, not hurting others, and the like. Good reasons are not adequate to convey the force of such practice. Good reasons are more likely to come in on those occasions in which overriding situational pressures—an emergency, in short—requires that we diverge from what we normally do—and with good reason. It is the exception that good reasons typically justify, not the rule, for the rule is not reducible to a single principle or set of principles. It is the living warp and woof of the interwoven thoughts and actions of the child's life.

The development by the child of such practice is an achievement of momentous importance. Once we fully realize how difficult it is to accomplish, we can have little patience with the superficial slogans everywhere offered in the name of moral education—"let kids talk it out," "get kids to see that there's really only one moral value—justice," "lay it on the line to kids—tell them the rules and wallop them if they disobey"—and so on.

To be effective, ethical education must be enormously patient, persistent and scrupulous; it must be carried on in a manner that is truly caring and benevolent, consistent rather than ambivalent, and with a concern for helping children to think, feel, act, and create for themselves. So far, our civilization has devised only one instrument that has even remotely approached serving as such an aegis, and that is the family. Today, with the family under enormous pressure, with its function in doubt and its structure changing, there are efforts to shift its moral function to other agencies, in particular to the school. Insofar as the school accepts this shift of responsibility, it should be fully aware of what it is taking on. The parent-child ratio was not 1 adult to 25 children—it was between 2 adults to 3 children and 2 adults to 7 children. This gave the family an opportunity to concentrate on moral education at virtually any moment of the day. And if parents have not always been intelligent, they have at least, more often than not, been concerned. If schools now presume to enter the ethical education domain, they must be prepared to enter it on a systematic and scrupulously careful basis—that is to say, with a commitment from kindergarten to grade 12, and with a view to the entirety of the school day, not just a moment devoted to moral inspiration. Such a commitment will in turn require an obligation to neutrality and nonindoctrination, on the one hand, and to strengthening the child's efforts at logical, creative, and moral practice, on the other. We see philosophy for children as the opening wedge of that commitment.

A final word of caution regarding the relationship of logic to moral education. We have stressed the importance of consistency between one's beliefs and one's actions, as well as among one's beliefs and one's actions. We have argued that the logic component of the philosophy for children program can be helpful in arousing in children an awareness of the criteria for such consistency, so as to mold more consistent habits and dispositions. We have contended that the philosophy for children program alerts children to the importance of good reasons in justifying their beliefs and in justifying departures from patterns of conduct they might normally have adopted.

There is always the danger that one or another of these elements will be taken out of context and overemphasized. We see a role for logic in helping chidren sort out and understand their own activities, even to the point of recognizing how some of the things they do can undermine their intentions and actions in other respects. But this is not to conceive of logic as a technique for decision making, as if one need only feed the data into the mechanism and the right answers will automatically pop out. To do so is seriously misleading. Some years ago, for example, we held a series of discussions with some high school students about the usefulness of philosophy, during which we presented a perhaps overly rosy view of the possible benefits of logical reasoning. As it happened, the students were at that moment engaged in a heated debate over the policy to be adopted toward drugs during the annual class encampment. To our surprise, there was an attempt to press the syllogism into service, as though *it* alone could demonstrate conclusively that certain policies were the right ones. When we tried to point out that one could examine the logic of any argument but that logic *alone* wouldn't solve their problem, the students were rather miffed, as if they had first been oversold and then betrayed.

Logic is only one part of philosophy, as moral education is only one aspect of education. Teachers should keep in mind not just the relation of logic to ethics but the relation of philosophy in its entirety to the total educational process—just as they should keep in mind what that total educational process can do for the whole of the child's life.

9. The Improvement of Moral Judgment

The problem of how to improve the moral judgment of the young is as complex as any that a society must cope with. The responsibility for dealing with the problem is of course part of the burden that parents assume in choosing to be parents. Teachers can rightly be apprehensive about being asked to assume even a portion of such a burden.

There is no lack of advice on the subject. There are experts aplenty when it comes to specifying ways of making children moral. There are those who would indoctrinate and those who would not, those who hold that there are moral principles and those who hold that there aren't, those who favor the development of "moral feelings," "moral character," "moral intuition," "moral sense," and those who decry such efforts as useless. Teachers thus find themselves in a most uncomfortable situation, with social pressure being exerted on them to guide the development of moral judgments among their students, while the required pedagogy turns out in fact to be a chaos of conflicting theories and pseudotheories.

Moreover, while none of the proposed approaches for developing excellence of moral judgment among children has appeared persuasive to the bulk of those concerned, neither has any been shown to be totally unworthy of consideration for at least one or another aspect of the matter. It has not been shown, for example, that habit formation is irrelevant, that rules and principles are irrelevant, that aesthetic considerations are irrelevant, that logic is irrelevant, that affective components are irrelevant, and so on. Nor is it likely that any such demonstration of irrelevance will be forthcoming.

Consequently, teachers are being left with the task of deciding which of these many approaches to employ or emphasize and in what fashion. It should be evident that teachers are going to need a good deal more guidance than they have been given if they are to deal effectively with a problem as vast and as bewildering as the explicit introduction of a moral dimension into the educational process. The philosophy for children approach, in this respect, can be helpful.

To interpret the ethical component of philosophy for children as merely an effort to strengthen children's cognitive powers or *reason* (so that their reason can dominate their emotions) would be to distort our approach enormously. Even if we were to hold (which we most certainly do not) that reason is somehow civilized and human emotions are somehow primitive and barbaric, the notion that reason is some kind of equipment by which emotions can be tamed and dominated is quite misconceived. The image of the rational thinker coolly keeping his head and making perfect deductions while emotions swirl all about him is a vestige of a psychology that should have been recognized as obsolete long ago.

One of the most perceptive classic philosophers put the matter succinctly when he observed that it is not by reason that a passion can be conquered but by another and still stronger passion. From which it follows that what should be encouraged in children—if we wish to help them control their inclinations to irrationality—is their impulse to rationality, their natural love of meaning, their desire for understanding, their feeling for wholeness, and their passion for investigating the endless byways of their own consciousness. The current flurry of interest among philosophers in the notion of "rational passions" is a healthy antidote to the morbid and futile effort to strengthen the intellect at the expense of the emotions.

Indeed, nothing seems more evident than the educability of the emotions—yet few things are so hotly disputed. But if passions are susceptible to becoming more rational, then one would suppose that this should indeed be the primary objective of moral education, rather than child-obedience training in respect for so-called universal moral truths, or teaching children something so indefeasibly cerebral and cognitive as "critical thinking."

That our feelings and desires and appetites do in fact become more sensitive, more knowing, more selective—in short, more judicious—seems difficult to deny. It is not our "minds" that compel our raw, untutored desires to prefer better works of art, better friends, better jobs, nobler deeds; it is rather the growing judiciousness of our desires themselves. If we want children to prefer noble actions to ignoble ones, we do well to devote ourselves to the cultivation of their developing tastes and preferences and to the guidance of their budding appetites instead of merely belaboring them with moral advice. If we can help children desire more intelligently, have more cultivated tastes and appetites and form more rational preferences, we will accomplish far more toward making them moral beings than if we merely equip them with a smattering of logic, exhort them to love or respect one another, and induce in them a docile attitude towards our favorite doctrines and ideologies.

The cultivation of children's moral dispositions and the improvement of their moral judgment should result from our provoking them in a variety of ingenious and surprising ways to exercise their natural powers of taste, discrimination, reflection, and analysis in the countless forms and phases of making, saying, and doing. But teachers nonetheless need to have spelled out for them the basic distinction between what it is appropriate for them to do and what it is proper for them to refrain from doing, in advancing the moral growth of the student. It is particularly useful for teachers to grasp the distinction between the procedural and the substantive and to exhibit that grasp so that their students will also likewise acquire it and use it in their own deliberations.

We have elsewhere noted the particular usefulness of the distinction between substantive and procedural considerations in classroom instruction. The teacher, we have pointed out, should normally be neutral when moderating discussions among students about specific substantive issues in which value questions predominate. But the teacher in such discussions should definitely be partial to and insistent on the rules of procedure by which the discussion is carried on. Should these rules happen to become themselves the substance of the discussion, then the teacher should endeavor once again to assume a neutral attitude towards them. For example, the teacher may make a practice of limiting the amount of time allowed for an individual student's contribution to a discussion. But this practice may be criticized by the class and become a matter for philosophical discussion—in which case, it would seem, the time-limitation should be suspended until the issue is resolved.

We have also observed elsewhere that it is unrealistic to expect judicious moral conduct from children who are uncaring or morally unconcerned. Now the primary focus of care in a person exercising moral judgment is on procedural rather than on substantive matters. Moral judgment is careful, scrupulous judgment—its opposite is careless judgment, characterized by lack of attention to procedures because procedures are considered unimportant. Adequate moral judgment therefore manifests itself in care for the procedural principles of inquiry, rather than in insistence on the rightness of this or that substantive principle of morality. There is an enormous difference between allegiance to, say, *'justice'* as a substantive principle of moral conduct, and allegiance to fair, nondiscriminatory procedures in resolving disputes. Unless there is care for the means or instruments necessary for the implementation of justice, we can be sure that justice will not be implemented. Nor is it fair of us to hold children responsible when we have never shown them how to be attentive to the procedures that moral conduct involves.

If care and concern for procedures are among the objectives of philosophy for children, then it is obvious that the objectives of philosophy for children are not limited to purely cognitive matters. Care and concern are primarily affective and character dependent. They are, moreover, the result of continual practice and habit-formation. There is in all education a balance between discovery and instruction, freedom and discipline, order and innovation, practice and creativity, and to these there must be added the balance between procedure and substance. It is far better to be clear about the domain of the teacher's neutrality and the domain of unneutrality, about the region of student independence and the region of routine learning, than to be permanently confused about the differences between these contexts and about the criteria for distinguishing between them.

What philosophy for children can best do is improve moral judgment by developing in children the techniques involved in making such judgments, and by developing in them at the same time the love of and the care for such techniques. The judiciousness of the average person in moral matters is highly precarious. Our critical dispositions are easily deflected by self-interest, and our foresight regarding the untoward consequences of our actions is readily blinded by wishful thinking. It is indeed remarkable how persons of character, normally scrupulous in adhering to proper procedures of moral inquiry, can casually ignore considerations of the greatest gravity for other persons involved when their own advancement is at stake. It is not so much callousness as fecklessness that marks the morally injudicious person, not inconsiderateness towards persons so much as disrespect for procedures. We can inveigh endlessly to such individuals about the need for interpersonal respect, but such exhortations are likely to be no more relevant today than the edifying essays of our more puritanical ancestors.

Attention to procedure, become part and parcel of the child's character, will do more to develop that child's moral judgment than all the edifying discourses ever written. At the same time, we must bear in mind that the infinitely varied nuances and subleties of human intercourse cannot be conveyed didactically. Only literature has shown the delicacy and flexibility needed to penetrate and communicate the many-layered multiplicity of human relationships. Consequently the improvement of moral judgment will require for its effectiveness the construction of a special body of literary works that will embody and display the modes of moral awareness, the nature of moral integrity, the techniques of moral inquiry and the alternative structures of ethical understanding. Philosophy for children, to be an effective curriculum for ethical education, must consequently stress the conjoint employment of literary texts, together with philosophical procedures aimed at developing logical proficiency, aesthetic sensitivity, epistemological insight, and metaphysical comprehension. Children who care about such procedures are children whose moral judgment is most likely to be improved in the course of their education.

✍ CLYDE EVANS

University of Massachusetts, Boston

Philosophical Thinking: An Ally for Parental Values

In recent times, educators have given much attention to the area of values education. I believe there is a great need among students for such attention, and I believe there is enormous benefit to be derived from such attention. There is, however, a serious concern, which I have encountered in many diverse situations, regarding the influence and effect of such values education on values taught by parents in the home. Parents ask, "How will values education in the school affect what I am teaching my child at home?"

The answer obviously depends on the kind of values education program envisioned. There are many possibilities.[1] The type of approach to values education that I consider most appropriate for the pluralistic public schools in this country is one in which the teacher does not teach or promulgate any particular values. Rather, the teacher facilitates the students' attempts to formulate values of their own. The key to this approach is to focus critically on the thinking and reasoning that takes place during such a formulation.

It can be seen, in this approach, that the emphasis is not solely on the values being considered. Major attention is also given to the critical thinking taking place. Thus, what we really have is an exercise in critical thinking *as applied* to values. This same kind of exercise in critical thinking could clearly also be applied to social studies, literature, science, and so forth. It just happens—very naturally, in the normal flow of events—that sometimes the topic of discussion will be values. In this sense, it seems more appropriate and accurate to describe such a practice as teaching critical thinking rather than teaching values.

The question to which I shall direct my attention here is whether such a practice—teaching critical thinking and applying that learning to the area of values—poses any danger to the values cherished and taught in the home. I do not believe that values education (thought of in the way described above) in any way threatens parental teaching. Indeed, I shall attempt to show that it is only by means of such an approach as I propose, one anchored in critical thinking, that parental teaching can be ultimately successful.

For the purposes of our discussion, I will take it as given that it is undesirable to attempt to undermine, reverse, or actively oppose the values taught to a student at home. I realize that this is a complex and subtle issue. Yet, although it is of great importance, it cannot be pursued here. So we will assume that such opposition is undesirable and ask, Are critical discussions such as those proposed here subversive of parental teaching?

Our analysis will be aided by the following distinction. We can distinguish (with regard to values) between teaching that is *substantive* and that that is *procedural*. The teaching in the home (compared with what is proposed for the classroom) tends to be substantive; children are told, "This is right, that is wrong," "This is good, that is bad," "This is proper, appropriate, acceptable; that is not," "You should do this; you should not do that," "You ought not act or be that way; you ought to act or be this way." In most homes, children are taught not so much what it means to be moral or immoral but rather what is or is not acceptable behavior from the parents' point of view. Again, children are not so much taught how one goes about trying to determine if a particular action falls into the category of 'moral' or the category of 'immoral' but are provided with a more or less detailed list in which categories have already been assigned once and for all. In short, children are not so much taught what *procedures* they can usefully employ in attempting to answer questions of values as they are supplied with the answers, ready-made. The balance between these two kinds of teaching will vary widely from home to home, but usually the predominance is in the direction of prescribed behaviors. (Another interesting question, which cannot be pursued here, is whether such a balance in parental teaching is "good." It would appear desirable to have both kinds: substantive ('This is wrong'.) and procedural ('This is how you go about deciding'.) Either one alone usually proves insufficient and undesirable.)

I do not wish in any way here to challenge or question such practices by parents. I believe strongly that such substantive direction is, in principle, appropriate and indispensable. However, what is appropriate for parents is not necessarily appropriate for teachers. And from my brief description above, the reader will see that it is a more procedural approach that I recommend for the classroom—an approach which focuses on *how* a reasonable, mature individual sets about making sound personal decisions on issues that intimately involve values.

Since we have distinguished between substantive and procedural parental teaching, our question has now become whether critical discussions undermine such substantive parental teaching. (I will take it for granted that no one will be concerned that a procedural approach in the classroom will in any way threaten the *procedural* teachings of parents.) This could be done by either (1) teaching different substantive values incompatible with and contradictory to those taught in the home; or (2) simply teaching the students that the values taught to them at home are "wrong" without trying to replace them with any other different set of substantive values. (The second practice can be very effectively carried out by the subtle, and sometimes not so subtle, use of innuendo, indirection, sarcasm, facial expressions, and other forms of nonverbal cues and communication. In this form, such a practice is even more insidious than open subversion.) That is, substantive parental teaching could be undermined by attempts either to *replace* parental values or to remove and *uproot* those values.

Either practice would, I believe, constitute "undermining." The teacher must refrain from promulgating his or her own values. The entire character of classroom discussions should be one of inquiry, not of decree. Hence, if the teacher never proselytizes for any values, then *a fortiori* the teacher would never proselytize for any particular set of values that happen to be incompatible with those taught in a given home or in any home.

Hence, the observant teacher would never be in a position to undermine parental values in the first way.

What about undermining parental values in the second way? Teachers must be cautioned not to adopt a judgmental position or attitude and to refrain from rendering judgments on the values held or expressed by any of the students. Again, if this advice is followed, a teacher would never render any kind of judgment on any value expressed by a student and hence once more would never be in the position of having rendered a negative judgment on a specific parental value. So again, the procedural features provide an effective safeguard—both for parents and teachers—against something that is considered undesirable by all concerned.

There is yet a third way in which substantive parental teaching could be undermined. Such teaching could be effectively undermined if, in some way, the students were given the message that either (3) all values are relative and it really doesn't matter which ones you adopt, or (4) values are just not important and need not occupy our attention. I think it is clear that though this would not threaten parental teaching in either of the above two ways, it does indeed constitute a clear and present danger to the entire enterprise of parental teaching of values in that it attacks the very foundation upon which *commitment* to values is based. I believe that in most homes either (3) or (4) would go counter to the totality of what parents are attempting to teach their children. This is because usually parents are attempting to teach not only that their children should have this or that particular value but that they should be persons who "have" values. Or again, not *only* that their children take *this* to be moral and *that* to be immoral, but that they be "moral" persons. Thus, the idea that values are crucially important and that one should have some *commitment* to one's values forms an indispensable part of the totality of parental teaching. It can be seen, therefore, that anything that undermines this idea thereby undermines parental teaching.

Again, although this is a danger (just as in (1) and (2) above) I think it can be effectively avoided. Below, I speak of the teacher's attitude as it engages with the students. That attitude is also important here, for if a teacher freely and sincerely engages in such discussion with students because she or he is convinced of the benefit of such an enterprise, then I see no way that message (4), that values are just not important, could ever be communicated to the students. And regarding message (3), let me simply state that it is possible to find a middle ground between saying (A) there is only one correct set of values or (B) it doesn't matter at all which set of values you choose. Thus, it *is* possible to avoid sending message (3) *without* succumbing to the "evil" contained in practice (1) above.

Hence, it does appear that the kind of critical discussion proposed here does not undermine parental teaching in any of the ways indicated. Nevertheless, there remains still another important concern. A parent may say, "I agree that such discussions, if properly conducted, do not undermine what I'm trying to teach my child at home, in the sense that he or she is not taught either that our family values are wrong or that other values are better. But my teaching still seems to be undermined in one way: these discussions, by their very nature, not only permit but encourage my child to question the things he or she is taught at home. And as far as I am concerned, there are certain things that are not open to question, not open for discussion. Some things are just wrong, Period. And I don't want my child being taught that it is just a matter of opinion."

There can be little doubt that these discussions encourage the child to question, for their very character is to ask the child to critically question, critically assess, and then critically accept or reject the values at issue. So there is virtually no way that one could deny the charge above. Perhaps the only defense possible would be to show that there is nothing harmful or undesirable about such a state of affairs. In particular, it must be shown that encouraging a child to question critically does not, in and of itself, necessarily lead to undermining parental values by the teacher or to rejection of parental values by the children. We shall attempt to do this by clarifying the full objective of parental teaching. But before we do this, there is another point to consider briefly.

In the "real world"—that is, that world jointly inhabited on a daily basis by teachers in the classroom, parents of children, principals, administrators, and members of the board of education—there is more than just passing concern with the phrase, "if properly conducted." Sensitivity to this feature is especially great among parents who either devoutly resist or who are merely cautiously concerned about the whole idea of "teaching values." Let me say emphatically and categorically that I believe the success or failure of such an enterprise as recommended here will stand or fall on whether or not it *is* "properly conducted." That is the cornerstone of the entire structure. It is not my objective here to consider what "properly conducted" might mean. (Elsewhere I have discussed, in summary fashion, some of the concrete, practical steps involved in what I take to be a "properly conducted" critical discussion of values. These practical guidelines are also accompanied by a bit of the rationale which underlies them.)² Secondly, I would like to suggest that the secret to having a "properly conducted" session lies in two things: the attitude of the teacher herself and the preparation undergone by the teacher (in the form of reading, peer-group discussions, workshops, in-service training programs, dry-runs with self-evaluation and assessment and feedback from others, and so on). This issue needs a separate article all by itself, but these scant remarks must suffice for now.

Parents, teachers—adults generally—are not interested merely and solely in the *behavior* of children. Adults have as their objective not merely that children or students should behave in certain "appropriate" ways in certain specifiable circumstances. I believe this to be true not only of the behavior involved in what might be called fairly superficial situations such as opening a door for someone, or raising one's hand to speak in class, or speaking respectfully to a teacher. I believe this to be just as true of the behavior involved in more serious situations such as pulling a knife on a teacher, or joining classmates in a couple of joints of marijuana brought to a party. Even in these more serious situations, I still claim that it is not *merely* the behavior that is of interest to parents, teachers, and other adults.

This assumption—that parents and teachers are not interested solely in behavior—is of vital significance. If adults are interested merely in having students exhibit certain behavior in certain circumstances, there are simpler and more effective ways of achieving such conformity than by trying to teach "values." A great deal is known about how to control the behavior of human beings—either by eliciting the behavior we wish or by eliminating the behavior we do not wish. A wide spectrum of techniques is available: punishment for "bad" behavior and/or reward for "good" behavior; the use of fear of being caught to discourage "bad" behavior (the idea of the chaperone); or simple physical constraint upon the activity of the persons involved, precluding the need to worry about their behavior in that case ("I will not allow you to go on a weekend skiing trip without any adults along"). These techniques are all very common, fairly crude, and notoriously unsuccessful.

More sophisticated and more dependable ways are available to insure "proper" behavior. Human beings have a high degree of programmability—culturally, psychologically, emotionally, physiologically. Techniques are well-known and well-established on how to brainwash a person, how to produce operant conditioning in an individual (such as through aversion therapy), how to affect behavior by means of surgical procedures, chemical therapy, or electrical stimulation of the brain. It is even known how to modify behavior without the subject's ever knowing that the modification was anything but his or her own idea. Hence, if it were purely behavioral responses under certain conditions that adults wanted, ways are available to obtain these responses. But the very perversity of these techniques brings into stark relief the truth that it is not merely behavior that is of concern to adults. Why is this? And what else is of concern?

The answers to these questions begin to appear when it is noticed that with the suggested techniques above, the resultant behavior becomes progressively less and less the behavior of a human person and more and more the behavior of a robot or automaton, with the robot having no control or choice in what it does. It is this feature that accounts for the feeling of perversity in such practices from which caring adults so strongly and instinctively recoil. Clearly, this is not what parents want for their children. No parents want their children to be so programmed that whenever they find themselves in a certain situation, a kind of switch is thrown inside their heads and they proceed to execute the program built into them by performing in certain ways. No parents wish their children to be robots, regardless of who implanted the program.

No humanely concerned adult wants children to be slaves to any prior programming any more than they want them to be slaves to their youthful impulses. What adults truly wish is that in a given situation boys and girls will do the right thing, not because they were programmed to do so but because they believe it to be right and because they choose to do it. And this is possible only if they are free: they must be free to act, thus they must be free from physical restraint, free from fear, free from "programming." They also must be free to choose; thus, they must be given the autonomy to accept or reject for themselves.

Hence, the only way to get truly human behavior (and not robot behavior) is to allow a person to exercise that absolutely essential human characteristic of free choice. And since it is this truly human behavior that adults really wish of children, then parents, teachers, and all adults must allow children this opportunity to be free, morally autonomous beings. Adults must, that is, allow boys and girls to ask questions and to choose for themselves.

Looking closely at what adults are really trying to accomplish with their children and their students reassures us that encouraging a child to question is not detrimental to the parental objective of teaching them values. On the contrary, such questioning by the child is indispensible for the attainment of that end that provided the rationale for the parental teaching in the first place, namely, producing persons who will do the right thing because they believe the choice to be right and because they choose to do it.

Only by thus allowing children to assess and then accept values for themselves can adults ever expect them to act responsibly in accord with those values. If one acts only out of fear of parents, that is not responsible, values-motivated action. And obviously, parents will not be around in every instance or for all time. Thus, mere parental enforcement of behavior in accord with certain values is neither effective (indefinitely) nor desirable. Likewise, if one acts merely because certain values have been imprinted upon them by parents, this action is not a morally responsible action, one motivated by the values of *that* individual. It is action motivated by the values of the parents. Again, it is necessary for a child, at some point, to make these values his or her own. Only then can that child's subsequent action be said to flow from a person acting in a truly human way, on the basis of values held by that person.

In conclusion, even if adults as parents have certain clear, firm, well-defined, nonnegotiable beliefs and values, they cannot just take that entire package and make it a part of their children. First, if they do that, these will never be the beliefs and values of the individual child; they will remain forever the parents' beliefs and values. Second, adult conviction in the rightness of certain beliefs, values, and consequent behaviors is the product of many factors: experiences, teachings, thought and reflection, trial and error, maturation and growth. Present clear adult conviction is the result of a long process. No one can simply graft the result upon youth without their experiencing at least some of the process. Finally, a great danger is inherent in trying to impose an entire set of beliefs and values *en bloc* without allowing for assessment and then critical acceptance by children. Almost inevitably at some point a child will reject some particular teachings of his or her parents. If these teachings are part of a total set of teachings which were merely passed *en bloc* to the child, it is quite likely that the child will tend to reject the entire set of teachings *en bloc*. If, on the other hand, the child has been encouraged to assess critically each and everything he or she is taught, then it follows automatically that the rejection of one particular teaching of itself in no way necessarily threatens the acceptance of other teachings. If each teaching is critically assessed on its own merits, then the rejection of one teaching in no way affects the merits of another teaching.

So it seems that encouraging students to question does not, in and of itself, undermine parental teaching. It does not oppose any of the particular values that parents wish to teach. It does not even lessen the commitment a student might have to those values. On the contrary, such questioning is the only way in which the student can hold values *with commitment*. In reality, encouraging a student to question does not undermine parental teaching but rather encourages a student to follow the only path that will make the parental teaching ultimately successful.

NOTES

1. See Clyde Evans, Critical Thinking and Reasoning: A *Handbook for Teachers*, published by New York State Department of Education, 1976.
2. Clyde Evans, "Facing Up to Values," *Teacher* (December 1974).

ও§ RICHARD M. HARE

Oxford University

Value Education in a Pluralist Society

I must start by explaining the scope of this paper. I am going to discuss the problem of how educators in our society (which makes it so difficult for them and their charges) are to help people to face, in as rational a way as possible, the bewildering choices of values, principles, ideologies, ways of life, etc., with which they are confronted. As an example of a kind of approach to this problem which I wish to defend, I have chosen the Humanities Curriculum Project because it is well known and has attracted much criticism. But, since there are many who would subscribe to the general approach which I shall be defending but would criticize the Project's particular way of following this approach, I must explain that in this paper I shall be defending the approach in general against those who criticize it in general. There may well be criticisms of the practical execution of the Project with which I should agree, if I knew enough about educational practice to venture an opinion. But I shall leave these practical questions to others more qualified than myself.

The Project, although it has aroused a great deal of controversy in Britain, may not be familiar to American readers; so I will describe it briefly. It was devised by John Elliott and Lawrence Stenhouse of the Centre for Applied Research in Education at the University of East Anglia, Norwich. Its aim is to help children to think for themselves about questions of value. The equipment for the system consists of packs of material (newspaper cuttings, extracts from stories and articles, cartoons, photographs, and the like, and a few films and tapes); there are enough copies of the printed material for everybody in the class to have one. The teacher's pack, which contains some instructions as well, is two inches or so thick. There are different packs for a variety of subjects, comprising for the most part controversial topics such as war and society, education, the family, relations between the sexes, people and work, law and order, and living in cities. The items vary widely in difficulty, ranging from simple pictures to literary texts with a fairly rich vocabulary and to quite closely reasoned articles. The teacher is encouraged to select material suited to the capacity of the class but is not supposed to select it in order to favor particular answers to the questions at issue. The packs themselves in their entirety represent a wide range of views on these questions and can fairly claim to be unslanted. This neutrality, which is the keynote of the whole system, is a feature also of the teaching method recommended. The teacher is required to act as a 'neutral chairman' while the children discuss the material that they have read. The teacher is allowed to insist on standards of fairness in argument, relevance, and other purely intellectual disciplines but must not seek to impose or even voice personal views on the matter at issue. The children are thus encouraged to develop their own views in discussion with one another.

The project has been attacked by people who think that the teacher should play a more positive role in moral education, deliberately leading children toward acceptance of values thought by most people in society to be the right ones. Elliott and Stenhouse are most emphatic in rejecting this view; they think, rather, that teachers must abdicate from their position of 'authority' before they can help the children to learn how to think for themselves about such controversial questions. The authors are, of course, not alone in this opinion, and there have been other somewhat simpler systems devised for putting it into effect. I should like to mention, besides the 'Harry' and 'Lisa' books of the Institute for the Advancement of Philosophy for Children, a very interesting experiment currently being conducted by John Wilson of Oxford and Alan Harris of the British Open University in which much simpler materials (just a book of extracts with a number of penetrating questions for discussion after each of them) are used with the same purpose and, broadly speaking, the same teaching method. An objective comparative assessment of the results of these different methods would be of great interest, if there could be any such thing. I should guess that Elliott and Stenhouse would think the IAPC method too structured and pedagogic, and the Harris method insufficiently equipped for its purpose; but one could only judge by results.

Let me start by describing the problem to which all these methods address themselves. Perhaps there are some who need convincing that there *is* a problem, or who think that, if there is one, it is created by school teachers and education authorities. On this view there is, or was, a set of values (the *right* or *best* values) in which people used to be brought up, so that, as is said, they 'knew the difference between right and wrong', and lived accordingly. If, it is said, this happy state of affairs no longer obtains, it is only because of the malign influence of a few people in our own and preceding generations, who have, acting partly through the colleges of education, won the ears of a very large number of school teachers, who as a result are now systematically corrupting the youth, and producing an ever-increasing number of criminals, vandals, hooligans, drifters and dropouts.

According to this view the problem, if there is one, is a relatively simple one, to be solved by a return to the good old methods of education, which, if single-mindedly pursued by parents and teachers, will restore order and tone to our society. At this point I cannot forbear to read you an extract from Samuel Butler's *The Way of All Flesh*. What Butler says about parents could no doubt be said equally well, with but small changes, about schoolmasters of the same and earlier generations.

> To parents who wish to lead a quiet life I would say: Tell your children that they are very naughty—much naughtier than most children: point to the young people of some acquaintances as models of perfection, and impress your own children with a deep sense of their own inferiority. You carry so many more guns than they do that they cannot fight you. This is called moral influence and it will enable you to bounce them as much as you please: they think you know, and they will not have yet caught you lying often enough to suspect that you are not the un-

worldly, and scrupulously truthful person which you represent yourself to be; nor yet will they know how great a coward you are, nor how soon you will run away, if they fight you with persistency and judgment. You keep the dice, and throw them, both for your children and yourself; load them, then, for you can easily manage to stop your children from examining them. . . . Feed them spiritually upon such brimstone and treacle as the late Bishop of Winchester's Sunday stories. You hold all the trump cards, or if not you can filch them; if you play them with anything like judgment you will find yourselves heads of happy united God-fearing families even as did my old friend Mr. Pontifex. True your children will probably find out all about it some day, but not until too late to be of much service to them or inconvenience to yourself.[1]

Mr. Pontifex, it will be remembered, 'thrashed his boys two or three times a week and some weeks a good deal oftener, but in those days fathers were always thrashing their boys'.[2] Liberals are still busily reacting against the wickednesses of those bad old days; but those parents and school teachers who are in contact with the real situation must give a wry smile when they read that 'You carry so many more guns than they do that they cannot fight you'.

We do, indeed, find Mr. Stenhouse repeatedly saying things rather like this, when he speaks of 'the inescapable authority position of the teacher'.[3] But I do not think that he really means to dissent from what I have been saying. He means by 'authority' something much more limited, namely the ability of the teacher to prevent the expression of views contrary to his own *in the classroom*. This a teacher who knows his job may well possess. But I am talking about what the children will think when they are a few years older. 'We asked a teacher', Stenhouse reports, ' "Do you meet the problem of pregnancy often with your pupils?" Her reply was: "Almost never, and you'd be surprised the number who get pregnant in the year after they leave school". She said this with satisfaction.'[4] A teacher who, in our present society, wished to use his position of authority in order to determine what his pupils would think about sex, or about anything else, *in five or ten years' time*, would be taking on an impossible task. I know this, because I see in the universities the results of unsuccessful indoctrination in the schools.

Perhaps there was a time when the methods of Mr. Pontifex really did work. But it is indeed laughable to compare his happy situation with that of most modern parents. Why was it so easy for him, and so difficult for us now, to bring up our children in the way we think that they should go?

The answer lies in the completely different social situation. There may be, even now, parts of the world in which methods like those of Mr. Pontifex are possible. I should guess that these include certain socially isolated parts of the U.S.A., Russia, China, and a few primitive tribes in out-of-the-way places where the young still have access to only one set of values, those of their elders. In such places somebody (and who it is differs in my different examples) is in a position to dictate the set of values that are to be inculcated in the young, and the inculcation is on the whole fairly successful. We have psychologists who claim that this situation might be restored in our own society by humaner and more effective methods.[5]

But actually we have opted for a wholly different, pluralist, liberal society; and it would be impossible, short of some kind of totalitarian revolution of the right or the left, to alter this. You would have to ban, not just *Lady Chatterley*, but all the works of D. H. Lawrence and most of the other writers that the young read. In practice it is not possible to insulate them from the voices, some wise and some quite crazy, according to one's point of view, which compete for their attention. I do not, therefore, feel called upon to answer the question of whether it would be a good thing to put the clock back; we cannot. For as long ahead as it is possible to foresee, there will be no chance, even if it were a good thing, of seeing to it that only one set of values is available to the children in our society. We have got to try to fit them to make, *for themselves*, the choices with which they will inevitably be faced. And these will be choices, not just of hair styles, but of some of the most fundamental elements in their ways of life. The choices may be made explicitly and with an understanding of what is happening, or they may be made by going with the crowd, which nowadays means the crowd of their own age-group; but they will be made. It is this situation to which, as I understand it, the Humanities Project is addressed.

I should like at this point to rub in the fact that there is a problem by giving you some statistics which, although I am only an amateur in that field, I am sure are extremely reliable. Let us suppose that you got married, or started on a career as a teacher, at the age of 24. And suppose that by the time you are 30 you have a five-year-old child in your care—either your own or somebody else's—and are worried about how to bring him up. The statistics establish that by the time that child is 15, you, if you survive that long, will have (believe it or not) a 100% chance of being 40; and by the time he is 25, you will have, if you are still here, a 100% chance of being 50. (You will have to ask the actuaries what your chances are of *being* still here.) By the time your child is 45, and making some of the most crucial decisions in his career, you, if you are still alive, will be 70. And by that time the child will not be paying all that much attention to what you say. Parents and teachers are all on the way out.

It follows from these statistics that you are not going to be able to do the child's thinking for him for ever. He will in the end have to do it. All you can do is prepare him for the task. But it does *not* follow that the policy of the Humanities Project is the only possible one. One might admit all that I have said so far, and still claim that the best policy, since complete thought-control is impossible, is to do what one can; that is to say, one should, while recognizing that the child will have to make his own decisions in later life, go as far as the situation permits in determining what those decisions will be. On this view we ought (to adapt Charles Lamb's phrase to a new use) to 'seize every occasion to inculcate something useful'.[6] By this means we can, it might be hoped, make it as least probable that the reactions of the child to new situations when he is grown up will be such as we would ourselves approve of. Granted, he will have to confront a lot of extremely diverse opinions about questions of value in a lot of extremely diverse situations, and we do not even know what these will be; but the grounding which we shall have given him will prepare him to sort out the wheat from the tares.

This policy has been called indoctrination; but I have no wish to condemn it simply by name-calling. We want to know why such a policy is a bad one, if it is.[7] But is it? I have no doubt that this policy is used even today with success in many places on many children, and that in most cases the children turn out well. So what is wrong with adopting this as our universal method of education in values?

It may well be that it is a good thing for all of us, however intellectually sophisticated we later become, to have been brought up in sound general principles selected for us by our elders, as Plato brought up the subordinate classes in his Republic, and indeed the highest class too until they reached mature years.[8] But our environment is not either simple or static (especially nowadays) and what were sound principles may be so no longer. Moreover, if somebody claims that he can tell us better principles, and attracts a following, we need to be able to argue with him and decide whether to accept his opinions. As Plato well realized, it is necessary, if our 'sound principles' are to survive, or even be changed for the better, that *somebody* in society (and, whatever Plato may have thought, I would say for as many people as possible in society) to be able to ask and answer deeper questions about values than 'Is this in accord with the way of life which we have absorbed from our elders?' In a pluralist society like our own, in which nobody has the power to indoctrinate everybody, the only solution is to teach as many people as possible to think as well as possible. And this means, inescapably, leading a double intellectual life. On the one hand we have to absorb and try to propagate what we think are sound values; but on the other we have to be ready to ask whether they really are sound, and answer the questions and criticisms of those who say that they are not.[9]

It seems to me that the approach to this problem of Stenhouse and other advocates of discussion in the classroom (and I am sure that he would not wish to claim that his Project is the only source of this doctrine[10]) is a fruitful one. I now wish to point out that its success depends absolutely on understanding a distinction which has its roots deep in moral philosophy. The Project has been criticized for asking the teacher to remain neutral on questions about which nobody ought to be neutral. If we look carefully at what Stenhouse and others have said, we shall find that they are more aware of the distinction than are many of their critics. It is the distinction between what I will call substantial values and methodological values. Stenhouse is advocating 'a pattern of discussion teaching in which students review evidence under the chairmanship of a teacher who represents educational values and critical standards, but maintains neutrality on the controversial issues under discussion'.[11]

If we are discussing, say, race relations, we have before us questions about how members of one race ought to treat members of another, and of what controls legislators ought to impose on their behavior. Stenhouse is telling us that when we are discussing these substantive questions in the classroom, nobody ought to set himself up as an authority on the right answers to them. In saying this, he is only saying something with which anybody must agree who wishes these moral questions to be discussed as moral questions; for there are not authorities on moral questions. That is to say, the question whether it is right to keep blacks in a position of inferiority is not to be decided by asking what X thinks about the question, whoever X is. This is one of the most important things that children have to learn about the nature of morality, and the classroom is one place in which they can learn it.

But Stenhouse is not necessarily confusing the many different senses of the word 'authority' that there are. Nor, even if we stick to one sense at a time, is he confusing two different fields over which authority can be exercised, as my last quotation shows—the field of substantial questions and the field of the procedure used in discussing them. He is not saying that classroom or any other discussion of such questions ought to be a free-for-all without any intellectual discipline whatever. He is saying, rather, that if the right intellectual discipline, embodied in sound rules of procedure, is imposed, we shall have done the best we can to fit the children, now and later, to answer such questions for themselves. It is a presumption of this method that a distinction can be drawn between the methodological principles or values—the logic of the argument—and the substantial views or values that the participants may come to hold about the questions at issue. People who disagree about these substantive questions may yet agree about the methodology and the logic, and the best way to help children to answer the substantive questions is to teach them a method of arguing fairly and clearly and logically about them.

There are two classes of people (both of which include, I am sorry to say, a great many philosophers) who with the best of intentions attempt to break down this distinction and others (as we shall see more than one distinction is involved), a grasp of which is essential to the rational discussion of questions of value. The first class says that, because questions of value are all subjective, argument about them cannot be governed by any rules or any methodological discipline. I will not now go into the meaning of that terrible word 'subjective' or its near neighbor 'relative'. Actually, if anybody says that values are subjective *or* that they are objective there is a very high probability that he is deeply confused about the whole matter. What most people who say either of these things think they mean is false. But that question must be left for another occasion.[12] All I will say now is that to think that, because value judgments are not statements of fact in the ordinary sense (which is *different* from their being subjective) we therefore can have no rules for argument about them, is like thinking that, because the laws passed by Parliament are not statements of fact, there is no point in having rules of Parliamentary procedure, or things like democratic elections and restrictions on the arbitrary power of governments, to make as sure as we can that laws are made only after careful and thorough deliberation in the light of the facts; or that because the sentence of a court is not a statement of fact, there is nothing to choose between different rules of procedure, or no rules at all, for the trial of cases in court.

It may be true (I believe it *is* true) that on questions of value we have ultimately to make up our own minds. But it does not follow that in arguing with one another there is nothing to learn about what makes an argument a good one. Is there no difference between two arguments, in one of which the disputants are careful to understand the question that they are disputing about, and especially what the terms in which it is posed *mean*, and to understand fully each other's point of view, and to look carefully at the facts which the other side adduces as relevant, and in the other of which they just go at each other without any regard for such niceties? Not from the way some people talk. But it seems to me that, although we have to reach our own decisions about values, the methods for reaching and discussing them are determined by the natures of the values in question (for example morality), that is, by the meanings of the value-words; and these can be taught.

The second class of people who blur the important distinction I am speaking of are those who deny that factual questions can be distinguished from evaluative ones. This second class is divisible into two sub-classes. We have, first of all, those who do not think that it is possible to make value-free or evaluatively neutral statements about social and other human concerns. This has become the orthodox opinion among sociologists, at least among left-wing sociologists (and I think a great many right-wingers too). I have never seen any attempt to defend this opinion by arguments that was not riddled with confusions (that may only be because I am not well-read enough). It must at once be granted that social scientists write about what they think important, and select the things to say about it that they think relevant. This must be so in any piece of writing of finite length. Therefore certain judgments of value are involved in the selection of their topics, and in the selection of facts to adduce. That a sociologist chooses to talk about the effects of horror comics on the attitudes of children to the use of firearms tells us something about his values; he thinks it important to know what effects they have. If he tells us that, of children who have read a certain serial, *n* per cent buy toy guns, compared with *m* per cent of a control group, that shows that he thinks facts about the buying of toy guns relevant to the questions in which he is interested. This does not stop the facts that the children read the comics and buy the guns being 'value-neutral' facts. They may of course reveal the *children's* values; but that has nothing to do with the question whether the statements of the *sociologist* are value-free. The statement, by X, that Y's values are of a certain description, may be itself a descriptive statement of fact.

It may also be granted that sociologists often do have certain values of their own which they wish to propagate, and that they may seek to do this by emphasizing certain facts and neglecting others, if not by other purely rhetorical devices. They may also use, in 'describing' what goes on, words which are overtly or covertly evaluative. However, the fact that it is *possible* for social scientists to do this does not show that it is inevitable—only that they and their readers ought to be on their guard against it. Nor is it a sin for the social scientist to have values of his own; if he is concerned about the state of affairs in his society, he will. But when he is doing social science he is under an obligation (another value!) to be critically aware of them and keep them scrupulously distinct from the statements of fact that he makes. If he does not do this, his scientific statements will be of little help, in their thinking, to those who do not share his values.

I do not need to rub in the relevance of what I have said to the discussion of values in the classroom. Even if children are set a bad example by some sociologists, it is *possible*, if they are clear-headed and have clear-headed teachers, for them to learn to distinguish the facts of the situation they are discussing from the value-judgments which they may come to make in the light of those facts. In other words, the situation, what courses of policy are possible, and the results of those policies, are all factual questions, ascertainable with greater or less probability from the evidence; but what policies they are to choose when they have surveyed these facts is not a factual question. They have to choose. It is no help towards an education in rational thinking to suggest that this distinction cannot be made. Nor is it a help to suggest, as do the people I discussed earlier, that, the distinction once made, we should stop arguing about values altogether and forget about the facts which determine *between what* we have to choose. Both of these views might be covered by a phrase which I think Collingwood used of the logical positivists, but which can with justice be used more generally: 'the propaganda of irrationalism'.[13]

However, it will be said at this point that we *cannot* separate questions of fact from questions of value because they just are not distinct. This brings me to the second sub-class of my second class of Aunt Sallies. It consists of those moral philosophers (usually belonging loosely to the school known as the Naturalists) who say that no distinction can be drawn, because questions of value just are a species of factual questions. *What* species will of course vary from philosopher to philosopher. A popular view is that at any rate moral value-judgments are really factual statements about what will or will not conduce to good or harm to human beings. I hope you will not ask me how these latter are to be interpreted as factual statements (what evidence, for example, would count for or against them); that is a task for the proponents of such views. I wish merely to point out that if such a view were accepted, it would strike at the root of the Humanities Project.

If questions of value are just one kind of questions of fact, then there is a right answer to them, and a teacher can say authoritatively, sometimes, what it is.[14] He can, that is to say, not merely teach authoritatively the method to be used in discussing them (for I agree that he can and should do that), but teach authoritatively the right answers to the questions. We are here up against one of the deepest disputes in moral philosophy. On one side of it are those who say that if we understand what morality is and what the moral words mean, we can derive from this knowledge, in conjunction with factual data about particular situations, answers to every moral question. On the other side are those like me who think that, although the nature of morality and the meanings of the moral words establish the canons of moral argument, they do not by themselves uniquely determine its conclusions, given the facts.

At this point, however, we must be careful to avoid confusing two different distinctions; otherwise we shall be overstating the case. There is first of all the distinction between the teacher who expects the children to take his word for it that the facts are as they are, on his authority, and the teacher who wishes the children to believe what they come to believe for the reasons which really make it rational to believe that. This distinction is implicit in the title of one of Stenhouse's articles: 'Pupils into Students'.[15] University students of mathematics, we hope, do not believe that seven eights are fifty-six because that is how the seven-times table goes, which they learnt by rote from their schoolteachers, but because it can be shown to be a theorem provable in arithmetic. And students of history ought to require better assurance that George I succeeded Anne than the fact that their teachers all said so. It is an empirical matter, on which I am not competent to pronounce, to what extent a style of teaching which is general in universities can be introduced with the same sort of results in schools. But this is not the most important distinction for our purposes, if only because its importance is generally recognized and therefore needs no emphasis. It is a distinction which separates, not one subject from another, but one method of teaching from another. It will therefore not serve to distinguish subjects for which the methods of the Humanities Project should be used from those where they would be inappropriate. In spite of the existence of this distinction of method, it might be possible and desirable, in handling the subject of race in the classroom—and for that matter in handling subjects like mathematics— for the teacher to remain neutral for reasons of pedagogical tactics, and let the children discover as much as they can for themselves, given certain materials and evidence. I think that this *is* a good method in mathematics.

The more important, because frequently neglected, distinction is that between different kinds of subjects, which vary in the reliance they place, not on mere authority, but on the ability by established methods, which are themselves determined by the nature and definition of the subject in question, to arrive at determinate answers to questions within the subject. In mathematics and French and physics and (in spite of what some have said) history, if you are doing *those* subjects, you must apply *those* methods, and will get *those* answers. For example, if you are studying French, and want to know how '*avoir*' is conjugated, you have to study the speech of Frenchmen by the methods of the linguists. It follows from this (though this is not really the important point) that teachers who have access to these methods or their results *can* speak with authority to their pupils who have not; but all the same it might be the aim of a good teacher to *give* the pupil access to the methods, thereby renouncing his own authority and turning the pupil into a student.

But are all subjects governed by methods of this sort, which yield determinate answers? What about subjects which contain uneliminable questions of value (for example moral questions)? These are the questions with which the Humanities Project deals, and so we have now come to the really crucial point in appraising it. And it is crucial also to keep clear my earlier distinction between a determinate *method* and determinate *conclusions*. I agree that there is a determinate method which has to be used in discussing and arguing about moral questions, such that, if you understand what a moral question is, you must know which arguments are legitimate, in the same way in which, in mathematics, if you know what mathematics is, you know that certain arguments in that field are legitimate and certain arguments not. But does this method by itself, or in conjunction with factual data, lead inevitably to a determinate set of evaluative conclusions?

It can at any rate be said in passing that the method in question is one which itself requires the participation of the pupils. This participation, which in other subjects may be only desirable or perhaps not even that, in moral issues is essential and indispensable. But I do not wish to exaggerate. In other subjects, too, if what you want to teach *are* their methods, you will have to get your pupils to participate in applying them, otherwise they will not learn. That is why we have laboratories for science teaching. And in morality, you could teach what *you thought* were the right answers somewhat as one teaches the seven-times table. I say 'what *you thought* were the right answers' because what is at issue is whether there are determinate unique right answers, as there are in science or mathematics. But at least there is this difference, that in morality it is much more important that the children should get hold of the method, because they will have to decide moral questions in later life, whereas, since they are not going, most of them, to be advanced mathematicians, the seven-times table will perhaps do. Be that as it may, *if* you are going to teach children how to think, and not merely what to think, about moral and other evaluative questions, you will have to get them to participate in discussing them, and familiarize them with the rules of reasoning in this field. I think that that is the aim of the Humanities Project.

The question remains, however, of whether the method will yield unique and determinate answers. This divides into two questions. The first is, will it yield determinate answers if we go on discussing long enough and familiarize ourselves with all the relevant evidence? I am inclined to say that that depends on whether you are seeking practical agreement or theoretical irrefutability. There are theoretical difficulties, connected with the possible existence of amoralists and fanatics, which I have discussed in my philosophical writings,[16] and which prevent us from speaking of a derivation of moral conclusions from factual data by means of the logic of the moral concepts. But in practice, if we explore the possible answers in the light of the facts and of an understanding of the questions, we are likely to reach agreement in any careful and fair and clear discussion between people that we are likely to meet. So the answer to this first question is, for practical purposes, 'Yes', but with the proviso that in practice we shall never have gone on discussing long enough, or familiarized ourselves with all the relevant evidence. So, paradoxically, the conditions that would in practice yield a determinate answer will never in practice be realized. But this should not alarm us too much; it is true in history too, and even in certain branches of science, for example cosmology. The children when they grow up will have to reach the answers that they think best, and these may differ, not because of uneliminable disagreements about value but because of the finitude of our grasp of the facts. That is why our society is likely to remain a pluralist one, and why it is so important that the children should absorb at school the canons of moral argument, so that the views which hold the field at any one time will at least be reasonably tenable.

The second question is, Will the method yield determinate answers within the confines of forty-minute discussions in the classroom? To this the answer is obviously 'No'. But this does not terribly matter if our aim is to teach the children how to think and not what to think. If in later life they think more rationally about moral questions, we shall have succeeded, whatever they think now.

I wish now to revert to the position of the teacher in all this, and to the question of his authority. I think I agree substantially with Stenhouse, but with a marked difference of emphasis. Stenhouse is (surprisingly to me) so impressed with the power of teachers to impose their authority in the classroom that he counsels them to abdicate from this authority without, perhaps, making it clear enough (or at any rate without getting the message over) that there are certain questions on which authority is still in place. These are the questions of method and procedure and logic. Now that class teachers are not normally allowed to thrash their pupils physically, I see no reason why they should not thrash them verbally if they are guilty of rambling off the point, or going on too long when others are wanting to speak, or appealing to prejudices, or using rhetoric when argument is required. It may be that if these disciplines were practised more in schools, we should have better students in the universities. But I do not wish to imply that a good teacher cannot impart them by gentler methods.

In practice, though, it is difficult to be a disciplinarian about method and procedure without creating the impression that you are forcing your own substantive opinions down your pupils' throats. No doubt that is one reason why Stenhouse is cautious. But, that said, I am for more discipline in discussion rather than less; I am old-fashioned enough to believe that people *can* be got to speak and write and think coherently and logically, and that one good ingredient in the recipe for this is to insist on them speaking and writing the English language correctly. It is this power of coherent thought, rather than explosions of sentiments arising from prejudices, that teachers ought to be trying to bring about. But that is another topic.

I have been discussing the Project, as befits a philosopher, from a rather exalted level, and have said little about practical difficulties that have arisen. May I end with a few more down-to-earth comments? First, there are two things about which I have been agreeably surprised. The first is that by all accounts discussions in classes doing the Project have not, in general, polarized into a state in which the pupils all take one view (a left-wing one, perhaps) and the teacher has either to let the opposite position go by default or, in order to get it a hearing, put it himself, contrary to the rules of the Project and contrary perhaps even to his own views. I say that I am surprised, because this is what often happens in discussions with university students.[17]

The second agreeably surprising thing is that the Project seems to have had some success with classes of quite limited or even low ability, and with quite young children. If you had asked me before the Project was tried out, I would have said that these methods were fine with university students or sixth forms, but might be too advanced for younger or less able children. But there is some evidence that they work lower down the school and in places like approved schools.[18]

Next, there is a real danger in the method which needs to be watched. The compilation of, or the selection from, the 'packs' of evidence may be consciously or unconsciously biased in one direction. There have already been complaints of this—I do not know how well justified.[19] Obviously this could be used as a subtle means of indoctrination. There is the same danger, even, if the more palatable and easy items in the pack are mostly from one side. I should like in this connexion to voice a warning about the use of fictional materials, valuable as these may be for stimulating interest. It is easy for a fictional writer to distort (perhaps for good artistic reasons) the picture of life that he gives. Classes which use fictional materials should be constantly invited to ask whether real life *is* like it is in the novels they are reading, and *how often* it is like that. In this, the Project has an advantage over other uses of fiction, in that the factual evidence is there in the pack too.

Lastly, if children learn the virtues needed for rational discussion of values, it will be above all by example. Rules of procedure and well-balanced and informative packs of evidence are no substitute for fairmindedness and clearheadedness in the individual teacher, any more than the best rules of court procedure are a substitute for these same qualities in a judge. And there is something else of which a teacher has to set an example: the strenuous desire to find the answers. It would be a pity if teachers created the impression that it does not matter what you say about these questions. Neutrality, or even impartiality, ought not to be interpreted to mean *that*. It is part of the example which the teacher has to set, that he has views, or at least is trying to reach them, on the questions at issue. Admitting, therefore, the initial merits of the 'neutral' approach, I should like to add, *pace* Stenhouse, that, if the class progresses, and if it becomes accepted that the teacher is not trying to put over a doctrine by means of his authority or by other irrational means, but that he is in the discussion as an equal, then he ought to give his own substantive opinion and his reasons for it.

It may be objected that this is an impossible ideal in schools (it is certainly realized at universities). It may also be objected that participation in the discussion is incompatible with the position of chairman. But it may be that, when the children have *internalized* the rules of procedure (the respect for each others' opinions and for the evidence, and for clear and logical thinking) they will be to some extent able to do the chairman's job for themselves and for each other; and *then* the teacher may, without incurring the dangers which Stenhouse foresees, be able actually to join in the discussion. I hope so.

NOTES

1. *Ernest Pontifex, or the Way of All Flesh*, by Samuel Butler (London, 1964), pp. 25f. (written 1873 onwards and first published posthumously 1903).
2. Ibid., p. 21.
3. The Humanities Curriculum Project: The Rationale, *Theory into Practice*, vol. 10, no. 3, June 1971, p. 155.
4. 'Open-minded teaching', *New Society*, 24 July 1969.
5. See my 'Platonism in Moral Education: Two Varieties', *Monist*, vol. 58 (1974), p. 573.
6. 'The Old and the New Schoolmaster', *Essays of Elia*.
7. See my 'Adolescents into Adults' in my *Applications of Moral Philosophy* (London, 1972).
8. See my 'Platonism in Moral Education' cited above.
9. See my 'Principles', *Proc. of Aristotelian Society*, vol. 72 (1972/3).
10. See the discussion of the materials compiled by Alan Harris at the beginning of this article.
11. 'Pupils into Students', *Dialogue*, Schools Council Newsletter no. 5.
12. See my 'Some Confusions about Subjectivity', Lindley Lecture at University of Kansas, 1974, forthcoming.
13. I have been unable to locate this phrase in Collingwood's writings; it may be from a lecture. But cf. his *Metaphysics* (index s.v. 'Logical Positivism') for evidence of his sentiments.
14. Cf. Mary Warnock, 'The Neutral Teacher' in Proc. of Royal Inst. of Philosophy conference, Exeter, 1973, *Philosophers Discuss Education* (London, Macmillan, 1975), and my comments in the same volume.
15. Cited above.
16. See my 'Wrongness and Harm' in my *Essays on the Moral Concepts* (London, 1972), s.f.
17. See *People in Classrooms*, ed. J. Elliott and B. Macdonald (Norwich, 1975), for accounts of practical experience with the Project.
18. Ibid., p. 129. The evidence as yet is anecdotal only.
19. *Daily Telegraph*, 3 July 1969, commenting on a prospectus for the Project; it is not clear that the writer had inspected the 'pack' itself.

ঙ§ 12 ৡ৯

THE ROLE OF THE

TEACHER IN THE PHILOSOPHICAL

EDUCATION OF

THE CHILD

ঙ§ SAMUEL SCOLNICOV

The Hebrew University of Jerusalem

Truth, Neutrality and the Philosophy Teacher

For Haggai—a new start, if there ever was any.

Perhaps no subject is more controversial than philosophy.[1] Some subjects are said to be controversial because they are value-laden, as the arts, for example, or moral education. Others are considered so because their specialists cannot agree about the rules and paradigms they are supposed to follow: this seems to be the case with psychology or the social sciences. Possibly both factors are involved to some degree in most cases, as is the case with history.[2] Philosophy, however, seems to have got the worst of all worlds: there is no agreement about procedures and paradigms, there is no agreement about proper subject matter, and, at least in some of its areas if not in all, it deals specifically, and many would say exclusively, with values.

When doing or teaching science we know, of course, most of the time, what counts as evidence and how it is to be interpreted. In fact, when teaching our students physics or biology, we want to teach them what counts as evidence for physics or biology according to the accepted paradigm of that science. Problems arise, no doubt, where there is more than one overall paradigm (as in the social sciences), or where one can hardly speak of a paradigm that is roughly valid for all cases (as in the arts or in art criticism). Philosophy, however, seems to be precisely *about* these questions that are taken for granted, to a greater or smaller extent, in the other areas of intellectual activity. If we have already made up our minds for, say, behavioristic (as against introspectivistic) data, or for reductionistic (as against organismic) interpretations, thus far we do not have a philosophical problem any more.

Values pose a particular problem to the teacher of philosophy. In some areas, as in ethics, values are either the very subject of inquiry or are very closely bound to it—much more so than, for example, in sociology or history. The question itself, "Why should I be moral?" and the readiness to ask moral questions and engage in discussions on morality, already implies something of a moral point of view, at least in the sense that a moral universe of discourse exists.[3] Moreover, even the distinction between value-free and value-laden, or between value and fact, or between the methodological principles of argumentation and the particular values that are the subject of the argument—these distinctions themselves are not presupposed by philosophy but rather are held up for examination and criticism.

No wonder, then, that the problem of the teacher's neutrality should arise within the province of the philosophy teacher in a particularly acute form. The teacher of physics can afford a definite partiality towards 'his' version of Gay-Lussac's Law of Compression of the Gases and press his arguments for it against the student's sometimes garbled version. He would still have to have the student understand why he is right and not attempt to force it down the student's throat mainly on his authority. Nonetheless, the teacher would be justified in promoting his point of view, insofar as he has the consensus of the scientific community to fall back upon. The teacher of history may not be allowed in all fairness to bring all his students around to his own appreciation of Napoleon, but he may and should still be quite strict concerning the use of certain generally approved methods of historical interpretation and what does and what does not count as historical evidence. Again, he may rely on some broad agreement among historians on the scope and methods of history. Even the teacher of literature, who comes quite low on this list,[4] may and should make his students relate their interpretations to the text and rule out some attempts at interpretation as irrelevant.[5] The teacher of philosophy, so it seems, has nothing left: his doctrines, his procedures, his evidence, his subject-matter, everything is open to questioning. Moreover, it is precisely this openness to questioning and doubt that the teacher of philosophy wants to develop in his students.

Some would say that the best way of fostering this openness is through a studied neutrality. In a philosophical discussion in class, as opposed, say, to the interpretation of a philosophical text,[6] the teacher should not side with one position rather than another. He should ensure suitable conditions for the discussion, he should see to it that the subject under consideration is clearly articulated and that the opinions discussed are adequately represented, that the evidence is relevant and is appropriately introduced, that the arguments are clear and valid, that the discussion as a whole is well-orchestrated and purposeful and does not degenerate into dinner-table talk, or worse, into a shouting-match.[7]

However, neutrality of this sort[8] may sometimes not be as neutral as it seems. Fortuitous factors in the make-up of the class or in the course of the discussion may cause one position to be developed better than another, or some positions not to be presented at all, which may be worth considering. In such cases, the teacher may find it necessary to redress the balance by injecting into the discussion a new point of view or by reinforcing an under-developed one. In fact, one may expect disagreement between the students often to be confined to the range of disagreement current in their more immediate society. The teacher of philosophy may legitimately see his role as widening the scope of alternatives available to the students, beyond what is at hand.[9] He would probably hope that someone in the class would pick up his clue, adopt the new point of view and try to defend it on his own. But if this does not happen straightaway—and there is no assurance that it will—the teacher may want to promote that position himself for a while (it is not necessarily, or even typically, his own position). On other occasions he may decide to aid (sparingly) one side in the discussion rather than the other, so as not to leave the discussion lopsided. But in all these cases he still would not be promoting *his* own view, at any rate not because it is his view. The position which happens to be poorly represented in class may coincide with the teacher's private views on the topic, but this is not the reason why he promotes it. He is *neutral*,[10] and he makes a point of his neutrality being felt by all participating in the discussion.

Of course, there are aspects of the discussion toward which the teacher will not be neutral. He will insist on proper speaking procedures, he will demand reasons for holding certain views rather than others, he will press for consistency and reject fallacies, and so forth. On substantive issues, however, so this position goes, he will not press his own views.[11]

Furthermore, neutrality of the type we have been looking into so far does not mean that the teacher has no views of his own on the subject under discussion. This would be impossible. It just means that, as a teacher, he is careful to separate what views he subscribes to from what views he does, or rather does not, teach.[12]

It has been rightly pointed out that one must distinguish between the subject under discussion and the purpose of the discussion.[13] The teacher may set his class to discuss race relations in order to get some more clarity and insight into the problem, or in order to get them some training in argumentation and discussion technique and to develop their critical thinking. In both cases, the subject under discussion is the same; the purpose, however, is different (although I suspect that in most cases the teacher would set himself both purposes at the same time).

In philosophy we seem to have a case of double purpose: we want the students to gain insight into the issue discussed and to clarify their thinking about it and, at the same time, we want to develop, in a more general way, their critical acumen and their competence in argumentation and in the giving and the evaluating of reasons.

The teacher stands in a different relationship to the class than any other member of the class stands to it. So does a chairman or a coordinator. But the teacher is *teaching* the class, and therefore he specifically has "a teaching responsibility"[14] toward the class (collectively and distributively). Thus, the teacher cannot be indifferent to *what* he is teaching. If he is teaching Gay-Lussac's Law he has a responsibility toward the class that they learn it. If he is teaching them (or rather trying to develop in them) critical thinking, he has a responsibility toward them that their thinking indeed becomes somewhat more critical. This responsibility may turn out to have been fulfilled only partially or even not at all, but without reference to it the act of teaching is unintelligible.[15]

The view we have been following would have it that one way, perhaps the best way, of fostering critical thinking is letting students argue between themselves, indeed encouraging them to do so. However, good as this procedure may be, the differences in the level of critical thinking between the students may not be great. In fact, if left to themselves, they may sometimes confuse the issue rather than clarify it. Obviously, the teacher should help them out, and I do not think anyone has seriously proposed that he shouldn't.

Like a good instructor, however, he should not only correct their mistakes but also stretch their capabilities by sometimes playing the game himself. One becomes a good player by playing good players. And another manner in which the teacher can help the student develop critical acumen is to engage him sometimes directly in discussion, setting him both an example and a challenge. However, part of the teacher's art consists in hitting the student only as hard as he can take—and then perhaps just a little bit harder. In the same way, the tennis instructor will send the ball so as to make his trainee move that much faster than the day before—but not so as to put it totally beyond his reach.

Nevertheless, there is an important difference between the tennis instructor and the philosophy teacher. We might call it the eduational factor. The instructor as such intends to instruct his student in a particular skill or set of skills: say, striking backhand or, more generally, playing tennis. It is not his intent, as a tennis instructor, to make his student care for playing tennis. He is only concerned with putting him in such a position that, should he ever want to play tennis, he would be able to play it properly.

Now, it is perfectly possible to instruct someone in the skills of logic or of philosophical argumentation, so that should he ever want to give reasons for his views, he would know how to go about it. The teacher of philosophy, however, especially in school, wants more than merely to open before his students the possibility of thinking or acting rationally. He wants in fact to make him prefer rationality over irrationality, the giving of reasons over the plumping for unexamined views. The tennis instructor does not educate because he is in fact saying to his trainee, "Should you ever want to play, this is how you do it." If he makes good his promise, his "teaching responsibility" is fulfilled. The teacher of philosophy, on the other hand, does not say, "Should you ever want to look for good reasons, this is how you know good reasons from bad ones." Rather, he is committed to inculcating in his students a drive toward preferring reasons over no reasons, and good reasons over bad ones.

The ground of the difference between the teacher of philosophy and the tennis instructor, or even between the teacher of philosophy and the teacher of mathematics, seems to be this: The question, "Why should I care about mathematics?" can be dealt with without resorting to the rules and procedures of mathematics (except, perhaps, as examples); whereas consideration of the question, "Why should I be rational?" cannot be carried out without submitting to the very rules and procedures under discussion. There is therefore no difference between the teacher who is trying to get his students to care about rationality and the teacher who wants them "only" to be in the best position to decide for themselves whether they care or not. For, in this particular case, the best position is one in which the decision has already been pre-empted. Every meaningful discussion presupposes standards of argumentation, and the only alternative to submitting to some such standards is not to engage in discussions at all.

Bringing students to care about reasons and about good reasons necessitates presenting them with alternative arguments and making them evaluate the respective strengths and weaknesses of these arguments. This, in turn, implies some standard for comparing arguments. Evidently, some arguments will be faulted on trivial grounds, such as undue appeal to authority or simple logical blunders. Others, however, will be more difficult to evaluate because the disagreement at their root is genuinely philosophical. For example, a not unreasonable argument can be put forward for a utilitarian morality, and a not less reasonable one can be advanced for a morality of duty. Here the teacher faces the real question of neutrality in the philosophy class: Should he be neutral regarding these two sets of arguments? Should he content himself with bringing his class to an equilibrium between the two?

If he does just that, he might create in his students the impression it doesn't really matter which way one decides—and that effectively means that after all the question may not really be that important. And if arguments cannot settle it anyway, then why bother about arguing at all—except, of course, for the fun of it.

On the other hand, if he pushes one position too hard at the expense of the other, he might be accused of forcing his view on authority rather than on rational grounds. And this is a procedure that defeats the whole purpose of teaching philosophy.

Possibly, the main educational factor in teaching is getting the student to care about the truth. The difference between teaching and indoctrination seems to be mainly that, while through the latter the student comes to believe something on extrinsic grounds, through the former the student comes to believe something because he has come to think—to the best of his discernment—that it is true. The role of the teacher is not so much to teach the truth as he sees it as to make his students care about it.

As for what grounds *are* legitimate for a belief and what are not, this is a matter that has to be settled separately for each domain of knowledge and even for each specific case. Clearly some types of purported grounds are

398 GROWING UP WITH PHILOSOPHY

more often than not irrelevant to most classes of beliefs, such as the social approval a certain belief is expected to encounter. Accepting a belief on authority is a rather more complicated case. In some cases, no doubt, to accept a belief on someone else's authority is to make up one's mind on grounds irrelevant to that belief's truth or falsehood, as, say, coming to believe that the square root of 289 is 17 because John Doe said so. On the other hand, we do accept a great many statements on the basis of authority, when the source we rely on is especially qualified for backing them up with evidence which presumably is not readily available to ourselves. In such cases, we are, as it were, shifting the burden of the proof onto our source. In fact, most of our information on history, physics, current affairs, and the like is of this latter type. And so far, this is unobjectionable. But the deceivingly small step is too easily taken from accepting a belief on authority because of the source's credentials to accepting it as if the authority's vouching for it *made* it true. Except perhaps for extreme cases (as in the case of a person being our authority for his own states of consciousness), authority is only second best to direct evidence. This sense that something more lies beyond every textbook or encyclopedia—or beyond every teacher, for that matter—has to linger around every appeal to authority. And although the teacher's authority in class is not to be dismissed too lightly,[16] yet a teacher who is mindful of these pitfalls can go quite a long way toward implanting in his students that residual discomfort with any and every authority, for, in principle, every authority *should* be checked, although, in practice, not every authority *can* be checked. Thus, there is a minimal sense in which accepting a belief on authority is not strictly compatible with caring about the truth. This minimal sense includes at least: relying on authority when this is irrelevant or unnecessary, and tending to forget the secondary character of almost all authority.

Some of what has been said up to this point may read like a naïve, pre-Kantian conception of knowledge. Truth is there to be discovered and only what conforms to this self-subsisting Truth is valid knowledge. After Kant, if not to some extent before him too, we ought to know better: reality (at least in science) is a construct, and truth and objectivity come at the end of the inquiry, not at its beginning. The Copernican Revolution is the inversion of the classical order of priorities: epistemology now takes precedence. The question, "How do I know?" becomes primary; the question, "What is the case?" is derivative. This, however, is not to say that the second question becomes meaningless or superfluous. Truth after Kant has become more complicated, but it has certainly not become less important.

It is precisely the question of the *grounds* on which a belief is accepted or rejected that has since come to the fore.[17]

Thus, these new epistemological considerations demand a much greater degree of tolerance toward views opposed to one's own. If truth is not given at the outset but found only in the end, so long as the inquiry is not concluded there is always the possibility that the opposed view will come out true. And is a philosophical inquiry ever concluded once for all? One can never take one's own position for granted.

Two good reasons for the teacher's being neutral in class would be (1) that he is meant to set an example of tolerance under which each view can be examined for what it is worth, and (2) that he hopes by his neutrality to create in the class as a whole and in each student individually some such tolerance.

Now, tolerance towards other people's views may be of different types: One kind of tolerance—it might be called 'pluralistic tolerance'—is that in which views opposed to mine do not really bother me. The opposition between my views and other people's is not really felt by me as threatening or bothering in any way. In a sense, this tolerance is superficial for, although I understand the opposition, I do not in fact care very much about it.

Another type of tolerance is that which stems from respect for my opponent as a person even though in this particular case I have overwhelming grounds to believe him in error. This is clearly a situation in which the teacher finds himself time and again. Nevertheless, I may still respect my opponent's erroneous opinion because I respect him as a person, one capable of using his reason. "On this"—says Kant—"there is based . . . a duty not to censure his error by calling it absurdity, poor judgment and so forth, but rather to suppose that his error must yet contain some truth and to seek this out, uncovering, at the same time, the deceptive appearance . . . , and so, by explaining to him the possibility of his having erred, to preserve his respect for his own reason. For if . . . we deny all understanding to the man who opposes us in a certain opinion, how can we make him understand that he has erred in it?"[18]

The last type of tolerance in this list is more complex and much more problematic. I feel the differences between the opposing views very acutely, and they bother me because they cannot all be true but they are all worthy of serious consideration. The view opposed to mine is a threat to my convictions—philosophical, religious, moral—and perhaps with very tangible consequences. Nevertheless, I am willing to consider the possibility that I am in the wrong and my opponent is in the right, in which case perhaps I would have to give up some of my deepest beliefs. A commitment to truth is a commitment to tolerance in this stronger sense. If to be tolerant means just letting potentially conflicting opinions co-exist peacefully side by side with no interaction between them, then this may mean no more than being indifferent to which opinion is true. If it means active disagreement for the sake of the mutual testing of opinions, then it implies, firstly, holding on to one's opinions as long as one honestly believes oneself to have better rational support for them than for their alternatives, but also, secondly, being ready to relinquish them when one's reasons for holding them cease to seem compelling. Socrates, for one, was well aware of the difference between these types of tolerance.[19]

Demanding from the student that he accept or reject opinions on intrinsic grounds and that he weigh the reasons and decide himself following his own judgment involves a great deal of respect for the student, as well as considerable trust in his capabilities. Kant's Copernican Revolution and his humanistic ethics are branches of the same tree.

On the pedagogical level, respect for the student means more than giving him full opportunity to develop his views. The student's views do not develop in a vacuum and interaction with his age peers and classmates is an important factor in their formation. But another important factor should be the effort expended by the student in trying to understand the complexities of the views which the teacher presents him with, in confronting them, and eventually in delineating his own positions vis-à-vis his teacher's. And the more complex the positions with which the student will successfully struggle, the richer and the more complex his own views will emerge in the end. Respect for the student's views means taking them seriously enough to think them deserving an honest answer, to the measure that the student can take it in without being overrun by it. To take the student's views seriously is to counter them with opinions that are seriously held too, in the sense that the teacher cares about the matter, even when he has no view of his own on it. This is not to say that a philosophy teacher should not present arguments that are merely hypothetical or dialectical (in Aristotle's sense). It only means that the student must feel that behind the elusiveness of the teacher's shifting arguments there is a position entertained in earnest—even if this position is not disclosed to him in its entirety.

This irony of partial concealment is another of the great difficulties in the teaching of philosophy. If the teacher conceals too much and presents to the students only masks with no face behind them, the student will most probably get the message that philosophy is a game for sharp wits and no one opinion is really worth more than any other. On the other hand, if the teacher presses his own view too hard, he may overrun the student's defences and overwhelm him at a time when he is not yet capable of forming his own opinions. Teaching philosophy is a kind of balancing art. Socrates was a master of it. The later Sceptics and Academicians were not. Socrates wanted to change his interlocutors' personalities, to transform their irrationality into rationality. The Academicians wanted to win people over to their doctrines, and the Sceptics wanted to teach people how to counter each argument with another argument of equivalent force, for the sake of a spurious imperturbability.

One may learn to think rationally without becoming in any way more rational. We could call this "external" rationality. One may learn how to argue successfully, how to defend any position, for the sake of paradox. External rationality becomes an excuse for noncommitment, a defence mechanism against the necessity of taking a stand. There are good arguments on each side of the question, so why take sides?

"Internal" rationality, on the other hand, is rationality that is structured into the personality. By this is meant rationality that relates to other aspects of the student's personality and is integrated with them, rather than being a feature apart with no relation to his other patterns of thought and behavior. As in other areas, here too, learning is genuine or authentic only if it does not remain detached from the student's own problems.[20]

We all know the student who knows how to solve a problem in long division once it is put to him in the canonic form but is incapable of recognizing everyday situations which call for long division or for the application of simple principles of mechanics. The same is true of rational skills. One may be perfectly proficient in them but nevertheless fail to use them in situations which for once are not exercises in argumentation. However, the educational dimension in teaching philosophy—as in all teaching—includes as well the formation of the capability and the willingness to use one's acquired intellectual skills out of classroom-like contexts and in ways that are more integrated into one's life and more meaningful to it than whetting wits for wits' sake. This willingness to use one's abilities is part of what we normally call *character*.

Such an integration of character cannot be achieved if the student cannot see in the teacher an example not only of logical rigor and clearness of thought and expression but also of a strenuous desire to use his skills in keeping with a commitment to find what is the case.

We started by considering the possibility and the desirability of neutrality on the part of the philosophy teacher. We pointed out some of the difficulties specific to the teaching of philosophy that make it much less feasible for the teacher to assume a neutral position toward the problems discussed in the philosophy class as compared with other subjects. Then, we gradually restricted the concept of neutrality applicable to the teaching of philosophy, with the help of the notion of procedural neutrality and of the distinction between public and private neutrality. But further consideration showed that the model of the philosophy teacher as a chairman or a facilitator cannot be wholly accepted, and we then tried to analyse his role by his responsibility to develop critical thinking in his students. We stressed, however, that the teacher of philosophy also has the *educational* function of bringing his students to *care* about truth and rationality. This function is not compatible with full-fledged neutrality. We then argued that, in order to fulfill this function, the teacher cannot always or typically shrink away from confronting the students with his own views and reasons. At the same time, we emphasized that one of the main difficulties of teaching philosophy lies in putting the right amount of intellectual pressure on the students, so as neither to overwhelm them nor to create in them an uncommitted frame of mind. Teaching philosophy has an educational aspect that has to do with the formation of character alongside the development of intellectual skills, and this educational aspect at least does not seem compatible with neutrality in the classroom as it is normally understood.[21]

NOTES

1. The discussion about whether and how far the neutrality of the teacher is feasible or desirable has been rekindled within the last twenty years, in the United States by Robert Ennis and in England by the Humanities Project team headed by Lawrence Stenhouse. It has since taken many turns and branched off in several directions, that cannot be summarized here. See, for example, Robert H. Ennis, "The 'Impossibility' of Neutrality," *Harvard Educational Review* 29 (no. 2, 1959): 128–136; "The Possibility of Neutrality," *Educational Theory* 19 (no. 4, 1969): 347–356; Jerome Eckstein, "Is It Possible for the Schools to Be Neutral?" *Educational Theory* 19 (no. 4, 1969): 337–346; Lawrence Stenhouse: *Culture and Education*, 2d ed., (London: Nelson, 1970); *The Humanities Project: an Introduction* (London: Heinemann Educational Books, 1970); Kenneth Strike, "The Logic of Neutrality Discussions: Can a University Be Neutral?" *Studies in Philosophy and Education* 8 (no. 1, 1973): 62–91; Charles Bailey, "Teaching by Discussion and the Neutral Teacher," *Proceedings of the Philosophy of Education Society of Great Britain* 7 (no. 1, 1973): 26–38; John Elliott, "Neutrality, Rationality and the Role of the Teacher," *ibid.*, 39–65; Mary Warnock and Richard Norman, "The Neutral Teacher," Proceedings of the Royal Institute of Philosophy

1973: *Philosophers Discuss Education*, (Macmillan, 1975); R. M. Hare, "Value Education in a Pluralist Society", *Proc. Phil. Ed. Soc. G. B.* 10 (1976), 7–23 (reprinted in chap. 11 above); P. D. Walsh, "Value Education in a Pluralist Society: A Reply to R. M. Hare", ibid., 24–33.

2. The Humanities Project team characterized a controversial issue as "one which divides students, parents and teachers because it involves an element of value judgment which prevents the issue's being settled by evidence and experiment" (Introduction, p. 6). The Humanities Project team is concerned with issues, not with subjects or disciplines, but the difference is not crucial. They seem to assume that evidence is not controversial and only value is. However, it will suffice to consider what on different views is considered evidence in, say, psychology. What counts as evidence, how is evidence to be interpreted, how are conclusions to be derived from the interpreted evidence, and what degree of reliability is to be assumed for these conclusions—these too are "controversial" questions, even if they do not have to do with values in the same sense that the social sciences and art criticism have to do with them.

3. I wonder what value-free premises could be agreed upon for a discussion in class of the views expressed in the following letter, printed in *The New York Times*, July 6, 1976:

"The press, the Times included, is arguing strongly for a tightening of ethical standards in both government and business. But when, and to what extent should morality prevail over other, amoral considerations? That is, what price are we as a nation willing to pay? And will the costs be equitably shared with due regard for individual rights? . . .

"The Watergate affair clearly weakened the ability of the executive branch to conduct foreign policy, and we may well have sacrificed too much efficiency in international policy-making for too small an increase in the openness and thoroughness of the policy debate. Also because of Watergate, we have already incurred a substantial decline in foreign prestige and policy leverage in return for the mere prospect of a reduction in official lawlessness and immorality. . . .

"Furthermore, myopic moralism is limiting the pool of available political talent while jeopardizing individual careers. . . . Moral pressure of these kinds represents an illibertarian form of collectivism—and could perhaps be countered by a "moral equal rights" amendment. Its purpose would be to protect the private and public rights of deviant moral minorities, to the benefit of those who like to sin in private, or find the American ambitions toward international moral leadership pretentious and foolish. Meanwhile, civil libertarians ought to take up the cause of the consciencious objectors to this new, pervasive moralism."

4. Cf. Bailey, "Teaching by Discussion and the Neutral Teacher," p. 30.

5. Creative art is on a different scale, since the relationship to the "content" to be mastered is different from that in history or algebra. But surely even in creative art the teacher must confront the student with some sort of standards for the evaluation of his or her performance.

6. In this paper I shall consider only the philosophical discussion. The reading of philosophical texts raises some interesting pedagogical questions that I cannot go into here. Not the least of them is the question of the relation between the reading and interpretation of texts and the discussion.

7. Cf. *The Humanities Project: an Introduction*, p. 20; M. Lipman, A. M. Sharp and F. S. Oscanyan: *Philosophy in the Classroom* (Upper Montclair, N.J.: Institute for the Advancement of Philosophy for Children, 1977), chap. 6. The Humanities Project has among the roles of the teacher "Introduce [s] appropriate evidence" but not "introduces new approaches." My exceptions to their views should be plain from what follows.

8. This is already more than Ennis' neutrality of the basketball referee.

9. Dewey, for one, saw clearly the function of "subject-matter" or "discipline," as accumu-

lated body of knowledge, in expanding the student's experience. And why shouldn't *the teacher* introduce it to the students?

10. Stenhouse later preferred the term 'impartial'.

11. This has been termed "procedural neutrality'. Cf. *The Humanities Project: an Introduction*, pp. 7–8, and Stenhouse, p. 159. But see n. 7 above.

12. This is "public" as opposed to "private" neutrality, Cf. Ennis, "The 'Impossibility' of Neutrality," p. 129.

13. Cf. Bailey, "Teaching by Discussion and the Neutral Teacher," p. 26.

14. Ibid., p. 28.

15. Cf. Israel Scheffler, *The Language of Education* (Springfield, Ill.: Charles C. Thomas, 1960), p. 99, who makes much the same point in different words.

16. For a recent discussion of the concept of authority in education, see David N. Silk, "Aspects of the Concept of Authority in Education," *Educational Theory* 26 (no. 3, 1976): 271–278.

17. Cf. Ernest Gellner, *Legitimation of Belief* (Cambridge: at the University Press, 1974), pp. 27–28.

18. Cf., e.g., Immanuel Kant: *The Metaphysics of Morals*, pt. 2: The Doctrine of Virtue, note to sections 37–39; tr. by M. J. Gregor (New York: Harper and Row, 1964), p. 133.

19. See my "Three Aspects of Plato's Philosophy of Learning and Instruction," *Paideia* (1976).

20. On authentic learning, see Carl Frankenstein, "On the Authenticity of Values and Teaching," *Sdemot* 57 (1976): 38–45 (Hebrew); on structurization of the personality see his *Roots of the Ego* (Baltimore: Williams & Wilkins, 1966), ch. 5, esp. p. 66.

21. I am grateful to Steve Katz, Robert Nozick, and Nathan Rotenstreich for having read an earlier draft of this paper and forcing me to reconsider several points I thought self-evident.

BIBLIOGRAPHY

Anderson, R. C. "Learning in Discussions: A Resume of the Authoritarian-Democratic Studies." *Harvard Educational Review* 29 (1959): 201.

Ausubel, D. P. "Learning by Discovery: Rationale and Mystique." *Bulletin of the National Association of Secondary School Principals* 45 (1961): 18.

Bayles, Ernest E. *Pragmatism in Education.* New York: Harper and Row, 1966.

Berlyne, D. E. "Children's Reasoning and Thinking." In *Carmichael's Manual of Child Psychology*, 3d ed., p. 939. Edited by Paul Mussen. New York: John Wiley and Sons, 1970.

Bloom, L. "A Reappraisal of Piaget's Theory of Moral Judgment." *Journal of Genetic Psychology* 5 (1959): 3.

Boas, G. *The Cult of Childhood.* London: Warburg Institute, University of London, 1966.

Braine, M. S. "The Ontogeny of Certain Logical Operations: Piaget's Formulation Examined by Nonverbal Methods." *Psychological Monographs* 5 (1959): 73.

Brown, S. C., ed. *Philosophers Discuss Education.* Totowa, N.J.: Rowman and Littlefield, 1975.

Bruner, J. S. "Inhelder and Piaget's *The Growth of Logical Thinking*: A Psychologist's Viewpoint." *British Journal of Psychology* 29 (1959): 363.

Bruner, Jerome S. *Toward a Theory of Instruction.* New York: W. W. Norton, 1968.

Bruner, J. S.; Goodnow, J. J.; and Austin, G. A. *A Study of Thinking.* New York: John Wiley, 1956.

Buchler, Justus. "What Is a Discussion?" *Journal of General Education* 8 (October 1954): 7.

Bunge, M. "Levels: A Semantical Preliminary." *Rev. Metaphysics* 13 (1960): 396.

Chomsky, N. "Review of B. F. Skinner, *Verbal Learning*." *Language* 35 (1959): 26.

Dewey, John. *The Child and the Curriculum.* New York, Macmillan, 1955.

————. *Democracy and Education.* New York: Macmillan, 1944.

————. *Experience and Education.* New York: Collier Books, 1971.

————. *Human Nature and Conduct.* New York: Modern Library, 1950.

————. *John Dewey: The Middle Works*, vol. 1. Edited by Jo Ann Boydston. Carbondale and Edwardsville: Southern Illinois University Press, 1976.

————. *Logic: The Theory of Inquiry.* New York: Henry Holt, 1938.

————. *On Experience, Nature, and Freedom.* Edited by Richard J. Bernstein. New York: Liberal Arts Press, 1960.

————. *The Philosophy of John Dewey,* vol. 1 and 2. Edited by John J. McDermott. New York: G. P. Putnam's Sons, Capricorn Books, 1973.

————.*The Quest for Certainty: A Study of the Relation of Knowledge and Action.* New York: G. P. Putnam's Sons, Capricorn Books, 1960.

————. *Sources of a Science of Education.* New York: Liveright, 1929.

————.*Theory of the Moral Life.* New York: Holt, Rinehart, and Winston, 1908.

————. *Theory of Valuation.* Chicago: University of Chicago Press, 1939.

Dolle, Jean-Marie. *Politique et Pedagogie.* Paris: Ligbairie Philosophique J Vrin, 1973.

Doyle, J. *Educational Judgments.* London: Routledge and Kegan Paul, 1972.

Durkheim, Emile. *Moral Education, Selections.* New York: Teachers College Press, 1959.

Edel, Abraham. *Ethical Judgement.* Glencoe, Illinois: The Free Press, 1964.

Ennis, R. H. "A Concept of Critical Thinking: A Proposed Basis for Research in the Teaching and Evaluation of Critical Thinking Ability." In *Psychological Concepts in Education,* edited by B. P. Komisar and C.J.B. Macmillan. Chicago: Rand McNally, 1967, p. 116.

Ennis, Robert H. *Logic in Teaching.* Englewood Cliffs, N.J.: Prentice-Hall, 1969.

Erikson, Erik H. *Childhood and Society.* New York: W. W. Norton, 1950.

————. *Insight and Responsibility.* New York: W. W. Norton, 1964.

Ervin, S. M. "Training and a Logical Operation by Children." *Child Development* 31 (1960): 555.

Featherstone, Joseph. *Schools Where Children Learn.* New York: Liveright, 1971.

Feffer, N. H., and Gourevitch, V. "Cognitive Aspects of Role-Taking in Children." *Journal of Personality* 28 (1960): 383.

Flavell, J. H. *The Developmental Psychology of Jean Piaget.* Princeton, N.J.: Van Nostrand Co., 1963.

Foot, Phillippa R. "When Is a Principal a Moral Principle?" *Proceedings of the Aristotelian Society, Supplementary Volume,* 1954.

Gowin, D. B. "Teaching, Learning and Thirdness." *Studies in Philosophy and Education* 1 (1961): 87.

Gutek, Gerald. "Philosophy for Children." *Phi Delta Kappan* (April 1976).

Haas, Hope J. "Philosophical Thinking in the Elementary Schools: An Evaluation of the Education Program, Philosophy for Children." Mimeographed. Institute for Cognitive Studies, Rutgers University, 1976.

Hall, Robert, and Davis, John. *Moral Education in Theory and Practice.* Buffalo, New York: Prometheus Books, 1975.

Hare, R. M. "Adolescents into Adults." In *Aims in Education: The Philosophic Approach*, edited by T. H. B. Hollins. Manchester: Manchester University Press, 1964.

Hare, Richard M. *Freedom and Reason.* London: Oxford University Press, 1964.

Harvard Educational Review 44 (February 1974). "The Rights of Children," A Special Issue, pt. 2.

Hazlitt, V. 'Children's Thinking." *British Journal of Psychology* 20 (1930): 354.

Inhelder, B., and Piaget, J. *The Growth of Logical Thinking from Childhood to Adolescence.* New York: Basic Books, 1958.

Isaacs, Susan. *Intellectual Growth in Young Children.* New York: Harcourt, Brace and World, 1931.

James, William. *Talks to Teachers on Psychology: And to Students on Some of Life's Ideals.* New York: Henry Holt, 1898.

Jersild, A. T. *The Psychology of Adolescence.* New York: Macmillan, 1957.

Jordan, J. A. "Socratic Teaching?" *Harvard Educational Review* 33 (1963): 96.

Kagan, Jerome, and Kogan, Nathan. "Individuality and Cognitive Performance." In *Carmichaels's Manual of Child Psychology*, 3d ed, p. 1273. Edited by Paul Mussen. New York: John Wiley and Sons, 1970.

Kaufman, A. "On Some Philosophic Grounds for Understanding Teaching." *Studies in Philosophy and Education* 5 (1967): 347.

Koffka, Kurt. *The Growth of the Mind.* New York: Harcourt, Brace and Co., 1924.

Kohlberg, Lawrence, and Turiel, Elliot. "Moral Development and Moral Education." In *Psychology and Educational Practice*, edited by Gerald Lesser. Chicago: Scott Foresman, 1971.

Langford, Glen, and O'Connor, D. J. *New Essays in the Philosophy of Education.* London: Routledge and Kegan Paul, 1973.

Lipman, Matthew. "Philosophy for Children." *Metaphilosophy* 7 (no. 1, January 1976).

―――. "Philosophy Is Also for the Young: At Least Possibly." *New York Times* (News of the Week in Review), October 20, 1974.

Mandelbaum, Maurice. The *Phenomenology of Moral Experience.* Glencoe, Ill.: The Free Press, 1955.

Martin, J. R. "Can There Be Universally Applicable Criteria of Good Teaching?" *Harvard Educational Review* 33 (1963): 484.

Martin, Jane R. *Explaining, Understanding, and Teaching.* New York: McGraw-Hill Co., 1970.

Matthews, Gareth B. "Philosophy and Children's Literature." *Metaphilosophy* 7 (no. 1, 1976).

Miller, G. A.; Galanter, E.; and Pribram, K. *Plans and the Structure of Behavior.* New York: Henry Holt, 1960.

The Monist 58 (no. 4, 1974). "The Philosophy of Moral Education," Special Issue.

Morris, Van Cleve. *Modern Movements in Educational Philosophy.* Boston: Houghton Mifflin, 1969.

Nelson, Leonard. *Socratic Method and Critical Philosophy: Selected Essays.* Translated by Thomas K. Brown III. New Haven: Yale University Press, 1949.

Nuthall, G. A. 'A Review of Some Selected Recent Studies of Classroom Interaction and Teaching Behavior." *American Educational Research Monograph* No. 6. Chicago: Rand McNally, 1970.

Nuthall, G. A., and Lawrence, P. J. *Thinking in the Classroom.* Wellington: New Zealand Council for Educational Research, 1965.

Opie, Iona, and Opie, Peter. *The Lore and Language of Schoolchildren.* London: Oxford University Press, 1967.

Osgood, C. E.; Suci, G. J.; and Tannenbaum, P. H. *The Measurement of Meaning.* Urbana: University of Illinois Press, 1957.

Parsons, C. "Inhelder and Piaget's *The Growth of Logical Thinking,* II: A Logician's Viewpoint." *British Journal of Psychology* 51 (1960): 75.

Peel, E. A. *The Pupil's Thinking.* London: Oldbourne Book Co., 1960.

Pestalozzi, Johann Heinrich. *How Gertrude Teaches Her Children and an Account of the Method.* Translated by Lucy Holland and Frances Turner. Syracuse, N.Y.: C. W. Bardeen, 1898.

Pestalozzi, J. H. *Letters on Early Education.* Syracuse, N.Y.: C. W. Bardeen, 1898.

Peters, R. S., ed. *The Concept of Education.* London: Routledge and Kegan Paul, 1967.

Phenix, P. H. "An Analytic View of the Process of Generalization." *Studies in Philosophy and Education* 5 (1967): 245.

Piaget, Jean. *The Birth of Logical Thinking from Childhood to Adolescence.* New York: Basic Books, 1958.

———. *The Early Growth of Logic in the Child.* London: Routledge and Kegan Paul, 1964.

———. *Judgment and Reasoning in the Child.* New York: Harcourt Brace, 1928.

————. *Language and Thought of the Child.* Cleveland, Ohio: World Publishing Co., 1959.

————. *Logic and Psychology.* New York: Basic Books, 1957.

————. *The Moral Judgment of the Child.* New York: Harcourt, Brace and World, 1932.

————. *The Origins of Intelligence in Children.* Translated by M. Cook. New York: International University Press, 1952.

————. *To Understand Is to Invent: The Future of Education.* New York: Viking Press, 1975.

Postman, Neil, and Weingartner, Charles. *Teaching as a Subversive Activity.* New York: Delacorte Press, 1969.

Radford, John, and Burton, Andrew. *Thinking: Its Nature and Development.* London: John Wiley and Sons, 1974.

Raths, Louis E.; Harmin, Merrill; and Simon, Sidney B. *Values and Teaching: Working with Values in the Classroom.* Columbus, Ohio: Charles E. Merrill Publishing Co., 1966.

Reeves, Joan Wynn. *Thinking about Thinking.* New York: George Braziller, 1965.

Ribble, Margaret A., M.D. *The Rights of Infants: Early Psychological Needs and Their Satisfaction,* 2d ed. New York and London: Columbia University Press, 1942.

Russell, David H. *Children's Thinking.* Waltham, Mass.: Blaisdell Publishing Company, 1956.

Sarason, Seymour. *The Culture of the School and the Problem of Change.* Boston: Allyn and Bacon, 1971.

Scheffler, I. *Conditions of Knowledge: An Introduction to Epistemology and Education.* Chicago: Scott Foresman, 1965.

Shaver, J. P. "Educational Research and Instruction for Critical Thinking." *Social Education* 26 (1962): 13.

Sigel, Irving E., and Hooper, Frank H., eds. *Logical Thinking in Children.* New York: Holt, Rinehart and Winston, 1968.

Sizer, Nancy F., and Sizer, Theodore R. *Moral Education: Five Lectures.* Cambridge, Mass.: Harvard University Press, 1973.

Smith, B. O. "A Concept of Teaching." *Teachers College Record* 61 (1960): 229.

————. "Logic, Thinking, and Teaching." *Educational Theory* 7 (1957): 225.

Smith, B. Othanel, and Ennis, Robert H. *Language and Concepts in Education.* Chicago: Rand McNally, 1968.

Smith, B. O.; Meux, M.; and Precians, P. *A Study of the Strategies of Teaching.* Urbana: University of Illinois Bureau of Educational Research, 1967.

Smith, B. O., and Meux, M. O. A *Study of the Logic of Teaching*. Urbana: University of Illinois Bureau of Educational Research, 1962.

Snook, I. A. "Teaching Pupils to Think." *Studies in Philosophy and Education* 8 (no. 2, 1973).

Suchman, J. R. "The Child and the Inquiry Process." In *Intellectual Development: Another Look*, edited by A. H. Passow. Washington, D.C.: Association for Supervision and Curriculum Development, 1964.

Taba, H.; Levine, S.; and Elzey, R. "Thinking in Elementary School Children." San Francisco: U.S. Office of Education, Cooperative Research Project No. 1574, San Francisco State College, 1964.

Thorndike, E. L. "Reading as Reasoning: A Study of Mistakes in Paragraph Reading." *Journal of Educational Psychology* 8 (1917): 323.

Tolstoy, Lev, *Childhood, Boyhood and Youth* trans. by Isabel F. Hapgood. New York: T. R. Crowell Co., 1886.

Toulmin, Stephen. *An Examination of the Place of Reason in Ethics*. Cambridge: At the University Press, 1950.

Wallach, Michael. "Creativity." In *Carmichael's Manual of Child Psychology*, 3d ed., p. 1211. Edited by Paul Mussen. New York: John Wiley and Sons, 1970.

———. "Creativity and the Expression of Possibilities." In *Creativity and Learning*, edited by Jerome Kagan. Boston: Houghton, Mifflin and Co., 1967, p. 36.

Werner, H. *Comparative Psychology of Mental Development*. Chicago: Follett, 1948.

———. "The Conception of Development from a Comparative and Organismic Point of View." In *The Concept of Development*, edited by D. Harris. Minneapolis: University of Minnesota Press, 1957.

Whitehead, Alfred North. *The Aims of Education*. New York: Macmillan Co., 1929.

Yolton, John W. *John Locke and Education*. New York: Random House, 1971.